AN INTRODUCTION TO EMPIRE
IN THE NEW TESTAMENT

RESOURCES FOR BIBLICAL STUDY

Editor
Tom Thatcher, New Testament

Number 84

AN INTRODUCTION TO EMPIRE
IN THE NEW TESTAMENT

Edited by

Adam Winn

SBL PRESS

Atlanta

Copyright © 2016 by SBL Press

Library of Congress Cataloging-in-Publication Data

Names: Winn, Adam, 1976– editor.
Title: An introduction to empire in the New Testament / edited by Adam Winn.
Description: Atlanta : SBL Press, 2016. | Series: Resources for biblical study ; Number 84 | Includes bibliographical references and index.
Identifiers: LCCN 2016012120 (print) | LCCN 2016014137 (ebook) | ISBN 9781628371338 (pbk. : alk. paper) | ISBN 9780884141525 (hardcover : alk. paper) | ISBN 9780884141518 (e-book)
Subjects: LCSH: Bible. New Testament—Criticism, interpretation, etc. | Rome—In the Bible.
Classification: LCC BS2545.R65 I58 2016 (print) | LCC BS2545.R65 (ebook) | DDC 225.6/7—dc23
LC record available at http://lccn.loc.gov/2016012120

Printed on acid-free paper.

Dedicated to the Memory of Ellen Aitken

Contents

A BRIEF WORD OF INTRODUCTION
AND ACKNOWLEDGMENT

Over the past twenty years, there has been an explosion of academic research and publication on the topic of the New Testament's engagement with the realities of Rome's empire. While there are certainly numerous precursors to this surge of scholarly activity, its primary point of origin seems to be the formation of the Paul and Politics consultation that began meeting (and still meets) at the Society of Biblical Literature Annual Meeting in the mid-nineties. Led by Richard Horsley and involving the noteworthy contributions of scholars such as Neil Elliot, Dieter Georgi, and Helmut Koester, this consultation produced a volume of collected essays on Paul's engagement with and challenge to Rome's empire (Horsley 1997). This seminal work led to the multiplication of monographs, journal articles, dissertations, and subsequent volumes of collected essays. The scope of research quickly expanded, as Horsley and others began to consider Jesus's response to empire, and Warren Carter began exploring the ways in which the Gospels might be challenging Rome's power. Today one can find "empire" studies on most books of the New Testament. The purpose of the present volume is both to introduce readers, particularly students and nonspecialists, to this growing subfield of New Testament studies, making them aware of the significant work that has already been produced, and to point them to new ways in which this field is moving forward. This volume includes a diverse group of interpreters who at times have differing presuppositions, methods, and concerns regarding how the texts of the New Testament engage the Roman Empire, but who all hold in common a belief that Rome's empire is a crucial foreground for reading and interpreting at least certain New Testament texts. The volume includes contributors who have been pioneers in "empire criticism" for the past twenty years and who continue to plow new ground, but it also includes the work of new scholars who, while often building on the work of those who have gone before them, bring new and fresh insights into the ways in which New Testament texts might be engaging the realities of Rome's empire.

While there have been a number of recent (and excellent) edited volumes that address the New Testament's response to and engagement with Rome's empire, this volume is particularly distinct in its scope, as the following essays cover virtually the entire New Testament canon. It is also distinct in its purpose to serve as an introduction to both students and nonspecialists within the field of New Testament studies and educated readers outside the field of New Testament studies. As a result of its introductory purpose, contributors have sought to avoid analysis and language that is overly technical and have minimized (where possible) the use of footnotes and excessive references to secondary literature. Each essays concludes with a section that directs interested readers to secondary literature in which they can find more thorough discussion and additional bibliographic information.

The volume begins with two introductory essays. The first, authored by myself, further discusses the development of "empire criticism" in the field of New Testament studies and considers the various strategies and methods employed in New Testament texts for engaging and responding to Rome's empire. The second, by Bruce W. Longenecker, Baylor University, introduces the reader to the nature and scope of the Roman Empire itself, demonstrating the ways and means by which the empire pervaded virtually every area of life in the ancient Mediterranean world. Following these two introductory essays, Richard A. Horsley offers an essay on the historical Jesus and his engagement with Roman imperial realities. The essays then progress through the canonical order of the New Testament: Warren Carter, Brite Divinity School, examines the Gospel of Matthew; I examine the Gospel of Mark; Eric D. Barreto, Luther Seminary, examines the Gospel of Luke and the Acts of the Apostles; Beth M. Sheppard, Duke Divinity School, examines the Gospel of John; Neil Elliot, Fortress Press, examines Romans and 1 and 2 Corinthians; James R. Harrison, Sydney College of Divinity, examines Galatians, 1 Thessalonians, and Philippians; Harry O. Maier, Vancouver School of Theology, examines Colossians and Ephesians; Deborah Krause, Eden Theological Seminary, examines the Pastoral Epistles; Jason A. Whitlark, Baylor University, examines Hebrews; Matthew Ryan Hauge, Azusa Pacific University, examines James; Kelly D. Liebengood, Letourneau University, examines 1 Peter; and Davina Lopez, Eckerd College, examines Revelation.

In the nascent stages of this project, Ellen Aitken of McGill University was committed to contribute the essay on Hebrews and empire, an area of study in which Ellen was a brilliant pioneer. Tragically, Ellen was diagnosed with a rare and aggressive form of cancer in early May 2014 and succumbed to the disease in the following month. Her all-too-sudden death at the age of fifty-three is a heartbreaking loss for her family and friends, but also for the guild of New Testament studies, which lost a dear and highly esteemed colleague, teacher, and scholar. This present volume is dedicated to Ellen's memory, and we hope it brings honor to her, her family, her friends, and her colleagues. You will be dearly missed, Ellen.

A project of this nature is always a significant undertaking, the success of which involves the hard work of many. I want to thank Tom Thatcher, the editor for the Society of Biblical Literature's Resources for Biblical Study series, who envisioned this project and asked if I would be willing to serve as its editor. His guidance and patience through what turned out to be a longer-than-intended process is greatly appreciated—without it the ship would have sunk! I would also like to thank my colleagues Tim Brookins (Houston Baptist University) and Alice Yafeh-Deigh (Azusa Pacific University), who both provided informal editorial and professional assistance with certain aspects of this project. Finally, I want to thank the thirteen excellent contributors who have provided superb essays for this volume, essays that contain first-rate scholarship that is deftly crafted to communicate to our intended audience of students and nonspecialists—not an easy task for many of us! Your patience, cooperation, and communication throughout this process has been commendable, and it has truly been a joy to work with you all. I hope the editorial work presented here is worthy of your significant contributions.

Adam Winn
Pasadena, California, 2015

ABBREVIATIONS

Primary Sources

Abr.	Philo, *De Abrahamo*
Acts Paul	Acts of Paul
Aen.	Virgil, *Aeneid*
Agr.	Tacitus, *Agricola*
Ann.	Tacitus, *Annales*
Ant.	Josephus, *Antiquities of the Jews*
Ant.	Sophocles, *Antigone*
Ant. rom.	Dionysius of Halicarnassus, *Antiquitates romanae*
Aug.	Suetonius, *Divus Augustus*
Bell. civ.	Appian, *Bella civilia*
Bib. hist.	Diodorus Siculus, *Bibliotheca historica*
Brut.	Cicero, *Brutus* or *De claris oratoribus*
Cat.	Lucian, *Cataplus*
Cher.	Philo, *De cherubim*
Claud.	Suetonius, *Divus Claudius*
Clem.	Seneca, *De clementia*
Dom.	Suetonius, *Domitianus*
Dreams	Philo, *On Dreams*
Eloc.	Demetrius, *De elocutione* (*Peri hermēneias*)
Ep.	*Epistulae*
Epict. diss.	Arrian, *Epicteti dissertationes*
Fug.	Lucian, *Fugitivi*
Haer.	Irenaeus, *Adversus haereses*
Hist.	Sallust, *Historiae*
Hist.	Tacitus, *Historiae*
Hist. eccl.	*Historia ecclesiastica*
Hist. rom.	Cassius Dio, *Historia romana* (*Roman History*)

Hom. Phil.	John Chrysostom, *Homiliae in epistulam ad Philippenses*
Il.	Homer, *Iliad*
Inst.	Quintilian, *Institutio oratoria*
Jub.	Jubilees
J.W.	Josephus, *Jewish War*
LAB	Liber antiquitatum biblicarum (Pseudo-Philo)
Leg.	Plato, *Leges*
Mand.	Shepherd of Hermas, Mandate(s)
Mart. Pol.	Martyrdom of Polycarp
Metam.	Apuleius, *Metamorphoses*
Nat.	Pliny the Elder, *Naturalis historia*
Nem.	Pindar, *Nemeonikai*
Num.	Plutarch, *Numa*
Off.	Cicero, *De officiis*
Ol.	Pindar, *Olympionikai*
Orest.	Euripides, *Orestes*
Pan.	Pliny the Younger, *Panegyricus*
PE	Pastoral Epistles
Pol.	Aristotle, *Politica*
Praec. ger. rei publ.	Plutarch, *Praecepta gerendae rei publicae*
Prog.	Libanius, *Progymnasmata*
Quaest. rom.	Plutarch, *Quaestiones romanae et graecae* (*Aetia romana et graeca*)
Rep.	Cicero, *De republica*
Res gest. divi Aug.	Res gestae divi Augusti
[*Rhet.*]	Dionysius of Halicarnassus, *Ars rhetorica*
Rom.	Plutarch, *Romulus*
Saec.	Horace, *Carmen saeculare*
Sim.	Shepherd of Hermas, Similitude(s)
Ti. C. Gracch.	Plutarch, *Tiberius et Caius Gracchus*
Tib.	Suetonius, *Tiberius*
Tim.	Plato, *Timaeus*
Vesp.	Suetonius, *Vespasianus*
Vis.	Shepherd of Hermas, Vision(s)

Secondary Sources

AJA	*American Journal of Archaeology*

AJEC	Ancient Judaism and Early Christianity
AJP	*American Journal of Philology*
ANF	*The Ante-Nicene Fathers: Translations of the Writings of the Fathers Down to A.D. 325.* Edited by Alexander Roberts and James Donaldson. 10 vols. Buffalo, NY: Christian Literature Publishing, 1987.
ANRW	*Aufstieg und Niedergang der römischen Welt: Geschichte und Kultur Roms im Spiegel der neueren Forschung.* Part 2, *Principat.* Edited by Hildegard Temporini and Wolfgang Haase. Berlin: de Gruyter, 1972–
AnSt	*Anatolian Studies*
AYB	Anchor Yale Bible
Bib	*Biblica*
BibInt	*Biblical Interpretation*
BibInt	Biblical Interpretation Series
BMC	*Coins of the Roman Empire in the British Museum*
BMW	Bible in the Modern World
BSGRT	Bibliotheca Scriptorum Graecorum et Romanorum Teubneriana
BurH	*Buried History*
BZNW	Beihefte zur Zeischrift für die neutestamentliche Wissenschaft
CBNTS	Coniectanea Biblica New Testament Series
CBQ	*Catholic Biblical Quarterly*
CIG	*Corpus Inscriptionum Graecarum.* Edited by August Boeckh. 4 vols. Berlin, 1828–1877
CIL	*Corpus Inscriptionum Latinarum.* Berlin, 1862–
CP	*Classical Philology*
CW	*Classical World*
Divinations	Divinations: Rereading Late Ancient Religion
ExpTim	*Expository Times*
GRBS	*Greek, Roman, and Byzantine Studies*
HSCP	*Harvard Studies in Classical Philology*
HTR	*Harvard Theological Review*
IBC	Interpretation: A Bible Commentary for Teaching and Preaching
IG	*Inscriptiones graecae. Editio Minor.* Berlin: de Gruyter, 1924–

IGR	*Inscriptiones Graecae ad Res Romanas Pertinentes*
ILS	*Inscriptiones Latinae selectae*
JBL	*Journal of Biblical Literature*
JETS	*Journal of the Evangelical Theological Society*
JGRChJ	*Journal of Greco-Roman Christianity and Judaism*
JHI	*Journal of the History of Ideas*
JHS	*Journal of Hellenic Studies*
JJS	*Journal of Jewish Studies*
JNES	*Journal of Near Eastern Studies*
JRASS	Journal of Roman Archaeology: Supplement Series
JRS	*Journal of Roman Studies*
JSJ	*Journal for the Study of Judaism in the Persian, Hellenistic, and Roman Periods*
JSNT	*Journal for the Study of the New Testament*
JSNTSup	Journal for the Study of the New Testament: Supplement Series
JSPSup	Journal for the Study of the Pseudepigrapha: Supplement Series
LCL	Loeb Classical Library
LNTS	Library of New Testament Studies
LSJ	Liddell, Henry George, Robert Scott, and Henry Stuart Jones. *A Greek-English Lexicon.* 9th ed. with revised supplement. Oxford: Clarendon, 1996
MAMA	*Monumenta Asiae Minoris Antiqua.* Manchester and London, 1928–1993
MNTSS	McMaster New Testament Studies Series
NIBCNT	New International Biblical Commentary on the New Testament
NICNT	New International Commentary on the New Testament
NIGTC	New International Greek Testament Commentary
NovTSup	Supplements to Novum Testamentum
NTL	New Testament Library
NTMS	New Testament Monographs
NTOA	Novum Testamentum et Orbis Antiquus
NTS	*New Testament Studies*
OGIS	*Orientis graeci inscriptions selectae.* Edited by Wilhelm Dittenberger. 2 vols. Leipzig: Hirzel, 1903–1905

Ph&Rh	*Philosophy and Rhetoric*
RBS	Resources for Biblical Study
RIC	*The Roman Imperial Coinage*
RPC	*Roman Provincial Coinage*
RSR	*Recherches de science religieuse*
SBLDS	Society of Biblical Literature Dissertation Series
SBLSP	Soceity of Biblical Literature Seminar Papers
SBT	Studies in Biblical Theology
SEG	Supplementum epigraphicum graecum
SemeiaSt	Semeia Studies
SNT	Studien zum Neuen Testament
SNTSMS	Society For New Testament Studies Monograph Series
SP	Sacra Pagina
SymS	Symposium Series
TAPS	*Transactions of the American Philosophical Society*
Thf	*Theoforum*
TynBul	*Tyndale Bulletin*
UBS	United Bible Society
USQR	*Union Seminary Quarterly Review*
VC	*Vigiiae christianae*
WBC	Word Biblical Commentary
WGRW	Writings from the Greco-Roman World
WGRWSup	Writings from the Greco-Roman World Supplement Series
WUNT	Wissenschaftliche Untersuchungen zum Neuen Testament

STRIKING BACK AT THE EMPIRE: EMPIRE THEORY AND RESPONSES TO EMPIRE IN THE NEW TESTAMENT

Adam Winn

As will become evident throughout this volume of essays, the Roman Empire dominated and pervaded virtually every aspect of life in the ancient Mediterranean world. Though Christianity was birthed under the power of this empire and every page of Christian Scripture was written under its shadow, the Roman Empire has played a relatively insignificant role in the history of modern New Testament scholarship. To be sure, realities of the empire were often recognized as a background for the Christian movement. Knowledge of Roman laws, rulers, and customs was certainly used to inform one's interpretation of Paul's mission and letters, the life of Jesus, the four Gospels, the Acts of the Apostles, and many aspects of the New Testament. To be sure, the history of religions school considered the impact of Roman religious ideas on the development and expression of early Christian theology. But few interpreters considered the way in which the Roman Empire and its ubiquitous power and influence might be a foreground for understanding Christian theological expression, mission, and practice. Few New Testament interpreters considered ways in which New Testament texts might be critiquing the evils of the Roman Empire. The prevailing assumption was that the writings of the New Testament were apolitical, that they were primarily concerned with spiritual realties rather than the worldly practices of ancient empires. The general conclusion of most interpreters was that Christians by and large accepted Roman authority, honored Roman rulers and laws, and only demonstrated resistance or critique when Roman power directly called Christians to violate their allegiance to God or his Christ.

While the reasons for such conclusions are numerous, I will note some prominent ones here. First, modern New Testament scholarship is a product of the modern Western world, a world in which the separation of religion and state is for many a foundational presupposition. This presupposition has two significant implications for the relationship between the Roman Empire and Christian Scriptures. The first implication is that the Roman Empire was understood in strictly political terms, as if it only incorporated political realities such as political officials, institutions, and laws. As such, it was presumed that the New Testament only engaged empire when it explicitly engaged these political realities—engagement that is relatively rare in the New Testament. The second implication is related to the fact that in the modern West, the New Testament was a book of the church and thus a distinctly religious book. Since the New Testament was a religious book and the Western world created a sharp divide between the interests of the state and religion, it was presumed that the New Testament would have little interest in political realities. Thus, by imposing its own dichotomy between religion and state onto the New Testament, the modern Western world was blinded to many ways in which the New Testament might be engaging or responding to Roman imperial realities.

Second, as a product of the modern West, modern New Testament scholarship belonged, and to a great extent still belongs, to the world's wealthy, powerful, and privileged. Because virtually all New Testament interpreters were citizens of powerful nations (empires?) and benefited from that power, they were (and still today often remain) predisposed to see themselves and their own situations in these texts. The authors, audiences, and characters are seen through the lens of privilege and are presumed to stand in the place of privilege. Thus the place of privilege held by many interpreters kept them from recognizing the primary players in the New Testament for what they actually were, namely, the poor, oppressed, powerless, and dominated people of the Roman Empire. Without recognizing the people of the New Testament as a dominated people, there was no real hope of seeing in their writings a critique of the powerful. One might conclude that the power and privilege of the modern Western interpreters themselves stand as a barrier to reading the text as a critique of the powerful and thus to see in the New Testament text critiques of Rome's empire.

Yet over the past three decades, there have been significant developments in the field of New Testament studies that have led to critiques of the previously held presumptions regarding the New Testament's relationship to the Roman Empire. Postmodern literary criticism led the way in recognizing the biases of readers and the ways in which those biases shape the meaning of literature. Subsequently, it did not take long for the dominant biases of privileged Western readers to be recognized and critiqued. Postcolonial criticism played a significant role in this process, recognizing biases of the privileged and powerful, the ways in which these biases oppress the colonized, and the ways in which the colonized respond to their subjugation. The application of postcolonial criticism to the New Testament led to the recognition that the primary actors of the New Testament (authors, audiences, characters, etc.) were distinctly different from the privileged Western interpreters that dominated the field of New Testament studies. The early Christians that both composed the New Testament and took center stage in it were not the powerful or privileged but the colonized poor who had little power to change their social condition. Such a recognition led interpreters to consider the ways in which early Christians might be responding to and resisting Roman colonization and imperial power. Strategies of response that were witnessed among modern colonized people were used to understand the behaviors and writings of early Christians.

Aided in part by postcolonial criticism and in part by developments in classical studies, New Testament scholars began to recognize the vast scope and pervasive nature of the Roman Empire (as seen in the following essay). These advances led many scholars to abandon the previously held presupposition regarding the separation of church and state. It became quite clear that Roman religion was inseparable from Roman politics, and vice versa. Likewise, the Roman economic system, social organization, architecture, and even literature were demonstrated to be inseparable from the political power of Rome. When Rome's empire is understood in this way, it does not take long to realize that virtually every dimension of Christian life would in some way be affected by Rome's empire and that engagement with and response to this empire would be a daily reality for all Christians.

As a result of these developments, the last two decades have seen numerous studies on the role that empire played in the life of early Christianity and in the composition and use of the New Testament. These studies have demonstrated that early Christian responses to the Roman Empire, responses found in the New Testament, were highly diverse in their estimation of empire, in their strategies for responding to empire, and the aspects of empire to which they respond. Here I consider this diversity and introduce the reader to various means and strategies employed in New Testament books to respond to Rome's empire.

Predicted and Imagined Judgment

Perhaps not surprisingly, the New Testament's estimation of Rome's empire is often negative. Central to much Christian proclamation was the return of Christ, an event that would bring with it the full establishment of God's righteous reign on earth (e.g., Acts 3:19–21; 1 Cor 15:23–28; Phil 3:20–21; 1 Thess 4:14–17). Implicit in the establishment of God's reign was the destruction of all earthly powers that opposed God, as well as the rulers that represented those powers. Since Rome was the current world power, its defeat and removal was implicit in Christian eschatological hope. Thus one way in which Christians responded to Roman power was to predict its removal and judgment. In 1 Cor 2:6, Paul claims that the "rulers of this age," presumably Roman rulers, "are doomed to perish."[1] Later, in 1 Cor 15:24, Paul says, "Then comes the end, when he [Christ] hands over the kingdom to God the Father, after he has destroyed every ruler and every authority and power." Though Paul does not specifically mention Rome here, the destruction of Roman power is clearly implied, and it would have been understood by Paul's earliest readers. Paul again predicts the judgment of Rome in 1 Thess 5:3: "When they say, 'There is peace and security,' then sudden destruction will come upon them, as labor pains come upon a pregnant woman, and there will be no escape!" "Peace and security" represents a common mantra of the Roman Empire (*pax et securitas*), one commonly found on coins and in imperial inscriptions. The mantra promised peace and safety to all those under the empire's power. Thus those saying "peace and security" are best identified as those who represent Roman power, that is, those who place these words on coins and inscribe them on walls and statues. Paul is claiming that these representatives of Roman power will experience sudden destruction at the return of God's messiah, Jesus.

These are examples of direct challenges to Roman power through the prediction of Roman destruction. While these are clearly direct challenges to Roman power, there is an element of "self-protection" to them. Self-protection is a common practice found in the response of the dominated

---

1. Unless otherwise noted, all scripture citations are from the NRSV.

to the dominant. There is much risk involved in challenging the dominant power, and as such, often measures are taken by the dominated to protect themselves. The first level of protection for these predictions of Rome's destruction is the medium by which they are conveyed, namely, through private letters. These letters would have been read by those who, by and large, shared Paul's opinion of Rome and thus would not have been scandalized by it. Such private correspondence would have been unlikely to create trouble for either Paul or his community. But even yet, it is noteworthy that in these predictions, Rome itself is never mentioned explicitly, though it is clearly implied. Implicit rather than explicit predictions of Rome's destruction likely reflect an element of self-protection in Paul's critique of Roman power.

The most powerful Christian prediction of the destruction of Roman power is likely found in Revelation. However, Revelation often goes beyond simply predicting the destruction of Rome by vividly imagining and describing this destruction. For example, in Rev 18, the author describes a vision in which an angel descends from heaven and cries, "Fallen, Fallen is Babylon the Great" (18:2). It is widely recognized that Babylon is a coded reference to Rome, which like Babylon destroyed the Jewish temple. The chapter describes the great sins of "Babylon," the Roman Empire, including fornication (perhaps a reference to idolatry), greed, arrogance, and the murder of the saints. Rome is described as a "dwelling place for demons" and a "haunt for every foul spirit, a haunt for every foul bird, and a haunt for every foul and hateful beast" (18:2). Its sins are said to be "as high as heaven" (18:5). To be sure, the outward greatness of Rome is not ignored, as the great economic wealth of Rome is thoroughly described, as is the wealth that Rome has brought to those who have "fornicated" with it (18:9–17). This wealth, obtained through unrighteous means, has led to arrogance as it claims, "I rule as a queen; I am no widow, and I will never see grief" (18:7). But Rome's wealth and arrogance only magnify the dramatic nature of its judgment and destruction, both of which are described as sudden and swift: "her plagues will come in a single day" (18:8) and "for in one hour your judgment has come" (18:10). The greatness of Rome is clearly juxtaposed with its shocking and sudden demise. Rome's great luxury will be matched by its great suffering: "Render to her as she herself has rendered, and repay her double for her deeds; mix a double draught for her in the cup she mixed. As she glorified herself and lived luxuriously, so give her a like measure of torment and grief" (18:6–7). God's judgment on Rome leaves it smoking and burning and the inhabitants weeping and mourning loudly (18:18–19). While the city is left void of music and laughter, the saints, prophets, and apostles rejoice over God's vindication the wrongs committed against them (18:20–23). Through such envisioned judgment, the powerless are able both to express their critique of their oppressors and to engender hope among their ranks by imagining the reversal of their current situation.

In this chapter, and throughout much of Revelation, we again see a strategy of self-protection, this time through the use of coded language. Rome is never explicitly mentioned in the chapter. The chapter speaks of the fall of Babylon, not the fall of Rome. To the outside reader, the harsh critique of Rome might be easily missed. But to the insider, Babylon is a well-known code word for Rome. Thus, through such coded language, the dominated find the courage to voice their critique of those who dominate them.

Critique through Co-opted Language

Another common way in which the New Testament responds to and critiques the Roman Empire is through co-opting the language of the empire and using that language to express loyalty to a competing power, ruler, and eschatological vision. Language that is both prominent and commonplace in the New Testament is equally so in the Roman imperial world. The word *euangelion*, which is often translated as "good news" or "gospel," was a word closely associated with Roman power and the Roman emperor. The word was used to describe the emperor's birth, ascension to power, and even victory in battle (A. Collins 2000, 85–100; Winn 2008, 97–99). To the Greco-Roman reader of the New Testament, the proclamation of the "gospel of Jesus Christ" and the eschatological vision it implied could be heard as a challenge to the "gospel of Caesar" and the present power of Rome. Titles that are frequently applied to Jesus, such as "Son of God," "savior," "lord," and "king," were all commonly attributed to Roman emperors. When in Mark's Gospel a Roman centurion bestows on Jesus the title "Son of God" (Mark 15:39), a title that such a figure would commonly bestow on his emperor, the Greco-Roman reader would at least pause to consider whether a subversive message was intended, namely, if Jesus is Son of God then is Caesar *not*? Additionally, words like "faith," "justice," "peace," and "hope" were regularly identified as prominent virtues of Roman emperors and Rome itself. The faithfulness of the Roman emperor to his people ensured them justice, peace, and hope for the future.

For Paul, the faithfulness of Jesus reveals and establishes God's *dikaiosynē* (Rom 1:16; 3:21–22; 5:1), a word that is often translated "righteousness" in our New Testament, but in the Greco-Roman world was often associated with the Roman imperial virtue "justice." But not only does the faith of Jesus bring about justice; it also brings about "peace" (Rom 5:1) and "hope" (Rom 5:2). This language pervades many of Paul's letters, and it continually plays a prominent role in Paul's presentation of the gospel of Jesus Christ. One could argue that Paul uses this language to subvert the gospel of Rome by showing the superiority of the gospel of Jesus; that is, in Jesus one finds the faithfulness of a superior Lord, who brings a superior justice, peace, and hope.

One would be remiss to ignore the fact that much of the language noted above finds significance and meaning in the world of Second Temple Judaism as well, and there is no attempt here to deny such significance. But when this language was read by Greeks and Romans, it no doubt called to mind, at least for some, the unavoidable imperial realities through which they daily saw this language (e.g., on Roman coins, Roman temples, Roman public inscriptions). Instead of choosing one background over the other, interpreters might be better served to recognize the multivalent nature of this language that makes it useful for contrasting the kingdom of the God of Israel with Rome's empire.

It is noteworthy that the co-opting of Roman imperial language still carries with it a measure of self-protection, as it generally does not convey any explicit critique of Rome or its rulers. In Mark's Gospel, the Roman centurion does not explicitly state that because Jesus is Son of God, Caesar is not, though such a meaning could either be implied by the reader or intended by the author. Yet co-opted language is likely more dangerous than the use of coded language, because it is more likely to raise the suspicions of the dominating power.

Hidden Transcripts

As noted above, postcolonial criticism played a significant role in paving the way for studying responses to empire in the New Testament. Of particular importance is the work of James C. Scott (1985, 1990), a professor of political science at Yale who has done extensive research on the way in which dominated people interact with and respond to a dominating power. Scott (1990, 18) has demonstrated that the dominating power usually has an organized narrative or ideology that explains its power, justifies its domination, and communicates the benefits of its power for the dominated. Scott refers to this narrative as a "public transcript" (2, 18). The public transcript is frequently communicated by the dominating power, and the dominated are expected both to know and affirm the public transcript (70). While the dominated often publicly affirm the public transcript, Scott argues that such public affirmation should not be understood as a sincere affirmation of the dominating power or the ideology they perpetuate (2–5). Because open resistance to the public transcript would likely result in an unpleasant outcome for the dominated, they often resist in secret by creating and promoting their own counternarrative or ideology. Scott refers to this counternarrative as a "hidden transcript" (5). The hidden transcript is usually only communicated in the private sphere of the dominated, "backstage" and out of the sight of the dominant power (5–8). However, at times the hidden transcript can break through into the public sphere. While such appearances of the hidden transcript are usually subtle, at times they can be overt.

Scott's work has provided a useful way forward in understanding and detecting ways in which New Testament texts might be engaging and responding to the Roman Empire. As Longenecker's essay in this volume demonstrates, Rome had a well-developed public transcript, one that presented Roman rule as divinely ordained and as a source of blessing to those who lived under its authority. Recognition of this public transcript has led scholars to mine the New Testament for evidence of a hidden transcript that functions to resist Roman power and that offers the reader a counternarrative. At times, the hidden transcript is blatant, such as Revelation's imagined judgment of Rome or Paul's prediction of the destruction of all earthly powers and rulers. Yet more often the hidden transcript is subtle and hard to detect if one is not looking for it. Is Paul's use of words like "faithfulness," "justice," "savior," and "peace" politically neutral, or is Paul advancing with these words a hidden transcript that subverts the public transcript of Rome in which these words are prominent? In the essays to follow, certain authors will use this concept of hidden transcript to identify ways in which a New Testament text might be responding to Roman power.

Formation of Alternative Communities and Subversion of Sociocultural Institutions

As Longenecker demonstrates in this volume, the Roman Empire was not simply the product of military and political might. While these two realities certainly had their place, the stability and power of the empire rested largely on the broad shoulders of Rome's social, cultural, and civic institutions. Roman governance over its many provinces was largely facilitated through intricate patron-client relationships. The social elites in provincial cities were clients of Rome and its emperor, and they worked hard to honor and support these patrons (e.g., through the building of honorific temples, the perpetuation of Roman propaganda, and the maintenance of civic peace and harmony). Such honor and support was rewarded by generous gifts from the patrons, which increased the wealth, power, and honor of the civic elite. But these civic elites were also supported by their own clients that worked to increase the honor of these patrons, for which the clients would receive generous gifts and benefits. Through this system of mutually beneficial relationships, Rome was able to maintain peace and stability throughout the provinces it ruled with relatively little need for the use of military force. Such a system was largely built on status and the proper recognition of one's social superiors. Threats to such notions of status would thus threaten the intricate web of client-patron relationships, which would in turn threaten the very stability of Rome's empire.

Roman stability was also closely tied to the stability of the family unit. Greeks and Romans linked the stability of families to the stability and success of the empire (Aristotle, *Pol.* 1.1.5–9; Cicero, *Off.* 1.54; Arimus Didymus, *Epitome* 148.5–13). The family unit was organized around the paterfamilias or "father of the family."[2] The father had full legal authority over everyone in his household, which would include his spouse, children, grandchildren, and slaves. The paterfamilias had complete imperium or authority over his home, just as the emperor, the father of the Roman people, had complete imperium over Rome and its provinces. A stable family required a stable father who ruled over his home with both wisdom and justice (Aristotle, *Pol.* 1.5.3–12). Any destabilization of the institution of the paterfamilias would be linked to the destabilization of Rome itself.

In addition to the cultural institutions of the family and patronage, the Roman legal system and its administration of justice was also seen as foundational to Roman power and stability. *Iustitia*, "justice," was a foun-

---

2. Technically, the paterfamilias was a Roman legal institution, and only Roman citizens could be recognized as a paterfamilias. But for non-Romans living in the Roman Empire (Greeks, Jews, etc.), the father essentially held the same authority over his family as that of the Roman paterfamilias.

dational Roman virtue. Cicero claims that justice is "the crowning glory of the virtues" (*Off.* 1.20 [Miller, LCL]). Rome perceived that its divine right to rule was largely predicated on the empire's (and emperor's) commitment to justice and the just rule of law (Rutilius, *De Reditu Suo* 63–66). Justice was largely facilitated by civic courts or councils where local magistrates, figures appointed either directly or indirectly by Roman authorities, would hear and adjudicate legal disputes (R. Collins 1999, 226). As such, subversion of these institutions could be perceived as a subversion of *iustitia* and ultimately the stability of Rome's empire.

When these social, familial, and civic realities are seen in their proper relationship to the success and stability of the Roman Empire, that is, as thoroughly imperial realities, New Testament passages that deal with such realities can be seen in radically new ways. Paul's instructions to "outdo another in showing honor," "bless those who persecute you," "extend hospitality to strangers," "associate with the lowly" (Rom 12:10–16), and the like all undermine the notions of status, honor, and obligation that are embedded in the Roman social institution of patronage. The teaching of the Lukan Jesus to invite to dinner only those who cannot reciprocate the invitation (Luke 14:12–14) or James's instruction not to show favoritism in one's home to the wealthy over against the poor (Jas 2:1–9) both subvert this institution as well and stand to threaten the client-patron social construct, a construct used by Rome to keep peace and stability throughout its empire.

Paul's declaration that the husband's body belongs to the wife (1 Cor 7:4) is radically egalitarian, and it implicitly challenges the rights and powers of (and thus the institution of) the paterfamilias. Similarly, Paul's declaration that in Christ there is neither male or female nor slave or free, presents an egalitarian principle that has significant implications for the institution of the paterfamilias (Gal 3:28). If the family is the model for the city and state, what kind of state would a family that adopted such egalitarian principles model? Certainly not a state that looked like imperial Rome.

Paul also urges the Christians of Corinth not to take their legal disputes to the courts of the gentiles but to act as their own arbitrators of such legal matters (1 Cor 6:1–11). While the specific courts that this Pauline text has in its purview might represent local civic authority in Corinth rather that the court of a Roman provincial governor (only significant cases would be brought to the provincial governor, while local magistrates would oversee less noteworthy cases [R. Collins 1999, 226]), Paul's basic premise that Christians should adjudicate their own legal disputes because of their superior wisdom to that of their pagan contemporaries would most certainly be applied to courts that more directly expressed Roman's authority, that is, the high court of either the provincial governor or the emperor. For Paul, Christians are able to provide a greater justice among themselves than what is offered by Rome's promise of *iustitia*.

Through such instructions, the authors of the New Testament are directing their readers to form alternative communities that stand in sharp contrast to those offered them by the Roman imperial order. Whether intentionally so or not, the formation of such communities was subversive to an empire that depended on social, familial, and civic institutions for its power and stability. Thus the formation of such alternative communities is a real and tangible way that New Testament texts engage and subvert Rome's empire.

Accommodation of Roman Imperial Power

Not all of the New Testament's engagement with and response to Roman power is subversive. Many New Testament texts seem to be accommodating or even supportive of Rome's empire. Perhaps most noteworthy are passages like Rom 13:1–7, in which Paul encourages submission to Roman power as it has been instituted by God, the payment of Roman taxes, and the giving of honor to political figures. First Peter 2:12–17 instructs the reader to honor all political institutions and figures, for it is the Lord who has instituted them for punishing those who do wrong and rewarding those who do good. Through such a response to imperial power, the authors hope that those who wield such power might honor God when he comes to judge the world.

In addition to such direct demands to submit to Roman authority, there are passages that seem to accommodate the social-familial institutions outlined above, institutions that undergirded Rome's power and success. While the undisputed letters of Paul seem to advance a radical egalitarianism and call for the formation of communities that stand in sharp contrast to those offered by the Roman imperial world, many of the disputed letters of Paul seem to embrace the social-familial realities that characterize the communities of imperial Rome. In Ephesians, the familial institution of the paterfamilias seems to be reinforced, as the author identifies the husband as the "head" of the wife and requires the wife to submit to her husband in everything (Eph 5:22–24). Likewise, the author appears to reinforce the institution of slavery, as slaves are told to obey their masters with "fear and trembling" (Eph 6:5–6). Similar teachings can also be found in the "household codes" of Colossians (Col 3:18–22). While some interpreters might argue that these passages do not reflect complete accommodation to Roman power (and that they might even reflect elements of resistance), one cannot deny the striking differences between the alternative communities that Paul's undisputed letters seek to form and the accommodation to Roman communal realities found in the disputed letters.

Hybridity: Ambivalent Response to Roman Power

Homi K. Bhabha, professor of English and American literature at Harvard University, is another significant voice in postcolonial criticism that continues to have a significant impact on the field of New Testament studies. Bhabha (1985, 144–65) has demonstrated that the responses of the colonized to their colonizers are rarely characterized by outright resistance or rejection but that such responses are quite often characterized by ambivalence. Even when colonization is resisted by the colonized, the colonized are inevitably affected by the realities of colonization. As a result, the colonized are in many ways hybrids of their own cultural realities and those imposed by their colonizers. Bhabha uses the term "hybridity" to describe this phenomenon and the responses to colonization that it creates (154–56). Hybrid responses to colonization often involve the colonized embracing some aspect of the colonial culture that has been imposed on them but then enacting or embodying that aspect of colonial culture in some new or different way (144–65). By accepting yet transforming a particular aspect of the colonial culture, the colonized are subtly subverting and resisting the colonial power.

One of the ways in which such hybridity is expressed is through what Bhabha (1984, 126–27) describes as "mimicry." The colonizers desire that the colonized resemble themselves in values, education, and other such cultural expressions. While the colonized regularly oblige these desires by embracing many aspects of the colonial culture, they frequently replicate such aspects imperfectly or incompletely (Moore 2006, 110). According to Bhabha (1984, 123), such imperfect mimicry of the colonizers combines both "resemblance and menace," as the imperfect imitation of the colonizers is a subtle form of resistance to colonization. Thus mimicry is an ambivalent form of responding to imperial power, as it maintains some resemblance of imperial/colonial realities, but it resists such realities by stopping short of complete or perfect imitation.

Such understanding of resistance to colonial/imperial power opens up radical new avenues for evaluating imperial responses found in New Testament writings. Texts that were long regarded as accommodating or embracing the realities of Roman imperial power can and should be reassessed in light of Bhabha's work on hybridity and mimicry. In such texts, are New Testament authors truly accommodating Roman imperial power, or is there evidence of imperfect accommodation and/or imitation that might function subversively? Luke and Acts have often been understood to demonstrate the commensurability between the Christian faith and Rome, and in so doing they present Rome, its empire, and its imperial actors in a positive light (Maddox 1982; Williams 1990, 15–16). But as the close reading of Luke and Acts in this volume will propose, the apparent pro-Roman aspects of these books are often tempered and subtle challenges to Rome's sociopolitical ideology. The concept of hybridity might also be helpful in analyzing a passage like Rom 13:1–7, a passage that, as we noted above, has often been interpreted in terms of Pauline accommodation of Roman power, yet stands in tension with other Pauline texts that seem to clearly critique and challenge that power (J. Marshall 2008, 157–78). Through the concept of hybridity, we are remind that there is rarely a "pure" and complete rejection of the colonial reality by the colonized but that most responses to colonization are ambivalent, combining both accommodation and resistance.

Summary

It is the hope of this essay to demonstrate the great diversity that characterizes the New Testament's engagement with empire as well as the resulting diversity in empire criticism. The New Testament's assessment of empire and Roman imperial realities clearly lacks uniformity. While some New Testament books directly critique and challenge Rome's empire, others offer attempts to accommodate it. Some books fall somewhere in between these two poles and offer hybrid or ambivalent responses to imperial realities. Strategies of response also vary widely, including coded language, co-opted language, imagined judgment, hidden transcripts, mimicry, and flattery among others. Also, due to the ubiquitous nature of the Roman Empire, the particular focus of any critique or engagement can be directed toward a wide range of "imperial" realities. While direct responses to Rome's political authority might be the most obvious examples of engagement with Rome's empire, some New Testament texts might completely ignore such political authority and instead choose to engage one or more of the many arms of Rome's imperial reach, including Roman religious, economic, social, and familial institutions.

The entirety of this diversity is reflected in the following essays, with some essays introducing the reader to methods and strategies for engaging empire that I have not addressed here and with other essays offering a more thorough discussion of issues I could only offer a cursory discussion of here.

For Further Reading

Bhabha, Homi K. 1994. *The Location of Culture.* New York: Routledge.

Carter, Warren. 2006. *The Roman Empire and the New Testament: An Essential Guide.* Nashville: Abingdon.

Horsley, Richard A., ed. 2004. *Hidden Transcripts and the Arts of Resistance: Applying the Work of James C. Scott to Jesus and Paul.* SemeiaSt 48. Atlanta: Society of Biblical Literature.

———, ed. 2008. *In the Shadow of Empire.* Louisville: Westminster John Knox.

Moore, Stephen D. 2006. *Empire and Apocalypse: Postcolonialism and the New Testament.* BMW. Sheffield: Sheffield Phoenix.

Porter, Stanley E., and Cynthia Long Westfall, eds. 2011. *Empire in the New Testament.* MNTSS 10. Eugene, OR: Wipf & Stock.

Scott, James C. 1990. *Domination and the Arts of Resistance.* New Haven: Yale University Press.

———. 1985. *Weapons of the Weak: Everyday Forms of Peasant Resistance.* New Haven: Yale University Press.

PEACE, PROSPERITY, AND PROPAGANDA: ADVERTISEMENT AND REALITY IN THE EARLY ROMAN EMPIRE

Bruce W. Longenecker

This essay surveys some of the key features of the Roman imperial order within which the Jesus movement first took root. The Roman Empire was propped up by people, places, and propaganda. An ideology of peace and prosperity undergirded the imperial project, and this ideology offers a compelling counterpoint to much of what we find in the texts of the early Jesus movement of the first century.

The Dawning of the Golden Age of the Roman Imperial Order

> He restored order when everything was disintegrating and falling into chaos, and he gave a new look to the whole world, a world which would have met destruction with the utmost pleasure if Caesar [Augustus] had not been born as a common blessing to all. (SEG 4.490, Priene Inscription[1])

The year 14 CE saw the end of the illustrious reign of Augustus, who had reigned as emperor of the Roman imperial order for more than forty years. Prior to his death, Augustus oversaw the process of constructing a public record regarding his own political legacy. That public record was published under the name Res gestae divi Augusti, or "The Deeds of the Divine Augustus." It offers a first-person account of Augustus's political accomplishments and demonstrates how he understood the character of the Roman imperial order that engulfed the Mediterranean basin.

---

1. For more on this inscription, see below.

Prior to Augustus's reign, the final years of the Roman Republic had been marked out by conflict between rival factions of political power. Prominent politicians took up arms against each other in an ongoing series of bids to accumulate power and prestige, with the result that some of Rome's most illustrious politicians were removed from the scene—either assassinated or killed in battle alongside the men conscripted to fight their battles. In the aftermath of the late Roman Republic, many would look back on this period as a time of instability and upheaval, of factionalism and warfare. In short, the final years of the Roman Republic were deemed to be an unproductive time that held back the progress and ideals that lay at the heart of the Roman project.

According to later advocates of Roman imperial ideology, the upheaval caused by the dying republic came to an end through one man, himself a son of (a) god. That man, heralded as divine, was Augustus. Accumulating a collection of lifelong powers awarded to him by the Senate of Rome, Augustus took the helm of power as Rome's primary arbitrator, overseeing the dramatic expansion of Rome's territory and the establishment of the *pax Romana* (the peace of Rome). Accomplishing much during the four decades of his reign, he was lavishly rewarded with honors as a consequence. Augustus's self-presentation in the Res gestae divi Augusti is styled in direct contrast to the character of the last days of the Roman Republic, prior to the establishment of the Roman Empire with Augustus's rise to power in 27 BCE.

To ensure that his legacy would not be forgotten, Augustus saw to it that the text of the Res gestae divi Augusti was spread throughout the empire after his death. Copies of it have been found throughout the empire, some on stone monuments and temples, in Latin and in Greek. Many of his accomplishments recorded in that account depict his abilities in conquest, while others depict his enormous generosity. Here are just a few examples.

With regard to conquest, Augustus says things along these lines:[2]

I extended the territory of all those provinces of the Roman people which had neighboring peoples who were not subject to our authority. I brought under control the Gallic and Spanish provinces, and similarly Germany, where Ocean forms a boundary from Cadiz to the mouth of

2. All translations for the Res gestae divi Augusti are taken from the Latin edition in Cooley 2009.

the River Elbe. I brought the Alps under control from the region which is nearest to the Adriatic Sea as far as the Tyrrhenian Sea. (26.1–3)

Augustus claims that he did all this for the benefit of the empire, adding that he "attacked no people unjustly."

With regard to generosity and beneficence, Augustus regularly says things along these lines:

> To the members of the Roman plebs I paid 300 sesterces each … and in my own name I gave 400 sesterces out of the plunder from warfare when I was consul for the fifth time, and also a second time in my tenth consulship out of my personal assets I paid out 400 sesterces each as a handout, and as consul for the eleventh time I bought up grain as a private individual and distributed twelve grain rations, and in my twelfth year of tribunician power I gave 400 sesterces each for a third time. These handouts of mine never reached fewer than 250,000 men. In my eighteenth year of tribunician power, as consul for the twelfth time, I gave 60 denarii each to 320,000 of the urban plebs. And as consul for the fifth time I gave to the colonists who had been my soldiers 1,000 sesterces each out of plunder; about 120,000 men in the colonies received this handout to mark my triumphs. As consul for the thirteenth time I gave 60 denarii each to the commoners who at that time were in receipt of public grain; these were a few more than 200,000 men. (15.1–4)

What emerges from Augustus's self-presentation is an astounding expansion of both the boundaries and the beneficence of the Roman imperial order—an order embodied in Augustus himself. With the establishment of the empire under the auspices of Rome's protecting deities, a new age had begun—an age of abundance, prosperity, generosity, concord, justice, and unity among all peoples.

Inscriptions from the time of the early Roman Empire reinforce the values evidenced in Res gestae divi Augusti. One says of Augustus that "the Emperor Caesar, son of god, god Sebastos has by his benefaction to all people outdone even the Olympian gods" (I. Olympia 53). The gods of Greece, this implies, cannot hold a candle to the gods of Rome (embodied in Augustus) in terms of their generosity toward humanity.

Another inscription that is particularly relevant comes from Priene (in modern-day Turkey), having been written in 9 BCE, when Augustus was almost twenty years into what would become a forty-year reign. The inscription, often called the Priene Inscription, proposes that the annual

calendar should be reordered in relation to the birthday of the divine
Augustus.

> Since Providence who has divinely ordered our existence has applied her
> energy and zeal and has brought to life the most perfect good in Augus-
> tus, whom she filled with virtues for the benefit of mankind, bestowing
> him upon us and our descendants as a savior—he who put an end to war
> and will order peace, Caesar [Augustus], who by his epiphany exceeded
> the hopes of those who prophesied good tidings— ... and since the birth-
> day of the god first brought to the world the good tidings resting in him
> ... the Greeks of Asia have decided that the New Year in all cities should
> begin on the twenty-third day of September, the birthday of Augustus.
> (SEG 4.490)

The "Greeks of Asia" who devised this inscription were proposing that
time itself should be reconfigured around Augustus, an epiphany of the
gods, a "savior" through whom wars cease and peace flows, all as part of
the "good tidings" or "good news" or "gospel" that has been brought to
the whole world. The salvation that Augustus brought to the world has
restored the created order, which had been falling into chaos prior to his
ascendancy. (This point was made clear earlier in the Priene Inscription,
as noted in the quotation that began this section of the essay.) It is little
wonder, then, that the Roman cult of the emperor spread like wildfire
throughout the empire, with worship of the emperor going hand in hand
with the perpetuation of the empire's success. Documenting the point
would itself require more than a single monograph. Indicative, however, is
a simple inscription on the base of a statue (now lost) in Acanthos (Macedonia), which reads: "The city, the association of Roman merchants, and
the inhabitants dedicate this to emperor Caesar Augustus, god, son of
god" (SEG 1.82). Similarly, when speaking of the emperor Caligula, the
late first-century Jewish historian Josephus can say that "all the subject
peoples in the Roman empire had dedicated alters and temples to Gaius
and had given him the same attentions in all other respects as they did the
gods" (*Ant.* 18.8.1 §258 [Feldman, LCL]).

The Priene Inscription imagines Emperor Augustus to have inaugurated a new age of blessing on the human race and the whole of the created
order. This sentiment is captured well in Horace's "Hymn for a New Age,"
written in 17 BCE and commissioned by emperor Augustus himself. The
new age has dawned, and all will be well, as the whole of the empire leans
in and contributes to the effort. Here is a glimpse of what that new age

looks like, through the vehicle of personification: "Now Good Faith, Peace, and Honor, along with old-fashioned Modesty and Virtue, who has been so long neglected, venture to return, and blessed Plenty with her full horn is seen by all" (Horace, *Saec.* 56–60 [Rudd, LCL]).

This, allegedly, was an era benevolently overseen by Augustus's successors as well, who were often highly praised for their generosity in inscriptions throughout the empire. Their rule continued to animate an empire in which everything operated at maximal efficiency. This is the view of the elite Roman historian Velleius Paterculus, who wrote the following regarding the empire overseen by Emperor Tiberius, his patron:

> Caesar [Tiberius] deified his father [Augustus], not by exercise of his imperial authority, but by his attitude of reverence; he did not call him a god, but made him one.
>
> Credit has been restored in the forum, strife has been banished from the forum, … discord from the senate-house; justice, equity, and industry, long buried in oblivion, have been restored to the state; the magistrates have regained their authority, the senate its majesty, the courts their dignity; rioting in the theatre has been suppressed; all citizens have either been impressed with the wish to do right, or have been forced to do so by necessity.
>
> Right is now honored, evil is punished; the humble man respects the great but does not fear him, the great has precedence over the lowly but does not despise him. When was the price of grain more reasonable, or when were the blessings of peace greater? The *pax Augusta*, which has spread to the regions of the east and of the west and to the bounds of the north and of the south, preserves every corner of the world safe from the fear of brigandage.
>
> The munificence of the emperor claims for its province the losses inflicted by fortune not merely on private citizens, but on whole cities. The cities of Asia have been restored, the provinces have been freed from the oppression of their magistrates. Honor ever awaits the worthy; for the wicked punishment is slow but sure; fair play has now precedence over influence, and merit over ambition, for the best of emperors teaches his citizens to do right by doing it, and though he is greatest among us in authority, he is still greater in the example which he sets. (Velleius Paterculus, *Compendium of Roman History* 2.126.1–4 [Shipley, LCL])

No doubt, Emperor Tiberius was pleased by political advertisements of this kind. The emperor is at the helm of a huge enterprise, in which any gestures of generosity that might occur throughout the Mediterranean basin are simply miniature versions of the generosity shown by the Roman emperors, who themselves "have attained heavenly glory and possess the eminence and power of gods" (*IGR* 4.39).

The depiction of divine prosperity and justice filling the whole of the empire was a transferable rhetoric, being seen as applicable to each emperor in turn. For instance, in the mid-first century, the Roman rhetor and philosopher Seneca, serving as one of Emperor Nero's advisers, had this to say about the glorious empire over which Nero ruled:

> Today your subjects one and all are constrained to confess that they are happy, and, too, that nothing further can be added to their blessings, except that these may last. Many facts force them to this confession, which more than any other a man is loath to make: a security deep and abounding, and justice enthroned above all injustice; before their eyes hovers the fairest vision of a state which lacks no element of complete liberty except the license of self-destruction. (*Clem.* 1.1.8 [Basor, LCL])

These aspects of Roman imperial ideology cannot be overemphasized, since they lie at the heart of the imperial project itself. An ideology concerning the expansive and bountiful empire was spreading like wildfire throughout the Mediterranean basin, and at its heart was an optimism that a new age had dawned, a golden age in which people were being united (often by marginalizing those who were not notably pro-Roman), war was out of place (except for the expansion of Rome's boundaries), and generosity flowed freely (especially to those who played a role in augmenting Roman interests).

This basic ideology, or "theology," was not wholly the concoction of Augustus himself (even if he was happy to nurture it and place himself firmly within it), nor was it without localized permutation and definition. But in its most basic form, it was an ideology that survived for more than three centuries, perhaps against all the odds. It proved to be a highly adaptable ideology that required the endorsement of both a religious narrative of legitimization and the political support of the urban elite. With each of these two aspects deserving attention, they will be outlined in the following two sections of this essay.

Legitimization of Rome by the Deities and Fate

> I [says the god Jupiter] have no fixed boundaries to their dominions [the dominions of the Romans], no fixed term to their rule. I have given them empire without end.... [The gods will show] favor to the Romans,

masters of the world, the people of the toga. This has been decreed. (*Aen.*
1.278–283, author's translation)

Probably the most popular story of the imperial age was the story of
the great hero Aeneas in the twelve-part epic *Aeneid* written by Virgil
(or Vergil). Commissioned by Emperor Augustus and composed over a
ten-year period (which ended with Virgil's death in 19 BCE), the *Aeneid*
recounts the story of the exploits of Aeneas, whose actions hundreds of
years before the reign of Augustus would ultimately lead to the establishment of the Roman Empire in the Augustan age. The story is full of the
wonders of epic storytelling, with closely fought battles between national
forces; relationships of love, jealousy, hatred, betrayal, and revenge between
characters; and conflicted characters who have to chose between the duty
to their calling and their own personal preferences. But at the heart of all
this, the *Aeneid* tells the story of Rome's prehistory, how events had been
set in play that ultimately resulted in the founding of Rome and the establishment of Roman rule. According to the story, the route to this outcome
would not be an easy one; there would be conflict, loss, carnage, death, and
sacrifice at every step of the way. But also according to the story, Roman
rule had always been a guaranteed outcome, an assured result.

It was assured because, as the story repeatedly makes clear, it was the
will of Fate that Rome would secure its place as the preeminent power in
the world. Because this was the will of Fate, so too it was the will of the
gods. In the *Aeneid*, history is depicted as having been overseen by the
gods in accordance with Fate's overarching plan. The story permits some
diversity on this matter initially, since throughout most of the story the
goddess Juno does everything in her power to prevent that outcome. But at
the end, even she falls in line with Fate's wishes and affirms, along with the
other gods, the rightness of the events that ultimately lead to the establishment of Rome and its rule over the world-that-mattered.

The story, then, is littered with divine prophecies foretelling the establishment of Rome, prophecies that would be fulfilled hundreds of years
later in the careers of Julius Caesar and his adopted son, Augustus Caesar.
For instance, a shield crafted by the god Vulcan is given to Aeneas to protect him in battle, and on its face Vulcan had inscribed notable moments
that would occur later with the founding of Rome as the imperial power
of the world (*Aen.* 8.626–731). So the shield's prophetic imagery includes
Augustus's famous victory at Actium in 31 BCE (when he was still known
as Octavian)—the last great battle of the Roman Republic when Augustus

defeated the combined forces of his opponents Mark Antony and Cleopa-
tra prior to acquiring imperial power for himself. In the *Aeneid*, Augustus
is the culmination of history that was unfolding according to an inevitable
plan, the fulfillment of all the significant events of the past.

Ultimately, the *Aeneid* propagates an ideology in which opposition to
Rome is opposition to the gods. One simple passage illustrates the point
from book 1, where the supreme god Jupiter speaks to his daughter Venus
about the Romans, "I have given them empire without end," as noted in the
quotation at the start of this section of the essay.

Virgil's story seems to have gripped the popular imagination from
the moment it was released. This is evidenced, for instance, in the city of
Pompeii. Covered by volcanic pumice and ash after the eruption of Mount
Vesuvius in 79 CE, Pompeii has been progressively uncovered through
archaeological excavations in the past three hundred years or so. Among
the huge number of graffiti found on the walls of Pompeii are thirty-six citations of the *Aeneid*—a number that far outstrips the graffiti that cite Homer,
the great epic Greek writer. Fourteen of these thirty-six citations recall the
famous opening line of the *Aeneid* in book 1: *arma virumque canto*, or "I
sing of arms and the man" (and another fourteen recall the opening line
of book 2: *contiquere omnes*, or "They all fell silent"). The man in question,
of course, is Aeneas, and the "arms" are his weapons of war that ultimately
pave the way for the founding of Rome. It has been suggested that these citations from the *Aeneid* might largely be attributed to schoolboys practicing
their writing exercises on the walls of the city, testifying to the *Aeneid*'s role
in forming young minds. But one way or another, the *Aeneid* played a pivotal role in bolstering Roman imperial ideology among the populace. Little
wonder, then, that when the dying Virgil asked that his unfinished epic be
burned instead of published, Augustus overruled his wish and ordered the
story to be lightly edited and circulated among the populace.

Implementation of the Roman Urban Project by the Elite

> History shows that the leading men in society have always dictated its
> character. Whenever there has been a transformation of morals and
> manners among the social leaders, the same transformation has followed
> among the people. (Cicero, *Leg.* 3.31 [Wallace-Hadrill 1990, 145])

It was, of course, self-evident in the first century that the golden age inaugurated by Augustus had not been fully implemented. But this was not

usually taken as a deterrent to the veracity of the ideology. It was all the more reason for others to invest themselves more fully into the imperial project, to shoulder more of the responsibilities in the task of implementing the vision. The entire world was invited to join in with the emperor, to imitate him, and to participate in the actualization of the imperial vision.

Those who participated most noticeably within the public arena were the civic elite. Although relatively few in number (i.e., they constituted about 3 percent of the urban population), they controlled vast resources and were magnificently wealthy. With wealth went responsibility. The elite were expected to use their economic resources for the enhancement of civic society. Accordingly, they undertook to develop their local urban settings, doing so at huge expense to themselves. This involved the construction and maintenance of central features in the urban environment, including monuments, statues, roads, pavements, public baths, gymnasiums, theaters, and temples. It also involved them in the provision of bread distribution to citizens and in the sponsorship of public spectacles such as gladiatorial contests. The elite also contributed further sums of money and other forms of assistance to people (usually men) who sought to ascend the ladder of social hierarchy and who themselves would seek to contribute to the well-being of the urban centers in whatever way they could. In all this, then, the vast wealth held by the few was intended to trickle down to others lower down the social ladder, benefiting them as it went and oiling the wheels of a benevolent and generous societyOf course, the elite did not undertake these responsibilities simply out of the kindness of their heart. There was something in it for them—honor, which meant status. The primary currency of the Greco-Roman world was not money per se, but honor. More precious than gold, honor was the most coveted social commodity. As noted by the Jewish philosopher of the first century Philo of Alexandria (20 BCE–50 CE), "those who are said to bestow benefits … are seeking praise or honor as their exchange" (*Cher.* 122 [Colson and Whitaker, LCL]).

Many factors were included in a person's "prosopographic profile"— the register of a person's public honor. When calculating a person's social reputation, wealth was only one indicator to take into account. Others included civic position, family heritage, citizenship, occupation, age, ethnic origins, position in relation to freedom (free, freed, slave), and sex. Although it was only one of many social indices, the economic factor was one of the most powerful formal indicators of one's public identity. This is because economic resources enabled the civic elite to "work the system" and open up advantageous opportunities for themselves in their quest to accumulate more honor.

Quite simply, then, it served the interests of the elite to be generous, to be known to be generous, to be seen to be generous. Bolstering society through expensive initiatives augmented the public reputations of the elite. This was seen as a win-win situation in which all parties benefited— including, of course, the elite themselves.

An exception to this win-win scenario might be found in Judea, where the local elite frequently catered to Roman interests at the expense of the indigenous Jewish sentiment. Here, for instance, is how Josephus depicts Herod the Great in his relationship both to Rome and to the Jewish people over whom he ruled:

> Because of [Herod's] ambition ... and the flattering attention which he gave to Caesar and the most influential Romans, he was forced to depart from the customs (of the Jews) and to alter many of their regulations, for in his ambitious spending he founded cities and erected temples ... in foreign and surrounding territory. To the Jews he made the excuse that he was doing these things not on his own account but by command and order, while he sought to please Caesar and the Romans by saying that he was less intent upon observing the customs of his own nation than upon honoring them. (Josephus, *Ant.* 15.9.5 §§328–330 [Marcus, LCL])

Herod's interest in honoring the Roman authorities (such as erecting a huge temple to Augustus in Jerusalem's harbor city, Caesarea Maritima) was one instance of a much larger system of patron-client relationships that lay at the heart of Greco-Roman urbanism in general. Patronage involved two people, being unequal in status, entering into a mutually enriching relationship. The patron, who was superior in status, provided financial and material support to the client, who was inferior in status. In return, the client was expected to augment the public prestige of the patron through public expressions of gratitude or in some other fashion. Publicly advertising the beneficence of one's patron was an enterprise that clients vigorously carried out, in fulfillment of their duties within the patronage relationship. For this reason, numerous inscriptions have been found in which clients praise their patron's "goodwill" (*eunoia*) and "grace" or "gift" (*charis*). Clients frequently followed their urban patron through the streets as an entourage, loudly acclaiming his greatness and generosity. They were frequently seen clustered at the entryway or within the central atrium of their patron's house, allowing passersby to catch a glimpse of the influence of the patron in generous support of his clients. In such ways, notoriety and enrichment were at the hub of the patronal relationship, to the benefit of both parties.

Although the Greco-Roman world was thoroughly patriarchal in its structures, on relatively rare occasions women slipped through the androcentric configuration and rose to civic prominence. Although women were not allowed to hold public office or even to vote, at times we find women at the heart of public benefaction, donating vast sums of wealth to enhance the civic environment and acting as financial patrons to associations of workers (for example, the women Eumachia and Mamia in Pompeii). Such women are few and far between, but they do exist in the literary and material record and testify to the manner in which embedded values (the prioritizing of maleness over femaleness) could at times be trumped by other values (i.e., the injection of resources into society).

Ascending the ladder of social honor was, of course, a highly competitive enterprise. Each of the elite attempted to manipulate the dynamics of honor-capture to the best of his (or her) ability, and consequently each was highly aware of where he (or she) stood in the register of social prestige, especially among social "equals." A person's own public initiatives could grease the wheels of social advancement or social slippage and therefore required careful consideration of the potential advantages and risks. So too, the initiatives of others were closely monitored in order to keep account of fluctuations in social prestige in the highly competitive contest of honor-capture. In essence, while the elite were yoked together in their efforts to enhance the public landscape, they also lived to outdo each other in attracting favorable public attention. The stakes were high, and the social antennae were always out, being attentive to every subtle indicator of success and failure.

Among the elite, then, friends were often competitors, and competitors were often friends. They would mix in the public arena (in the public baths, forums, temples, theaters, palestrae, and amphitheaters), but also in private dinner parties, where opulence was on display in order to impress peers and clients. Beyond that, the funding of ever-more-lavish games of gladiatorial combat and extravagant animal hunts became the order of the day among the elite, for the entertainment benefit of those within their city and neighboring cities. In all this, the elite sought to demonstrate the abundance of their reserves and the generosity of their character, seeking to acquire honor in return, in the never-ending quest for influence, prestige, and power.

At the center of this mix was Rome, the city that connected and governed the whole of the world that mattered. Among the elite of the provincial cities, there was usually an unabashed eagerness to align themselves (and consequently their cities) with the ideals of Rome. Advertising
the glory of Rome, its emperor, and its values was not done in newspaper
or television ads, of course, or on political flyers, websites, or social-net-
working services such as we might see today. One of the main media for
promoting Rome's merits and interests was stone. Cities in the first century were adorned with innumerable statues, inscriptions, temples, arenas,
and the like. Even when the "surface text" engraved on these erections did
not explicitly mention Rome and its interests, the "subtext" was almost
inevitably in line with Roman priorities. Beyond stone, Roman interests
were embedded within and advertised by civic ceremonies, gladiatorial
contests, dinner parties, and coinage.

Enabling a pro-Roman spirit to infiltrate every sector of their local
context, the urban elite hoped to endear their city to Rome. The more
successful they were in that endeavor, the more they and their city could
accrue benefits. Rome was eager to bestow honors on pro-Roman cities
and their administrators, thereby heightening the prospects of further
civic and individual success stories. Accordingly, the enthusiastic loyalty
to Rome that had taken hold in urban centers of the Greco-Roman world
went on to fuel the propagation of pro-Roman initiatives by the civic elite,
elevating their city's profile and enhancing their own prospects at the same
time. In a sense, the urban elite functioned as unpaid overseers in the
process of consolidating Roman expansion through the urban centers of
the Mediterranean basin. Roman imperialism relied on elite compliance,
involvement, and initiative. Success in these respects would be met with
further success in the quest for honor-capture.

A Case Study: Numerius Popidius Celsinus

One example brings some of these strands together. In the year 62 or 63
CE (ancient sources differ on the point), the city of Pompeii was devas-
tated by an earthquake—the foreshadowing of the volcanic eruption of
Mount Vesuvius that would destroy the city in the year 79 CE. After that
earthquake, a massive influx of funding was needed to rebuild many of
the edifices that had been heavily damaged within the city's central forum.
While some of those funds probably came from the city treasury and from
imperial funds in Rome, much of the rebuilding project was funded by

the city's elite—or in at least one instance, by a wealthy Pompeian "wannabe." This is illustrated by an inscription marking out the rebuilding of the Temple of Isis, which reads as follows:

> Numerius Popidius Celsinus, son of Numerius, rebuilt at his own expense from its foundations the Temple of Isis, which had collapsed in an earthquake; because of his generosity, although he was only 6 years old, the town councilors nominated him into their number free of charge. (*CIL* 10.846 [Cooley and Cooley 2013, 31])

The inscription gives the impression that a six-year-old boy rebuilt the temple with his own funds and that the city's governing administrators admitted the boy among their number as a result of his generosity.

The reality behind this appearance is probably different. The key figure here is the father of the boy, who is known to us from other inscriptions within the temple where he, Ampliatus, appears alongside his son Celsinus (the inscription being *CIL* 10.847–848, where a woman is also mentioned—a Corelia Celsa, presumably Ampliatus's wife). Ampliatus seems originally to have been a slave. He had taken his master's names when earning his freedom, and Ampliatus's son Celsinus had inherited the first two of those names (the *praenomen* Numerius and the *nomen* Popidius) when he was born in freedom. Meanwhile Ampliatus must have become successful in business, acquiring significant wealth. The destruction of the Temple of Isis in the earthquake allowed him a chance to advance the honor of his family. In an arrangement with civic officials, Ampliatus agreed to pay for the reconstruction of the temple in return for an opportunity to promote his family name. Since Ampliatus was a freedman and not freeborn, he was excluded from holding public office; his freeborn son Celsinus, however, had no such restrictions placed on him. So in return for the use of Ampliatus's money to restore the temple, the city's officials carved out a place for the six-year-old Celsinus on the city council, giving Ampliatus access to power through Celsinus's position. In this way Ampliatus, the former slave, had guaranteed a bright future for his freeborn son, ensuring a long-term place for him alongside other members of the civic elite—such as his former master's family, the *gens* Popidius, who had long been prominent in enhancing the city of Pompeii.

As a freedman with enormous amounts of wealth, Ampliatus would almost certainly have been one of the *Augustales* in Pompeii (and a man with this same name appears on a list of Augustus's "attendants" from the city, probably being the same man). The *Augustales* were found in most cities and large towns of the eastern Mediterranean basin. They primarily comprised freedmen who, due to their servile past, were excluded from securing official civic positions but who, upon gaining their freedom and in view of their notable economic resources, were willingly conscripted by elite patrons (in Ampliatus's case, probably one of the members of the Popidius family) to enhance local civic life. They seem frequently to have enhanced religious devotion to the emperor, perhaps simply by hosting meals (perhaps temple meals) in his honor or, more formally, by serving as local priests in the burgeoning imperial cult. Whether assisting in the worship of the emperor or simply promoting Roman imperial ideology locally, the *Augustales* demonstrate that being "upwardly mobile" went hand in hand with enhancing Rome's reputation within the sprawling urban centers of the Greco-Roman world.

Rome, Prosperity, and Poverty

> Cities now gleam in splendor and beauty, and the whole earth is arrayed like a paradise. (Aelius Aristides, *The Roman Oration* 99 [Wengst])

This sentiment of Rome's glorious achievements from the second-century pro-Roman rhetorician Aelius Aristides would have coincided with the sentiment of the *Augustales* of the first century, like Ampliatus. They themselves played an important symbolic role by reinforcing at least two values that were deeply entrenched within Greco-Roman society—the superiority of wealth to poverty and the inferiority of servile birth to free birth. (Similarly, they represent the fact that, in the Greco-Roman world, being male was superior to being female.)

But most who had been born into slavery could never expect to climb out of it like Ampliatus had done, let alone to become economically engorged, as he had done. Ampliatus and his son Celsinus were among a very small number of those who enjoyed a significant degree of economic security. Despite Aristides's glowing words about the wonders of urban living "in splendor and beauty" in a world "like a paradise," the reality was much different for huge numbers of people.

An approximation of the economic spread within a typical urban population of the first century appears in table 1 below. In it, seven strata are distinguished, each one labeled with an ES (for "economy scale") number. The most destitute are represented at the bottom of the scale, with the designator ES7, while the wealthiest are represented at that top of the scale, with the designators ES1, ES2, and ES3 (with ES3 being the stratum that might be most appropriate for someone like Ampliatus). Also a brief description and a fuller elaboration of the profiles of the various strata appear in the table, along with proposed population percentage for the various economic levels.

Table 1. Economy Scale

Scale	Description	Includes	%
ES1–ES3	Imperial, regional, and municipal elites	Imperial dynasty, Roman senatorial families, provincial officials, some retired military officers, some merchants	3
ES4	Those with moderate surplus	Some merchants, some traders, some freed persons, some artisans (especially those who employ others), and military veterans	15
ES5	Those with stable resources, with reasonable hope of remaining above the minimum level to sustain life	Many merchants and traders, regular wage earners, some artisans, large shop owners, freed persons, some farm families	27
ES6	Those whose resources provided for the everyday necessities of life	Small farm families, laborers (skilled and unskilled), artisans (esp. those employed by others), wage earners, most merchants and traders, small shop/tavern owners	30
ES7	Those with inadequate personal resources to sustain life in the long term	Unattached widows, orphans, beggars, disabled, unskilled day laborers, prisoners	25

The survival strategies employed by people at the various economic levels would have differed greatly. The elite of ES1–ES3 were busy enhancing the prospects for personal and civic honor, while the poor of ES6 and ES7 were desperately trying to eek out the most rudimentary form of existence—with ES7s being wholly dependent on the goodwill of others in order to keep from slipping into the inevitable.

Complicating the picture, however, are slaves. They would usually have fallen within the lower strata of this economy scale but, by nature of the fact that they belonged within household structures, they were not exposed to the harsh realities of poverty to the same extent as those in the lower strata who lived beyond household structures. But if the household offered slaves some level of economic security in one regard (i.e., the householder inevitably supported them), their economic security was nonetheless tenuously based, being dependent on the "goodwill" of the householder to maintain the slave in exchange for obedience and efficiency. Some slaves were able to earn money of their own in order to eventually purchase their freedom; for most, however, that must have been far beyond the scope of their situation. Some slaves were likely given their freedom when their health and abilities had deteriorated, making them no longer able to perform satisfactorily within the household; that "freedom" left them without the support of the household and without much to offer in terms of crafting out an economically secure livelihood. For ex-slaves who matched this profile, the lower strata of the economy scale had become a place where gloomy economic consequences were now more threatening than ever before.

While those who were enormously rich sank incredible amounts of money to enhance the fabric of the public space and to display their own opulence, at times they also undertook charitable initiatives on behalf of the poor. This was not the norm, however, since the people who mattered were their "middling-level" clients and the general public, not really the poor per se. But at certain times and in certain places, the elite donated money so that poor children would benefit from assistance schemes, for instance. We should also imagine occasions when a rich patron instructed members of his accompanying entourage to toss a few coins to beggars sitting along the roadside or standing at the entrance to a temple. Of course, such gestures would have been made with an eye to enhancing the status of the rich man, but we cannot altogether exclude more altruistic and "humanitarian" concerns from the motivational mix of the elite.

Nonetheless, when considered in relation to the other initiatives the elite funded, initiatives favoring the poor were usually insignificant in the amount of resources that they redistributed. Even the grain dole in the city of Rome was targeted not for the benefit of the poor in general but primarily for those within the middling groups who were also freeborn citizens; these provisions of grain may, in fact, have been intended more to prevent economic slippage among the middling groups than to foster the economic well-being of the destitute.

Meanwhile, the resources of the elite needed to be constantly restocked. Not only did the coffers of the elite require perpetual replenishment, but the Roman army also had to be paid and provided for at a massive expense. Controlling as many economic resources as possible was an imperative that the elite could not afford to compromise. Moreover, with approximately 85 percent of the empire's resources being based on agricultural harvests, the elite were heavily invested in land ownership. For the elite, acquiring ever-greater amounts of rural land held the prospect of ultimately acquiring even more honor through urban initiatives.

Often this involved the acquisition of land through lightly disguised forms of pilfering. Here is one way in which the elite acquired land from those less fortunate. A farmer experiences a financial setback due to bad weather damaging his crop. The farmer arranges to receive a loan of money from a rich man, although with a very high rate of interest attached to it. But through a combination of the high interest rate and continued bad luck, the farmer finds it impossible to pay back the loan on time. As a consequence, the rich man now acquires the farmer's land, taking possession of it as a result of the loan default. The farmer is offered the opportunity of renting the land from the rich man or working it as the rich man's manager, with the new owner expecting a profitable return either way. In this way, the rich man has captured prime resources and added to his long-term financial portfolio.

In scenarios of this kind, resources were squeezed out of the land with as much of it as possible moving upward to those urbanites who needed it to bolster their civic prospects. The economy of the Greco-Roman world was not only enmeshed within an honor system that took its cues from the political interests of Rome; it was also fine-tuned to ensure that economic surplus was stripped from those at the bottom of the economic scale and redistributed to those at the top.

If the system was run by and favored the elite, many of the poor survived at subsistence level for long periods of time, perhaps getting a bit of luck at times to help buffer them against the hardships of life, but also dropping below subsistence levels at other times. Some may have been able to pull themselves out of the grip of destitution, while others were not as fortunate. In urban centers, the poor would have included many merchants, traders, artisans, and shop or tavern owners, whose livelihood is characterized by Lucian of Samosata (ca. 125–80 CE) as "laborious

and barely able to supply them [i.e., the artisans] with just enough" (*Fug.*
12–13 [Harmon, Kilburn, and MacLeod, LCL]). For many, however, even
the harsh life of a struggling artisan might have seemed like comfort.
Unskilled laborers were ever-present, hoping to glean any kind of menial
labor in order to perpetuate their existence a little longer. Public provisions to assist those in need were (at best) few, far-between, and feeble.
The disadvantaged simply had to hope for an escape from the precarious
situations that they inevitably faced, and often the clutches of poverty
dragged them into the downward spire of ill-health leading to death.

More needs to be said about slavery—the institution that oiled the
machinery of the Greco-Roman world. Slaves were everywhere in the
ancient world, and without them, the "system of survival" would have
come crashing down. The best estimates for the city of Rome, for instance,
place the number of slaves at 400,000 in a city of 1,000,000—with two
slaves for every three nonslaves. The best estimates suggest that about
35 percent of urban centers comprised slaves. At one point, the Roman
Senate considered whether to pass a law requiring slaves to wear a certain
kind of clothing in order to distinguish them from the free and freed; the
motion failed when the senators realized that this would allow slaves to
realize how numerous (and therefore potentially dangerous to social stability) they really were (Seneca the Younger, *Clem.* 1.24.1).

Apart from a master's initial expense of purchase and the ongoing
maintenance costs, a slave provided relatively cheap labor. Even households running small shops might have purchased an inexpensive slave to
assist in the operating of that business (ES5 shop owners, for instance).
The higher up the economy scale, the more slaves would be found per
household. In the houses of the elite, slaves were ubiquitous, involved in
the running of every facet of the household's many operations and enter-
prises.

Some slaves were well-treated by their masters, on the basis that property serves its owner better if it is well cared for. But for many slaves, life
was harsh. Ill-treatment must have been common. So, for instance, Cicero,
a prominent Roman statesman and philosopher (106–43 BCE), thought
that while a father would care well for his own children, a master should
"coerce and break" his slaves with the whip (*Rep.* 3.37).

Being the property of their masters meant that slaves (especially low-
level slaves) were at his beck and call, being pawns to their masters' whims,
including sexual whims. An inscription from the basilica (or civic court-
room) in Pompeii reads *Prehende servam; cum voles, uti licet* (CIL 4.1863).

Translated this reads: "Take hold of your servant [for sexual purposes] whenever you want to; it is your right" (author's translation). The Latin poet Martial (40–ca. 103 CE) praises a certain Linus for his frugality when he (Linus) chose to have sex with his slaves' wives (for free) instead of purchasing prostitutes (*Ep.* 4.66). In the late fourth century, the theologian John Chrysostom testifies to occurrences of sexual abuse of slaves by their masters, a situation that would have prevailed as well in the first century: "Many [slave owners] have thus compelled their domestics and their slaves. Some have drawn them into marriage against their will, and others have forced them to minister to disgraceful services, to infamous love, to acts of rapine and fraud, and violence" (*Hom. Phil.* 1 [*ANF*]).

Since bestowing sexual favors on their master was a common experience for both male and female slaves, female slaves often gave birth to sons or daughters who were both offspring of the householder and new slaves within his household; some female slaves fathered by the householder would then have grown up and given birth to further slaves through impregnation by the same householder. This was a convenient way to increase a household's workforce and, presumably, productivity. If offspring of slaves were not wanted, they were "exposed." This involved placing the babies out on the road either to die or for someone else to pick up and make use of—usually using them later in life either as slaves or as beggars.

Slavery in the Greco-Roman world was not based on ethnic origins, as with the North American slavery of Africans in the seventeenth through nineteenth centuries (and beyond?). One became a slave either by being born into it or by misfortune. Slave traders could acquire more stock for their trade, for instance, by kidnapping children in one territory and selling them off as slaves in another territory. But one of the most lucrative sources of slaves was warfare. Conquered people became spoils of war to be sold off as slaves in order to ensure that the system would continue to run efficiently for those at the helm of power.

Rome, Peace, and Violence

There were always kingdoms and wars in Gaul right up until you submitted to our [Roman] laws. Although we have often suffered at your hands, we have (by right of conquest) imposed only this one thing on you, with which we keep the peace. For peace between nations is impossible without soldiers, and there are no soldiers without pay, and no pay

unless taxes are paid. Everything else we share with you. (Tacitus, *Hist.*
4.74 [Moore, LCL])

Everyone knew about Roman warfare. From the time of her ascendancy,
Rome had succeeded in conquering the nations, stamping out dissent, and
unifying the world by means of her military strength and acumen. Everyone knew these things, but not everyone agreed about how to interpret
them. While most extolled the virtues of the divinely legitimated Rome, a
few characterized the Roman project as the incarnation of evil.

Rome was, of course, hugely successful in realizing its goals. Never
before had such a socioeconomic and religiopolitical force enthralled
so much of the globe. Never before had so much been done for such a
single cause. For those who stood to benefit from her initiatives, Rome
was empowered and legitimated by the gods as a source of goodness on the
earth. Rome stood for the integration of all the people-who-mattered in a
system of peace, security, concord, and prosperity.

Tacitus (56–117 CE) articulated the official line of Roman expansion-
ism over what were termed "barbaric nations" when he wrote that Rome's
military conquests helped to ensure "that men who were scattered and
uncivilized (and for this reason naturally inclined to war) might become
accustomed to peace and quiet through pleasures" (*Agr.* 21 [Benario]).
Surely this was a grand and laudable vision in the eyes of those who promoted Rome's empire—first conquer the savage nations, then introduce
them to the abundant cultural pleasures offered by Roman society. Such
"humanizing" concerns permitted the extraction of taxes to enable Rome
to keep the peace through the imposition of its paid armies. The point is
given voice elsewhere in Tacitus's works, as noted in the quotation from
his *Histories* at the start of this section of the essay: "There are no soldiers
without pay, and no pay unless taxes are paid."

Such pro-Roman views cohere well with the view adopted by Josephus, the Jewish historian who, in an earlier phase of his life, had served as
a general of Jewish military forces in the uprising against Rome in 66–70
CE on the soils of Judea and Galilee. When he came to the recognition
that he was doomed if he continued to oppose Rome, he seized on an
opportunity to save his skin by becoming a vocal supporter of the Roman
general Vespasian, who was wiping out the Jewish forces and would later
be appointed as emperor in Rome. Josephus's enthrallment with Roman
power is evident in these words that he later penned: "For what was there
that had escaped the Romans.… Fortune, indeed, had from all quarters

passed over to them, and God who went the round of the nations, bringing
to each in turn the rod of empire, now rested over Italy" (*J. W.* 5.9.3 §§366–
367 [Thackeray, LCL]). Even Virgil would have struggled to say it better.

Josephus had more to say on the matter. He championed the view that
Rome was unwillingly drawn into war against the Jews. Jewish hotheads
had provoked Rome to act; Rome really sought "to save the city and the
temple," which were destroyed "contrary to Caesar's wishes" (*J. W.* pref. 11
§27–28 [Thackeray, LCL]) and by "the unwilling hands of Rome" (*J. W.*
pref. 4 §10 [Thackeray, LCL]). Since the war was provoked by extrem-
ists who do not represent the majority of Jews, Josephus can frame his
account of the Jewish war against Rome in terms that avoid blaming one
side or the other (*J. W.* pref. 1–4 §§1–11). Nonetheless, he might have done
more in that narrative to unmask why resentment was festering among
some Jews in the first place, prior to the outbreak of war. There was more
than one story to tell regarding that tragic conflict, but arguably Josephus
truncates the voice of those Jews whom he conveniently blames for the
onset of the conflict.

If some might have dared to ask the question, "What have the Romans
ever done for us?" a scripted answer is readily given by Epictetus, who had
this to say: "Caesar has obtained for us a profound peace. There are neither
wars nor battles, nor great robberies nor piracies, but we may travel at all
hours, and sail from east to west" (*Discourses* 3.13.9 [Oldfather, LCL]).
Similar are the words of this inscription:

> Land and sea have peace, the cities flourish under a good legal system,
> in harmony and with an abundance of food, there is an abundance of all
> good things, people are filled with happy hopes for the future and with
> delight at the present. (Hirschfeld 1893, inscription 894)

From what we have already seen, there is reason to doubt that this inscription's rhetoric matched reality; quite simply, all did not share bounty and
delight in harmony. The inscriber seems content to allow the experiences
of those at the upper echelons of society to inform much of his heavily
scripted propaganda.

Even someone like the author of the Johannine Apocalypse (i.e., Revelation) gives testimony to the magnificence of Rome's project when looked
at from one angle. Although he likens Rome to "Babylon the great, mother
of whores and of earth's abominations," and depicts it as being "drunk with
the blood of the saints and the blood of the witnesses to Jesus," when he

sees Rome revealed in her full splendor he admits that he even is "greatly amazed" at her greatness (Rev 17:5–6 NRSV, where a positive connotation resides with the notice of amazement). But this fleeting moment of awe in relation to Rome's greatness is countered with the Apocalypse's demarcation of Rome as "whorific," abominable, and bloodthirsty. So, only a few verses later, the author lists the commodities of "the merchants of the earth" in order of their perceived value, with the most valuable appearing first in the list and the least valuable appearing last (Rev 18:11–13). After listing twenty-seven more valuable commodities, the author adds his last entry—"slaves." The author then adds an ironic phrase identifying slaves not as mere chattel for the benefit of merchants and householders but, in fact, as "human lives" (or literally, "human souls"). For this author, the satanic dragon has infiltrated the whole of the Roman system—its religion, its economics, and its military power base (see, e.g., Rev 13).

Rome made no apology for the devastation that accompanied her campaign of world domination; it was simply collateral damage. So, for instance, Virgil says, "You, Roman, be sure to rule the world, to crown peace with justice, to spare the vanquished and to crush the proud" (*Aen.* 6.851–853 [Fairclough, LCL]). Pliny the Younger (61–112 CE) praises the emperor Trajan, speaking of the way that "terror" is now among the enemies of Rome. According to Pliny, the emperor's goals have resulted, legitimately and rightly, in the seas having been "stained with the bloodshed of victory" and the battlefields having been "piled high with the bodies of the dead" (*Pan.* 12 [Radice, LCL]). Plutarch (45–122 CE) speaks of Roman victories being won through a "multitude of corpses and spoils" (*Mor.* 324 [Babbitt, LCL]). Tacitus describes the invasion of Germany by Germanicus in 14 CE in this way: "For fifty miles around he wasted the country with sword and flame. Neither age nor sex inspired [his] pity; places sacred and profane were razed indifferently to the ground" (*Ann.* 1.51.1 [Jackson, LCL]). When describing the Roman invasion of Britain, he also speaks of the British tribes having "feared our peace" with good reason (*Ann.* 12.33).

One example of "neither age nor sex" inspiring the pity of Rome's warriors is recounted by Josephus. Recounting the invasion of Roman troops, Josephus recounts how the Roman general Florus commanded his soldiers

> to sack the agora known as the "upper market" and to kill any whom they encountered. The troops, whose lust for booty was thus backed by their general's order, not only plundered the quarter which they were sent to attack, but plunged into every house and slaughtered the inhabitants.

There ensued a stampede through the narrow alleys, massacre of all who were caught, every variety of pillage; many of the peaceable citizens were arrested and brought before Florus, who had them first scourged and then crucified. The total number of that day's victims, including women and children (for even infancy received no mercy), amounted to about three thousand six hundred. (*J. W.* 2.14.9 §§305–307 [Thackeray, LCL])

If the Roman way of bringing peace through bloody conquest of the nations was thought to be a laudable program, it was also one that was advertised extensively on the coinage that circulated throughout the empire. Coins commonly depicted Mars, the god of war, in full armor and in league with the goddess Victoria (i.e., victory), or they depicted Rome holding the goddess Victoria in one hand and stepping on the instruments of war of opposing nations. Other scenes common on coinage include Octavian Augustus in full military uniform holding a spear, or subjected people being crushed under the right foot of the goddess Pax (i.e., Peace), or simply subjected people in mourning.If Rome was engaged in a program of rapacious violence, it was a program ingrained within the founding myth of Rome itself. Romulus and Remus, the two twin brothers credited with founding the city of Rome, had been suckled in their infancy by a she-wolf, according to that myth. That the twins had inherited the voracious instincts of the wild predator who nurtured them was testified to within the fratricide of the myth, with Romulus killing his twin in order to gain exclusive control of the city. As one third-century writer puts it, the founders of Rome "were fed at the breast of a she-wolf, so now that whole people has the disposition of a wolf, insatiably bloodthirsty, hungry and lusting for mastery and riches" (Marcus Iunianus Iustinus, *Historiae Philippicae* 38.6.7–8 [author's translation]).

If the voracious appetites of the she-wolf became embodied within the ethos of the Roman imperial order itself, that same ethos frequently percolated down into the attitudes of Rome's most dedicated supporters. The process of bringing about Roman good by way of violence is evident in the oaths of allegiance to the emperor that were sworn annually throughout much of the Roman Empire. The following oath, from the beginning of the Common Era, indicates what such oaths normally consisted of:

I swear by Zeus, Earth, Sun, all the gods [and] goddesses, and by Augustus himself that I will be loyal to Caesar Augustus and his children and descendants for all the time of my life, in word, deed and thought, considering as friends whomever they [i.e., the imperial family] consider so, and reckoning as enemies whomever they themselves judge to be so; and that in their interests I shall spare neither body nor soul nor life nor children, but in every way for those things that pertain to them I shall endure every danger; and that if I see or hear anything hostile to them being either said or planned or carried out, I will report this and shall be the enemy of the person who is saying or planning or doing any of these things. And whomever they themselves may judge to be their enemies, these people I will pursue and defend them against, by land and sea, by sword and steel.

But if I do anything contrary to this oath or do not conform to the letter with the oath I swore, I bring down on myself and my body, soul and life, and on my children and all my family and all that belongs to me utter and total destruction down to my every last connection and all my descendants, and may neither the earth nor the sea receive the bodies of my family and descendants nor bear fruit for them. (translation Parkin and Pomeroy 2007, 9)

Devastation is all around this oath. Enemies of the emperor are deemed to be enemies of the one who swears the oath; the oath-taker commits himself to kill such imperial enemies "by sword and steel"; should the oath-taker fail in his murderous obligations, he commits his whole household to destruction. The extent to which the rhetoric would have matched reality is open to debate. But since such oaths had notable currency in the first century, it is at least clear that a vitriolic posture often went hand in hand with loyalty to Rome throughout much of the Mediterranean basin.

The same is demonstrable from Dionysius's *Roman Antiquities*, completed just prior to the birth of Jesus. In one episode (*Ant. rom.* 3.13–21), Dionysius recounts how two sisters each gave birth to triplets, one sister having married a Roman and the other an Alban. These six cousins, who had loved each other dearly in youth, are asked to act out the grievances of the two cities that they belong to, resulting in the cousins slaughtering each other until only one remains—a Roman. Adding to the pathos of the moment, the Roman survivor had a female sibling who was engaged to be married to one of the Albans who had been slaughtered. When that sibling mourned for her butchered Alban fiancé, the triumphant Roman slaughters her as well, touting that he is one "who loves his country and punishes those who wish her ill, whether they happen to be foreigners or his own people" (*Ant. rom.* 3.21.6 [Cary, LCL]). Her father refuses to allow his daughter to be buried and, instead, sponsors that very evening a marvelous banquet in honor of Rome and its triumphs.

The virus of destruction that often went hand in hand with Roman imperialism was the subject of occasional critique, when voices were brave enough to challenge Rome's modus operandi. This is evident from a variety of Jewish texts from the time, not least the Jewish apocalyptic text called 4 Ezra, probably composed in Judea at about 100 CE, thirty years after the destruction of Jerusalem in 70 CE. Fourth Ezra 11–12 contains an elaborate vision about an eagle that God opposes—with the eagle, of course, being the symbol of Rome, as advertised on the standards of the Roman military, which fought under its banner. The "vision" in 4 Ezra highlights the atrocities carried out by the machinery of the Roman system. In accord with Rome's own claims, the eagle is said to reign "over the whole earth," controlling "the whole earth." The vision is unsparing in its critique of Roman control. Rome's reign is carried out "with much oppression," "with great terror," "with grievous oppression," "with deceit," and "not with truth." The Roman eagle is depicted as having "terrifying wings," "evil little wings," "malicious heads," "most evil talons," and a "worthless body" because of the horrors perpetuated in the name of peace and security.

According to 4 Ezra's portrait of Rome, at the very heart of Rome lies "insolence" and "pride" that perpetuates atrocities. Convinced that Israel's God is opposed to Rome's ways, the author knows that Rome and its ways "will surely disappear" before the God of justice. The human (and humane) voice of "a lion," the messiah of Israel, speaks words of hope regarding the impending destruction of Rome and the establishment of the reign of God: "so that the whole earth, freed from your violence, may be refreshed and relieved, and may hope for the judgment and mercy of him who made it" (= 2 Esdras 11:46 NRSV). The empire of Rome, propped up at its core by violence, has opposed the "refreshing" and "relieving" empire of God, an empire of "judgment [against oppressors] and mercy."

The overthrow of Rome by means of an eschatological invasion of Israel's God was a sentiment widely shared among the Jewish people of the first century. Perhaps the best example of this comes from the Jews of the Qumran community on the edge of the Dead Sea. A scroll known as the War Scroll (1QM) articulates the community's great hope that "the rule of the Kittim [= the rule of Rome] will come to an end, wickedness having been defeated, with no remnant remaining, and there will be no escape for [any of the sons] of darkness" (1.6–7). Then a new era will transpire, as the God of Israel overthrows the darkness: "And [the sons of jus]tice shall shine to all the edges of the earth, they shall go on shining, up to the end of all the periods of darkness; and in the time of God, his exalted greatness will shine for all the et[ernal] times, for peace and blessing, glory and joy, and length of days for all the sons of light" (1.8–9 [García Martínez and Tigchelaar 1997–1998, 1:113]).

This sentiment, that Rome would one day be uprooted by the God of justice, was shared by one Jewish writer from whom such sentiment is least expected—Josephus, whom we have met several times already in this essay. Writing in the last quarter of the first century, Josephus had much to say that was positive about Rome (although this was probably not the case during his days as a leader of Jewish military forces against Rome). He even claimed that the Jewish prophet Daniel had predicted that Rome would be used by God to punish God's own people (*Ant.* 10.11.7 §267). It is, then, extremely revealing to see how Josephus interprets Dan 2 for his first-century audiences. Noting various features of Dan 2 that correspond with various political regimes throughout history, one would expect Josephus to offer an interpretation of the "stone" that destroys the kingdom of iron, a key component of Dan 2. But at precisely that point in his interpretation, Josephus writes this:

> I have not thought it proper to relate this [i.e., the meaning of the stone], since I am expected to write of what is past and done, and not of what is yet to be; if, however, there is anyone who has so keen a desire for exact information that he will not stop short of inquiring more closely but wishes to learn about the hidden things that are to come, let him take the trouble to read the Book of Daniel, which he will find among the sacred writings. (*Ant.* 10.10.4 §210 [Marcus, LCL])

The fact that Josephus broke off his interpretation of Dan 2 at this juncture is extremely telling, since it enabled him to avoid discussing the toppling of an immovable empire by divine fiat—something that belongs to "what is yet to be" and "the hidden things that are to come." Evidently Josephus's posture toward Rome was multilayered. An empire of unbreakable iron that has already served as an instrument of Israel's God, Rome was ultimately destined to be overthrown by Israel's God of justice by means of a "stone"—that is, a messiah or a messianic age.[3] It is not surprising, then, to find a few paragraphs later that Josephus's overview of the book of Daniel skips from Dan 6 to Dan 8, entirely omitting any mention of Dan 7, a passage that others of his day were interpreting as a messianic prediction of

---

3. On this common interpretation of the passage, see Wright 2013, 1316.

the toppling of Rome by a Jewish messiah (as Josephus himself notes in *J.W.* 6.5.4 §§312–314; see also 4 Ezra 12:32–34).

Criticism of Rome was not simply restricted to some who expected that the God of Israel would overthrow Roman rule when he ultimately invades the world in eschatological glory. There are indications that people at the very heart of the Roman system knew of similar criticisms of Roman brutality.

This is evident from Tacitus's *Agricola*. Although that text praises Rome (as shown above) and is pro-Roman in its intent, it also contains passages in which opponents of Rome are allowed to articulate their point of view. For instance, Tacitus permits criticisms of Rome to be voiced within his text by Calgacus, a leader of the indigenous British tribes, who as a general of the "barbarian" forces naturally opposes Roman attempts to conquer his native land. Calgacus criticizes the notion that the end justifies the means—more specifically, he criticizes the notion that Roman violence is legitimate if it results in Roman conquest and occupation of new lands. Calgacus depicts Roman encroachment past its boundaries as driven by a lust for power, resulting in the degradation and exploitation of indigenous communities. According to Calgacus, Rome's way is "to make a devastation and call it peace." With Roman leaders as "harriers of the world," Calgacus protests against them in this way:

> Now that the earth fails their all-devastating hands, they probe even the sea. If their enemy has wealth, they have greed. If he is poor, they are ambitious. East and West have glutted them. Alone amongst humanity they behold with the same passion of concupiscence waste and need alike.
>
> To plunder, butcher, steal, these things they misname empire. They make a desolation and call it peace. Children and kin … are swept away from us by conscription to be slaves in other lands. Our wives and sisters, even when they escape a soldier's lust, are debauched by self-styled friends and guests. Our goods and chattels go for tribute. Our lands and harvests are taken in requisitions of grain. Life and limb themselves are used up in leveling marsh and forest to the accompaniment of gibes and blows. Slaves born to slavery are sold off forever. (*Agr.* 30.3–31.2 [Hutton, LCL])

Here, criticism of Rome appears within the text of an elite Roman. Importantly, in his speech (not recorded fully here), Calgacus assumes a knowledge of Rome that he himself, as a non-Roman general, could simply not have had. This shows Calgacus to be Tacitus's literary construct, a mouthpiece for criticisms of Rome that were known not merely on the periphery of the empire (e.g., in barbaric Britain) but within the very heartland of Rome itself.[4]

That Rome's ways were questionable is evident also in the work of the Roman satirist Juvenal in the late first century CE. He characterized the day in which he lives as "an age more evil than that of iron, one for whose wickedness nature herself can find no name, no metal from which to call it" (*Sat.* 13.3 [Ramsay, LCL]). According to Juvenal, "luxury, more deadly than any foe, has laid her hand upon us and avenges a conquered world"; he notes that "since the day when Roman poverty perished, no deed of crime or lust has been wanting to us" (*Sat.* 6.37 [Ramsay, LCL]). The poet Propertius, writing during the time of Emperor Augustus, recognized that the "lust for hateful gold" had propelled Rome to worldwide domination: "Now o'er such wide seas are we tempest-tossed; we seek out a foe, and pile fresh war on war" (*Elegies* 3.5.10–12 [Butler, LCL]). So too, the Roman historian Sallust (86–35 BCE) constructs a fictionalized letter sent from Mithridates to the emperor of Parthia in which the militarism of the Roman Republican era is strongly condemned.

> Or are you not aware that the Romans turned their arms in this direction only after the Ocean put an end to their westward progress? That from the beginning they have possessed nothing except what they have stolen: their homes, wives, lands, and dominion? That having been once upon a time refugees without a native land or parents, they have been established to serve as a plague upon the whole world, being men who are prevented by nothing human or divine from plundering and destroying allies and friends—those situated far away or nearby, weak and powerful too—and from considering as their enemies all powers not subservient to them and especially monarchies. (*Hist.* 4.69.17 [Ramsey, LCL])

Even the great Plutarch, with his strong connections to Roman power, asks at one point whether Rome's reputation is shamed by its violence. "That is a question," he says, "that would need a long answer, if I am to satisfy men who hold that betterment consists in wealth, luxury and empire, rather than in safety, gentleness and that independence that is attended by righteousness" (Plutarch, *Num.* 26 [Perrin, LCL]). Although he never provides

---

4. For similar knowledge of such criticisms within Roman halls of power, see Caesar, *Gaelic War* 7.77.14–16.

a direct answer, his contrast here of the violence of "empire" versus the gentleness of "righteousness" seems indicative of how he would provide an answer, if boldness permitted.

From this survey, we can see that the *Pax Romana*, the peace of Rome, involved what one scholar has called a "hostile confrontation" between Rome and indigenous cultures; in that confrontation, peace was "brought about by blood and iron and the use of every fighting weapon of the state imaginable" and was "based on a politics of compulsion; and in each individual instance there lay behind it an unbounded desire to preserve its own advantage" (Fuchs 1965, 201; trans. from Wengst 1987, 176 n. 31).

A Case Study: The Renovation of Herculaneum's Waterfront Profile

Herculaneum, a town about one hundred miles south of Rome, under-went extensive renovations during the Augustan age, and those renova-tions were carried out in order to align the city with the Roman imperial ideologies of peace and prosperity and to advertise those values within its civic architecture.

Whereas the city's waterfront had earlier been dominated by a military garrison advertising the city's strength and impregnability, just prior to the first century CE the waterfront was completely overhauled. Central to this project was the construction of at least two magnificent dwellings at either end of the city's seafront limits and a tower connected to some of the city's baths. What had once been a military façade was transformed in order to publicize peace and prosperity.

This transformation was probably orchestrated by a leading resident of the city, Nonius Balbus, a strong supporter and friend of the emperor Augustus. The extensive and expensive task of first demolishing and then reconstructing the waterfront profile of this Greco-Roman town was prompted by the eagerness of the civic elite to align Herculaneum with Augustan ideology and be an embodied advertisement of that ideology. In Nonius Balbus's hopes, Herculaneum was to be seen as showcasing all that the exciting and eternal empire of Rome was inaugurating throughout the world-that-mattered.[5]

---

5. For more on this, see Wallace-Hadrill 2011, 252–53.

In Brief

In order to overview the ideological and practical aspects of the Roman imperial order, the preceding sections of this essay have had to truncate some issues and overlook others. But enough has been said to signal what could be demonstrated in far greater length concerning the Roman imperial order.

In essence, there was a double nature to the Roman imperial order. On the one hand, the Roman Empire had an obvious greatness about it; that much cannot be denied, nor should we attempt to detract from that fact. On the other hand, the greatness of Rome had an objectionable underbelly that is all too often lost from view—not least, perhaps, because the majority of data informing us about that time come to us from the privileged elite.

Undergirding both the greatness and the contestability of Rome lay a widespread belief in the essential goodness and appropriateness of Roman rule, a rule bestowed with a legitimating mandate from the gods. Advertising peace and prosperity, the Roman imperial order engaged in an ideological universalizing program that favored those who mattered, especially the wealthy Roman elite, while often spawning injustices against those who were deemed not to matter.

For Further Reading

On what kept the Roman Empire together over such a long period of time:

Woolf, Greg. 2012. *Rome: An Empire's Story*. Oxford: Oxford University Press.

On the age of Augustus:

Galinsky, Karl. 1996. *Augustan Culture: An Interpretive Introduction.* Princeton: Princeton University Press.
Wallace-Hadrill, Andrew. 2005. "*Mutatas Formas*: The Augustan Transformation of Roman Knowledge." Pages 55–84 in *The Cambridge Companion to the Age of Augustus*. Edited by Karl Galinsky. Cambridge: Cambridge University Press.
Zanker, Paul. 1988. *The Power of Images in the Age of Augustus*. Translated by Alan Shapiro. Ann Arbor: University of Michigan Press.

On the Res gestae divi Augusti:

Ridley, Aaron. 2004. *The Emperor's Retrospect: Augustus' Res Gestae in Epigraphy, Historiography, and Commentary*. Leuven: Peeters.

On the *Aeneid*:

Harrison, S. J., ed. 1990. *Oxford Readings in Vergil's Aeneid*. Oxford: Oxford University Press.
Martindale, Charles, ed. 1997. *The Cambridge Companion to Virgil*. Cambridge: Cambridge University Press.

On the Greco-Roman economy and a defense of the approach adopted in part of this essay:

Longenecker, Bruce W. 2010. *Remember the Poor: Paul, Poverty, and the Greco-Roman World*. Grand Rapids: Eerdmans. Especially chapters 1–4.
———. Forthcoming. "The Politicized Graeco-Roman Economy and the Economic Ethos of Paul's Mission." In *Oxford Handbook of Pauline Studies*. Edited by R. Barry Matlock. Oxford: Oxford University Press.
Scheidel, Walter, ed. 2012. *The Cambridge Companion to the Roman Economy*. Cambridge: Cambridge University Press.

On the Roman peace, war, and security and the emerging Jesus movement:

Wengst, Klaus. 1987. *Pax Romana and the Peace of Jesus Christ*. London: SCM.
Wright, N. T. 2013. *Paul and the Faithfulness of God*. Minneapolis: Fortress. Especially 279–347 and 1271–1319.

For a "novel" approach to the Greco-Roman world in the first century:

Longenecker, Bruce W. 2003. *The Lost Letters of Pergamum: A Story from the New Testament World*. Grand Rapids: Baker Academic. 2nd ed., 2016.

Jesus-in-Movement and the Roman Imperial (Dis)order

Richard A. Horsley

The basic assumptions and controlling concepts of the field of New Testament studies obscured the Roman Empire as the historical context of Jesus and the Gospels. New Testament studies developed in Western Europe as the division of theology that interpreted the sacred texts of the Christian religion. Religion was understood as separate from political-economic affairs. Religion was also increasingly understood as individual faith or belief. Correspondingly, New Testament books were defined as religious texts about religion, the Gospels viewed as merely collections of the sayings of and stories about Jesus, and Jesus understood as an individual teacher of individuals.

At the center of New Testament studies was a Christian scheme of the origins of Christianity as a more universal and spiritual religion than the more parochial religion of Judaism. Jesus was the unique teacher-revealer who preached the good news of love to individual followers and broke with the restrictive Jewish law. Only after he appeared as resurrected did his disciples organize a community in Jerusalem, from which the movement spread among gentiles in the more universal Hellenistic culture. Thus Jesus was an individual religious teacher in the context of and opposed to Judaism. Little attention was given to the Roman conquest and the Roman imperial order that dominated Palestine.

About a century ago, New Testament scholars became convinced that "(late, or now early) Judaism" and "(early) Christianity" were dominated by "apocalypticism." This also distracted attention from Roman imperial rule, since "apocalypticism" was understood apolitically, as focused on the imminent "end of the world" in "cosmic catastrophe."

Some New Testament introductory textbooks did mention the Hellenistic and the Roman empires as part of the broad historical framework within which Jesus and Paul and the Gospels and Letters were then discussed as religious leaders and texts. But imperial rule of Palestine did not appear to have a serious impact on Jesus's "ministry." Although they were appointed by the Romans, the high priests were the "religious leaders" and the temple was the central "religious" institution of Judaism. Jesus's action in the temple was merely a "cleansing." Interpreters found no conflict between God and Caesar in Jesus's response to the question about the tribute to Rome, which was read through the lens of the separation of religion and politics ("church and state").

Innovative adaptation of concepts from social science (e.g., "honor-shame" or "patron-client") or development of critical new perspectives (e.g., feminist criticism) did not necessarily lead to questioning of the standard assumptions and concepts that still shape the field in the questions posed and the interpretations offered.

In the last few decades, however, there has been growing recognition of how the Roman conquest and imperial rule of Palestine was the determining context of Jesus's mission and of how Jesus's mission and movement(s) opposed Roman imperial rule. In retrospect, it would appear to have been a critical rereading of "background" sources for life in Roman Palestine during the 1970s and 1980s that led to a break with some of the standard constructs and assumptions and the initial recognition that Jesus was not opposed to and by "Judaism" but the Roman imperial order in Palestine. Then in the last twenty-five years separate lines of research on a number of fronts have led to an ever more complex and precise understanding of the imperial context in which Jesus worked and of the how the gospel sources portray him in resistance to the Roman imperial order.

Recognition of the Roman Imperial (Dis)order in Palestine and Jesus's Response

The Historical Context: Roman Conquest, Imperial Rule, and Popular Resistance

A broader and closer reading of the Judean texts that are the primary sources for life in Roman Palestine and attention to modern anticolonial movements would appear to be the main factors that led to discernment of how Roman imperial rule was the determining factor in Jesus's mission.

First, reading of sustained historical narratives in sources for "the Jewish background" of Jesus opened up the ways in which imperial armies and rulers had dominated the life of the Judean (and Galilean) people for centuries. Reading those sources also made clear that more than other peoples subject to the Hellenistic and Roman imperial rule, Judeans and Galileans had mounted repeated resistance and periodic rebellion. The visionary sections in the book of Daniel, for example, narrate the history of the wars between the Ptolemaic and Seleucid kings for control of Syria-Palestine that climaxed in the emperor Antiochus IV Epiphanes's violent attacks on Jerusalem in support of the Hellenizing high priesthood and the resistance by a group of learned scribes (the *maskilim*).

Most important was a critical rereading of the extensive historical accounts of the wealthy Judean priest Flavius Josephus, which provided the most extensive and precise portrayal of Roman Palestine (*Jewish War*; *Ant.* books 14–20). The principal division was not between "Judaism" and "Hellenism" but between the Roman officers and their client Herodian and high-priestly rulers, on the one hand, and the people in Judea and Galilee on the other (Horsley 1981, 1984, 1985, 1986, 1987; Goodman 1987). Not long after the initial Roman conquest, the Roman Senate installed the military strongman Herod as "king of the Judeans." After his death, the imperial court set his son Antipas as ruler over Galilee and Herod's four high-priestly families as rulers over Judea, under the oversight of a Roman governor. The people, however, living in hundreds of village communities, formed movements of resistance and periodically mounted widespread revolts. The revolts in 4 BCE and 66–70 CE provide a significant historical framing of the mission of Jesus. Josephus's accounts indicate a disintegration of the social fabric and an increase in conflict between the people and their Rome-maintained rulers in the immediate historical context of Jesus's mission: increasing debts, popular protests, repressive military attacks by the Roman governor, and predatory exploitation of their own people by high-priestly and Herodian families (Horsley 1981, 1987).

It is clear from sources such as Dan 10–12; Pss. Sol. 2 and 17; and Josephus's histories that the high-priestly families and Herodians were not "Jewish leaders." They certainly had no followers. They were rather the Roman-supported rulers of the people. The temple-state in Jerusalem was indeed the central religious institution in Judea. But it was also the central political-economic institution, supported by revenues taken from the people and charged with maintaining social order and collecting the tribute for Rome. Far from ever defending the people against Roman abuses, the priestly aristocracy exacerbated the exploitation of the people for their own advantage (Horsley 1986). The high priests (appointed by the Roman governor) and temple were the face-and-form of the Roman Empire in Judea, just as Herod Antipas and his newly built capital cities of Sepphoris and Tiberias were in Galilee.

Second, prominent in "current events" in the 1950s through the 1980s were anticolonial movements and revolts among African, Southeast Asian, and Latin American peoples and military "counterinsurgency" campaigns by the colonial and neocolonial powers. Since these belonged in the sphere of politics, they did not seem relevant to most biblical interpreters. But students in western Europe and North America protested their own governments' repressive violence against the anticolonial movements. It hardly seems coincidental that in these decades, leading New Testament scholars lumped the many different Galilean and Judean peasant movements and scribal protest groups together as a kind of ancient Jewish "national liberation front" advocating violent revolt, "the Zealots" (Hengel 1961). In fact, as student protests escalated, leading New Testament scholars published pamphlets using "the Zealots" as a foil for their interpretation of Jesus as an apolitical teacher and advocate of nonresistance (Cullmann 1970; Hengel 1971; 1973).

The sources, however, especially the historical accounts of Josephus, read more critically, indicated a far more complex resistance to Roman imperial rule that was also suggestive in comparison with the portrayal of Jesus in the Gospels (Horsley 1984, 1985, 1987). The revolts and resistance movements formed mostly among the peasants in hundreds of villages in Judea, Samaria, and/or Galilee. It was not a case of movements or revolts of "the Jews" against "the Romans," but rather of the Judean and Galilean people against the Herodian and high-priestly rulers installed by the Romans as well as the Roman military sent out against them. The villagers proved themselves capable of mounting collective action under their own leadership. As Josephus's accounts often indicate, their resistance was clearly rooted in Israelite tradition.

A telling example of the conflict between the people and Roman imperial rule is the Galilean villagers' organization of a peasant "strike" in protest of a Roman army moving through their area with a statue of the emperor Gaius that he had ordered installed in the temple. In collective action across many villages, the peasants refused to plant their fields (*Ant.* 18.8.2–6 §§261–284; Horsley 1987, 110–16). As the anxious Herodian officers pointed out to the Roman legate of Syria, this action would result in a "harvest of banditry." That is, with no crops that year, there would be no harvest from which the Romans could take their tribute, but also no food for the peasants themselves, who would resort to banditry. The collective peasant action was clearly taken in defense of the second commandment in the Mosaic covenant: the command not to "bow down and serve" a ruler (or god, other than God, i.e., Caesar) with tithes, taxes, or tribute from the crops that were needed to feed families.

More significant in comparison with the Gospels' portrayal of Jesus as a messiah or a prophet like Moses or Elijah is that much of the revolt or resistance took the distinctively Israelite forms of movements led by a leader acclaimed as "king" by his followers or movements led by a prophet (Josephus, *J.W.* 2.4.1–5.2, 13.4–5 §§56–75, 259–263; 422–442; *Ant.* 17.10.5–8 §§271–285; 18.4.1 §§85–87; 20.5.1, 8.6 §§97–98, 168–171; Horsley 1984, 1985). The widespread revolts of 4 BCE in the three major districts of Israelite heritage of Judea, Galilee, and the Transjordan and the revolt in southern Judea in 67–70 CE all took the form of a "messianic" movement patterned after the traditions of the Israelites' "anointing" the young David as their king to lead them in resistance against the Philistines (2 Sam 2:1–4; 5:1–4). In the movements of resistance and renewal in Samaria and Judea in the decades immediately following Jesus's mission, a prophet led his followers out to experience some new act of deliverance clearly patterned after the great acts of deliverance led by Moses and/or Joshua.

A critical reading of Josephus's accounts of these movements suggests that stories both of the young David as the messiah leading struggles against invasive outside rulers and of Moses as the prophet of the people's deliverance from bondage under foreign rulers were so vibrant in village communities that they provided the social forms taken by new movements of resistance. There is no indication, however, that these stories were derived from written texts such as Exodus or Joshua or 2 Samuel. The popular "kings" of 4 BCE or 67–70 CE bear little resemblance to the elaborate psalmic anticipation of the more "royal" or "imperial" anointed son of David in the scribal Ps. Sol. 17. These movements were rooted in the Israelite popular tradition, comparable to the "little tradition" that anthropologists and historians find in other agrarian societies, in contrast to the (often partly written) "great tradition" of the ruling class (Scott 1977).

Many sources indicate that some groups of scribes also took up opposition to imperial rule. The previously standard construction of Judaism included the four "philosophies" or "factions" (Josephus, *J.W.* 2.8.2–14

§§119–166; *Ant.* 18.1.2–6 §§11–25; sometimes called "sects" by modern scholars): the legalist Pharisees, the aristocratic Sadducees, the monastic Essenes, and the "fourth philosophy" (sometimes identified as the early "Zealots"). The accounts of Josephus explain that the Pharisees were a large faction of advisers or assistants who served the high-priestly heads of the temple-state (*Ant.* 13.10.5–6, 16.2 §§288–298, 408), what historical sociologists sometimes termed intellectual or scribal "retainers" of the rulers (Horsley 1987, 16–19, 68–71; Saldarini 1988). Insofar as Pharisees and other scribes served the priestly aristocracy and were economically dependent on it, they had a stake in the temple-state and would be expected to be loyal. Indeed, "the leading Pharisees" worked hand in hand with high-priestly figures to keep a lid on the insurrection after the summer of 66 CE until they could negotiate with the Romans to regain their position in the imperial rule of Judea.

But the scribes serving the temple-state were also the guardians of (official) Israelite tradition. When the imperial rulers and/or their own high-priestly patrons violated Israelite tradition too egregiously, circles of scribes mounted serious resistance (Dan 11:33–35). It is clear from examination of the Dead Sea Scrolls that the covenanters who withdrew to Qumran were a group of dissident scribes and priests who opposed the Hasmonean high priests' abuse of power. At the end of Herod's reign, two prominent (scribal) teachers in Jerusalem inspired their students to cut down the Roman eagle that the king had erected above the gate of the temple and were brutally killed (*J. W.* 1.33.2 §§650–655; *Ant.* 17.6.2–3 §§150–160). As the Romans were installing the high-priestly aristocracy to keep order and collect the tribute under the oversight of a Roman governor, the scribes and Pharisees of the "fourth philosophy" organized resistance to payment of the tribute, which the Romans viewed as tantamount to rebellion (*Ant.* 18.1.1, 6 §§4–10, 23–24). As with the popular movements of resistance, the scribal protests were motivated by Israelite tradition, particularly how the Roman eagle and especially the tribute to Caesar violated the first two covenantal commandments ("No other god/master/king" and "do not bow down and serve another god/master/king").

In sum, from a critical reading of primary sources with reflection stimulated by current colonial rule and anticolonial movements, it became clear that the historical context in which Jesus worked was not "Judaism" as constructed in the field of New Testament studies. The historical context was rather peoples of Israelite heritage in Judea, Samaria, and Galilee conquered by Roman warlords and ruled by Rome-appointed and Rome-maintained client rulers in the Jerusalem temple-state and Herodian kingship. The people of Israelite heritage, however, rooted in a deep tradition of resistance to unjust and imperial rulers, mounted move-ments of resistance and periodic revolts. Most important for consider-ation of Jesus's mission, the people formed movements of renewal and/ or resistance rooted in Israelite popular tradition, the best known led by prophets. Even a few scribal circles trained to serve the temple-state chose instead to oppose their high-priestly patrons and their imperial overlords on the basis of their loyalty to the principles of Israelite tradition.

Constructing Jesus's Mission as a Response to the Roman Imperial (Dis)order in Palestine

By the mid-1980s, it was possible to see that, as presented in the Synoptic Gospel tradition, Jesus fits just this context and these conditions imposed by Roman imperial rule (Horsley 1987). His proclamation of the direct rule of God offered an alternative to imperial rule, and his healing of the personal and collective body addressed the impact of imperial violence and exploitation. In contrast to the Christian scheme of Christian origins in which Jesus was only an individual teacher and a movement began only after the resurrection appearances, key Jesus traditions in the Gospels por-tray Jesus as generating a movement in the villages of Galilee (Horsley 1987, chs. 8–9). In contrast to the previous scholarly emphasis on how he addressed mainly "tax collectors and prostitutes and (other) sinners," his teachings address the poor in general, that is, the peasant villagers who were hungry and in debt. If we attend to the context indicated in the content of the "love your enemies, do good, and lend" complex of say-ings, they are addressed to local social-economic interaction and cannot be taken, as previously claimed, as admonitions of nonresistance to the Romans. Indeed, insofar as these sayings make many allusions to Mosaic covenantal social-economic laws and teachings, it is evident that Jesus was restating covenantal demands for mutual aid and cooperation among vil-lagers who, indebted to one another, had fallen into divisive quarreling. Jesus was not teaching individuals but was addressing communities that had been disintegrating under the pressure of violence, tribute and taxa-tion, and high-interest loans.

    Among the aspects of imperial rule in Palestine that became evident from a closer reading of Josephus's histories was that the high-priestly aristocracy set in power by the Romans in 6 CE had little legitimacy and exercised little power in Judea other than what the Roman governor provided by (threat of) military action (Horsley 1986; Goodman 1987). The four high-priestly families were all creatures of the hated Herod, who had massively rebuilt the temple in Hellenistic-Roman style. Dependent on the favor of the Roman governor, they never protested outrageous Roman actions against the people. The annual Passover festival, which celebrated the people's liberation from bondage, was fraught with potential conflict and became the occasion for popular protest of imperial domination. Symbolic of the temple as the face-and-form of Roman rule, the governors posted Roman soldiers atop the colonnades of the newly constructed courtyard—which would only have exacerbated the conflict (Horsley 1987, 34, 93–99). In the revolt of 66 CE, once the Roman troops took shelter in the Antonia fortress and were then driven out of Jerusalem, the people attacked the house of the high priest Ananias and later attacked other high-priestly figures (Josephus, *J. W.* 2.17.6 §§427–429).

Jesus's prophetic pronouncements and prophetic demonstration against the temple and high priesthood fit this context of opposition to the face-and-form of Roman imperial rule in Judea. The previously standard interpretation of Jesus's action in the temple as a "cleansing" is an anachronistic projection of the modern separation of religion and politics. It appears rather to have been a prophetic demonstration of God's condemnation of the temple as an institution that oppressed the people, particularly in its allusion to the famous prophecy of Jeremiah that God would destroy the Jerusalem temple because of its violation of the covenantal commandments.

This interpretation of the action in the temple is confirmed by the multiple attestation of Jesus's prophetic pronouncements of judgment against the temple and/or the high priests or the ruling "house" of Jerusalem. As in the demonstration in the temple, Jesus again acts in the traditional role of an Israelite prophet. His prophecy of the impending desolation of the ruling house of Jerusalem paralleled in Matthew and Luke (Matt 23:37–39 // Luke 13:34–35; presumably from Q) takes the traditional form of a prophetic lament. His pronouncements of the destruction of the temple, attested three times in Mark (13:1–2; 14:58; 15:29), as well as in John (2:14–22) and in Gospel of Thomas (71), again takes the poetic form of a prophetic oracle: of the destruction of the temple/house of God ("made with hands"), followed by the rebuilding of the temple/house of God ("not made with hands"). Several attempts had been made to blunt the political impact of this prophecy. The argument by E. P. Sanders (1985) that Jesus was anticipating a literally rebuilt temple in Jerusalem was based on a (surprisingly literalistic) misreading of prophetic and "apocalyptic" texts. Those texts suggest rather that the "house of God" to be restored following God's judgment of the temple and imperial rule referred to the renewal of the people. This is unmistakable in the Animal Vision (1 En. 85–90), in which "the house" symbolizes the people, the (second) temple is represented by "the tower" (which has "polluted bread" on its altar), and, following the judgment of the oppressive imperial forces, the rebuilding of "the house" symbolizes the renewal of the people.

The previously standard interpretation of Jesus's response to the Pharisees' question whether it was lawful to pay tribute to Caesar, meant to entrap Jesus, was similarly an anachronistic projection of the modern separation of religion and politics. In this separation, no conflict is seen between loyalty to God and paying tribute to Caesar. In the Roman Empire, however, Caesar was served (honored/worshiped) as the sole Lord and Savior of the world and "son of God" in shrines, monuments, festivals, and temples, including those that had been built in his honor by Herod, king of the Judeans (not to mention the loyalty oath imposed by Herod and the Roman eagle erected above the temple gate). The "fourth philosophy," led by the Pharisee Saddok and the scribal teacher Judas of Gamla, refused to pay the tribute, because it meant violation of the first two commandments, that is, the prohibitions of serving any Lord and Master other than God. The Pharisees, whose basic views the "fourth philosophy" shared (according to Josephus, Ant. 18.1.6 §23), similarly knew that it was not lawful according to the Mosaic covenant to render tribute to Caesar. That was how they thought to entrap Jesus into declaring that payment of the tribute was not lawful, which would lead the Roman governor to execute him, since the Romans viewed refusal to pay the tribute as tantamount to rebellion. Jesus does not say in so many words "it is unlawful, so don't pay." But he cleverly indicates, in no uncertain terms, that the people do not owe and should not pay tribute. (What belongs to God? Everything. What belongs to Caesar? Nothing.)

In this construction of Jesus's mission as a response to the conditions created by Roman imperial conquest and domination and as opposition to and by the institutions and agents of Roman imperial rule in Palestine, there is no problem explaining why he would have been arrested by the high priests and ordered executed by crucifixion by the Roman governor. The Roman authorities did not allow the high priests the power of execution (the customary form was stoning). Crucifixion, a slow, agonizing, torturous death purposely staged in public places for its "demonstration affect" to terrorize people, was the form of execution used by the Romans for recalcitrant slaves in Italy and leaders of rebellion among subject peoples. In their maintenance of the imperial order locally, however, by sending out the military or ordering crucifixions, Roman officers did not bother to differentiate among bandits making raids, popular kings leading revolts, and popular prophets leading nonviolent movements of renewal. Judging from the Gospels' portrayal, Jesus would appear to have been among those prophets, except that he focused on catalyzing a renewed, independent, and alternative covenantal community in the villages, while pronouncing God's judgment of the institutions of Roman imperial rule. Jesus was leading a renewal of the people of Israel in opposition to the rulers of Israel.

This summary of an initial construction of "Jesus and empire" is based on recognition of two historical realities that are fundamental for further refinement of our understanding of the mission of Jesus in its historical context. First, judging from the sources for the historical situation in "Roman" Palestine, the fundamental division was not between "Judaism" and "Hellenism" but between Roman and Roman-appointed rulers and the people in the villages struggling to survive destructive conquest, multiple taxation, debt, and the resulting disintegration of village community. Second, there was persistent resistance to Roman domination among people of Israelite heritage. Thus, like other (prophetic) leaders of popular movements, Jesus was not engaged in a conflict with "Judaism" (which had not yet emerged historically as a religion-and-ethnic group) but in opposition to and by the Roman and Roman-appointed client rulers and their impact on the people.

Confirmation and Complexification from
Further Historical Investigations

In the last twenty-five years, our understanding of Roman imperial rule as the context of Jesus's mission and of Jesus's mission as a response to imperial rule in Palestine has become more complex and multidimensional as the result of many lines of research into political-economic and cultural aspects of life under Roman imperial rule (Horsley 2014).

Roman Conquest and Imperial Rule

Recognition that Roman conquest and imperial rule in Palestine was the context of Jesus's mission was confirmed and reinforced by the increasing recognition that the Roman Empire was the context of Paul's mission and his letters and of other texts later included in the New Testament. This was particularly important with regard to the mission of Paul and his letters insofar as it had long been standard in New Testament studies to understand the great apostle in opposition to "Judaism" (see esp. Georgi 1991; N. Elliott 1994; Horsley 1997). The empire was recognized as the context of Paul's mission, and the book of Revelation became vivid from archaeologists' and art historians' investigations of the shrines, temples, festivals, and inscriptions in honor of the emperor, whose presence came to "pervade public space" in the very cities to which Paul's and "John's" letters were addressed (Price 1984; Zanker 1988; both abbreviated in Horsley 1997). Similarly, it seemed clear that the "infancy narratives" in Matthew and Luke portrayed the newborn Jesus as a "Savior" and messianic leader of the (independent, renewed) people (of Israel) as an alternative to the imperial Savior and a serious threat to the imperial rulers and their client king Herod (Horsley 1989a).

Meanwhile, Roman historians began to present far more candid accounts of the brutality of Roman military conquests, as the warlords deliberately destroyed villages, slaughtered and enslaved people, and crucified leaders of resistance in order to terrorize subject peoples into submission (Mattern 1999; Kallet-Marx 1995; summarized in Horsley 2003, 26–31). These studies confirmed the veracity of Josephus's accounts of the brutal Roman reconquests of Judea and especially Galilee and opened toward an appreciation of the concrete devastation, slaughter, and resulting social trauma that would have been experienced by Galileans and Judeans in the decades before and after Jesus's mission.

The Roman reconquest that directly affected Jesus of Nazareth and the people among whom he worked was the military suppression of the popular revolts in 4 BCE. The Roman appointment of Antipas as tetrarch following the reconquest had a much greater and lasting impact on Galileans. For the first time historically, the ruler of Galilee was located in Galilee. Antipas, moreover, built two capital cities within twenty years. Resources were needed to fund the massive building projects, and tax collection became far more "efficient," with nearly all of the villages of Lower Galilee within sight of either Sepphoris or Tiberias. These new cities would have been foreign bodies imposed on the landscape culturally as well as politically and economically (Horsley 1995, 158–85). Without reflecting on the dramatic change that these newly constructed cities brought to Galilee in the lifetime of Jesus, some archaeologists hypothesized that

Galilee had become "urbanized," which in turn led to the notion that Galilee was culturally cosmopolitan (Crossan 1991, 18–19). More sober estimates of the population of the new cities soon followed (Reed 1992). Moreover, culture in the new cities would hardly have been "cosmopolitan," certainly not "Hellenism" versus "Judaism." These cities rather represented the consolidation of the Roman imperial order of client rulers. Whatever the mix of elite Judean and (Hellenistic) Roman culture that was imposed onto Galilee in these cities (Antipas had been raised at the imperial court in Rome), the Galileans were or became sharply hostile, as Josephus's accounts of their attacks on the cities in the great revolt indicate (Horsley 1995, 76–88; 2002).

The new awareness of how "the presence of the emperor pervaded public space" in the Greek cities sharpened sensitivity to the imposition of cities and temples constructed in honor of Caesar in Palestine, begun on a massive scale by Herod and continued by his sons and successors. The presence of Caesar in the seaport city of Caesarea, seat of the Roman governor, further represented by the Roman eagle over the gate of the temple and Caesar's soldiers atop the porticoes of the temple at the Passover festival. It cannot be simply coincidental that gospel stories locate Peter's "confession" that Jesus is "the messiah" in "Caesarea Philippi," near which yet another temple to Caesar was constructed.

Parallel to the increasing awareness of the culture of Roman imperialism was the dawning awareness in the 1990s of the modern culture of imperialism. Edward Said's 1993 book *Culture and Imperialism* had a profound impact on several academic fields.[1] One of the principal features of the modern culture of imperialism was that cultural criticism blocked awareness of the imperial power relations in which cultural expressions were rooted. As Said pointed out, for example, academic interpretation of English literature self-consciously articulated as a cultural antidote to dehumanizing industrialization ignored how the families featured in nineteenth-century novels lived from exploitation of colonized peoples. Following Said's analysis, the lack of attention in New Testament studies to the Roman imperial order as the determinative context of Jesus can be seen as a symptom of the more general "disconnect" between modern

---

1. The development of postcolonial criticism owes a good deal to Said's groundbreaking analysis. Like Said's analysis, however, some postcolonial criticism is narrowly cultural and not grounded in analysis of the political-economic relations in which cultural expressions are based.

Western culture and modern Western imperialism. This makes it all the more imperative for critical inquiry into the gospel sources and Jesus-in-movement to include criticism of the field in which we interpreters have been "trained" and of its elision of Roman imperial domination of subject peoples among whom Jesus and the Gospels originated.

This elision, however, was soon seriously affected by current events. As Said noted, while the French and British were proud of their empires, people in the United States were ambivalent or even embarrassed, which subdued public discussion. Considerable public dissent and critical academic discussion arose over the Vietnam War. But it was the George W. Bush administration's response to the events of September 11, 2001, that evoked more serious academic attention to American empire, which in turn led to wider critical consideration of the Roman Empire as the dominant context of Jesus's mission and of New Testament texts in general. "Neoconservative" intellectuals, several prominent in the Bush administration, had been insisting that the United States had an empire and should use its military power accordingly. It was clear that the Bush administration would mount major military action. Given that United States administrations seek (Judeo-Christian) religious justification for military action, it seemed important to bring critical analysis of Jesus's opposition to Roman imperial rule to the fore by focusing *explicitly* on Jesus and empire (as in the 2001 Rauschenbusch Lectures at Colgate Rochester in October, revised as Horsley 2003). It was then the Bush administration's invasion of Iraq in 2003, despite worldwide protests against it, provoked wider interest among New Testament scholars in the realities of empire in the programs of the Society of Biblical Literature and an increasing number of publications.

The Jerusalem Temple-State and the Deeper Conflicts in the Imperial (Dis)order

Several separate lines of recent research have revealed the deeper historical roots of the multiple conflicts that came to a head under Roman domination of Palestine. The rebuilding of the temple by the previously "exiled" Judeans has often been touted as the beginning of Judaism. The "second" temple, where sacrifices were made to "the god who is in Jerusalem," however, was sponsored by the Persians as the local representative of the imperial administration that would maintain order and gather revenues both as tribute to the Persian regime and as support for the priesthood that headed the temple. The books of Ezra and Nehemiah, named for imperial officials sent by the Persian court, explain in some detail how difficult it was to consolidate the temple-state's control in Judea (Horsley 2007, building on many recent studies).

More extensive recent investigations of the intellectual retainers of the temple-state suggest that scribal opposition to the priestly aristocracy and the imperial regimes who kept them in power was long-standing and more intense than previously understood. A critical rereading of the Judean texts usually classified as "apocalyptic," in Dan 7–12 and most sections of 1 Enoch, indicates that they do not articulate an apocalyptic scenario of the end of the world in "cosmic catastrophe." They are not evidence that "the Jews" at the time of Jesus were caught up in "apocalypticism." Rather they are visionary reviews of the history of imperial rule over Judea that climax in the scribes' own resistance, God's judgment of imperial rulers, and a restoration of the people (Horsley 2007, chs. 7–9).

With regard to the mission of Jesus in the context of imperial rule, these texts rather indicate how deep the division was between the people and the rulers of the temple-state and its imperial sponsors, in three ways. First, the Jerusalem temple-state was the long-standing face-and-form of imperial rule in Second Temple Judea that was then exacerbated by the Roman conquest, imposition of Herod, and restoration of the priestly aristocracy that had little legitimacy among the people. Second, even some circles of the scribes who were dependent on the high priests mounted resistance to the local face of imperial rule, resistance that paralleled that of the people, as in the Maccabean revolt. Third, these texts indicate that yearning for the renewal of the people had been vividly alive in scribal circles for two centuries before Jesus's mission. As noted above, moreover, their image of the restoration of the people either did not include or specifically excluded the temple and (presumably) its priestly aristocracy (Dan 7; 10–12; 1 En. 85–90).

Directly related to the course of Jesus's mission, which focused on Galilean villages but then climaxed in Jerusalem, is recent historical investigation into the different histories of the different regions of Israelite heritage (Horsley 1995, chs. 1–2). The Galileans had come under Jerusalem rule only a hundred years before the birth of Jesus and during the lifetime of Jesus were no longer under Jerusalem rule. For the many centuries before that, the Galileans (presumably descendants of the most northerly tribes of Israel) had been under different kings or different Persian and Hellenistic imperial jurisdictions. As the Seleucid regime weakened, the Hasmonean high priests in Jerusalem, after conquering Samaria and Idumea, took control of Galilee and required the inhabitants to submit to "the laws of the Judeans" (Josephus, *Ant.* 13.11.3 §§318–319). Galileans may thus have experienced Jerusalem rule as empire-like. It is certainly difficult to discern how and when the Galileans might have become loyal to the temple-state.

On the other hand, it is conceivable that Galileans became more aware of their affinity with Judean and Samaritan villagers and their common Israelite heritage once they were brought under the same Jerusalem rulers, who then became the face of Roman imperial rule in Palestine. It is clear from "insider" sources such as Josephus that people were distinguished by the region in which they lived (or from which they originated), "the Judeans" in Judea proper, "the Samaritans" in Samaria, and "the Galileans" in Galilee (Freyne 1999). But insider sources (such as Josephus or rabbinic texts) also refer to all of these people as "Israel." "Outsiders" evidently thought of all people subject to Jerusalem rule as "Judeans."[2] As Israelites, they all would have shared the same Israelite tradition: of the liberation from foreign rule in the exodus, of the leadership of the founding prophet Moses and their common bond in the Mosaic covenant, and of the common struggle against the invasion of the Philistines. During the lifetime of Jesus itself, after the Romans set Antipas over Galilee, the Jerusalem temple-state no longer had jurisdiction over the Galileans. But during the prior century under Jerusalem rule, Galileans could have come to view Jerusalem as the capital from which Israel was ruled. Would a popular prophet pursuing the renewal of Israel in Galilee have viewed the temple and high priesthood as the rulers of Israel whom it was part of a prophet's role to confront?

Several separate recent lines of research are confirming, directly or indirectly, that there was a cultural division in Palestine that corresponded to the political-economic divide and that popular leaders and movements were rooted in what I have been calling Israelite popular tradition. Text-critical analysis of the manuscripts of books later included in the Hebrew Bible that were found among the Dead Sea Scrolls has reached two significant related conclusions about the state of books of the Torah in the late Second Temple period: the books existed in multiple versions, and the

---

2. This may explain why, in the Gospel of Mark, Pontius Pilate mocks the Galilean Jesus as "king of the Judeans," while the high priests, at the foot of the cross, mock him as "the king of Israel."

different versions were still undergoing development (Ulrich 1999). This text criticism is showing that, contrary to previous assumption, there was no stable, much less standard text of *the* Torah, even in the scribal circles, that could provide a solid basis for our knowledge of "(early) Judaism."

Considering that literacy and written scrolls were confined basically to scribal circles, it is unclear that nonliterate villagers would have had any direct knowledge of books of Torah (Hezser 2001; Horsley 2011b, 126–29). In a traditional society in which it was rare, writing had an almost numinous authority. Judean and even Galilean villagers may have known that the scrolls laid up in the temple included certain Israelite traditions (exodus stories, covenantal commandments and teachings). What scholars with modern print-cultural assumptions assume were "quotations" in the Gospels from written texts were rather appeals to the authority of what "is written" (usually commonly known phrases of psalms or combinations of lines from different prophets or a version of a story different from what appears in the scribal or "biblical" version; see Horsley 2001, 59–61, 162–66). The combination of these lines of research thus confirm that popular leaders of movements such as Jesus were informed by and working from the Israelite popular tradition cultivated orally in village communities, parallel to but often different from the official or scribal Judean tradition, some of which was written on scrolls kept in the temple or in scribal circles (Horsley with Draper 1999, ch. 5; building on Scott 1977).

The Gospels as Sources and a
Relational Approach to Jesus-in-Interaction

In my initial attempt to understand Jesus's mission as response to the Roman imperial order in Palestine, I followed what had been the standard focus on "Jesus traditions," particularly the teachings, separated from the gospel "collections" and analyzed by form criticism. Most of the scholarly studies of "the historical Jesus" that mushroomed in the 1990s focused even more narrowly on individual sayings as the sources ("data") for Jesus. The liberal scholars of the Jesus Seminar, further refining form criticism, rejected most of the judgmental sayings as "inauthentic" and constructed Jesus as an itinerant teacher of other individuals, a "sage" (Crossan 1991). Those who, like Albert Schweitzer a century ago, still interpreted Jesus as an "apocalyptic" preacher (of the end of the world) judged a wider range of sayings as "authentic," but also focused on individual sayings (Allison 1998).

Isolating individual sayings from the Gospels, however, separates them from the principal literary context that might serve as an indication of their meaning in historical context. Individual sayings are thought to have been uttered separately, remembered by individuals who then transmitted them to other individuals and so forth, somewhat like the old game of "telephone." Imagined as (remembered) isolated artifacts, Jesus's sayings evidently involved no (genuine) communication, no resonance with hearers in the context. Individual sayings are also thus isolated from particular cultural tradition in which people live and work.[3] Put bluntly, it is not clear that any person, much less a historically significant leader, could have communicated in isolated individual sayings. But is there any reason, other than that the assumptions of form criticism had become habitual, for thinking that isolated individual sayings are the sources or "data" for the historical Jesus?

While Jesus interpreters were focused narrowly on refining their assessment of individual sayings many interpreters of the gospels were recognizing that the Gospels were not mere collections of traditions but sustained stories comprising a sequence of episodes that are integral to the overall story (Kelber 1979; Rhoads and Michie 1982; Moore 1989). The recognition of the Gospels as stories and the development of narrative criticism prepared the way for efforts to read these stories in their historical context(s) (e.g., Horsley 2001; Winn 2008). Since a gospel story and the Jesus traditions it incorporated may have developed from their origins closer to the context of Jesus-in-interaction but then was addressed to communities of a Jesus movement expanding into areas beyond the frontiers of Galilee and Judea, however, it may be necessary to consider shifting contexts. Yet it is striking that however a gospel may have developed, the basic story of each gospel, in its setting, characters, and plot, fits the historical context of Roman Palestine in the mid-first century, as known from other sources such as Josephus's histories (Horsley and Thatcher 2013).

Now that the Gospels have been recognized as sustained stories, it is only appropriate to recognize also that the gospel stories, and not sayings isolated from narrative context, are the sources for the historical Jesus. In contrast with the individual teacher or apocalyptic preacher constructed by Jesus scholars, the Gospels portray Jesus as engaged in conflicts with

---

3. The old criterion of "double dissimilarity" is very telling in this regard. Sayings were not "authentic" if they fit too closely into the "Jewish" cultural context or fit too readily into the "early Christian" interpretation of Jesus.

the high priests and their scribal and Pharisaic representatives, and the conflict is political or rather inseparably political-economic-religious. By no means can we read the historical Jesus-in-interaction directly off the surface of the gospel narratives. By attending to the portrayal of Jesus-in-interaction in each gospel, however, and then comparing those portrayals, we can gain a sense of what may have been the main features and agenda of Jesus-in-movement.

A parallel shift from individual sayings to fuller "speeches" is appropriate for the speeches in Matthew and Luke that are closely parallel, indeed often virtually verbatim. It has been standard to posit a "sayings source," Q (for *Quelle*, "source"), from which Matthew and Luke derived this material. In both Matthew and Luke, however, this parallel teaching and prophecy of Jesus has the form of shorter or longer speeches, not individual sayings. What is incorporated into the respective gospel stories thus must have consisted of a series of speeches on issues of concern to a Jesus movement, such as covenant renewal, commission of Jesus's envoys to extend his mission in village communities, faithful confession when placed on trial, woes against the scribes and Pharisees, and prophetic pronouncements against the Jerusalem ruling house. Thus in a way somewhat similar to how we can discern the portrayal of Jesus-in-interaction in Mark or Matthew, we can gain a sense of the portrayal of Jesus-in-interaction in the Q speeches and then compare that portrayal with those of the gospel stories. Since it seems that Matthew and Luke followed Mark and the Q speeches, we would give greater weight to the portrayals of Jesus in the earlier texts.

Insofar as the Gospels as sustained stories are the sources for Jesus-in-interaction, then the Gospel of John would be included (Horsley and Thatcher 2013), and its portrayal be compared to the other gospels' portrayals in attempting to discern what would appear to have been the main features and agenda of Jesus-in-movement.

As should be evident from all of the contingencies discussed above, attempting to understand Jesus's mission in the historical context of Roman Palestine requires development of a complex relational approach. An individual teacher of individuals unencumbered by involvement in the fundamental social forms of life and political conflicts would hardly have become a significant historical figure. We would know nothing about him if he had not been remembered by people with whom he interacted. He would not have been executed by crucifixion if he had been as innocuous as often presented by New Testament interpreters. Like other significant historical figures, Jesus addressed a historical crisis of his people in the contingencies of the historical context, in interaction with the forces, institutions, and agents prominent in the context and in a way that resonated with people who formed a movement focused on his leadership (see further Horsley 2003, ch. 3). Two further factors require attention as well: like other leaders around whom a movement coalesced, Jesus addressed the crisis and pursued an agenda rooted in the people's cultural tradition, and he acted in and they responded in terms of (a) social-political role(s) given in that tradition.

Critical analyses of the interrelationship of political-economic domination and the culture and politics of subordinated people offer suggestive possibilities for the further development of a more comprehensive relational approach to Jesus in the Roman imperial context. Increasingly sophisticated critical feminist analysis, both outside and inside the New Testament field, offers insights into the subtle cultural and psychological as well as not-so-subtle political-economic way in which women and other subordinate people have been dominated by more powerful men, both in political-economic structures and in the operation of cultural symbols and patterns (Schüssler Fiorenza 1983). Also particularly suggestive for analysis of gospel portrayals and Jesus-in-interaction is the developing theory of "domination and the arts of resistance" by political scientist James C. Scott (1990; cf. Horsley 2004), who draws on a wide range of studies of how peasants and/or slaves responded culturally and politically to their domination by masters, lords, and rulers. Scott opens up insights into a range of peasant politics that can replace the distorting dichotomy between passive acquiescence and active revolt.

The Gospels' Portrayal of Jesus's Renewal of the People, Which Was Also Resistance to the Rulers

Study of the overall gospels' portrayals of Jesus's mission, in contrast to the narrow focus on separate individual sayings, further reinforces previous discernment (from the context indicated in the content of Jesus's sayings) that his mission focused on villages and emphasized the renewal of covenantal village communities.

Gospel narratives repeatedly portray Jesus and his disciples as working in villages and their assemblies (*synagōgai*). This brings to the fore what has been generally ignored by interpreters of Jesus and gospel traditions, that the fundamental social-economic form in Galilean and Judean society (or in any agrarian society) was the village community composed of many households. Archaeological surface surveys confirm Josephus's estimate that there were two hundred villages in Galilee. In the Roman imperial order in Palestine, these villages and their households were the focus of the struggle between the rulers and the villagers for control of the resources produced by the labor of villagers on what had traditionally been their ancestral land (Horsley 1995). Those in control of surplus wealth, mainly the wealthy priests and the Herodian officers, made loans to desperate families in order to gain control over their land and labor (Broshi 1987; Goodman 1982). A variety of sources indicate that those village communities were beginning to disintegrate under the impact of Roman conquest and their client rulers' exploitation. The cumulative impact of these forces would have brought about the conditions that Jesus addresses in the gospel sources: debts, hunger, and quarreling in village communities from people borrowing to feed their families after surrendering produce in tribute and taxes (Horsley 1989b, 2003, 2011a).

Jesus addressed these conditions not in separate sayings but in terms of the most fundamental pattern of Israelite culture, the Mosaic covenant, the pattern in which the commandments and customs that guided community life were deeply embedded. Recognition that the gospel sources have the form of sustained stories and longer or shorter speeches on key issues for a movement enable us to discern the covenantal pattern in them. Not only is the "love your enemies" cluster of sayings in Luke 6:27–36 // Matt 5:38–48 renewed covenantal teaching, as discerned in its many allusions to Mosaic covenantal laws (Horsley 1987), but also the overall speech of which this renewed covenantal teaching is the central component, in Luke 6:20–49, expanded in Matt 5–7, has the form of a renewed covenant in which the covenantal demands are prefaced by a declaration of deliverance and followed by positive and negative sanctions (Horsley 2003). This traditional pattern of the Mosaic covenant is evident in the official written texts in Exod 20 and Josh 24. That the Mosaic covenant was still the fundamental form of Israelite community at the time of Jesus is evident in the Community Rule from Qumran. The Community Rule, moreover, enables us to see that (Q's/Matthew's/Luke's) Jesus enacts a renewed Mosaic covenant. Like the Qumran community, he transforms the blessings and curses that had been the sanctions on keeping the demands and had led to self-blame by the poor and hungry, into the new declaration of deliverance: "blessed are you poor." This transformation of despair into hope then gave the poor and hungry the basis for responding to Jesus renewal of the covenantal demands for mutual aid and cooperation in village communities: "love your enemies, do good, and lend."

Analysis of the overall gospel story opened up recognition that renewal of covenantal community was also an integral part of Jesus's mission in the Gospel of Mark (Horsley 2001, 2003). The most obvious clues are the explicit references to most of the "ten commandments" in his dialogue with the wealthy man (10:17–22) and his appeal to "the basic commandment of God" in dispute with the scribes and Pharisees (7:1–13). This opens toward recognition that the series of dialogues in Mark 10:2–45, with their law-like pronouncements of principles, constitute a covenantal charter for the communities of the Jesus movement. This charter of renewed covenantal community comes at a crucial juncture in the story, after Jesus has been working in the villages of Galilee and beyond and before he marches up to Jerusalem for direct confrontation with the rulers. It is prefigured in Jesus's pronouncement about "familial" community that is also covenantal (doing "the will of God"; 3:31–35). It is ceremonially confirmed in Jesus's transformation of the Passover meal (celebrating the exodus liberation) into a covenant-renewal meal (in the words over the cup in Mark 14:24 that allude to the original covenantal ceremony on Sinai, Exod 24:3–8).

That renewal of covenantal community was central in Jesus's mission in the villages of Galilee and beyond is confirmed by how references to covenantal commandments and customs crop up elsewhere in both the gospel story (appeal to the basic commandment of God in Mark 7:1–13) and the Q series of speeches (such as cancellation of debts in the Lord's Prayer, Luke/Q 11:2–4). That the covenant-renewal speech in (the Q source of) both Matt 5–7 and Luke 6:20–49 is "performative speech" (and not just "teaching") suggests that the "Jesus-speakers" in Jesus movements, and perhaps Jesus-in-movement, were enacting the renewal of covenant community. Such renewal of mutual aid and cooperation, that is, renewal of community solidarity in the villages, would have enabled them to resist the further debilitating impact of the forces of Roman imperial rule in Palestine on their families and their collective life together.

The Gospels' Portrayals of Jesus's Mission in Active Opposition to and by the Rulers

Even without attention to the overall gospel stories, it was possible to argue, on the basis of critical examination of Jesus's prophetic pronouncements and prophetic demonstration in the temple, that he was speaking and acting in opposition to Roman domination, especially to its face-and-form in the high-priestly aristocracy based in the centralizing institution of the temple (Horsley 1987, ch. 10). Recognition that the sustained gospel stories and series of Jesus speeches are the sources for Jesus-in-interaction strongly reinforces this conclusion.

The Gospel of Mark, of course, includes an account of Jesus's demonstration against the temple, his prophetic parable against the high priests, three references to his prophecy of God's condemnation of the temple, and his crafty statement that the people do not owe tribute to Caesar. Beyond those particular episodes and references, however, the gospel presents a sustained story of Jesus's renewal of the people in opposition to the rulers in Jerusalem, the face of Roman imperial rule, or a story in opposition to Flavian imperial propaganda in Rome (Horsley 2001; Winn 2008). From early in the story, the scribes and Pharisees come "down from Jerusalem" as representatives of the high priests to confront, accuse, and plot against Jesus. He not only fires right back at them but also condemns them for their exploitation of the people on behalf of the temple (esp. Mark 7:1–13).

Matthew and Luke follow and compound the basic gospel story of conflict with stories of Jesus's birth as the messiah who will liberate the people of Israel from Herodian and Roman imperial rule and Jesus's woes against the scribes and Pharisees and prophecy against the Jerusalem ruling house, those who have traditionally killed prophets like him.

Recent rereadings of the Gospel of John have cut through the previous mystification of the "spiritual" gospel to the fundamental narrative of Jesus's actions and pronouncements in a portrayal of Jesus that is even more active and adamant in his opposition to the rulers of the Judeans than the portrayals in Mark and the Q speeches (Carter 2008; Richey 2007; Thatcher 2009; Horsley and Thatcher 2013). It seems clear in John as in Mark that Jesus is engaged in a renewal of Israel, insofar as he works among all of the peoples of Israelite heritage, "the Judeans" and "the Samaritans" as well as "the Galileans," with many becoming "loyal to" Jesus (the meaning of *pistuein eis* in the Roman imperial context). John mainly presents Jesus in a series of journeys up to Jerusalem on the occasions of one of "the festivals of the Judeans," where he stages a confrontation against the high priests and the Pharisees (whom John also refers to as "the Judeans" (meaning the rulers of "the Judeans"). The boldest and most blatant confrontation is the first, the forcible demonstration in the temple, at the Passover festival "of the Judeans" (the people at the head of the temple). After the high priests and Pharisees, threatened by his expanding movement, finally decide to take action against him, he marches up to Jerusalem with his followers acclaiming him as "the king of Israel," which leads to his arrest and his crucifixion by Pilate.

Each of the gospel stories articulates a distinctive stance of Jesus-in-interaction vis-à-vis Roman imperial rule, especially against its face-and-form in the Jerusalem temple-state. We should not imagine that events happened in just the way one or another of the gospels portrays. But they all present Jesus in opposition to and by the rulers. The gospel stories that emerged from and were addressed to Jesus movements had reasons to downplay the opposition. But they persist in their portrayal of their prophet (and/or messiah) as having both formed a movement of renewal of Israel and adamantly opposed the Roman imperial order in Palestine—and having been crucified as a leader of resistance.

For Further Reading

Crossan, John Dominic. 1991. *The Historical Jesus: The Life of a Mediter-ranean Jewish Peasant*. San Francisco: HarperSanFrancisco.

Hezser, Catherine. 2001. *Jewish Literacy in Roman Palestine*. Tübingen: Mohr Siebeck.

Horsley, Richard A. 1987. *Jesus and the Spiral of Violence: Popular Jewish Resistance in Roman Palestine*. San Francisco: Harper & Row.

———. 2014. *Jesus and the Politics of Roman Palestine*. Columbia: University of South Carolina Press.

Mattern, Susan P. 1999. *Rome and the Enemy: Imperial Strategy in the Prin-cipate*. Berkeley: University of California Press.

Saldarini, Anthony J. 1988. *Pharisees, Scribes, and Sadducees in Palestinian Society: A Sociological Approach*. Wilmington, DE: Michael Glazier.

An Imperial-Critical Reading of Matthew

Warren Carter

Interpretive methods ask questions and employ particular perspectives, highlighting some areas for inquiry and relegating others. What is an imperial-critical reading of Matthew? What questions does it ask? What is its focus, and how does it carry out the investigation? What insights does it produce?

An imperial-critical reading of Matthew's Gospel foregrounds the power and structures of the Roman Empire. This approach takes seriously the very obvious, but frequently ignored, observation that Matthew's Gospel originated from and negotiated the Roman imperial world. It recognizes that Matthew assumes this everyday world of empire throughout. It makes evident and foregrounds for twenty-first-century interpreters of the gospel (some of) the experience and knowledge that was obvious to or assumed by first-century people.

The term *critical* does not mean forcing Matthew's Gospel, or any other New Testament writing, into an exclusively or primarily oppositional stance "over against" the empire. Some imperial-critical work has tried to do so but fails to recognize multivalent interactions with the empire that include numerous dynamics such as participation, imitation, accommodation, competition, opposition, contesting, fantasy, and reversal (Carter 2006b, 2008).

While this approach includes historical and literary methods, it especially resonates with contemporary approaches such as postcolonial criticism (Segovia 2005). Postcolonial work focuses on the emergence, representation, and consequences of imperial power including interconnected issues of power, gender, class, race/ethnicity, and sexual orientation. It engages biblical texts across a spectrum embracing their origin in contexts of empire through to their current reception and interpretation, often in contexts of various contemporary expressions of empire. In addressing "the needs and aspirations of the exploited" (Sugirtharajah 2001, 547, 552), postcolonial work both thinks about and *does* justice. It concerns ways of reading and ways of living on our planet that are good for all people. Space limits here mean a focus on reading the gospel in terms of its origin and textual negotiation of the Roman Empire. Such a reading offers a sustained critique of and alternative to much standard interpretation of Matthew (Carter 2013). Informing this limited focus are larger commitments to justice that disclose the investments and limits of spiritualized and individualized readings.

This restrictive, text-and-context focus opens up imperial-critical work to the criticism from some critics that it neglects the contemporary structures, practices, and legacy of empires (Schüssler Fiorenza 2007, 5–6). This criticism, though, ignores the reality that pervasive, Western, "spiritualized," individualized, and depoliticized readings of New Testament texts avoid societal and imperial dimensions of the texts. Imperial-critical readings expose and challenge such readings of the New Testament texts and the spiritualized understandings and "practices" they foster in faith communities. By foregrounding the integral role of imperial power in shaping and interpreting the New Testament texts, imperial-critical readings enact a societally engaged reading strategy that fosters among contemporary readers active, politically engaged communities and practices.

Section 1 elaborates an imperial-critical approach. Section 2 identifies points of interaction between Matthew and the empire's structures, means of exercising power, and visions of societal life and structure. Section 3 identifies some of the ways that the gospel evaluates the Roman Empire.

An Imperial-Critical Approach: Sources and Methods

The Roman Empire comprised the territory and people around the Mediterranean Sea. Centered in Rome, it stretched from Britain in the northwest, through present-day France and Spain in the west, across to Turkey and Syria in the east, and to northern Africa in the south. Its population comprised some 55–60 million people. Wealth, power, and status resided with a very small ruling elite. Most people were, to varying degrees, poor.

How do we understand this complex imperial world? How did the small groups of Jesus believers that came into existence through the first century CE make their way in it?

Primary and secondary sources provide insight into the Roman Empire. Primary sources comprise written works of various genres that originated mostly from elite males in the ancient world. We have, for example, histories (Livy, Dionysus of Halicarnassus, Josephus, Tacitus), biographies (Suetonius, Plutarch), philosophical writings (Plutarch, Seneca), letters (Pliny), epic poems (Virgil, Statius, Silius Italicus), witty and often acerbic satirical writing (Juvenal, Martial), geographical writings (Strabo), agricultural treatises (Varro, Columella), architectural treatises (Vitruvius), and recipe books (Apicius) to name but a few.

Other written sources include graffiti and collections of papyrus (an ancient form of paper) comprising material as diverse as magical spells and rituals and tax records and contracts. Very important are stone inscriptions from tombs, statues, and other monuments, as well as honorary or commemorative inscriptions that celebrated a wealthy person's civic benefaction such as constructing a building or sponsoring a feast or festival.

Primary sources also include material or physical remains such as buildings and cities like Ephesus, Corinth, and Rome. Excavations of the towns of Pompeii and Herculaneum, buried by the eruption of Mount Vesuvius in 79 CE, provide insight into urban life. Across the empire are arches, amphitheaters, temples, bath houses, markets, stadia, and so on (MacDonald 1982–1986; Wallace-Hadrill 1994). Physical or material artifacts also include small items like pottery, coins, bones of animals and people, textiles, jewelry, household items, children's toys, tools, weapons, and so on.

While these sources offer valuable insight, they are limited and provide us with a partial and skewed record at best. Not everything, of course, has survived. What has survived—whether material or literary remains—has done so by accident or by being durable enough and/or by being deemed by someone to be significant enough to be preserved over several thousands of years. Most commonly those sources that have survived provide a "top-down" perspective, reflecting particularly the interests of elite males, especially political and military matters from which elite males gained honor and power. Receiving much less attention are the relatively powerless or insignificant such as women, slaves, the poor, peasant farmers, manual workers, beggars, and so on.

Classical scholars work on interpreting these existing sources. Secondary sources connect the partial data or investigate areas that are often peripheral to the primary sources. For instance, a "bottom-up" approach, such as that of "peoples' history" or postcolonial approaches, explores the lives of peasant farmers, women, poor urban dwellers, or slaves even though the elite-male-dominated primary sources are not especially interested in such people. From disparate pieces, scholars try to construct a larger understanding.

For example, Steven Friesen (2004) has constructed a poverty scale to understand the empire's enormous range of wealth and poverty).[1] To form his poverty scale, Freisen links together "sparse data, the judgment of specialists, reasoned conjecture, and comparison with other pre-industrial economies" (347). The data include estimates of population, percentages of urban dwellers, calorific needs, comparative urban and nutritional studies of pre-industrial Europe, annual incomes, and prices paid for slaves. From this partial and comparative data, Friesen creates a poverty scale for Roman society.

What does Roman society look like? Friesen's scale posits seven gradations or divisions. Levels 1–3 encompass imperial, regional, and municipal elites (including some wealthy veterans and merchants), comprising some 2–3 percent of the population. Level 4, about 7 percent, consists of those with "moderate surplus resources" such as more prosperous merchants, traders, artisans, and veterans. Level 5—merchants, traders, artisans, shop owners, some farmers—lived near subsistence levels "defined as the resources needed to procure enough calories in food to maintain the human body" (Friesen 2004, 343). Level 6—farmers, laborers, artisans, small shop owners—lived at or below subsistence levels. Level 7 comprised the most vulnerable members of society, namely, those who lived below subsistence levels: some farmers, day laborers, orphans, beggars, prisoners, unattached widows, the physically and emotionally damaged. Levels 5–7, then, comprise different gradations of the poor, some 90 percent of society, who struggled continually for survival around or below subsistence level. This scale provides an "economic map" for the world of Matthew's Gospel.

Other secondary sources come from disciplines beyond classical studies. Scholars supplement the existing partial primary record by borrowing theories and models developed in other contexts and disciplines and apply them to the ancient world. For instance, social scientists who study the structures and functions of societies often construct "models" that link disparate pieces of information, fill in gaps with comparative studies from other societies, and create a larger societal picture. Useful in imperial-critical work, for example, have been models of imperial societies constructed

---

1. See also Longenecker 2010 and the essay by Longenecker in this volume.

by social scientists such as Michael Mann, Gerhard Lenski, and John Kautsky (see Duling 2005). Mann (1986, 1–33, 250–340)," for example, studies structures of power and posits four interrelated spheres of power in Rome's world: economic, ideological, political, and military. These "big-picture" perspectives can be elaborated and finessed with specific content from classical studies.

Lenski (1984, 189–296), for his part, develops an intercultural model by studying agrarian empires from different periods of time and regions (Roman, Byzantine, Ottoman, Chinese). He formulates his model of social stratification in answering the question, "who gets what and how?" Lenski identifies features of the Roman Empire that help us understand something of the experiences of early Jesus believers.

First, the Roman Empire is hierarchical, with power, wealth, and status concentrated in the small ruling elite. With the emperor, this small ruling group of civic and military leaders comprises three groups (senators, equestrians, decurions) that form levels 1–3 on Friesen's economic scale. This ruling group in Rome and throughout its provinces sustains and creates their lifestyles through the services and expertise of retainers (about 3 percent of the population) comprising officials, soldiers, priests, and domestic servants. They receive economic and social benefits in return for their service.

Second, the Roman Empire is an agrarian society. Wealth, status, and power are based in land. Urban centers, along with trade, and commerce are important, as Kautsky (1984) emphasizes, but land, often controlled from such centers, is the most important commodity.

Third, the Roman Empire is a military power. Rome's foundational epic, Virgil's *Aeneid*, identifies Rome's mission in the world as establishing an "empire without end" (*Aen.* 1.279) marked by peace. This *pax Romana* was established by and reflected Roman dominance over the nations, whether by negotiated submission or military conquest (*Aen.* 6.853). Rome's military power, both the threat of intervention and actual campaigns, protected and extended Rome's rule.

Fourth, the empire operates with a "proprietary theory of the state." This means that elite control, usually founded on tradition and hereditary, reinforced by military power and taxation, and based in urban centers, assures an unequal distribution of power, privilege, and wealth in elite favor. Elites control economic production through resources of land and slave labor. They transfer wealth to themselves through taxes, tribute, and rents. Social inequality expresses and maintains elite values such as scorn for manual work and workers, ostentatious consumption and display of wealth, societal benefactions through various good works ("euergetism"), a sense of aristocratic superiority, and elite privilege through the administration of justice. This hierarchical social system benefited elites, not general societal well-being.

Fifth, Lenski emphasizes the empire's vertical social structure. A significant division existed between the small number who govern and the rest, who are governed. There was no "Roman dream" whereby those of lower orders—levels 4–7 on Friesen's scale—jumped up to a much higher status. While a few gained wealth and elevation as merchants, most struggled to maintain their current living around subsistence levels.

Sixth, the Roman Empire depended on slave labor. Slaves comprised those defeated in battle and those born in or kidnapped into slavery or who sold themselves into it. Some slaves had significant skills (economic management, medical knowledge, pedagogy). Others exercised considerable power and received honor as the slaves of a high-status person. Others provided labor in houses, fields, or mines. Many knew a miserable and short-lived existence marked by hard work, minimal comforts, and sexual exploitation.

Seventh, Lenski (1984, 209) notes that empires "harness the powers of religion in the service of the state." Ruling elites sanction and mystify structures of social inequality and strategies of control with imperial theology. This "theology" proclaims that the gods have chosen Rome as agents of their rule, will, blessings, and presence among human subjects. The imperial structures and goals are thereby legitimated as "natural," "inevitable," or "divinely sanctioned." In the *Aeneid*, for example, the poet Virgil has Jupiter declare, "I set no bounds in space or time; but have given empire without end" to the Romans to be "lords of the world" (*Aen.* 1.254–282 [Fairclough, LCL]). This mission "to rule the world" means to "crown peace with justice, to spare the vanquished and to crush the proud" (*Aen.* 6.851–853 [Fairclough, LCL]). To submit to Rome is to submit to the gods. To reject Rome is to reject the gods' will. Imperial cult observances, often involving games, festivals, processions, offerings to images of imperial figures, temples, and so on and funded and led by provincial elites who functioned as high priests and priestesses, enacted and reinforced this divine sanction.

Lenski's model supplies a useful big-picture, heuristic map of the Roman Empire's social, political, and economic system. Lenski answers the "who got what and how?" question by focusing on the elite and their strategies. Classical studies refine and elaborate the model with specific data.

There are, though, some significant omissions from Lenski's model. Lenski pays little attention to complex gender roles. Likewise he undervalues commercial activity. Kautsky (1984) more helpfully distinguishes the role of land in agrarian and commercial activities. In the former, elites withdraw the production surplus from peasant land, while in the latter, elites understand the land itself as a commodity and find ways through high rents, taxes, debt, and foreclosure to acquire it. Classical studies are able to offer more nuance, highlighting, for example, regional differences, gender performances, and economic and social dimensions. Moreover, while Lenski's brief discussion recognizes that resistance is inevitable where power is exerted, he does not elaborate forms of resistance with sufficient nuance.

Postcolonial work has foregrounded the question of how local peoples negotiate imperial power and its legacy. Cultural anthropologist James C. Scott (1990) has also insightfully investigated how powerless people in various cultures negotiate the imbalance of power in societies like that of Rome's empire. Scott counters the simplistic equation of resistance with violence and the assertion that the absence of violence means passive consent. Such claims have marked studies of Jesus and Matthew's Gospel, with scholars falsely concluding that if Jesus did not violently resist Roman rule, he was not interested in political matters. Scott, however, shows that the binary of violence or compliance is simplistic and misleading. He argues that powerless people negotiate power in numerous ways. Negotiation is often self-protective, disguised, and ambiguous, aimed less at changing the system and more at asserting dignity in its midst and expressing dissent in anonymous and self-protective ways. Scott (1994, v) quotes an Ethiopian proverb that highlights this self-protective mix of accommodation and disguised dissent: "When the great Lord passes by, the wise peasant bows deeply and silently farts."

Scott examines the ambiguous strategies often constituting this "third space" between submission and open revolt. Powerless people can simultaneously embrace cooperation, submission, pragmatism, obedience, and self-assertion, along with imitation of and competition with the ruling power, and self-protective acts of dissent and defiance. The powerless mimic yet also lust for the very power that they resist. As Frantz Fanon (1968, 53) observes, "The native is an oppressed person whose permanent dream is to become the persecutor." They express anger in rumors and in imagining reversals or worlds turned upside down in which they occupy the role of the powerful. They construct different social narratives and develop rituals that sustain their own dignity and sanction self-protective and anonymous acts of dissent in the face of oppressive and humiliating power. Scott identifies such strategies as "weapons of the weak."

Direct and open confrontations between the powerless poor and elites are rare and frequently avoided, because powerless folks know they will probably lose. With leadership and "offstage" protected space away from the scrutiny of ruling powers, they engage in world-constructing/contesting/imitating work that creates a "hidden transcript," or alternative way of viewing the world. By these means, they protectively contest the dominant structures and affirm their own dignity against dehumanizing exploitation even while they find ways to accommodate the assertions of imperial power. Matthew's Gospel can be seen as such a work of dissent and disguised accommodation (Carter 2000, 2001, 2005b; Horsley 2004).

Matthew and the Roman Empire

In this section I highlight ways in which Matthew's Gospel inscribes, participates in, and contests the political, economic, social, and ideological spheres of Roman power. Often these expressions of Roman power go unnoticed by readers who are not aware of the various ways Roman power pervaded the gospel's narrative world.

In an exchange between Jesus and some Pharisees (Matt 22:15–22), the Roman emperor's image, and the taxes he requires, render him present. He is also made present in territory under his control that bears his name. Caesarea Philippi, located north of the Sea of Galilee (Matt 16:13), was named by Herod's son Herod Philip in honor of the emperor Caesar Augustus for whom a temple was dedicated there (Josephus, *Ant.* 15.10.3 §363). Subsequently, it was renamed Neronias in honor of the emperor Nero (Josephus, *Ant.* 20.9.4 §211). Jesus's ministry begins in Galilee owned or possessed by "the gentiles," an oblique reference to Roman control (Matt 4:15; Carter 2000, 115).

Pontius Pilate, governor of Judea from 26–37 CE, represents Roman interests with life-and-death power (Matt 27:2; Josephus, *J.W.* 2.8.1 §117). In crucifying Jesus, he maintains order and enacts Roman "justice" to protect the status quo of elite interests against this "king of the Jews" (Matt 27:11, 29, 37). Rome ruled in alliance with local rulers, including kings sanctioned by Rome. The unsanctioned Jesus is understood to challenge Roman authority in claiming a kingdom or empire—the Greek could be translated in either way (4:17)—and in being perceived as "king of the

Jews" when Rome has not granted him any such title or authority (2:2; 21:5, 9). Matthew's Jesus recognizes that his proclamation and practices of an alternative empire, along with his identity as a king, put him on a collision course with Roman power that will inevitably cost him his life (16:21; 17:22; 20:18–19).

The gospel's references to the Herods reflect the Roman practice of governing by alliances with local leaders and rulers. Herod "the Great" (Matt 2) ruled as king of the Jews from 37–4 BCE by Rome's sanction. He secured his power by honoring his Roman overlords and viciously removing internal threats. The historicity of the events of Matt 2 seems dubious, but Herod's actions of protecting his power with Jerusalem allies, lies, spies (2:7–8), and military violence (2:16) are standard strategies of maintaining Roman interests through local alliances.

Herod's son Archelaus succeeds him (Matt 2:22), causing the frightened Joseph to bypass Jerusalem and travel to Galilee. Extensive unrest forced the emperor Augustus to remove Archelaus and exile him in 6 CE. Thereafter Rome appointed governors like Pilate to rule Judea until the war of 66–70 CE. Another of Herod's sons, Herod Antipas, was appointed to rule Galilee. He built the cities of Sepphoris and Tiberias, the former four miles north of Nazareth (2:23), the latter some eight miles southwest of Capernaum (4:13). Herod knows of Jesus and thinks that he is John the Baptist raised from the dead (14:1–2). He had imprisoned and beheaded John for opposition to Herod's liaison with Herodias (14:3–12).

The gospel also reflects Rome's alliance with the leaders based in Jerusalem's temple. It is easy for contemporary readers to interpret the gospel's references to the temple, priests, and groups such as scribes and Pharisees as religious figures like modern-day churches and ministers. But in Rome's world, religion, politics, and economics are intertwined. Josephus describes the Jerusalem high priests as the nation's rulers (*Ant.* 20.10.1 §251). Yet they ruled by Rome's consent and as Rome's allies. Roman governors appointed the high priests (Josephus, *Ant.* 18.2.2, 4.3 §§33–35, 95), and the chief's priestly garments were kept in the Antonia fortress next to the Jerusalem temple. The temple was also "big business," dependent on taxes and tithes under the oversight of wealthy and powerful priests (Hanson and Oakman 1998, 131–59). Their allies, the scribes were interpreters of the tradition who enjoy "eminence in the public assembly," make legal decisions, associate "among the rulers," "maintain the fabric of the world," and "serve among the great and appear before rulers" (Sir 38:24–39:11). The alliance of Jerusalem leaders is political and economic, embedded in and shapers and protectors of the larger political-societal structures in alliance with Rome.

The "chief priests and scribes" first appear in Matt 2:4 as Herod's allies. Jesus exposes their alliance with Rome in announcing that "the elders, chief priests, and scribes" will put him to death (16:21; 20:18). In Jerusalem, "chief priests and elders" confront Jesus over his authority for his actions and teachings (21:23). In Matt 21:33–45, Jesus attacks the "chief priests and Pharisees" for rejecting him as God's agent and for failing to represent God's reign for the common good. Angered by his attacks on their temple (21; 24; 26:57–68), they cooperate with Rome's governor Pilate to arrest and crucify Jesus (21:45; 26:3, 47, 61–65; 27:1–2, 11–31).

The linking of the chief priests with the Pharisees in Jerusalem in Matt 21:45 significantly presents these two groups as allies and in alliance with Rome against Jesus. The Pharisees have been Jesus's main opponents in Galilee, committed to destroying him (12:14). Jesus declares their leadership and teaching as illegitimate (9:34; 15:8–9, 13; 16:5–12). He denounces them for various practices, including neglect of "the weightier matters of the law, justice and mercy and faithfulness" (23:23). Given that they are embedded in and cooperative with elite societal-political structures, it is very misleading to think of their teachings and practices as "religious" matters. They involve societal visions and practices that Jesus contests as contrary to God's purposes. Hence they conflict over social interactions (eating, 9:10–13), transforming actions (exorcisms, 9:32–34), doing mercy (Sabbath observance, 12:1–14), and care for the elderly (15:1–14). The gospel links Pharisees, chief priests, and Pilate in upholding the hierarchy and elite-centered imperial world.

The gospel highlights the ruling and economic strategies of elite personnel. These practices include control of land, use of slaves, absentee land-owners, collection of taxes, and military force. Jesus's parables employ these structures and practices, thereby presenting God's reign or empire as often imitating and embracing imperial ways. So Jesus tells the story of a king who uses his aristocratic allies and retainers to collect taxes and tributes to the sum of ten thousand talents, the amount that the Romans levied from Judea in 63 BCE (Matt 18:23–35; Josephus, *Ant.* 14.4.5 §78). Another king uses military power against the town of those who dishonor him by not attending his son's wedding (Matt 22:1–11). A landowner with a large vineyard hires day laborers (20:1–16). Another landowner establishes a vineyard and hires it out to tenants who refuse to pay the rent and suffer a military backlash (21:33–45). Absentee landlords use slaves with economic management skills to run their estates in their absence (24:45–51; 25:14–30). Several scenes concern tax collectors (5:46; 18:17; 21:31) and tax collection (17:24–27; Carter 2001; 22:15–22). Jesus calls a tax collector, Matthew, to be a disciple (9:9; 10:3) and eats with tax collectors (9:10–13; 11:19). Wealthy household-ers (13:52), a rich young man (19:16–30), and the dominating ruling elites (20:24–26) people the narrative.

Military violence is present in other ways. One involves the practice of *angaria*. Roman soldiers could requisition bodies, labor, possessions (sup-plies, means of transport), and lodging. In Matt 5:42 ("if any one forces you to go one mile, go also the second mile"), carrying a soldier's pack or equipment, is probably in view (see Josephus, *J. W.* 3.5.5 §95). The Gospel narrates the practice when Simon of Cyrene is compelled to carry Jesus's cross (Matt 27:32). Soldiers, including auxiliaries and those of the Hero-dian allies, appear commonly in the narrative (2:16; 5:42; 8:5–13; 14:9–11; 22:7; 24:6–7; 27:27–31, 54, 62–66; 28:11–15).

The nonelites of this imperial world also appear in the gospel. They live in the villages of Galilee (Matt 9:35; 14:15) and "districts" or "regions" surrounding the towns of Tyre and Sidon (15:21) and Caesarea Philippi (16:13). They are the "crowds" who inhabit "Galilee, the Decapolis, Jeru-salem, Judea and from beyond the Jordan" (4:25; 5:1; 8:1, 18). Matthew describes "Galilee under the Gentiles" (Rome) as a place of "darkness … the region and shadow of death" (4:16), appropriating Isaiah's description of life under Assyrian imperial power to describe Rome's world (Isa 9:1–2; Carter 2000, 93–107). The crowds include "the poor" (Matt 11:5) whose material poverty has so eaten away at their very being and dignity as human beings that they are both poor materially and "poor in spirit" (5:3; Carter 2000, 131–32). Their poverty places them in need of redistributed resources (19:21; 26:9). They include fishermen (4:18–22), slaves (8:5–13), the homeless (8:28–34), swineherds (8:33), tax collectors (9:9–13), labor-ers (9:37), farmers (13:3–9), harvesters (13:30, 39), merchants (13:45), artisans (stone, wood, and metal workers; 13:55), shepherds (18:10–14), day laborers (20:1–16), beggars (20:29–34), prostitutes (21:31), builders (21:42). They mostly belong to levels 5–7 on Friesen's scale and daily strug-gle, to varying degrees, for survival.

The embeddedness of nonelites in Rome's world can be seen, for example, in elaborating structures surrounding fishing (Hanson and Oakman 1998, 106–11). When Jesus calls four fishermen to follow him as disciples (Matt 4:18–22), he intervenes in the Sea of Galilee's impe-rial fishing economy. Numerous writers name the emperor as "lord of land and sea," attesting imperial "proprietary" control over the sea. Local brokers, representing the emperor and local rulers, sold fishermen fishing rights. Fishermen were contracted to supply quantities of fish. To fish required the skills and labor of boat builders, sail and net makers, as well as farmers to supply flax, and stonemasons to create anchors. The catch needed a labor force of processors and supplies of salt, wine, and stone jars, along with distributors, buyers, and sellers, activities that were taxed. Matthew the tax collector from Capernaum also participated in this economy (9:9). Fishing, like farming and artisan work, was deeply embedded in the imperial economy.

Matthew presents the crowds suffering the harmful effect of imperial rule: they are "harassed and helpless" (Matt 9:36). The first verb denotes violence and plunder, while the second describes those who are downtrodden and beaten up (Carter 2000, 230). Jesus locates responsibility for this damage with the ruling elite, who have failed to live up to their calling as shepherds or leaders. Echoing Ezekiel's condemnation of Israel's leaders (Ezek 34) for prospering themselves at the expense and neglect of the people, Jesus declares that these societal leaders have failed so badly that the crowds are leaderless, "like sheep without a shepherd" (Matt 9:36).

How have these leaders failed? What sort of world has their maintenance of and support for hierarchical imperial structures and unjust practices created? In addition to the oppressive world of hard labor and relative deprivations noted above, another startling feature of the imperial world that the gospel constructs is the prevalence of sickness. Sick people appear in summary scenes: "They brought to him all the sick, those who were afflicted with various diseases and pains, demoniacs, epileptics, and paralytics, and he cured them," including "the lame, the maimed, the blind, the mute and many others" (Matt 4:23–25; 9:35; 11:4–5; 14:35–36; 15:29–31). Individual encounters narrate Jesus healing leprosy (8:1–4), paralysis (8:5–13; 9:1–8), fever (8:14–15), hemorrhage (9:20–22), blindness (9:27–31; 20:29–34; 21:14), a withered hand (12:9–14), and lameness (21:14).

Why are there so many sick and disabled people in the gospel world? What do they have to do with Roman power? Many in the Roman world struggled for access to adequate nutrition. The food supply was controlled by elites through landownership and taxes on production, transportation, and distribution. With daily stress and harsh living conditions, diseases of deficiency and contagion were pervasive. Peter Garnsey (1999, 43–61) highlights the pervasive impact of poor nutrition in the Roman Empire, arguing that the grain-based diet of many nonelites was deficient in vitamins A, C, and D. A lack of vitamin A contributes to blindness, deformed bones, growth retardation, and low immunity. A deficiency of vitamin C impedes bone and teeth development. It also causes scurvy with symptoms of lethargy, shortness of breath, pains, skin and gum disease, and fever. Vitamin D deficiency results in rickets, comprising muscle pain, bone and dental weakness, impaired growth, and deformities.

Diseases of deficiency were accompanied by infectious diseases. Inadequately nutritioned bodies have low immunity. The spread of infectious diseases was facilitated by overcrowded urban living, unhygienic sewage disposal, lack of understanding of basic hygiene, inadequate water supply and storage, disease-carrying insects and animals, and a lack of appropriate medical understanding and interventions.

Related are the numerous "demoniacs," or demon-possessed (Matt 8:16, 18–36; 9:32; 12:22). This phenomenon can be interpreted in diverse ways. In Matthew's world, demons are agents of the devil, who opposes Jesus's ministry (4:1–11) and who claims to control "all the empires of the earth" including Rome (4:8). The demon-possessed embody those in the devil's power; Jesus's exorcisms enact God's victory over the devil and the empire (8:28–34). Another perspective sees demon possession as a way of coping with and protesting harsh (crazy) circumstances, a refusal to adjust to and accept such circumstances as normal. Scott (1990, 141–42) understands spirit or demon possession in contexts of domination and socioeconomic exploitation as preserving anonymity and inviting a lack of attention while expressing dissent or criticism. Giving voice or enacting grievances under the guise of possession disavows personal responsibility. Yet it can also function as social control whereby labeling "demonic" those who defy or depart from imperial norms marginalizes them. Elites label Jesus as demon-possessed in 9:34 and 12:24. The sick and demon-possessed who pervade the gospel bear the somatic impact of imperial hierarchies and inequalities of access to adequate food resources.

Other signs of the destructive impact of imperial structures are evident in instructions to "give to the one who begs" (5:42) and to practice almsgiving (6:2–4). The gospel recognizes the existence of debt and the need for its "forgiveness" (6:12). It also names situations of need and deprivation in requiring the hungry to be fed, the thirsty supplied with drink, the stranger welcomed, the naked clothed, the sick cared for, and the imprisoned visited (25:31–46).

Imperial structures and practices pervade the gospel world. The gospel presents Jesus engaging this world in his ministry. How does it evaluate this imperial world?

Evaluations of the Empire and Alternative Practices

The gospel assumes the imperial world on every page. Often it takes it for granted, employing imperial structures and practices to exemplify aspects of God's reign or empire. So in Matt 18:23–35, a parable about forgiveness (or more accurately, unforgiveness), the kingdom/empire of the heavens is compared to imperial structures of tax or tribute collection presided over by a kingly tyrant and peopled by subservient slaves or officials. In Matt 20:1–16, God's empire is compared to a wealthy landowner who hires day laborers to work in his extensive vineyard. These structures of kingly power, taxation, slavery, large landholdings, and the vulnerability of unskilled day laborers are assumed as normal everyday life, imitated without critique to exhibit God's reign.

Likewise, the gospel mirrors and mimics the empire's theological claims to be the chosen agent of the gods. The gospel presents God, not Jupiter or the emperor, as "our Father" (6:9) and "Lord of heaven and earth" (11:25). God's will and empire/kingdom prevail in heaven, and disciples are to pray that God establishes God's ruling presence and will "on earth" (6:10) in place of Rome's or Jupiter's ruling power. In designating Jesus as the "Son of God," chosen and sanctioned by God (1:18–25; 2:15; 4:1–11) as God's agent to manifest God's saving presence and reign among humans (1:21–23; 4:17), the gospel borrows and redeploys a title commonly used for the emperor. The gospel presents Jesus as manifesting God's blessings (5:3–12) and representing God's authority over heaven and earth (28:18), contesting but imitating imperial claims. The gospel competes with and copies Roman imperial ideology in presenting Jesus as greater than the emperor.

Three Perspectives

The gospel offers further evaluations of Rome's empire. The opening genealogy references "the deportation [or exile] to Babylon" in 597/587 BCE (Matt 1:11–12). The language evokes several Hebrew Bible perspectives on imperial power. One perspective sees God using the Babylonian Empire to punish Judea's kings for their failure to represent God's just rule (1 Kgs 9:6–9; 2 Kgs 24:16; 1 Chr 5:22). Another perspective sees Babylon reaching beyond this punitive role, so God punishes Babylon and frees the people from Babylonian rule. God does so by using another empire, Persia, to overcome Babylon and free some of the people to return the land (Isa 44:28–45:1). The continuation of the genealogy after verse 12—"And after the deportation to Babylon"—indicates that empires (including Rome's) are both agents of yet subservient to God's purposes.

These initial perspectives on the Babylonian Empire are repeated in Matt 4:12–16 by evoking the Assyrian Empire. Jesus's withdrawal to Galilee is interpreted by citing Isa 9:1–2. Along with other Isaianic texts, this eighth-century BCE text promises God's saving of Judea from Israel and Syria by using the Assyrian Empire (Isa 7:17–20). Assyria oversteps this role, though, and God punishes Assyria (Isa 10:5–19; 14:24–27). Quoting Isa 9:1–2 in Matt 4:12–16 evokes and evaluates the Roman Empire, the current ruling power of Galilee, and sets Jesus's ministry in relation to it.

These references to the Babylonian (Matt 1:11–12) and Assyrian Empires (Matt 4:12–16) employ a paradigm about imperial power that comprises three elements in tension: God opposes empires, God uses empires, and God punishes empires. Evoking the Babylonian and Assyrian traditions provides perspective on Roman power, the contemporary empire. God opposes it (20:24–28); God uses it to punish Jerusalem's leaders (22:7); yet God punishes Rome and brings about the downfall of the so-called eternal empire (24:27–31). Rome's power is temporary and doomed.

Violence

The first "face" of the Roman Empire in the narrative is Herod, Rome's client king. The scene reveals Herod's violent opposition to Jesus (Matt 2:3). Herod uses his Jerusalem allies, the chief priests and scribes, to identify Jesus's place of birth (2:4–6). With lies he recruits the magi as spies (2:7–12). He sends troops to murder boys "two years old and under in and around Bethlehem" (2:16). Allies, lies, spies, and murderous violence are standard imperial strategies, as is lineage—Archelaus rules "in place of his father Herod" (2:22).

Subsequently, other faces of Roman power employ violence. Herod Antipas murders John the Baptist (14:1–10). Pilate crucifies Jesus (26–27). Jesus uses verbal violence to condemn the Jerusalem leaders, client rulers, and Rome's allies, cursing them repeatedly in Matt 23. He accuses them of exploiting the people so that they "were harassed and helpless [oppressed and downtrodden], like sheep without a shepherd" (9:36).

Condemned

In addition to violence, the gospel highlights and condemns other dimensions of the imperial structures. In Matt 19:16–30, the text personifies the extremes of wealth that pervade the empire when a "rich person" asks Jesus, "What good deed must I do to have eternal life?" (19:16, 23). Jesus reminds him of the societal vision offered by the Decalogue—forbidding murder, adultery, theft, false witness but honoring parents and loving neighbors—to which Jesus adds the instruction to sell his possessions and "give the money to the poor" (19:18–21). Jesus requires him to redistribute his wealth and dismantle a marker of elite status and power. The man, defined by his wealth as "a rich man" (19:23), prefers to maintain the elite status quo.

Matthew's Jesus condemns the "power over" that marks the imperial structure. In Matt 20:24–28, he constructs the power of gentile rulers and "great ones/men" (like the emperor, Pilate, Herod, and the Jerusalem elite) in terms of lording it over and being tyrants. The scene presents the imperial structure as tyranny and evaluates it negatively by forbidding this structure among Jesus followers: "it shall not be so among you" (20:26). Ironically, his prohibition reinscribes an aspect of the imperial system among Jesus followers, constituting their identity and lifestyle as slaves. The scene borrows and redeploys the imperial structure of slavery without critique. Resistance and accommodation, opposition and mimicry go hand in hand.

Under the Power of the Devil

The gospel also presents the empire as being in the power of the devil. In the temptation scene, the devil shows Jesus "all the empires of the world and their glory" and promises, "All these I will give you, if you will fall down and worship me" (4:8–9). Jesus as God's son or agent, loyal to God, refuses. The scene constructs the devil as controlling the Roman Empire and directing its destiny. It presents the empire as fundamentally opposed to God's purposes.

Under Judgment

The gospel also constructs Rome's empire as under judgment. It presents Rome's allies, the Jerusalem leaders, as condemned by God. In 15:13, Matthew's Jesus condemns them with a plant image as leaders whom God "has not planted" ("uprooted"; cf. Jer 1:10). Once Jesus enters Jerusalem, he attacks the center of their power, the temple (Matt 21:12–17). A cursed and withered fig tree, an image borrowed from the prophets (Isa 34:4; Jer 8:12–13), symbolizes their judgment. Their judgment for rejecting Jesus and his revelation of God's good purposes is delivered, interestingly, by their allies, Rome, who destroy Jerusalem, where Jesus meets his death on a Roman cross (Matt 21:33–44; 22:1–11, esp. 22:7). In Matt 23, Jesus curses "the scribes and the Pharisees" for their role in mis-structuring society by neglecting "the weightier matters of the law: justice and mercy and faithfulness" (23:23). These denunciations reject their rule.

Matthew 24, part of the eschatological discourse, presents the ultimate verdict. God's judgment on Rome means the end of Rome's world. This scenario expresses a fantasy of anger against and revenge on Rome, anger often suppressed in daily imperial life to ensure survival (Scott 1990, 36–37). The chapter gives it full expression, envisioning the collapse of their world and Jesus's imminent and victorious return to a transformed world.

The cosmic implications of Jesus's return, for example, are depicted in Matt 24:27–31 (Carter 2003). The scene identifies Jesus as Son of Man, evoking the (anti-?)imperial traditions of Dan 7 concerning the Son of Man as an agent of God's judgment and universal rule. Lightning accompanies his return (Matt 24:27), an ambiguous sign associated both with Jupiter, whose sovereignty the emperors manifest, and with manifestations of Israel's God (Exod 19:16; Ezek 1:13). Matthew 24:28 denotes Rome's defeat that Jesus's coming effects. Translations mistakenly render the term *aetoi* as "vultures" instead of the much better-attested term "eagle." The eagle symbolized Roman power; soldiers carried an image of an eagle into battle. Now at Jesus's coming, the eagles are gathered with the corpses as Roman power is destroyed. In Matt 24:29, the heavenly powers that emperors were said to manifest are "shaken," God's created order restored, and God's reign and people finally established (24:30–31). The nations are judged before God for vindication or condemnation (25:31–32) on the basis of whether they have provided "the least of these" with food, drink, clothing, shelter, and companionship (25:31–46). The judgment reverses the imperial privileging of elite interests by foregrounding the needs of the poor and powerless. The vision reveals the imperial structures not to be divinely sanctioned or "natural," but creations of and for the imperial elite (Scott 1990, 168)—and under God's judgment.

God's Alternative (and Imitative) Empire

This eschatological scenario also exhibits a profound irony. As much as it opposes Rome's empire, it also imitates it. Matthew attributes the things of Rome to God in constructing God's empire to be like Rome's in asserting power over all. Like Rome, it coerces participation with the threat of violent condemnation for noncompliance. God's empire has cosmic reach with God as "Lord of heaven and earth" (11:25). God's empire out-Romes Rome, imitating and exceeding the very power it resists. Such ambiguities reflect how deeply the gospel is embedded in, imitative of, and accommodated to imperial culture.

The same ambiguities are evident in the prayer that Matthew's Jesus teaches his followers (6:9–13). The prayer is deeply embedded in and reflective of imperial realities even while it is imperially contestive in addressing "our Father in heaven," not the emperor as "Father of the Fatherland" (*pater patriae*). It prays for God's empire to come, God's will to be done, and for God to supply daily bread and forgiveness of debts. For God to answer these petitions fully and finally means the end of Rome's empire. Yet these petitions also imitate imperial structures, replacing one empire with a superior one.

Resurrection and God's Purposes

Jesus's crucifixion and resurrection demonstrate a similar range of perspectives. Jesus's crucifixion as "king of the Jews" (Matt 27:11, 29, 37) is the apparent victory of Rome and its provincial allies. To claim or to be understood to be a king without Rome's sanction was an act of rebellion that Rome met with crucifixion. Pilate and his Jerusalem allies exercise their ultimate power in killing Jesus.

But Matthew presents the victory as empty. While the crucifixion story exhibits Rome's supreme life-and-death power over Jesus, it also presents Jesus as controlling his own death and participation in God's purposes, which were bigger than Rome's will and power (Matt 16:21; 20:17–19; 26:2). Likewise, the narrative mocks Roman power with two scenes concerning the futile attempts of Pilate and the priests to keep Jesus dead by sealing Jesus's tomb against rumors of attempts to steal Jesus's body (27:62–66; 28:11–15). God's resurrecting power, though, is not thwarted. At the empty tomb (28:6), the angel announces God has raised Jesus from the dead, giving him—in imperially imitative style—"all authority in heaven and earth" (28:18).

The conviction that God raises those who died in faithful relationship to God emerged in a context of imperial oppression. The earliest and clearest affirmations of resurrection in Dan 12 and 2 Macc 7 concern those who, in the second century BCE, faithfully resisted the tyranny of Antiochus Epiphanes and were martyred. The affirmation of resurrection understood that death-dealing imperial tyranny could not break relationship with God or thwart divine purposes. Resurrection asserted God's justice-bringing and life-giving work over imperial tyranny.

Conclusion

The personnel, structures, and practices of the Roman Empire pervade Matthew's Gospel. The gospel constructs it as being in the devil's control and under God's judgment, fantasizes its demise, and prays for God's empire to rule in its place. Yet the gospel also imitates and accommodates Rome's empire. It assumes imperial structures as the world Jesus followers negotiate each day. The gospel forbids them to resist it violently (5:39), leaving that option to God alone (Carter 2005a). They are to love their enemies, expressing practical mercy and concern for the well-being of even the hostile other (5:44; 25:31–46). They are to pay taxes, outwardly cooperating with Rome's demand even while regarding the act as testifying to God's purposes. They work, shop, marry, give birth, and die in Rome's world. The gospel fosters a community centered on Jesus's teaching, which requires practical love (22:37–39), acts of mercy (6:1–18), justice (6:34), and torah as interpreted by Jesus (5:17–48). But never does it require followers to abandon this imperial world. In imperially imitative style, it entrusts them with worldwide mission (28:18–20), a mission lived in the "third space" between dissent and accommodation.

For Further Reading

Carter, Warren. 2000. *Matthew and the Margins*. Maryknoll, NY: Orbis.
———. 2001. *Matthew and Empire*. Harrisburg, PA: Trinity Press International.

Garnsey, Peter, and Richard Saller. 2015. *The Roman Empire: Economy, Society, and Culture.* 2nd ed. Oakland: University of California Press.

Huskinson, Janet. 2000. *Experiencing Rome: Culture, Identity and Power in the Roman Empire.* New York: Routledge.

Kelly, Christopher. 2006. *The Roman Empire: A Very Short Introduction.* Oxford: Oxford University Press.

Riches, John, and David C. Sims. 2005. *The Gospel of Matthew in Its Roman Imperial Context*, LNTS. London: T&T Clark.

Scott, James C. 1990. *Domination and the Arts of Resistance.* New Haven: Yale University Press.

The Gospel of Mark:
A Response to Imperial Propaganda

Adam Winn

Despite traditional assumptions, the canonical gospels were not written merely for the purpose of recording for posterity the events in the life of Jesus. In fact, it is widely recognized in the field of New Testament studies that these gospel narratives about Jesus were crafted to address the various realities and situations facing their first-century audiences. As the introductory essay of this volume demonstrated, many of these realities and situations were related to an empire that permeated the whole of first-century existence. As such, it should not be surprising that in early Christian gospels we find intentional responses to that empire. It is the purpose of this essay to determine whether the Gospel of Mark might contain such a response and, if so, what the nature and purpose of that response might be.

We will begin by looking for indicators in Mark's Gospel that suggest an intentional response to empire. After identifying and considering such indicators, we will then consider specific imperial realities that Mark's Gospel might be responding to—realities that are consistent with proposed settings for the composition for Mark's Gospel. We will then consider how reading Mark from a particular historical vantage point might lead us to recognize additional Markan texts as intentionally responding to empire. We will conclude by pulling all of these pieces together and proposing a unified anti-imperial reading of Mark's Gospel.

Markan Responses to Empire

To detect possible responses to empire in Mark's Gospel, we begin by looking for a variety of features that might signal such a response. Such features include Roman imperial language; references or allusions to

Roman imperial actions, institutions, and policies; and the portrayal of Roman officials or rulers. Since many of these features were simply a part of the world in which both Jesus lived and also the evangelist wrote, their mere presence in Mark's Gospel does not demonstrate an intentional response to empire. However, such features provide starting points for analysis, analysis that evaluates the purpose and function of these features in Mark's Gospel.

Mark's Incipit[1]

One does not have to go far in Mark's Gospel to find a feature that signals a possible response to the Roman Empire. Mark's opening line, "The beginning of the good news of Jesus Christ, the Son of God" (Mark 1:1), is pregnant with Roman imperial language.[2] The Greek word *euangelion*, translated "good news" or "gospel," was closely associated with Roman emperors, as it was frequently used to describe the emperor's birth, political ascension, or victory in battle. Describing the spread of the news that Vespasian had been declared emperor in the Roman East, the Roman historian Josephus writes, "Every city kept festivals for the good news [*euangelia*] and offered sacrifices on his behalf" (*J.W.* 4.10.6 §618 [Thackeray, LCL]). Josephus also writes, "On reaching Alexandria, Vespasian was greeted by the good news [*euangelia*] from Rome and by embassies of congratulations from every quarter of the world, now his own" (*J.W.* 4.11.5 §656 [Thackeray, LCL]). But even more significant are the striking parallels between the language of Mark's incipit and the Priene Inscription honoring Caesar Augustus.

> Since providence, which has ordered all things and is deeply interested in our life, has set in most perfect order by giving us Augustus whom she filled with virtue that he might benefit humankind, sending him as a savior, both for us and for our descendants, that he might end war and arrange all things, and since he, Caesar, by his appearance excelled even our anticipations, surpassing all previous benefactors, and not even leaving to posterity any hope of surpassing what he has done, and since the

---

1. An incipit is a title of sorts that often functioned as a programmatic statement for an entire piece of ancient literature (see D. Smith 1990, 1–9).

2. Unless otherwise stated, all biblical translations follow the NRSV. It should be noted that "Son of God" is missing in some early manuscripts, and thus its place in the Markan text is uncertain. For discussion, see Metzger 2002, 62.

birthday of the *god* Augustus was the *beginning* of the *good news* [*euangelion*] for the world that came by reason of him. (trans. Evans 2000, 69)

Perhaps most striking is the shared phrase "beginning of the good news." While in this inscription Augustus is identified as "god," he, along with other Roman emperors, was also regularly identified as "son of God," an identification that creates another parallel with Mark's incipit (Evans 2000; Winn 2008, 97).

First-century Greco-Roman readers would certainly recognize these strong parallels between the language of Mark's incipit and the language used to describe the Roman emperor. It seems equally certain that they would detect in this parallel a bold challenge to the identity of the Roman emperor. The Markan evangelist has taken a phrase that would be commonplace in the ubiquitous propaganda of Roman emperors and within that phrase has substituted the name "Jesus Christ" for that of Caesar; that is, he has replaced Caesar "Son of God" with Jesus "Son of God." An implied religiopolitical challenge seems hard to deny.

In all fairness, many Markan scholars have also pointed out similarities between the language of Mark's incipit and that found in Isaiah's "servant song" (Isa 42–53 LXX; see, e.g., Watts 2000, 96–99). In these chapters, "the one who proclaims the good news" (*euangelizō*, the verbal form of *euangelion*) of God's victory and reign figures prominently (Isa 40:9 [2x]; 41:27; 52:7 [2x]; 60:6; 61:1). In Mark's Gospel, it is Jesus who proclaims the "good news" of God's kingdom, and thus these verses from Isaiah are arguably an intended backdrop against which Mark's incipit should be read. Such a conclusion is strengthened by the fact that the incipit is immediately followed by a quotation from Isa 40:3 (Mark 1:3), a passage that comes only a few verses before Isaiah's first reference to "the one who proclaims *good news.*"

In light of the similarities that Mark's incipit shares with both the language of Isaiah and the Roman imperial world, many interpreters feel the need to choose one background over the other. While choosing only one of these two backgrounds for understanding the Markan incipit seems natural, perhaps a third option is possible. It may be that the Markan evangelist *intended* to bring these two backgrounds together (Evans 2000, 77; Winn 2008, 98–99), and thus ignoring either would be a significant mistake. We will move forward with the recognition that both backgrounds are important and will return to the significance of such a solution below.

Thus I conclude that Mark's readers would hear in the Markan incipit a direct challenge to the identity of the Roman emperor and the "good news" of the Roman Empire that he ruled. That such a challenge appears in Mark's incipit is tremendously significant, as an incipit functioned to indicate the overall purpose of a literary work. Thus, in light of Mark's explicit challenge to both Rome and its emperor, the reader would be attuned to ways in which the rest of the gospel might carry this challenge forward. Through the incipit, the Markan evangelist establishes the claims and power of the Roman Empire, and perhaps its emperors, as a background against which the gospel should be read.

The Gerasene Demoniac

In Mark's account of the Gerasene demoniac (5:1–20), we find a clear reference to a distinctly Roman institution. In Jesus's dialogue with the demoniac, the demoniac answers a question about his name by saying, "My name is Legion; for we are many" (Mark 5:9). The use of the name Legion is noteworthy, as this word represents an institution closely related to Roman imperial power. A Roman legion was the largest Roman military unit, numbering between five thousand and six thousand soldiers. The commander of these legions was the Roman emperor, and it was through these legions that Rome both expanded and controlled its empire. On the surface, such a reference may look innocuous and might simply be understood as a generic reference meaning "many." But there are many details in this story that strongly suggest Mark's use of the word "legion" is an intentional reference to Roman imperial power, particularly military power. Pigs play a prominent role in this story, as Jesus casts this "legion" of demons into a herd of swine. It is thus noteworthy that the tenth Roman legion, the legion stationed in Palestine, fought under the symbol of a boar, with soldiers having the symbol of a boar on their shields. Additionally, the story uses language that is commonly associated with military/combat. Mark uses the word *agelē* to describe the herd of pigs, a word that is more commonly used to describe military forces. Mark also uses the word *hōrmēsen* to describe the pigs "rushing" over the cliff into the sea, but this word is often used to describe charging soldiers. It appears that Mark may be intentionally using language to draw parallels between demon-possessed pigs and charging soldiers. It is also noteworthy that the demons plead with Jesus not to make them leave the "territory," a request that evokes the image of soldiers occupying an assigned region. Finally, the city associated with this pericope, most plausibly Gerasa, is also closely linked with Roman military power. During the Jewish Revolt (66–70 CE), Roman legions, under the command of the general (and eventual emperor) Vespasian, burned Gerasa and ravaged the villages of the region. In light of all these details, it seems that Mark has crafted this pericope into a purposeful response to Roman imperial power. The Markan Jesus does not merely exorcise demons but engages in the symbolic defeat of Roman military might—perhaps a defeat that in some way reverses Vespasian's victory over the city of Gerasa. Thus the challenge to Roman imperial power communicated in Mark's incipit finds further expression in Jesus's encounter with the Gerasene demoniac.[3]

A Centurion's Declaration

The Markan passion narrative culminates with the proclamation of a figure closely associated with Roman imperial power, a Roman centurion. A Roman *centuria* was the smallest military unit within a Roman legion and was composed of sixty to eighty soldiers. A centurion was the commander of a *centuria*, though experienced centurions commanded cohorts (composed of six *centuriae*). It seems undeniable that such a figure would represent Roman imperial power in Mark's Gospel. What is striking, then, is the claim that is made by this representative of Roman power after he has observed the events surrounding Jesus's death. The centurion claims, "Truly this man was [a] son of God" (15:39, author's translation). As I noted above, the title "son of god" was a title closely associated with Roman emperors. The Greek phrase *huios theou*, "son of god," that we see here in Mark is the common translation of the Latin imperial title *divi filius*, "son of god." A centurion would commonly hail the reigning emperor, who commanded the Roman military, "son of god." But to the first-century reader, the centurion shockingly applies this title to the crucified Jesus rather than Caesar. As at the beginning of the gospel, again the evangelist co-opts common imperial language by replacing the normal

---

3. For similar readings of this passage, see Myers 1992, 190–93; Horsley 2001, 141–48. This analysis might lead some to conclude that the pericope of the Gerasene demoniac was a creation of the Markan evangelist. While such a conclusion is possible, it is not necessary, as one could also conclude that the evangelist has simply adapted a well-known Jesus tradition for the purpose of responding to Roman imperial power. The same rationale could be used in the evaluation for all pericopes discussed below.

and expected recipient Caesar with Jesus. The challenge that is issued to Caesar in the incipit is repeated (or culminates?) with a Roman centurion declaring Jesus rather than Caesar to be "son of God."

Markan Responses to Empire: A Summary

Here I have shown three different texts in Mark's Gospel that clearly challenge Roman imperial realities. These texts suggest to us that Mark's Gospel indeed has an interest in critiquing the Roman Empire and presumably the claims of Rome's emperors. But how central is such a critique to Mark's Gospel? The presence of a challenge to Roman power in the Markan incipit might suggest that such a critique is quite central to the entire gospel. But does the rest of the gospel evince a critique/challenge of Roman power, or can such only be found in these isolated texts? Are there any specific historical realities or situations that might help us better understand this critique? To this point I have provided enough evidence to demonstrate that Mark's Gospel contains challenges to Rome's empire, and from these starting points, I will explore further the possible nature and purpose of these challenges.

The Roman Empire and the Setting of Mark's Gospel

It is widely accepted by Markan interpreters that the gospel was written in temporal proximity to the destruction of the Jewish temple in 70 CE, with interpreters somewhat evenly divided over whether the gospel was written before or after this event.[4] Despite this debate, a commonly accepted time frame for the composition of Mark is 67–72 CE. Less consensus exists with provenance or place of origin for Mark's Gospel, with scholarly opinion divided over whether Mark was written in the Roman West (Rome) or East (Syria or Galilee).[5] For our purposes, there is no need to settle these debates here. Instead, I will simply consider the historical situation of the Roman Empire and its emperors during the generally accepted time frame of 67–72 CE, realities that would be significant in both the West and the East. Such realities present plausible contexts for a Markan challenges to the Roman Empire.

---

4. For discussion and bibliography on this debate, see Winn 2008, 43–76. It is the opinion of this interpreter that Mark was written after the destruction of Jerusalem and the temple in 70 CE.

5. For discussion and bibliography on this debate, see ibid., 76–91.

The Latter Years of Nero's Reign (67–68 CE)

Nero ruled as Rome's emperor from 54 to 68 CE. While the early years of Nero's reign were promising, the later years are described by Roman historians as tyrannical. Nero killed indiscriminately, confiscated property illegally, spent state resources excessively and wastefully, and taxed both the city of Rome and its provinces heavily (Suetonius, *Nero* 30–35). His poor governance led to political and economic instability in the empire and ultimately resulted in open rebellion in the Roman provinces. It is not hard to imagine that Mark 10:42, "You know that among the Gentiles those whom they recognize as their rulers lord it over them, and their great ones are tyrants over them," would have evoked thoughts of Nero for those who first read it. Such a conclusion seems all the more likely given the antagonistic relationship between Nero and Roman Christians. Nero instituted the first formal and systematic persecution of Christians in the first century, persecution that is described by the historian Tacitus in the following way:

> First, then, the confessed members of the sect were arrested; next on their disclosures, vast numbers were convicted, not so much on the count of arson as for hatred of the human race. And derision accompanied their end: they were covered with wild beasts' skins and torn to death by dogs; or they were fastened on crosses, and, when daylight failed were burned to serve as lamps by night. (Tacitus, *Ann.* 15.44 [Jackson, LCL])

In addition, Nero was aggressive in promoting his own worship. He presented himself as Apollo incarnate and styled himself "son of the greatest of the gods" (Suetonius, *Nero* 25, 53; Evans 2001, lxxxiii). Certainly the tyrannical emperor Nero and the Rome he governed might have evoked a challenge from Christians. Could Mark's Gospel be such a challenge? Could Mark's incipit be contrasting Jesus "Son of God" with Nero who claimed to be the "son of the greatest of the gods"? It seems that the reign of Nero presents a plausible background against which one might read Mark's challenges to the Roman Empire.

The Year of the Four Emperors (68–69 CE)

Nero died in 68 CE, after his servant helped him commit suicide. He left no male heir to replace him as Rome's emperor. Thus with the death of Nero and no succession plan in place, there was a significant power vacuum in the Roman Empire. The first to claim power and to be declared as emperor by the Roman Senate was Galba, the governor of Spain, who had begun a rebellion against Nero in 68 CE. Galba's popularity did not last long, and he remained emperor for only six months, when he was killed by the prae-torian guard, the very soldiers that were meant to protect him. On the day that Galba was killed, the Senate recognized Otho, the governor of Lusita-nia, as Rome's next emperor. However, Otho's reign was almost immedi-ately challenged by the general Vitellius, who was commanding the legions in Germania Inferior. After three months as Rome's emperor, Otho's armies had been defeated by Vitellius, and Otho committed suicide. On the day of Otho's death, Vitellius was recognized as emperor by the Senate. But only three months after Vitellius was declared emperor, Vespasian, the general of the Roman legions in the East, was declared emperor by his own sol-diers. Five months later, Vespasian's legions defeated those of Vitellius, and Vespasian was declared emperor by the Senate. Craig Evans suggests that Mark's Gospel may have been written during this turbulent year and that Mark is putting forward Jesus as a rival to the numerous figures vying for the control of the empire (2001, lxxxix). The challenges to empire that we observed above would certainly make sense against this political backdrop.

The Rise of Vespasian

As noted above, the "year of the four emperors" culminated with the gen-eral Vespasian becoming Rome's emperor. Vespasian's ascension to power is noteworthy, because he was the first emperor who did not come from the patrician upper class. Vespasian was a "new man" in Roman politics, and he held power because he held the most powerful legions. Knowing that it would take more than legions to secure both his position and Rome's peace, Vespasian sought to demonstrate that his reign was the divine will of the gods and not merely the result of his military might. The new emperor sought to achieve this goal through a significant propagandis-tic campaign. It was widely circulated that from Vespasian's youth, divine portents had signaled his eventual rise to power, portents even witnessed by the emperor Nero himself (Suetonius, *Vesp.* 5). In addition to these por-tents, prophecies were made that predicted Vespasian's rise to power. It was also reported that while in Alexandria, Vespasian had a supernatural vision in the Temple of Serapis, which assured him that he would be suc-cessful in his imperial ambitions (Tacitus, *Hist.* 4.82; Suetonius, *Vesp.* 7.1). Vespasian also performed two supernatural healings while in Alexandria, including the healing of a blind man by means of spittle and the healing of a man's withered hand (Tacitus, *Hist.* 4.81.1–3; Suetonius, *Vesp.* 7.2; Cassius Dio, *Hist. rom.* 66.8.1). Such miracles were seen as evidence of divine favor on the soon-to-be emperor.

However, perhaps more significant for our purposes than any of the previous pieces of propaganda is the claim that Vespasian was the true fulfillment of Jewish sacred Scriptures, Scriptures the Jews believed pointed toward a messianic world ruler. The Jewish historian Josephus writes:

> But what more than all else incited them [the Jews] to war was an ambiguous oracle, likewise found in their sacred scriptures, to the effect that at that time one from their own country would become ruler of the world. This they understood to mean that someone from their own race, and many of their wise men went astray in their interpretation of it. The oracle, however, in reality signified the sovereignty of Vespasian, who was proclaimed Emperor on Jewish soil. (Josephus, *J. W.* 6.5.4 §§312–313 [Thackeray, LCL])

Similar claims are made by two Roman historians (Tacitus, *Hist.* 5.13.1–2; Suetonius, *Vesp.* 4.5). Such a belief finds its most plausible origin in the propagandistic campaign of Vespasian, a campaign that sought to secure Vespasian position as Rome's emperor.[6] It is important to note that Vespasian is not claiming to be the Jewish "messiah," but rather is claiming that the Jews had misunderstood their own Scriptures. While Jews believed that their Scriptures foretold of a world ruler arising from among the Jewish people, Vespasian is claiming that the world ruler foretold by such Scriptures was actually himself! This claim by Vespasian certainly presented a challenge to the early Jesus movement, as Vespasian was usurping the claims of its "Christ." One might expect that such a challenge would call forth a Christian response. As I have argued elsewhere, we may find just such a response in Mark's Gospel.[7]

Additional Responses to Empire in Mark's Gospel

We now return to Mark's Gospel in order to consider how additional pericopes might function as responses to the Roman Empire. These Markan

---

6. For discussion on this point, see ibid., 161–63.

7. For further discussion on Vespasian's rise to power and the possibility that Mark's Gospel is responding to this situation, see ibid., 178–201.

texts may not be as explicit in their challenge to empire as those we considered previously, but when read against the historical situations outlined above, their challenge to imperial power becomes more evident.

Similar Healings

As noted above, the emperor Vespasian famously healed two individuals while in Alexandria. The first individual Vespasian healed was a blind man. The man's sight was restored by the application of Vespasian's spittle to the man's eyes. Such a healing finds a striking parallel in Mark's Gospel, as Jesus also heals a blind man by applying spittle to the blind man's eyes (8:22–26). The second individual Vespasian healed was a man with a disfigured hand. Vespasian touched the hand with his foot, and the hand was restored. This miracle also finds a parallel in Mark's Gospel, as Jesus encounters a man with a withered hand in the synagogue (3:1–6). Jesus asks the man to stretch out his hand, and the hand is immediately restored. These healings of Vespasian were well known, as evidenced by the fact that the Roman historian Tacitus claimed that these stories were still being reported even during his day, thirty years after the events occurred (Tacitus, *Hist.* 4.81.1–3). Given the popularity of these stories, it seems likely that Mark's readers (if Mark's Gospel was composed after these events) would have quickly perceived the similarities between the healings of Jesus and those of Vespasian. They would have perceived Jesus not only matching the miracles of Vespasian but also surpassing them. Jesus heals the blind twice, opens the ears of the deaf, raises the paralyzed, cleanses skin diseases, and even raises the dead. If Mark's opening verse presents a challenge to the claims of the Roman emperor, than it seems probable that Mark's readers would understand both these Vespasian-like miracles and those miracles unique to Jesus as a part of that challenge; that is, they serve as examples of Jesus's superiority over Rome's reigning emperor.[8]

Stilling Storms

Mark includes two pericopes in which Jesus demonstrates his power over the winds and the sea. In Mark 4:35–41, Jesus, while at sea, calms a

---

8. Such arguments can be found in Incigneri 2003, 170–71; and Winn 2008, 184–85.

great storm simply with a verbal command, and in Mark 6:45–52, Jesus both walks on the sea and calms the winds. Interpreters have provided a number of plausible backgrounds for these two Markan pericope, including the Jonah narrative, God's primordial conquest of the sea at creation, and even the Homeric epics. While all of these possible backgrounds have merit and might inform our reading of these Markan pericopes (and perhaps those found in other gospels), one background has particular significance for our purposes. The calming of storms and seas was a motif that was closely associated with Greco-Roman rulers. In 2 Macc 9:8, Antiochus IV is described as one who believed he had the power to "command the waves of the sea." The Roman emperor Augustus claimed to have brought peace to the seas by ridding them of pirates (Res gest. divi Aug. 4.25). Philo describes this achievement in the following way: "This is the Caesar who calmed the torrential storms on every side.... This is he who cleared the sea of pirate ships and filled it with merchant vessels" (*Embassy* 145–146 [Colson, LCL]). In light of this motif, we can clearly see a political dimension to Jesus's nature miracles. By calming the storms and the seas, Jesus is being cast alongside the great rulers of the Greco-Roman world. Yet while such rulers might metaphorically provide peaceful seas or arrogantly believe they have the power over the winds and waves, the Markan Jesus demonstrates this power by literally calming storms and walking on the water. If Mark is presenting Jesus as a challenger to the emperors of Rome, the ability to calm storms would be an impressive piece of evidence indeed![9]

Feeding the Five Thousand and the Four Thousand

Mark includes two pericopes in which Jesus uses a meager amount of food to miraculously feed a multitude of people. Like Jesus's nature miracles, numerous backgrounds have been provided for understanding these Markan pericopes (e.g., God's provision of manna in the wilderness, Elisha's multiplication of barely loaves, eucharistic symbolism, Homeric banquets). While all of these traditions might inform our reading of these Markan pericopes (as well as parallel accounts found in other gospels), I suggest that these pericopes might also be read in light of a Markan

---

9. For further discussion on this motif in the Greco-Roman world, see Bolt 2003, 134–35; Cotter 1999, 131–48; and Winn 2008, 185–86.

challenge to the Roman emperor. In a world in which all people found themselves playing the role of a client to some and a patron to others, the Roman emperor was regarded as a patron to all and a client to none, save the gods. As such, it fell upon the Roman emperor to provide benefaction for his clients, particularly if those clients were in need. One significant way in which the Roman emperor functioned as benefactor was in the distribution of grain. The emperor Augustus claims to have provided grain to over 100,000 Roman plebeians on multiple occasions (Res gest. divi Aug. 3.15, 18). When Vespasian secured the city of Rome, the city was in dire need of food, as its granaries held only a ten-day supply (Levick 1999, 124–25). Vespasian immediately had grain sent from Egypt to meet the food shortage in Rome. Jesus's distribution of food to a hungry multitude could certainly be understood against this common practice of Roman benefaction—particularly if Mark's readers were aware of challenges to empire found elsewhere in the gospel. But in these pericopes, Jesus does not simply match the benefaction of Rome's emperors; he surpasses it. While emperors like Vespasian take from their abundance to provide for scarcity, the Markan Jesus takes scarcity and creates abundance. Again, Jesus is shown to out-Caesar the Caesar![10]

Jesus's Passion and the Roman Triumph

A Roman triumph was a celebratory parade that most often commemorated the military victory of a general or emperor. Such triumphs have a number of stock features, and Thomas E. Schmidt (1995, 1–18) has made a compelling case that many of these features are paralleled in Mark's passion narrative. The similarities begin in Mark 15:16, when the text describes the location to which the Roman soldiers brought Jesus as the "praetorian." While this word might adequately describe the governor's palace, it is also a word that describes the personal guard of the Roman emperor, a unit that numbered approximately nine thousand soldiers. This Markan reference calls to mind the praetorian guard that would certainly have been present at a Roman triumph. In this same verse, Mark also references the presence of an entire cohort. A cohort was a subdivision of a Roman legion and numbered between five hundred and a thousand

---

10. For more thorough discussion of such arguments, see Winn 2008, 166–67 and 188–90.

soldiers. Many have noted that the presence of an entire cohort at Jesus's execution is historically implausible, and thus a Markan exaggeration.[11] Schmidt (1995, 6) has argued that Mark's reference to a cohort intends to draw a parallel to a Roman triumph, an event for which an entire cohort would have been present.

In Mark 15:17, a purple garment is placed on Jesus. Again, this detail is historically implausible, as purple garments were incredibly expensive and were worn only by the social elite. That such a garment would have been available to place on the bloodied shoulders of a criminal seems highly unlikely. Even the Gospel of Matthew changes the color of this garment from purple to crimson, the color of the garments worn by Roman soldiers. Schmidt (1995, 7) suggests that Mark purposefully includes this detail of a purple garment to draw a parallel between Jesus's passion and a Roman triumph. Mark is presenting Jesus as a Roman triumphator who would have been dressed in a purple robe. In addition to the purple robe, the Markan Jesus is adorned with a crown of thorns (15:17), a detail that is paralleled by the crown made of laurel leaves that would have been worn by the Roman triumphator. In Mark 15:18–19, the Roman soldiers pay homage to Jesus and hail him as a ruler. While such homage is clearly mockery, it parallels the homage that would have been paid to a Roman emperor during a triumph (Schmidt 1995, 8).

The location of Jesus's crucifixion shares a striking similarity to the location where a Roman triumph would have come to an end. Mark tells us that Jesus was crucified at a location known as "Golgotha" (likely an Aramaic word), which the text translates as "place of the skull." A Roman triumph culminated at the *Capitalium*, a word derived from the Latin word *caput*, "head." Roman legend claims that this name originated from a skull that was found while the *Capitalium* was being built. Thus both a Roman triumph and Jesus's passion narrative culminate at the place of the "skull" (Schmidt 1995, 10–11).

In Mark 15:23, Jesus is offered (presumably by the Roman soldiers) wine mixed with myrrh, a drink Jesus refuses. Again, this detail in Mark's passion narrative, a detail that has been altered by Matthew, finds a significant parallel in a Roman triumph. When the triumphator had reached the *Capitalium*, he was offered a cup of wine to drink, but he customarily refused the wine. Immediately after the triumphator's refusal, a bull

---

11. See Hooker 1991, 370; France 2002, 637; etc.

was sacrificed. Immediately after the Markan Jesus refuses the wine, the text states, "and they crucified him" (15:24). Again Schmidt (1995, 11–12) argues that this is a striking parallel between Mark's passion narrative and Roman triumph.

Mark also reports that Jesus was crucified between two thieves. After the procession of a triumph had come to a stop at the *Capitalium*, the triumphator would be elevated in a ten-feet-high seat. Yet there are numerous examples in which two individuals were seated at the triumphator's right and left. For example, Tiberius sat between Rome's two consuls (Suetonius, *Tib.* 17), Claudius between his two sons-in-law (Cassius Dio, *Hist. rom.* 60.23.1), and Vespasian between his sons Titus and Domitian (Josephus, *J. W.* 7.5.5 §152). Again, we see Jesus's passion paralleling a Roman triumph (Schmidt 1995, 14–15).

In light of these parallels, Mark's concluding his passion narrative with a Roman centurion declaring Jesus to be "son of God" takes on even greater significance (15:39). Mark tells us that the centurion makes this declaration after he saw the manner in which Jesus "breathed his last," a euphemism for dying. We might conclude then that centurion's declaration of Jesus's identity as "son of God," a declaration a centurion would normally make about the emperor, results from the centurion's recognition that Jesus's death parallels a Roman triumph.

In light of these similarities, a compelling case can be made that the Markan passion narrative presents Jesus's death as a Roman triumph. Such a presentation functions well as a capstone to what could be argued is a thoroughgoing response to Roman imperial power in Mark's Gospel. On the surface, this narrative presents Roman imperial power as the agent that takes Jesus's life; that is, Jesus dies on a Roman cross. But with the use of dramatic irony, Mark mocks those who execute this power. While the Roman actors believe they are defeating Jesus through a shameful execution, Mark presents them as unwittingly giving Jesus a triumph in the process. Thus even in death, the Markan Jesus subverts Roman power and outdoes the Roman emperor. As the passion narrative comes to a close, one Markan character, a Roman centurion, recognizes the irony and declares Jesus "Son of God."

Pulling the Pieces Together: Jesus versus Vespasian

When these various pieces of Mark's narrative are taken as a whole, there emerges a clear and discernable response to the power and propaganda of

Rome's empire and emperors. While such a response might fit any one of the historical setting I described above, I argue here (and elsewhere, Winn 2008) that it fits particularly well with the propaganda that surrounded Vespasian's rise to power. Unlike his predecessors, Vespasian merged Jewish messianic expectations with his own thoroughly Greco-Roman propaganda. Perhaps it is not coincidental, then, that in the Markan incipit we find the merging of Roman imperial language together with language of Jewish messianic hope. When read against the backdrop of Vespasian's propaganda, Mark's incipit seems tailor-made for rebutting Roman imperial claims that usurp the commitments of the early Jesus movement. But Mark's incipit is only the first blow the gospel strikes against Rome's new emperor. Much of Mark's Gospel can be read as a résumé of Jesus that counters the impressive résumé of Vespasian. While Vespasian performed miraculous healings, the Markan Jesus not only matches those healings but also surpasses them. While Vespasian commands Rome's powerful legions, the Markan Jesus commands and destroys legions of supernatural demons—an act that may symbolize God's defeat of Roman power. By commanding the winds and the waves, the Markan Jesus is shown to be superior not only to Vespasian but also to any world ruler who presumed to hold such power. Mark also demonstrates that Jesus is a superior benefactor to Vespasian. While Vespasian takes from his abundant grain supply in Egypt to address a food shortage in Rome, Jesus takes what is a food shortage and transforms it into abundance. Finally, even in death, Jesus is given a triumph by Roman authorities, a triumph that leads a Roman centurion to recognize Jesus rather than Caesar as Son of God. Thus one might argue that from beginning to end, Mark is a gospel that directly challenges the claims of Rome's emperor and presents Jesus, not Caesar, as the true and superior ruler of the world.[12]

For Further Reading

Evans, Craig A. 2000. "Mark's Incipit and the Priene Calendar Inscription: From Jewish Gospel to Greco-Roman Gospel." *JGRChJ* 1:67–81.
———. 2006. "The Beginning of the Good News and the Fulfillment of Scripture in Mark's Gospel." Pages 83–103 in *Hearing the Old Testa-*

---

12. For a more thorough presentation of these conclusions, see Winn 2008.

ment in the New Testament. Edited by Stanley E. Porter. Grand Rapids: Eerdmans.

Horsley, Richard. 2001. *Hearing the Whole Story: The Politics of Plot in Mark's Gospel.* Louisville: Westminster John Knox.

Incigneri, Brian J. 2003. *The Gospel to the Romans: The Setting and Rhetoric of Mark's Gospel.* BibInt 65. Leiden: Brill.

Myers, Ched. 1992. *Binding the Strong Man: A Political Reading of Mark's Story of Jesus.* Maryknoll, NY: Orbis.

Winn, Adam. 2008. *The Purpose of Mark's Gospel: An Early Christian Response to Roman Imperial Propaganda.* WUNT 2/245. Tübingen: Mohr Siebeck.

———. 2014a. "Resisting Honor: The Markan Secrecy Motif and Roman Imperial Ideology." *JBL* 133:583–601.

———. 2014b. "Tyrant or Servant: Roman Political Ideology and Mark 10:42–45." *JSNT* 36:325–52.

CRAFTING COLONIAL IDENTITIES:
HYBRIDITY AND THE ROMAN EMPIRE IN LUKE-ACTS

Eric D. Barreto

How do you resist the forces of empire when you lack power or even a voice? When resistance is not tolerated by the powerful, how can the weak resist the incursions of empire, even in subtle ways? That is, how do you stand against an empire in a way that critiques its deployment of power but also preserves some modicum of safety or self-preservation? One way to do so is to reject imperial power in ways that the empire will not recognize as betrayal. That is, you use the propaganda and ideologies of empire as a weapon against oppression. You speak and act in ways that look like accommodation in the eyes of the empire but are actually inimical if you know what you are looking for. If you know the code, you note the subtle subterfuge underlying discourse that appears to accommodate and not resist. Luke-Acts does precisely this. These texts narrate a hybrid form of resistance that subtly—but no less powerfully—challenges the claims of imperial domination.

Questions about the purpose and genre of Acts in particular have long revolved around the author's perspective on the Roman Empire.[1] Was this text primarily apologetic, defending the commensurability of Christian faith with Roman rule? That is, does Acts embrace the Roman Empire, defending it as a benign ally of those who would follow Jesus? Or does this text contain a critique of Rome's power? Do the early Christian communities narrated in Acts embody an active resistance to Roman hegemony? In both cases, what tends to be underdeveloped is how these conclusions about Acts then shape our reading of the Third Gospel. That is, how do Luke and Acts together

---

1. For example, see the distinct approaches of Gilbert 2004, 233–56; and Walasky 1983.

grapple with questions of empire? Do the Gospel of Luke and the Acts of the Apostles contain a consistent perspective on empire?

Perhaps, then, Luke's theology of empire requires some critical nuance, for the binary options of accommodation and resistance cannot fully comprehend the negotiation of empire we see in Luke-Acts. With a postcolonial optic of *hybridity*, we can recover a number of ways in which Luke draws on imperial discourses of power in order to undercut their claims in this two-volume work. Hybridity is a way to understand colonial responses to imperial power. Specifically, hybridity connotes the ambivalent posture colonized communities may elect, a posture that seemingly sanctions the identity imposed by the colonizer while simultaneously undermining this very same identity. The notion of hybridity opens a valuable, complex, in-between space that can better comprehend the gradation evident in colonial contexts between resistance and accommodation, between the rejection of one's former identity and an identity imposed by the colonizer.

So, where do we turn to find Luke's deployment of such hybrid forms of discourse? Of course, Luke never exposits directly a thesis or theology of empire. Instead, in narrative form, Luke creates literary and theological spaces within which to narrate the many encounters Jesus and his followers have with Rome and its many outgrowths around the Mediterranean. So, we search these narratives and experience the world they project, a world in which empire is stripped of its ostentatious claims to power though the empire remains unaware.

Luke-Acts, therefore, remains a powerful resource as a theological reflection on the pursuit of justice, identity, and community within the bounds of a powerful empire. There are two primary strategies of hybridity I would like to highlight. First, Luke draws on a hybrid posture when grappling with the power and influence of Rome. In doing so, Luke challenges the prerogatives of Roman power in a seemingly innocuous manner. In other words, this first theme looks at an external force that presses in from the outside on the Christian communities Luke-Acts describes. Second, hybridity is a valuable strategy for positing and constructing complex, overlapping, and flexible ethnic identities. That is, Luke-Acts crafts a hybrid theological and ethnic space in which difference is treasured as a gift from God not an obstacle to be overcome. In the formation of these forms of identity, the hegemony of Rome is undercut. This second theme is more internal. In light of this imperial force in the world, how then do we, the people God has gathered, live together? How do we embrace community? How do we "belong" in a contested world?

So, I will turn to an exegetical treatment of key texts in Luke-Acts, including Luke's tendency to synchronize the events of his narrative with larger historical event along with the regular appearances of faithful tax collectors and centurions. Throughout, I contend that hybridity characterizes both Luke's perspective on the Roman Empire and the identity of these inchoate Christian communities. Luke-Acts crafts a hybrid theological and ethnic space in which difference is treasured as a gift from God and the power of Rome is undercut. That is, Luke's engagement with ethnic discourse is yet another way that he provides a theological imagination of resistance.

Empire Defined

First, however, we might wonder what we mean by this notion of "empire."[2] By empire, we certainly refer to the powerful leaders, complex bureaucracies, military might, and pervasive propaganda that signal the long reach of imperial force. Empire is certainly represented by these physical instantiations of power, especially the freedom to create and propagate massive historical and ideological narratives that sanction and perpetuate imperial claims to authority and legitimacy. At core, empires weave a narrative of order and hierarchy, of belonging and exclusion. These stories determine who is superior and who should submit to them. It is perhaps precisely for this reason that the narratives of Luke-Acts are so powerfully yet so subtly subversive. In them, Luke engages in storytelling that forms the identity of a people and their communities.

It may be more helpful to imagine the central meaning of empire not in its symbolic representations or its most explicit manifestations. Empires are more ideological than they are physical. Or better yet, the manifestation of empire is deeply rooted in all-encompassing ideologies. So we might define "empire" as an external system of identity and belonging that predetermines our way of life so much so that the system seems natural and inherent but is actually constructed and ultimately destructive to human life. In short, empire is not defined by thrones, emperors, and armies but by the many ways in which empire shapes how we view the world and how we live in it. For these reasons, when Luke narrates the stories of Jesus and

---

2. My colleague Cameron B. R. Howard's insights were critical in developing this perspective on empire.

his earliest followers, he is criticizing the constructed orderliness Rome had projected. By demonstrating its frailties and shortcomings, Luke provides a theological counterpoint to such imperial assertions. By imagining a new way of belonging, of being in communities gathered by faith not by the wielding of power or the propagation of corrupt wealth, Luke weaves a very different kind of story than Rome was propounding.

Hybridity and Resistance

Fortunately, there are some helpful tools available to help us conceptualize how Luke's subtle form of resistance works. Having established what we mean by empire, "hybridity" helps us understand the ways Luke wrestles with the Roman Empire.

Much could and has been said about the notion of hybridity.[3] In brief, hybridity is a powerful heuristic for our reflections on the Bible and empire. Hybridity is a strategic posture that resists easy binaries and uses the liminal space between purportedly clear delineations of identity in order to undercut the power of colonial thinking. Otherwise stated, hybridity is a rubric for understanding colonial responses to imperial power. Specifically, hybridity connotes the ambivalent posture colonized communities may elect, a posture that sanctions the identity imposed by the colonizer while simultaneously undermining this very same identity.

In the mode of hybridity, resistance and accommodation are false choices, as these are not the only alternatives available to a colonized people. Between these radical alternatives lies a third way. This third way eschews this false binary and imagines how acts of resistance may yet *appear* to be modes of accommodation. Hybridity is not mere resistance. It is not a full-throated rejection of empire. So we ought not look for violent overthrows of the powerful or vocal protests of the same. Hybridity is not mere accommodation. It does not find communities resigned to the status quo. So we ought not look for communities sloughing off their previous identities in favor of imperial identities or peoples simply going along to get along, so to speak. Instead, hybridity encompasses some of both strategies. Hybridity resists power precisely by seeming to embrace the parameters of belonging staked out by empire. In such strategic postures,

---

3. For example, see Jervis 2004, 173–93; J. Marshall 2008, 157–78; and Sals 2008, 315–35.

communities may *appear* to accommodate the demands of the powerful. However, in these seemingly innocent performances of imperial identity, we can also discover an undercurrent of resistance and critique. In this way, the postcolonial notion of hybridity is a significant help in reading texts in which empires and their colonies, the center of power and its margins, as well as the contestations of local and empire-wide identities are a central component of the texture of the narrative.

Such theoretical reflections are necessary, of course, but the ubiquity of hybrid strategies and their import in exegesis become evident in the reading of our texts. As such, let us first turn to the Gospel of Luke.

"In Those Days": Historical Synchronicity in the Narrative of the Gospel of Luke

One of the many distinctive features of the Third Gospel is the way Luke synchronizes the story of Jesus with important political and historical events. Luke at several points will set the events of the gospel within the temporal measure of imperial time. Why would he do this? At first glance, these markers appear to serve a largely chronological function; they tell the reader what time it is, so to speak. When is it that these events occurred? However, these markers are not just historical connections meant to anchor Luke's narrative at a particular place and time. Instead, they are symbolic points of resistance. Especially by saturating the opening chapters of the gospel with these historical synchronicities, Luke appears to embrace the ways in which Rome marks time and space; that is, the very organization of history revolves around these powerful political figures and moments. However, by tying these momentous figures within the Roman world to the exploits of a mere Galilean, Luke is making a rather bold claim. Though received by mere shepherds, the news of Jesus's birth ought to reverberate in the halls of Herod and Caesar. In fact, the birth of Jesus places him not just on the same level as the powerful Herod and Caesar but actually as their superior.

The first instance of such synchronicities is found a mere five verses into the gospel. Luke 1:5 begins with "In the days of King Herod of Judea"; in this way, Luke introduces the story of Elizabeth and Zechariah. In the rest of this opening chapter, Luke provides a number of chronological markers (1:8, 21, 24, 26, 39, 56, 57, 80) that move the narrative from one moment to the next. In this introduction, these chronological points almost serve as chapter divisions, noting the major transitions in the story of John's birth. Paralleling the birth of a preacher in the wilderness with the great power of Herod is audacious. What do these two figures possibly have in common? This subtle chronological alignment thus serves to indicate not just the measure of time but also the measure of this man. There is a great contrast established too. Despite Herod's great efforts as a builder of impressive edifices, his cruelty is perhaps his prevailing legacy in the ancient world. The mere mention of his name is a whispered augur of threat. Aligning Herod's reign with John's birth and ministry reverberates even more when we learn in 3:19 that Herod's son orders John's execution. That is, the Herodian family provides a narrative but also a theological frame around John's story. This framing is not just a chronological aid but a strategy of hybridity. In conjoining Herod and John, the empire sees a concession where the astute reader notes a counterimperial tone. The naming of the Herods is not only a chronological marker but also stands as a marked contrast between the servants of God and the imperial forces that fear them.

As Luke turns to Jesus in chapter 2, however, local royalty gives way to the countenance of the emperor. John's birth and life are framed by mention of Herod and his son. In a parallel structure that also marks Jesus's superiority, 2:1–2 begins by setting Jesus's birth alongside the reign of Emperor Augustus. That Augustus is a threat to Jesus and his neighbors is only emphasized by Luke's noting of the census Augustus demands. Like the mention of Herod in introducing John's origins, the census of Augustus is an augur of empire's power. A census, we must remember, is not just a demographic study meant to give social scientists crucial data. Augustus's census is a means of control and a platform for taxation. Knowing the population is a prerequisite for their taxation, and taxation is not an innocuous matter but a potent symbol of imperial control. Yet this act of imperial force backfires. In trying to count his tax base, Augustus unwittingly delivers the messiah, the savior, the Lord (2:11) into the household of David.

Luke 3:1 provides an even more extensive set of chronological markers. A litany of five Roman rulers and a pair of high priests of controversial appointment (cf. Acts 4:6) in quick succession here provide the chronological setting for this new chapter in the narrative. These historical markers, however, are quickly subsumed under the citation of the prophet Isaiah in 3:4–6. That litany of rulers and priest is not driving this narrative; God is, as told long ago by God's prophet.

Yet it may be a scene in these earliest chapters of the gospel that does not refer directly to Rome and its leadership that provides our clearest view into Luke's perspective on the undisputed political power of his time. Driven by the Holy Spirit, Jesus endures a set of temptations from the devil designed, narratively speaking, to test and then confirm the prophetic declarations of the opening chapters. In the second temptation (4:5–8), the devil projects a panoramic display of all the world's kingdoms and promises: "To you I will give their glory and all this authority; *for it has been given over to me*, and I give it to anyone I please" (4:6).[4] That is, Luke here suggests that behind the machinations of Rome's great empire is the devil, who has received and now controls the reins of power (see Green 1997, 194–95). That the devil may be lying is, of course, possible. At the same time, the temptations of Jesus are not so much to give in to the deceptions the devil propounds but to buy into their implications.

In light of this connection to the source of the empire's power, Jesus's response in 4:8 takes on a vivid valence: "It is written, 'Worship the Lord your God, and serve only him.'" His response is not just a commitment to monotheism or a dogmatic confession but a statement of political allegiance as well. There is only one God, and God does not sit on a throne in Rome. There is only one God to serve, and God is not the deployer of tax collectors and soldiers who will oppress the people. Yet this true God does not exclude these agents of the empire's power. This God invites them in.

"And We, What Should We Do?":
Tax Collectors, Centurions, and the Local Faces of Rome

The narrative of Luke-Acts is regularly punctuated by the appearance and pivotal roles of a number of individuals who represent the local faces of Rome's power. Maligned by their neighbors as traitorous and corrupt, tax collectors stand in a more favorable light in Luke-Acts than we might expect. Though representatives of Rome's military might, soldiers and centurions play similar roles in these texts. Again, a seeming concession to the presence of Roman power far from the imperial capital may actually be a subversive critique through the lens of hybridity.

Let us start with the earliest chapters of the gospel. In Luke 3, we find John the Baptist "proclaiming a baptism of repentance for the forgiveness of sins" (3:3). In response to his preaching, the crowds wonder how they ought to react to this call for repentance. This set of three questions is

---

4. All translations are from the NRSV; italics added by the author.

unique to Luke and thus likely represents a particularly Lukan perspective. To the gathered crowds, John broadly calls for generous care of the neighbor, especially those lacking clothes and nourishment (3:11). Even today, this call to radical generosity shakes us from the typically self-concerned ways we dispose of our possessions (see Johnson 2011).

But then two specifically named groups ask John the same question. Perhaps the general admonition to generosity is insufficient in the case of these two groups. First are tax collectors. It is important here to remember the disruptive role tax collectors would have played in their communities. Charged with collecting taxes from their neighbors, tax collectors were looked at suspiciously precisely because such power too often devolved into corruption and the enriching of themselves at the expense of the meager provisions of their neighbors. So it may be little surprise that John instructs these tax collectors seeking forgiveness to "collect no more than the amount prescribed for you" (3:13). That is, do your jobs with honesty. Similarly, when soldiers come to John, he commends honorable service that rejects the ways corruption and power so easily work together. In essence, John calls these soldiers to complete their duties with honor and without abusing those over whom they wield the threat of force.

Without the rubric of hybridity, John has seemingly two contrasting choices when confronted by tax collectors and soldiers alike. On the one hand, he could have called them to leave their vocations behind, for in continuing to serve the financial and military arms of Rome, they aided and abetted continuing oppression. He could have called them to resist the siren call of imperial power, status, and wealth. On the other hand, he could have invited them to be kinder, more generous tax collectors and soldiers. There is no way around the realities of the status quo. All we can do is work as best we can within the limitations of the regnant system, as oppressive as it might be. At first glance, this latter alternative appears to be what John says. Hybridity, however, allows for another interpretive possibility.

The admonitions John presents are not just accommodations or ways to continue living within the realm of the status quo. Instead, the seeking of forgiveness paired with the behaviors John calls for together represent a transformation of power and one's relationship with one's neighbors. Hybridity creates space for tax collectors and soldiers alike to "bear fruits worthy of repentance" (3:8). Simply leaving these vocations behind may not have been even remotely plausible for these coming to seek John's baptism. But in inhabiting these offices in the way John advocates, the world may just be transformed as the empire's claim to power is undercut not by outside forces violently imposing a new narrative of belonging but from the inside as people seeking repentance begin to see the other as kin rather than as means for self-aggrandizing wealth and power.

Such transformations are present in both Luke and Acts. In Luke 7, we hear of a faithful centurion seeking the healing of a valued servant. This centurion never meets Jesus, instead relying on "friends" to serve as intermediaries between him and Jesus. Through these friends, the centurion calls himself unworthy to host Jesus in his home. Instead, he recognizes in Jesus the power to heal. This is a power that the centurion recognizes as someone whose commands are heeded, not questioned (see 7:8). However, this is a power that cannot deliver life; such power only resides with Jesus. Hearing this testimony, Jesus deems the centurion an exemplar of faith (7:9). But why? What faith did Jesus see in this centurion?

The centurion believed and recognized Jesus's power over the forces of death. As a military officer, he likely understood well how powerful raw force could be. He knows how swords and masses of trained men can create massive destruction in their wake. He recognizes such power in Jesus, but there is a difference in Jesus's power, a difference the centurion believes can make all the difference in the world. Military might cannot heal the sick or raise the dead. An army cannot heal his faithful servant. Imperial power cannot gain the affections of a people only their fear. Jesus's power is unlike that wielded by Rome or any other empire. Jesus's power heals peoples and communities; it brings the powerful down from their thrones and lifts up the lowly. That is, Jesus's power turns the world upside down and inside out. That a centurion would recognize this power is the very essence of faith; faith is seeing the world with God's eyes, seeing the possibilities of a world renewed by God's love and grace.

Like John's encounter with the soldiers, Jesus does not instruct this centurion to lay down his sword or divest himself of the power Rome had granted him. Instead, the centurion's recognition of Jesus's power demonstrates that military force pales in comparison to the power Jesus wields.

Paralleling this centurion is Cornelius, yet another faithful centurion who stands at a narrative fulcrum in Acts. In Acts 10, Peter encounters Cornelius and his household after a litany of visions precipitate this unlikely meeting. There the Holy Spirit interrupts Peter's sermon in order to fall upon the household of Cornelius. Stunned by the receipt of this divine gift, Peter and his entourage realize the full magnitude of the gospel's inclusiveness. No power, no difference, no form of identity, no empire can stand in the way of God's activity in the world.

"All Together in One Place":
Hybrid Identities and a Theology of Difference

Difference and identity are yet other forms of hybridity in Luke-Acts. Ethnic identities are at the center of the theology of the book of Acts. After all, one of the critical narrative arcs in the book is the bridging of Jews/ Judeans and Greeks in a new alignment of kinship and belonging, a kinship of hybrid identities that undercut imperial order.

Much could be said about the ethnic negotiations Luke engages in and the kind of theological argument these narratives of difference promulgate (see Barreto 2010; 2013, 97–106). In brief, what we find in Acts is a steady negotiation of difference within a particular set of theological convictions. As I have argued elsewhere,

> The Acts of the Apostles is a natural home for exegetes hoping to make sense of the rich ethnic diversity of God's people. At root, Acts narrates the intrusion of the gospel into the myriad populations that dotted the landscape around the Mediterranean in antiquity. Propelled by persecution and the Spirit's guidance, these first followers of Jesus carry the gospel message to the very ends of the earth. A number of cultural boundaries are crossed in Acts, but at no point does Luke narrate the cessation of ethnic difference. Instead, the text invites us to enter a world in which ethnic difference and faithful unity coexist. (Barreto 2013, 97)

For many, Pentecost remains a powerful symbol of human unity in the midst of great linguistic and cultural difference. We often assume that this purported reversal of Babel saves us from the problem of many languages and the incomprehension and disagreement they create. Such a reading misses a critical component of this story.

After all, when the Spirit descends on the gathered Judeans/Jews from every corner of the world, Acts reports that they hear the gospel preached "in the native language of each" (2:4). That is, the Spirit did not revert this multilingual crowd into a pre-Babel existence where everyone has "one language and the same words" (Gen 11:1). Instead, the Spirit embodies the linguistic diversity present at Pentecost, embracing the complexities and particularities of every human tongue spoken that day. In short, at Pentecost, the Spirit dwells in the midst of difference, not over against it.

Now, what does this all have to do with empire? Much in every way. One of empire's most powerful tools is imposed homogeneity, the smoothing of ethnic, cultural, religious, and linguistic distinctives for the sake of unity. After all, a homogeneous people is far easier to control than a panoply of diverse communities and peoples. Alexander the Great recognized this well, enacting a project of hellenization that reshaped the ancient world as Greek culture and language became standards by which lands and people could be linked and thus ruled.

How then does Luke respond to such striving toward cultural homogeneity? By embracing difference as a critical component of community, not as an obstacle in its construction. These interpretive and theological trends come together with questions of empire rather well in Acts 21–22.

Let us start with a seemingly straightforward question. What is Paul's ethnicity in Acts? At first glance, we might point to Acts 21:39 and 22:3, where Paul calls himself a Jew/Judean (Greek *Ioudaios*) and declare the query easily solved. Yet the complexities of the ethnic discourse we find in the wider narrative context of these verses (21:27–22:30) suggests that a more complex negotiation of hybrid identities is at play. In the span of these two chapters, Paul claims no fewer than three ethnic identities: as a Judean/Jew, a citizen of Tarsus, and a Roman. Moreover, this complex of ethnic identities in which Paul claims to dwell is not just an insight into Pauline biography according to Luke. Instead, what we discover is Luke's embedded vision of difference as embodied by Paul, a profoundly theological vision that runs throughout Luke-Acts.

In the midst of the tumult around his arrest in Acts 21–22, Paul's linguistic abilities precipitate a great deal of confusion. His captor, later identified as Claudius Lysias (23:26), is surprised that Paul can speak Greek. Apparently, the tribune had assumed that Paul was a certain Egyptian who had led an insurgency against the Romans (21:38). Likely affronted by the tribune's assigning of mistaken identity and not so implicit accusation of fomenting rebellion, Paul lays out a series of ethnic identities as a defense. He is among his people; he is a Jew/Judean. To that local identity, Paul adds his hometown of Tarsus. That is, Paul is a person of significant ethnic status, not a common criminal or a foreigner looking to stir up local hostilities. In light of his status and perhaps chagrined by his misapprehension of Paul's identity, the tribune grants an opportunity for him to speak to the gathered people. In this way, Paul's dexterity in language provides vital leverage, first with his captor and then with the gathered crowd.

Paul engages a linguistic switch, turns to his people, and speaks their common language. This linguistic switch is mentioned twice, both in 21:40 and 22:2, the latter emphasizing the power that this linguistic connection creates between Paul and his audience, even if its effect is temporary. In the span of only a few verses, Paul rebuts the tribune's accusations by ably deploying Greek; now as he returns to his fellow Judeans/Jews, it is their common language that will enable Paul an audience. In these verses, Paul manages to move between porous ethnic boundaries.

Last, Paul deploys one further ethnic identity. Paul claims to captors about to torture him that he is indeed a Roman. Much scholarship and many translations have assumed that his claim here is largely a claim of certain legal rights. He is a Roman *citizen*. However, Paul's claim here is also and primarily ethnic. He is claiming to be a Roman, to belong in this imperial system and thus not able to be treated as a mere outsider.

In these few verses, Paul describes himself in a number of ways. He claims a number of identities. Paul is Jewish/Judean. He is a citizen of Tarsus. He is a Roman. Is Paul thus being dishonest, adapting to the situation only to save himself? Is he speaking one way to his captors and another to a rabid crowd in some sort of complex trick? How might we understand Paul's strategic posture?

Holding these three identities is not a contradiction, especially when understood under the rubric of hybridity. Paul's fungible ethnic identities are a powerful political tool, which provides a counternarrative to Roman hegemony. In the face of Rome's deadly injustice, Luke narrates Paul's negotiations of political power. This narrative is not alone in doing so, of course. The presence of righteous centurions in both Luke 7 and Acts 10 is not a concession to Roman power, though it may appear so on the surface. These centurions are exemplars of Rome's power, certainly, but more importantly, they represent the submission of these powerful individuals to the God of Israel. Luke's critique of the empire is subtle but no less powerful than a full-throated rejection of Roman arrogations. Paul's deployment of ethnic identities is thus a counternarrative to Roman imperial ideologies. While claiming his Roman identity, Paul's simultaneous and strategic deployments of two other forms of ethnic identity undercut any sense that Roman universalism or hegemony holds absolute sway in a world transformed by God's servant Jesus.

"With All Boldness and without Hindrance":
The End and the Ends of Acts

Rome simply cannot be anything but a villain at worst or an ambiguous presence at best as Acts closes. Paul's demise at the hands of the empire is certain; the readers of Acts would know of his execution whether through tradition or Paul's own prophetic pronouncements earlier in Acts 20:17–38. But Luke's critique of the empire is only evident if one knows how to read between the lines. Shrouded in a text seemingly accommodating Rome's claims are the seeds of its downfall, theologically speaking. If the God Luke describes can bridge linguistic barriers without imposing cultural hegemony, gather together people from every corner of the world without erasing their differences, compel soldiers to acts honorably and tax collectors honestly without the threat of violence, turn the world upside down without an army, then that God provides the most serious challenge to Roman power one could imagine. We only need the imagination to see it.

Yet hybridity is no panacea. Its practitioners do not dwell in some interstitial paradise. Hybridity and its practices exact a heavy cost. The strategy of hybridity Luke-Acts deploys requires some sanction of imperial ideology even as it is surreptitiously critiqued. That is, despite Luke's hybrid critiques of Roman power, he—as well as the communities he describes and addresses—becomes embroiled in Rome's imperial ideology, ensnared by its claims to supremacy. Hybridity is always a posture of necessary concession to the powerful even as it challenges their assertions of might. The "weapons of the weak"[5] are able but also inevitably dulled by imperial force. Hybridity does not leave the colonized unscathed. Embroiled in the narratives of empire, the colonized will always lose a piece of themselves even as they struggle to maintain the integrity of their identities and their communities. Hybridity always requires loss but a loss the colonized deem necessary, perhaps even indispensable.

So what does this mean for us today? To me, these exegetical insights are not just historical curiosities. Instead, reading Luke-Acts with the lens of hybridity invites profoundly theological implications about how Christians today function in complex political systems. Imperialism remains a powerful force, even (or maybe especially) in democratic political systems. As a theological educator, I am particularly concerned about how Scripture is heard, read, and interpreted in Christian communities. So also, I wonder how reading Scripture with these hermeneutical lenses might inspire a renewed imagination about how we relate to one another and the powers that rule the world, at least for now.

First, the hybrid discourses of Luke-Acts might inspire a renewed vigor for justice in a broken world. Too often, we imagine a pair of opposing

---

5. For more on this concept, see Scott 1985; Horsley 2004; and Kahl 2008, 137–56.

options in our struggle for justice. We can either reject the political and economic forces that thwart justice or embrace them as inevitable conditions. Both alternatives prove lacking in many ways. For one, we are so deeply entangled in oppressive political and economic systems that escaping their reach may prove impossible for many of us. Faced with the reality of oppression but also our apparent inability to escape the forces that propagate it, we might be frozen with an unavailing guilt. However, I would contend that guilt without grace is not the gospel. Neither does the gospel diagnose our common ills but then provide no means by which we can cooperate with God in the work of God's reign. On the other side, a naive embrace of unjust social and political systems is inconsistent with the good news. When we are unaware of how our actions, politics, and lifestyles impinge upon others, we entrench ourselves in systems of sinfulness.

Hybridity provides one path from this ethical morass. Between accommodation and full-throated resistance, there might be a space to reject oppressive forces while still being held by them. A hybrid reading of Luke-Acts might spark an imagination for how we can resist the forces of empire in small but influential ways. In addition, such awareness might allow us to open our eyes to moments of subtle resistance present all around us. Instead of seeing oppressed communities merely as sites for our compassion, we might learn from them how best to shine the light of the gospel in a dark world, for they might understand better what it means to live on the underside of history and still speak and act in a prophetic way.

Second, the hybrid discourses of Acts might inspire a wider imagination about identity, especially racial and ethnic identities. Too often we assume facile racial boundaries that do not admit the wide panoply of expressions of identity that communities and individuals embrace. Empires prefer to homogenize and thus pacify the vast swaths of peoples they hope to rule. Hybrid identities pose a challenge to such homogenizing forces and embrace the complexities and ambiguities in which ethnic negotiations are struck and restruck. Thus such a reading of Luke-Acts might invite us to reimagine diversity. Instead of a challenge we seek to solve by eliminating difference, we might begin to understand diversity as the very place where God exercises God's creative touch in our lives. In the midst of difference, we resist the universalizing forces of empire.

So, let us return to the question with which I began. How do you resist the forces of empire when you lack power or even a voice? Luke-Acts deploys a hybrid posture toward empire as well as hybrid identities to challenge the very premise of that question. The powerless indeed have power and voice, even when the effects of that power are subtle and that voice sounds innocuous in the ears of Caesar. In that mode of survival, we too may find an indispensable path for our resistance of empire's encroachments.

For Further Reading

Burrus, Virginia. 2007. "The Gospel of Luke and the Acts of the Apostles." Pages 133–55 in *A Postcolonial Commentary on the New Testament Writings*. Edited by Fernando F. Segovia and R. S. Sugirtharajah. London: T&T Clark.

Carey, Greg. 2009. *Sinners: Jesus and His Earliest Followers*. Waco, TX: Baylor University Press. Especially 79–96, 107–23, 125–35.

González, Justo L. 2010. *Luke*. Belief Theological Commentary on the Bible. Louisville: Westminster John Knox.

Kahl, Brigitte. 2008. "Acts of the Apostles: Pro(to)-imperial Script and Hidden Transcript." Pages 137–56 in *In the Shadow of Empire: Reclaiming the Bible as a History of Faithful Resistance*. Edited by Richard A. Horsley. Louisville: Westminster John Knox.

Rowe, C. Kavin. 2010. *World Upside Down: Reading Acts in the Graeco-Roman Age*. Oxford: Oxford University Press.

Skinner, Matthew L. 2010. *The Trial Narratives: Conflict, Power, and Identity in the New Testament*. Louisville: Westminster John Knox.

Taylor, Justin. "The Roman Empire in the Acts of the Apostles." *ANRW* 26.3:2436–500.

The Fourth Gospel, Romanization, and the Role of Women

Beth M. Sheppard

Just in front of the turnstile that marks the entrance to the current-day archaeological site of Ephesus, a city that tradition associates with the Fourth Evangelist, there is a series of souvenir shops. One displays a sign that proudly announces that its owner is a purveyor of "Genuine Fake Watches." Another sells sterling silver handcrafted jewelry, although a careful examination of some pieces reveals that they were made in Mexico rather than Turkey. These are just a few of the indicators of the complex tapestry of cultural influences that may be found in the region today. There are more. For instance, after touring the reconstructed first- and second-century ruins of the city, one can venture into the nearby modern town of Izmir (the province in which the Ephesus excavation is located) to stop into a Starbucks, purchase a stainless-steel cook pot manufactured in Germany at a housewares store, or pass some time in a Burger King. Clearly, present-day Turkey is globalized, not to mention a touch Americanized. Indeed, the souvenir vendors flanking the ruins of Ephesus are equally as happy to accept American dollars as they are Turkish lira or even euros for their wares, and they speak English (not to mention German and Turkish) fluently. Just as Turkey today is cosmopolitan, reflecting a variety of cultural strands, so, too, were the cities and lands of the ancient province of Asia (as the region in which Ephesus was located was called in the first century) and the wider Mediterranean region in the era in which the author of the Fourth Gospel lived and wrote. Prominent among those strands, in addition to the local culture, were the influences of Hellenization and Romanization. While it is obvious that Hellenistic culture had an impact on the Gospel—after all, the Gospel itself was written in Greek—

the Roman aspects may be a bit harder to tease out. But we are up for that challenge.

To add a twist, let us also try a different method for approaching the text and its Roman aspects than has recently been popular. To be sure, during the last few decades several scholars have explored John's Gospel against a backdrop of the political and social tensions inherent in Roman imperialism in order to illuminate how various aspects of its narrative may reveal resistance to Roman domination (Rensberger 1988; Cassidy 1992; Carter 2006a; Horsley and Thatcher 2013). But the process of Romanization does not always require that those investigating the past approach the text from the perspectives of political history or postcolonial history. There are many historical methods that may be used, such as social history, in which researchers are interested in customs and social conventions; economic history, in which investigators plumb texts and archaeological remains for evidence of how resources, labor, and production functioned in the ancient marketplace; cultural history, in which historians explore everyday life; and feminist history, in which scholars concentrate on discovering traces of a segment of the population that does not necessarily figure prominently in the written record. This project draws primarily on feminist history in its methodology, so little attention will be paid to issues of class conflicts or politics. Instead, I will explore how the portraits of the four main female characters in John's text—Jesus's mother, Mary Magdalene, the woman of Samaria, and Mary (with a few words about her sister Martha)[1]—stack up against sketches of Roman women that appear in the histories of Tacitus and Cassius Dio. Before plunging in, however, it is important to say a few words about the concept of Romanization.

Romanization: Texts and the Melting Pot

Romanization, like today's terms *globalization* and *Americanization*, is a complex phenomenon. Certainly there are obvious points at which Rome influenced the lands within its sphere. For example, Roman rulers encouraged the establishment of the state cult, which designated some emperors and members of their families as deities. The Senate even granted various

---

1. Minor female characters, such as the woman at the gate (John 18:17) and the mother of the man born blind (9:19–23), will not be treated, nor will the woman caught in adultery, since textual variants raise some question as to whether her story was original to the Gospel.

cities throughout the empire the right to serve as a *neokoros* (guardian of a temple dedicated to one of the caesars), a privilege that was viewed by the local residents as a prestigious honor. This particular right was accorded to Ephesus during the reign of Domitian, who was emperor from 81 to 96 CE, about the time the Gospel was likely taking shape.[2] Not only Asia but also Palestine, the land that is the setting for the action recounted in the Gospel, had a Roman flavor.

For his part, Herod the Great, who ruled Palestine as a client king who had received his throne from Rome, built a Roman-style city in his territory named Caesarea (Caesarea Maritima) in honor of Augustus and constructed a harbor that included Roman building techniques. There were so many innovations related to building the breakwater for Herod's new seaside city that the port might be described as "a monument to superior alien technology" (MacMullen 2000, 22). It is even possible that Herod and Augustus demonstrated how entwined the economies of Palestine and Rome happened to be by conspiring to build the harbor as a necessary way station for grain ships that were transporting that vital commodity from Egypt in order to feed Rome (Beebe 1983, 204–5). What is more, to add extra Roman flair to the city, Herod erected a temple to the goddess Roma and Augustus.

Even though no mention of Caesarea Maritima is made in the Fourth Gospel, nonetheless, following the Jewish War and the destruction of the temple in 70 CE (which may have occurred before John's text was written), that coastal city became a colony and the capital of Palestine, so its Roman pastiche was likely familiar to those who resided in the province.

Rome's influence was apparent not only in Ephesus and Palestine but also throughout the entire Mediterranean region through the establishment of Roman colonies, the bestowal of the rights of Roman citizenship, the promulgation of Roman rule and legal processes, and the distribution of luxury and other goods through trade and commerce. Certainly Roman roads and the use of Roman-style building techniques were present in Miletus, Pergamum, Ephesus, Sparta, Corinth, and elsewhere (MacMullen 2000, 21). Yet beyond these obvious examples, cultural dissemination is an extraordinarily subtle process, which makes untangling specific threads to determine how Roman civilization affected the everyday lives of women

---

2. For discussion of the early history of the Gospel, see, for example, von Wahlde (2010, 22–43, and the chart on 55), who proposes three editions of the Gospel dating between the mid-50s through the mid-90s CE.

during the period of the Fourth Gospel a difficult undertaking. Think about it. For a modern-day Turkish woman, does patronizing a Starbuck's coffee shop in Istanbul mean she is "Americanized," even if she purchases the Turkish coffee that is offered on the menu (a beverage that is not available in the United States versions of the franchise)?

Indeed, even classicists agree that just what is meant by the term *Romanization* is not clear (Alcock 1997, 1). The empire was a vast, sprawling entity, and accommodation and acculturation to Roman rule and culture proceeded at different paces during different periods of time and in various localities. Further, evidence of Roman influence in civic spaces, public architecture, and material culture aside, literature and history tend to develop conservatively and are prone to evidence direct continuity with the Greek past (Lamberton 1997, 151).[3] Certainly Rome itself was still profoundly Hellenized in the first century CE, so much so, as Grace Macurdy (1937, 7) was keen to point out, that the Roman satirist Juvenal, who was writing in the second and third decades of the second century, showed a distinct disdain for "Greek" Rome. Without knowing the exact provenance of the Fourth Gospel,[4] one is left only to speculate about the level of Romanization of John's readers or the women portrayed in his text.

The Fourth Gospel and Engagement with Empire

Nevertheless, undertaking a comparison of the female characters in the Gospel with the portraits of women in the Roman histories of the period is warranted, in part because the Gospel itself was written in the cosmopolitan milieu of the first century. In fact, there are sometimes overt, sometimes subtle ways that the Roman Empire is reflected in the Gospel. For example, Pontius Pilate is a Roman official and features prominently in Jesus's trial (John 18:29–40) along with Roman soldiers (18:3, 19:23). Elsewhere in the story, the author of the Fourth Gospel betrays sensitivity to the Roman aspects of the Galilee when he refers to the Sea of Galilee not only by that name but also by its Roman designation, the Sea of Tiberias (6:1).

---

3. In a study of Roman Syria, Lidewijde de Jong (2007, 23) cautions scholars about a "Hellenocentrism bias" that pervades many studies of the eastern Roman provinces.
4. The exact provenance of the Gospel is not known. Although traditionally associated with the city of Ephesus, Roman Palestine and even Egypt have been suggested. For a detailed discussion, see Keener 2003, 142-49.

The influence of Rome on the Fourth Evangelist may also be apparent in the episode of Jesus healing the son of a royal official who may have been Roman (4:46–54).[5] More clearly, a nod to Rome is evident when denarii, the Roman monetary unit, rather than shekels or talents are mentioned in relation to the possibility of buying food for the crowd of five thousand (6:7) and when Judas protests that the oil Mary uses to anoint Jesus should have been sold to generate funds for the poor (12:5). Perhaps the strongest evidence of all for the diverse nature of the culture is the statement that, in John's account of Jesus's death, the title displayed on the cross, "Jesus the Nazorean, King of the Jews," is said to have been rendered in Latin, the language of the Romans, as well as Greek and Aramaic (19:19–20). Clearly each of these passages reveals sensitivity to the realities of Roman languages, governance, and ways of life. Where there are such sensitivities, it becomes plausible to speculate about the extent that the portraits of the women in the Fourth Gospel—such as the Samaritan woman, Mary Magdalene, and Jesus's mother, to name a few—would also have been recognizable to contemporary Romans.[6] One place where sketches of Roman women may be found to serve as the basis for comparison is in the writings of the Roman historians.

Women and the Histories of the Imperial Period

When it comes to the genre of history, the Fourth Gospel (as will be seen later) bears some affinity with ancient biographies and accounts of the past. Although one must always remember that, even when parallels are found, the Roman historians were preoccupied with recording political history and the stories of the ruling elite, while the author of the Fourth Gospel had an entirely different agenda: to persuade his readers that Jesus was the Christ, the Son of God (20:31). Thus, even if the women in the Fourth Gospel do have some surface similarities to the women who grace the pages of the Roman historians, the women described by the evangelist also assist in promoting theological agendas that are outside of the scope of this particular essay.

---

5. Mark A. Chancey (2005, 52 n. 56) speculates that the official is not necessarily Roman but a member of Antipas's administration.

6. This method echoes that employed by Brigitte Egger (1988, 33–66) in relation to ancient novels.

So, how did the classical historians treat women and women's history? In his introduction to historical texts written during the Greco-Roman period, classicist Michael Grant (1995, 59) notes that, for the historians of that era, women were not center stage and did not feature prominently in accounts of the past. Still, the Latin and Greek works of Tacitus (born ca. 56 CE), Cassius Dio (born ca. 164 CE), Josephus (born 37/38 CE), and other historians who were active during the dawn and heyday of the Roman Empire do offer occasional glimpses into the everyday lives of women and the roles, both large and small, that a few of them played in current events. Exploring how the sketches of women in the Fourth Gospel compare with mentions of women as found on the pages of histories written during the first two centuries of the imperial period seems an interesting exercise on its own account, doubly so for a Gospel text that ultimately had appeal not only to its own initial audience, wherever that may have been located within the boundaries of the empire, but also eventually to the entirety of Christendom.

For the purpose of this study, the focus will center on comparing the Fourth Gospel with the works of classical historians who were Roman citizens and lived during the first two centuries of the empire.[7] This material will be supplemented with occasional references to texts written by earlier historians whose works influenced those of their successors. Thus a range of histories will be consulted regardless of whether the authors wrote in Greek or Latin or were born in Rome or the provinces, although Cassius Dio and Tacitus will feature more prominently.

A second methodological caution has to do with the fact that, not only were first- and early second-century CE histories a tangle of Greek and Roman influences, but in the case of Josephus and the Fourth Gospel itself, Jewish historiography undoubtedly was also influential and perhaps helped to predispose these authors who are heirs to the Jewish tradition to include women in their story lines. To be sure, the ancient Jewish account of the past found within Genesis to 2 Kings contains a narrative based on traditions that include the tales of strong women such as the matriarchs Deborah, Miriam, and Ruth, to name just a few.[8] The fact that Josephus

---

7. Josephus was granted Roman citizenship by Vespasian (*Vita* 423).

8. Eve = *Ant* 1.1.2–4 §§27–36; Sarah = *Ant.* 1.6.5 §§148–153; 1.7.1 §§154–157; 1.8.1 §§161–165; 1.10.4 §§186–190; 1.12.1-3 §§207–219; 1.14 §237; 1.17 §256 (the tale of Sarai's laughter is omitted from Josephus's version); Rebekah = *Ant.* 1.16.1-3 §§242–255; 1.18.6, 8 §§269–273, 276–277; 19.5 §§285–287; Rachel = *Ant.* 1.19.4-11

elected to incorporate rather than skip over these women in his *Jewish Antiquities* serves as testimony to the high level of esteem in which Josephus held his chief source.[9] Nonetheless, Roman sources are not shunned by this historian. Starting with book 13 of the *Antiquities*, he draws on the Roman historian Livy (59 BCE–17 CE) and also Strabo (born ca. 64 BCE), the geographer who supported Roman imperialism (Bilde 1988, 87–88).

This careful shading of the story and blending of cultural influences plays out, in part, in Josephus's account of Ruth (*Ant.* 5.9.1–4 §§318–337), the woman who was loyal to her mother-in-law and gleaned in the fields of Boaz. While remaining relatively faithful to the biblical account of this young woman and her subsequent marriage,[10] Josephus gives a nod to the fact that Roman historiography tended to be written by the aristocracy (those of the senatorial class) and focused on the lives of great men by offering an apology to his readers for including a story of a girl of such humble address, explaining that God worked through the otherwise insignificant couple to provide the great David as one of their descendants (*Ant.* 5.9.4 §337). As will be seen, the Fourth Gospel also tends to include sketches of women that appear in the text as boldly as the females of the Old Testament, but unlike in Josephus, they are presented in ways and roles that would be palatable to cosmopolitan audiences without the need to offer justification for their inclusion in the narrative.

The Fourth Gospel: Genre and Historical Consciousness

This observation, however, brings up the question of the nature of the Fourth Gospel vis-à-vis the Roman histories. Many have noted the similarities of the gospels with the ancient genres of biography in the field of history and encomium in rhetoric, which both focus on the deeds and actions of a central figure (Burridge 2004; Justin Smith 2007; Keener 2003,

---

§§285–324; Deborah = *Ant.* 5.5.2–4 §§200–209; Miriam = *Ant.* 2.9.4–5 §§217–227 (though in Josephus she does not sing on the banks of the Red Sea after the destruction of Pharaoh's army, but Moses composes a song in hexameter 2.16.4 §§345–346; Ruth = *Ant.* 5.9.1–4 §§318–337).

9. Laura S. Lieber (2012, 329–42) traces the tradition of strong Jewish women such as Esther and Judith in the Hellenistic era.

10. Bilde (1988, 82) notes Josephus's placement of the story of Ruth between material drawn from Judges and 1 Samuel, as in the LXX. Its more traditional placement is with the writings as one of the five Megilloth.

11-34). Finding an exact match, however, between the gospels and other types of ancient literature is a challenge. On the one hand, the extant biographies and encomiums were generally written by those with elite status, while the author of the Gospel is identified as one of Jesus's circle of followers known as the Beloved Disciple and is not portrayed in the Gospel as belonging to the upper class (John 21:20-24). On the other hand, since only a very small percentage of ancient literature has survived, generalizations and comparisons are difficult. The Gospel itself presents a further wrinkle: in John's text the characters tend to engage in dialogue. This is not a passing observation. By and large the characters do not converse in the histories of Josephus, Livy, Tacitus, and others. Generally the ancient authors of history preferred to write straight narration into which they sprinkled speeches to mark key turning points in the past or to highlight significant events. True, they might add the occasional incisive epigram or witticism uttered by key protagonists, but they tended to steer clear of episodes in which characters engage in interactive discourse. One rare exception to this rule is a short exchange between Augustus and his wife Livia that is found in Cassius Dio and will be unpacked in detail below.

This does not mean, however, that a comparison between the Roman histories and the Fourth Gospel is a futile effort. On the contrary, the evangelist has a well-developed historical consciousness that legitimizes the enterprise. This sensitivity to history is revealed in two ways: by showing concern for the veracity of the account he is recording and through the application of a key historian's storytelling convention about the need carefully to select material for inclusion in the text. Regarding the former, the author of the Fourth Gospel shows this keen regard for the truthfulness of a tale when he provides a narrative aside to verify the testimony about both blood and water flowing from Jesus's wound (John 19:34-35). Turning to the latter issue of selectivity, John actually employs a historian's storytelling gambit that also appears in the writing of Cassius Dio when in John 20:30 he asserts, "Jesus did many other signs before his disciples that are not written in this book," a sentiment echoed in the epilogue where it is noted again that Jesus did many other things that, if they had been selected and recorded, the world itself would not be able to contain the books that would be written (21:25).[11] For his part, Cassius Dio makes use of this same device in his account of the year 15 BCE, in

---

11. Unless otherwise stated, all biblical translations are my own.

which Augustus colonized many cities in Gaul and Spain, issued decrees related to the name change of a city, and provided earthquake relief. The Roman historian observes that, if all the various ways cities were aided during this period were mentioned, "the work involved in rendering them in writing would be boundless" (*Hist. rom.* 54.23.8 [my translation]). Clearly, then, the author of the Fourth Gospel appears to have at least a working familiarity with the conventions for recounting significant events that occurred in the past. With this in mind, we undertake a comparison of the female characters in the Gospel with the portraits of women in the Roman histories.

John's Women and the Women of the Roman Histories

When it comes to the presence of women in Roman histories, classicist Kristina Milnor observes, "Whereas the Greeks seem to have generally followed Pericles' famous dictum—that the mark of a good woman is not to be spoken of, for praise or blame—Roman historians offer us a number of depictions of good women behaving well, despite the political forces which drag them on to the stage of history" (Milnor 2009, 281). To be sure, some portraits of women are unflattering. For instance, in the *Annals* Tacitus relies on stereotypes to depict forceful women. One is the British queen Boudicca, who leads a military revolt against the Romans (*Ann.* 14.30–36). Another strong woman whom Tacitus views with chagrin is Agrippina the Younger, the mother of Nero, who upstages her husband Claudius at a military review of some captive Britons (12.37.4). In fact, the portrait of any woman who assumes masculine power and male prerogatives (the *dux femina*, or commanding woman) is a topos that occurs not only in Tacitus but also in Seneca, Virgil, and even Cicero (Santoro L'Hoir 1994, 24).[12]

Yet in his *Histories* Tacitus limits his pejorative portraits to only select women; others are depicted positively. For instance, the historian extols Vitellius's wife Galeria for her modesty and describes the emperor's mother Sextilla as a woman who never took advantage of the temptations posed by being related to an emperor. He notes that she even felt keenly any misfortunes that befell her family, much as did the women of high character from other eras (*Hist.* 2.6.4). This romanticized view of women aside, Tacitus,

---

12. For an example from Tacitus's *Histories*, see the comments regarding Triaria (*Hist.* 2.63).

Cassius Dio, and Josephus do briefly mention several women who may be compared to the female characters in the Fourth Gospel.

(1) Jesus's Mother and the Women at the Foot of the Cross (John 2:1-11 and 19:25-27)

For his part, the author of the Fourth Gospel provides brief glimpses of several women who take an active role in Jesus's ministry and life, but unlike Tacitus, who cannot resist a barb now and then, the evangelist tends to resist imputing negative characteristics to any of his female characters. The first woman to receive mention in the text is Jesus's mother, who prods her son into performing his first miracle at the wedding of Cana in Galilee (John 2:1-11) and is also present at the foot of the cross at the bitter end of his ministry (19:25, 26-27).

The motif of mothers intervening in the careers of their male progeny, similar to the way the mother of Jesus prods her son to action at the wedding, is not absent from Roman history. Cornelia Scipionis Africana (born ca. 190 BCE), for instance, was quite active in the careers of her adult sons. As early as 124 BCE, she wrote a letter indicating that her son C. Sempornius Gracchus should not stand for the office of tribune (Cicero, *Brut.* 211), and she also advised her son to withdraw a law that he had proposed that prohibited deposed magistrates from ever holding another office (Plutarch, *Ti. C. Gracch.* 4.1-3). Three-quarters of a century later, Servilia, the mother of Marcus Junius Brutus, the man who participated in the assassination of Julius Caesar, extended her *maternal auctoritas*, or maternal authority, over Brutus and even played a role in the councils of her family (Brennan 2012, 361).

Perhaps the role of mothers influencing their adult sons has its earliest precedent in an example provided by the historian Livy. Although he was writing during the death throes of the republic, he records an incident that occurred in 488-487 BCE about Veturia, the mother of Coriolanus. Coriolanus was a general who, after being exiled from Rome, turned and attacked the city. His mother, for her part, gathered a number of women in her home and arranged a delegation of children, wives, and mothers to accompany her outside of the city walls into the enemy camp. During the resulting confrontation between mother and son, Veturia expressed her shame over the behavior of her offspring and then castigated him for not considering that, while he had been exiled, his home, his mother, his wife, and his children were all still in Rome, the very city to which he was now laying siege. The delegation was successful and resulted in quite a bit of renown for the women involved in the event (Livy, *Ab urbe condita* 2.40.1–12).

Given all of these examples, from Veturia to Cornelia to Servilia, Milnor (2009, 278) hypothesizes that, with the fall of the republic and rise of the empire, women assumed a more prominent role in the public scene, including promoting the influence and interests of their families. In any event, by the time of the empire, the role of the woman who directs the career of her male offspring is well established. Indeed, it reaches its height with Agrippina the Younger, who manages to place her son Nero on the throne after convincing the emperor Claudius to adopt him (Cassius Dio, *Hist. rom.* epitome 61[60].32.2). When read against this background, then, the Johannine account of Jesus's mother (who is not named in the pericope in the Fourth Gospel)[13] urging Jesus to intercede when there is a shortage of wine at the wedding of Cana in Galilee (John 2:3–5) is not peculiar. Her actively pressing Jesus to solve the problem at the marital celebration may be viewed as a natural facet of her maternal authority in assisting with the launch of a son's career. At the same time, Jesus's "mild rebuke" (Reinhartz 2003, 18) at the wedding about the sphere of her influence and concern demonstrates that her authority is not greater than Jesus's own *imperium*, or ability to command, which he nonetheless chooses to exert when he completes the miracle of turning a vast quantity of water into first-rate wine. In other words, the maternal role is exercised appropriately and is not allowed to spill over into that of the domineering *dux femina* who usurps male privilege and is so reviled by Tacitus. Rather, Jesus's mother's actions remain within the bounds of matronly decorum.

In addition to promoting their sons' fledgling political and leadership ambitions, women in Roman histories are also depicted as playing a role in funerals and participating in acts of mourning in scenes that are not that dissimilar from the tableaux at Jesus's crucifixion. In John's account, during Jesus's final hours the mother of Jesus and Mary the wife of Clopas are both present at the cross along with Mary Magdalene (19:25). Just as the women are nearby for Jesus's last breaths and then later at his tomb, so also do Roman women witness the deaths of prominent or notorious individuals. For instance, in 14 CE Augustus's wife Livia kept her husband's death a

---

13. Mary Coloe (2013, 210) links the titles "mother" and "woman" with Gen 2:23 and 3:20.

secret for a period while she waited for his adopted son Tiberius to return to Rome from Dalmatia (Cassius Dio, *Hist. rom.* 56.31.2). Although Dio implies this was a bit suspicious, he does record additional details about the emperor's funeral demonstrating that women had prerogatives related to caring for remains and mourning the deceased. To be specific, when it came to the funeral rites for Augustus, not only the senators but also their wives (*gynaikes*) were permitted to march in the funeral procession (56.42.1). Then, after the cremation, when all others had departed, Livia remained with a few of Augustus's most trusted knights for an additional five days at the pyre before gathering up the bones to place them in the tomb (56.42.4). For its part, the Senate decided to mark the passing of the first Roman emperor with a decree stipulating that a few days of mourning were required for Roman men (who presumably then had to return to work after the brief period) but mandating the observance of a full year's worth of morning for women (56.43.1).

Apart from the death of Augustus, other episodes of women's role in burials and mourning have made it into the record of the Roman past. For example, Vitiellus's wife saw to his burial (Cassius Dio, *Hist. rom.* epitome 64[65].22.1), while Domitian's nurse, Phyllis, filched his body after his murder in order to ensure a proper burial for this reviled leader (67.18.2). Like Dio, the historian Tacitus recounted women's involvement with making funeral arrangements and the appropriate care for the dead. One example is that of Verania, the wife of Lucius Calpurnius Piso Frugi Licinianus, who along with Titus Vinius and Vinius's daughter Crispina paid a ransom for the head of her husband (who was killed by assassins of Otho during the Roman civil war in 69 CE) so that she could bury a full corpse rather than one that had been decapitated (Tacitus, *Hist.* 1.48).

In addition to details about interment of the dead, at least one of the authors who recorded the Roman past also indicated that bonds between a mother and son might prompt a man who was facing his last days or final hours to consider and plan for his mother's welfare after his death. Indeed, Tacitus, in a poignant episode similar to the scene in which Jesus commends his mother into the care of the Beloved Disciple (John 19:25-27), revealed the deep sentiments that the emperor Vitellius harbored for his mother. When his armies were defeated in the civil war of 69 CE and the ruler was about to be deposed, Vitellius was anxious for "his mother, who was bowed with years" (Tacitus, *Ann.* 3.67 [Jackson, LCL]). Consequently, the defeated emperor did not wish to struggle further against the victor lest Vespasian treat Vitellius's female dependents viciously in retaliation.

Ultimately, his worries about his mother were ungrounded, since, as Tacitus reports, his mother fortuitously predeceased him by a few days, "having gained nothing from the elevation of her son to the principate but sorrow and good repute" (3.67). Clearly, the impulse for a condemned leader to provide for his mother, as Jesus does in 19:25-27, is not unique to the Fourth Gospel.

All in all, then, the presence of the women at the cross—including Jesus's mother, for whom he provides in his final hour—all fall within the boundaries of the same type of roles that the classical historians ascribe to Roman women. As will become clear, the same may be said about one more scene in the Gospel: Mary Magdalene's encounter with the risen Jesus at the empty tomb. Mary's discovery that Jesus's body is missing and her subsequent conversation with Jesus, however, have additional dimensions in the Johannine account that deserve comment.

(2) Mary Magdalene (John 20:1-18)

The Gospel episode in which Mary Magdalene lingers in the garden following Jesus's burial contains a variety of steps. First she notices that the body of Jesus is missing from the tomb (20:1), and she reports her dismaying discovery to the disciples (20:2). Then, after Peter and the Beloved Disciple have verified that the remains are absent and return to their homes (20:10), she lingers by the tomb weeping. Subsequently, she has the opportunity to engage in a brief dialogue with two angels, only to turn around and participate in a short conversation with Jesus (during which her greeting using the Aramaic word "rabbi" is translated for an international readership by the author using the Greek word for "teacher"). As the next act in the scene, Jesus directs her to communicate a message to the disciples (20:17-20), after which she complies with this charge by telling Jesus's circle of students that she had encountered Jesus.

As illustrated in the discussion above related to women's roles in mourning, we see that depictions of women wandering to the vicinity of the tomb to continue to grieve (much as Mary does in the Fourth Gospel) or remaining in an attitude of sorrow after the men have returned to the tasks related to their daily lives are consonant with the model of Roman mourning provided by Livia upon the death of Augustus. In broad outline, then, there is nothing in this story that would shock Roman readers.

The other aspect of the scene—that Mary is commissioned as Jesus's agent to carry a message—also has links to or parallels in the Roman histories. Let us take a closer look at the issue of agency and women. Although not particularly frequent, there are some instances where the Roman historians record that women functioned as go-betweens in matters of court politics and business affairs. For example, Josephus preserves the information that Queen Bernice, of the Hasmonean dynasty and a client queen of Rome, attempted to intercede on behalf of the population of Jerusalem with the Roman procurator Florus during a period when her brother Herod Agrippa II was in Egypt. Florus had allowed his forces to sack the marketplace and pillage the city following riots upon his entrance into Jerusalem (*J. W.* 2.14.7–9 §§297–308); unfortunately, Bernice's efforts proved unsuccessful (2.15.1 §§309–314). Nonetheless, her role in matters of governance is indicated at other points in Josephus's narrative. For example, she wrote to Cestius on behalf of the citizens of Jerusalem (2.16.1 §333) and was placed "in a commanding position on the roof of the Palace of the Hasmonaeans" (2.16.3 §344 [Thackery, LCL]) in order to serve as an inspiring presence while Agrippa gave a speech in which he attempted to cool the passions of those Jews who were keen to embark on war in 66 CE. Her influence with those in power may be surmised, given that she was the intended recipient of a letter written by Phillip, a Roman refugee in the run-up to the war (*Vita* 11 §§48–49).

Although Bernice is associated with rule of the provinces, in Rome itself women occasionally served as agents or in positions of power in relation to government and business affairs. For example, during the reign of Claudius his wife Valeria Messalina was center stage in affairs of state since she took bribes on her husband's behalf, leveled accusations of treason against those whom she regarded as rivals, and even sold citizenships (Cassius Dio, *Hist. rom.* epitome 60.8.5–28.7). In addition, historians record that, a few years following Messalina's active role in her husband's rule, Vespasian, who became emperor in 70 CE, also conducted business through the agency of a woman. In this particular case his concubine Caenis had a photographic memory and functioned as a secretary in Vespasian's court. In that role, this gifted member of the emperor's retinue not only took dictation but also bolstered imperial revenue by selling governorships. Oddly enough, when it comes to these two women, Claudius's wife Messalina is portrayed by Dio as conspiring against her husband, engaging in adultery, and exercising authority beyond her due as a sort of *dux femina*, while Vespasian's paramour/secretary is mentioned with respect (*Hist. rom.* epitome 65[66].14.1). Clearly, although the roles these two Roman women exercised were similar, the historian came to two different assessments of their character—perhaps evidencing a political bias for Vespasian over Claudius that plays out in how the respective emperors' relationships with the women in their circles are characterized. Nonetheless, the idea that a woman might serve as a go-between on business for a man, much as how Mary Magdalene in the Fourth Gospel is assigned the task of taking a message to the disciples by Jesus when she sees him in the garden, would not be a foreign concept to Roman audiences.

In fact, given that Jesus had been resurrected from the dead (even if he had not yet ascended), one might regard the agency role assigned to Mary as similar to that assigned to a priestess or intermediary between the divine and human realms. In this regard, an episode involving Livia, the wife of the first emperor, is illuminating. According to Dio, the Senate accorded Livia the honor of serving as a priestess for her late husband. The account bears repeating here.

> At that time they declared Augustus immortal, assigned to him priests and sacred rites, and made Livia, who was already called Julia and Augusta, his priestess; they also permitted her to employ a lector when she exercised her sacred office. On her part, she bestowed a million sesterces upon a certain Numerius Atticus, a senator and ex-praetor, because he swore that he had seen Augustus ascending to heaven after the manner of which tradition tells concerning Proculus and Romulus. A shrine voted by the Senate and built by Livia and Tiberius was erected to the dead emperor in Rome. (56.56.1–2 [Cary and Foster, LCL])

Unlike Mary's encounter with Jesus in the garden, Livia herself did not speak with her resurrected husband; however, the widowed empress was instrumental in rewarding the individual who attested to her husband's ascension, and she also sponsored the construction of his temple to initiate the cult. It is apparent that both Mary from the Fourth Gospel and Livia as recorded by Dio, despite their gender, played a role in the sacred postmortem stories related to the men with whom they had been associated.

In addition to serving as agents in affairs of state, mourning the men in their lives, or serving as mothers who direct the careers of their sons, powerful aristocratic Roman women were also bold enough to spar intellectually with men. In this regard, Dio provides a single anecdote in which Livia engages in a philosophical conversation with her husband Augustus that may be used as a basis of comparison with the conversation between Jesus and the Samaritan woman in John 4.

(3) A Woman of Samaria (John 4:1-30 and 39-42)

The political shift from republic to empire had cultural implications that began to play out in the first century in terms of women's roles and their ability to interact more broadly with men intellectually. As Renate Johne (1996, 152) observes, with all power concentrated in the hands of a single ruler, a focus on private life, everyday events, and the home (in which women had already been prominent) meant that "women and girls [were] granted more opportunities to broaden their minds; women of the prosperous strata, because of their improved economic and legal situation, gained influence." Johne also notes that the Stoics began advocating greater access to philosophical education for women and that the Greco-Roman romance novels of the period introduced female characters whose feelings, views, and desires were more highly valued than they had been in prior eras (153). This dynamic seems to be reflected in the accounts of the conversation between Augustus and Livia and that between Jesus and the Samaritan woman.

First, however, it is important to mention that, according to both Dio and the author of Fourth Gospel, the dialogues in the respective writings took place in private. Livia and her husband are located at home in their bedroom, out of earshot of retainers and any government functionaries (*Hist. rom.* 55.14.2); similarly, the woman at the well encounters Jesus while he is sitting by himself, after his disciples left to purchase food in a nearby town (John 4:6-8). Given the relative isolation in which the respective conversations occur, one may conjecture that, while women were encouraged to exercise their intellect, during that time it may not have been appropriate for them to do so publicly.[14] Certainly when the disciples

---

14. What was permitted in the private sphere versus the public sphere was, according to Dio, a driving force behind Augustus's exiling his daughter Julia. Dio records that everyone was well aware of Julia's infidelity and wild ways, but it was not until she took part in "revels and drinking bouts at night in the Forum and on the very rostra" (*Hist. rom.* 55.10.2 [Cary and Foster, LCL]) that she was banished. Dio also looks askance at Agrippina the Younger's practice of attending the emperor in public when he was conducting business (*Hist. rom.* epitome 60[61].33.7).

return to find Jesus and the woman in conversation, they appear to be taken by surprise (4:27).

Be that as it may, another parallel between the two dialogues is that both women soft pedal their roles in their conversations with the men. The Samaritan woman, for example, wonders at the fact that Jesus is willing to engage with her, a woman of Samaria, in conversation and to request that she provide water for him (John 4:9). By the same token, in Dio's text the empress cautiously inquires whether Augustus is willing to accept input from her on the matter of Gnaeus Cornelius's conspiracy. The empress, who is as cautious as the woman of Samaria, states, "and I have some advice to give you,—that is, if you are willing to receive it, and will not censure me because I, though a woman, dare suggest to you something which no one else, even of your most intimate friends, would venture to suggest" (*Hist. rom.* 55.16.1 [Cary and Foster, LCL]).

However, the most interesting aspect of the two dialogues, the one Roman and the other related to the provinces, involves their outcomes. According to Dio, Augustus did heed the advice of Livia and treated the conspirator Cornelius with leniency. Dio even goes so far as to credit her with saving Cornelius's life (*Hist. rom.* 55.22.1-2). Likewise, the conversation between Jesus and the Samaritan woman also ends on a positive note. The woman herself invites others to come to meet Jesus, and on account of her testimony other residents of her village enter the initial stages of belief that Jesus is the Christ (John 4:39), which they later confirm as they grow in faith through their own personal encounters with him (4:42).

In sum, when these two conversations are compared, the one from John and the other from Dio, there is nothing about the depiction of the Samaritan woman that would appear to be radically different or incomprehensible to Roman readers familiar with the conventions of Roman histories. As will be demonstrated next, the story of Mary the sister of Martha also conforms with how Dio and Tacitus use the actions of women as foils to point out weaknesses in the behaviors of men.

(4) Mary the Sister of Martha (John 11:1-45 and 12:1-8)

The account of Martha and Mary grieving their brother Lazarus falls within the bounds of female mourning and loss that was discussed above in relation to women at the cross and Mary Magdalene. The extended conversation with Jesus and Martha, however, serves a Johannine agenda that extends beyond a historian's usual concerns for presenting a historical account. In that conversation, the Gospel author focuses on issues faith and belief, which are not characteristic of the political histories produced in the era of the early empire. Unlike the genre of the extant Roman histories, where character development is not paramount, throughout the course of the dialogue in the Fourth Gospel Martha is presented with an evolving and ever-deepening understanding of Jesus's identity and mission (Lee 2013, 205). Although there are no clear parallels between Jesus's conversation with Martha and Roman histories, the pericope in which her sister Mary anoints Jesus's feet with expensive nard (John 12:1–8) does resonate with several passages that appear in Dio and Tacitus.

The central point of contact between Mary and the women of the Roman histories does not occur at the narrative level of her action of anointing Jesus's feet with oil. Attention to the feet of guests is not really mentioned in the Roman histories. There is, however, one exception. Specifically, Dio, with a tone of incredulity, writes down the tale of an individual named Pomponius Secundus, who was serving as consul during the reign of Claudius. Despite holding the highest elected office, he demonstrated what to Dio was abhorrent and extreme sycophantic behavior by sitting at the emperor Claudius's feet and showering kisses on them during a banquet in the palace (*Hist. rom.* 59.29.5).

The ministration to Jesus's feet by perfuming them with expensive ointment, which unlike Dio's account of Pomponius Secundus is not portrayed by John as an act of debasement but rather as one of reverence, serves as a foil that contrasts Mary's level of devotion to Jesus with that of Judas. This particular disciple is identified as someone who misappropriated the funds that Jesus's followers had set aside for the poor (John 12:6); Judas would eventually hand Jesus over to the Roman authorities (13:26–30; 18:2–3). In essence, Mary, though a woman, has a higher standard of virtue and a better understanding of loyalty and discipleship than does Judas. Thus she serves as an exemplum, or figure that demonstrates high character traits, and it is this aspect of the story that matches several passages in the Roman histories.

Several women in the Roman histories function as exempla and, like Mary, possess virtues that are contrasted with men of status who behave inappropriately. For instance, a woman named Pythias, an attendant of Octavia, refused to utter lies about her mistress, even under torture. Because she upheld her principles in a climate where false testimony was common tender in the court, it turned out that Pythias was more loyal to the empress than Octavia's own husband, Nero, who would soon put his wife to death (Cassius Dio, *Hist. rom.* epitome 62.13.4). Another woman whose virtue outshone that of the men in her circle was named Epicharis. In 65 CE this freedwoman participated in the Pisonian conspiracy against Nero. Due to her involvement, she knew several details of the plot and the names of her accomplices but demonstrated her own exemplary character by holding fast to all of the secrets with which she had been entrusted even when being tortured. Ironically, at the very moment she was being stead-fast, however, the men who had been involved, many of whom were of noble rank and thus presumably would have had a more developed sense of honor than a mere freedwoman, were all informing against each other (Tacitus, *Ann.* 9.51; Cassius Dio, *Hist. rom.* epitome 62.27.3). The lesson? Epicharis was a shining example of the very virtues that should have been held by the men.

A final illustration of a woman who serves as an exemplum is a woman of the province of Liguria who bravely hid her son from Otho's Roman soldiers when they sacked the city of Albintimilium (present-day Ventimi-glia, Italy) during the civil war of 69 CE. Even under torture, she would not reveal where she had concealed him but pointed to her womb and declared, "Here is his hiding place" (Tacitus, *Hist.* 2.13 [Moore, LCL]). Tacitus describes her as an "outstanding example" (*praeclaro exemplo*) of good behavior, since the residents of Albintimilium were Roman citizens and the Roman soldiers should have been defending the population rather than pillaging the town. By protecting her son, even under torture and death and without the use of arms, the woman of Liguria was effectively a better soldier than the soldiers themselves.

In essence, then, the Roman historians include several stories of women who, like Mary, outshone men. The Johannine scholar Dorothy Lee (2013, 200) comments that, although Mary and Martha are rela-tively minor characters in the Gospel narrative, they play key roles and are clearly among Jesus's friends and disciples. They, like the Samaritan woman, Mary Magdalene, and Jesus's own mother, briefly step onto the stage of the Gospel and betray no particular characteristics that would dis-tinguish them from Roman women.

Conclusion

With the review of these Johannine women, the comparison of the female characters depicted in the Fourth Gospel with a few portraits of women in the Roman histories draws to a close. While a simple comparison of this nature is based on a limited number of Roman sources (which no doubt might be expanded with a more extensive treatment of the subject), the parallels drawn do appear to demonstrate that the basic characteristics and behaviors ascribed to women in the Gospel and the Roman sources are consistent in both traditions. Whether this fact demonstrates that the women of the Fourth Gospel were Romanized, however, is a difficult case to make without knowing the exact circumstances that surrounded the Gospel's origin and the location of its initial audience. But just like their Roman counterparts, these women were variously active in the careers of their sons, played a role in funerals and mourning, served as intermediaries or agents, and might be held up as foils to illustrate the failings of men who should have known better than to behave as they did. Given this, one may at least conclude that there was enough similarity between the community of the Fourth Gospel and the larger Roman world to enable a diverse body of readers to recognize and perhaps even relate to the women who appear in the Gospel. The universal, cosmopolitan nature of John's women perhaps contributed to the reception of the Gospel throughout the empire and ultimately the growth of Christianity. In a way, then, all of the women in John's text serve as witnesses with the potential to help his readers, whether Romanized or provincial, to understand the identity, mission, and message of the true Savior of the World.

For Further Reading

Feldherr, Andrew, ed. 2009. *Cambridge Companion to the Roman Historians*. Cambridge: Cambridge University Press.

James, Sharon L., and Shelia Dillon, eds. 2012. *A Companion to Women in the Ancient World*. Chichester, UK: Wiley-Blackwell.

Levine, Amy-Jill, and Marianne Blickenstaff, eds. 2003. *Feminist Companion to John*. 2 vols. Cleveland: Pilgrim.

Mehl, Andreas. 2011. *Roman Historiography: An Introduction to Its Basic Aspects and Development*. Translated by Hans-Friedrich Mueller. Chichester, UK: Wiley-Blackwell.

Pitcher, Luke. 2009. *Writing Ancient History: An Introduction to Classical Historiography*. New York: Tauris.

PAUL AND EMPIRE 1:
ROMANS, 1 CORINTHIANS, 2 CORINTHIANS

Neil Elliott

The Letters of Paul present us with distinctive challenges. As letters, they provide only occasional, partial, and often oblique references to any larger narrative that might allow interpreters to describe a coherent "theology" of Paul. They represent the apostle's responses to particular situations for which we have little evidence beyond Paul's own construal, which we must infer from his rhetoric. We have neither any communication from the assemblies he addressed nor a reliable representation of the message Paul may have originally presented to attract adherents to his "gospel" (though different scholars have suggested that one or another passage in his letters provide summaries of that message). The task of describing Paul's "theology" is thus both complex and elusive, requiring inference and conjecture. How much more challenging, then, even precarious, is the effort to infer Paul's general attitude toward the Roman Empire from the surviving letters, where he mentions the "governing authorities" explicitly only once (in Rom 13:1–7). This essay will discuss some of the issues involved in present discussion of "Paul and empire" and present observations that deserve consideration in the interpretation of 1 and 2 Corinthians and Romans.

On Interpreting "Paul and Empire"

Decades have passed since the late Edward Said, one of the pioneers of postcolonial criticism, issued his plea to "take empire seriously" in the interpretation of texts. The plea was all the more urgent given what Said (1993, xx and 303) described as "the astonishing sense of weightlessness" in Western academic life (to say nothing of popular culture) regarding "the gravity of history." The essays in the present volume give some sense of the erudition now being mobilized in contemporary biblical studies to "take empire seriously" in the interpretation of early Christian texts. That scholarship has surfaced a number of questions regarding substance and method in the interpretation of Paul's letters that deserve attention here.

Attention to Paul and empire appears to be a relatively recent phenomenon. In fact, however, already at the beginning of the twentieth century, scholars such as Adolf Deissmann (1908) and William Mitchell Ramsay (1907) recognized that the early Christian proclamation of Jesus as *kyrios*, or "lord," stood in sharp antithesis to the claims made in the imperial cult that Caesar was "lord." If that contrast is sometimes presented today as a recent rediscovery, it may be because the intervening decades were marked by relative inattention to empire as such, and to the Roman Empire in particular, in Pauline studies. Through most of the twentieth century, the emphasis was on *theological* interpretation, an emphasis often attributed to the enthusiastic reception (particularly in American Protestantism) of Karl Barth's work. That emphasis has also usually meant interpreting Paul's letters as an important strand in *biblical* theology, from which it follows that the relevant contexts are, first, the Scriptures of Israel, and secondarily, the currents of early Judaism up to and contemporary with Paul. On these terms, aspects of the Hellenistic environment or Roman imperial culture are, at best, "atmosphere" or "background." Indeed, it would seem even today that "theological" attention to Paul's use of Israel's Scripture or his relationship with Judaism (the focus of the "new perspective"), on the one hand, and focus on his place within Hellenistic culture in the Roman age, on the other, remain fairly exclusive alternatives, explored in different scholarly circles. Such polarization effectively excludes the notion that "political" interpretation might itself *be* theological interpretation.

Before the 1990s, it was customary for Paul's scholarly interpreters to address the Roman Empire only when it appeared as a topic in Rom 13:1–7 and, even then, to concentrate their remarks on explaining why Paul's appraisal of imperial power there appeared so benign. (The few exceptions were German-language studies in the 1980s, subsequently translated into English, which suggested that Paul's attitude to empire might have been more critical than those verses in Romans indicated.[1]) The late 1990s and 2000s saw multivolume efforts to describe the theologies of

---

1. For example, see Wengst 1987; Georgi 1991; Taubes 2004 (orig. 1987).

individual letters, published by Fortress Press (the work of the Society of Biblical Literature Pauline Theology Group published in Bassler, Hay, and Johnson 1991–1997) and Cambridge University Press (volumes in the New Testament Theology series), but *empire* as such appears only rarely in them as an object of reflection. When I ventured to explore "the politics of the apostle" in *Liberating Paul* (N. Elliott 1994), I could draw on important insights from a number of scholars, but these were generally isolated and had not been brought together with sustained attention to the question of Paul and empire. Indeed, such work did not get underway until the Society of Biblical Literature Paul and Politics Consultation was organized in 1995, under the indefatigable direction of Richard A. Horsley (see suggestions for further reading below).

If the "political" reading of Paul and, more specifically, attention to the relationship of Paul and empire are more established today, those inquiries have also evoked strong reaction and critique from other scholars. One categorical objection is that a "political" reading simply misses the point of Paul's letters, since Paul was concerned with proclaiming the gospel, which is a *theological*, not a political activity. On this view, those who claim to detect in Paul's letters a veiled critique of empire have simply committed the cardinal sin of projecting their own (presumably) left-wing concerns about contemporary political realities, which they decry under the banner of "imperialism," back onto Paul (see the works by Barclay and McKnight and Modica in the further reading section at the end of the essay). Another objection, arising from a different quarter, criticizes the anti-imperial reading of Paul as a dangerous attempt to render the apostle a heroic champion of a particular contemporary agenda. The attempt is dangerous precisely because another contemporary agenda, which seeks to counteract the prejudice, subjection, and violence that is perpetrated today in partial dependence on the presumed authority of Paul's letters, requires demystifying and neutralizing that authority (see Castelli 1991; Schüssler Fiorenza 1987; and Wire 1990).

My own previous work has regularly been named as one of the objects of these critiques, and I take them seriously as impetuses for greater precision and nuance in the discussion. My purpose here is not to advance an "anti-imperial" reading of Paul's letters or to adjudicate arguments for or against such a reading. It is, first, to offer several observations about the current state of discussion from which I believe we may draw helpful guiding principles for interpretation, and second, to describe considerations that are relevant to the interpretation of Paul's letters to the Roman and Corinthian assemblies in particular.

Principles for Interpreting "Paul and Empire"

I propose that scholarship to date on the question of Paul and empire offers the following "lessons learned."

(1) *It matters what we mean by "empire."* Some biblical and theological scholars use the term broadly, in what approaches a homiletical way, in order to draw parallels and analogies with aspects of contemporary reality. This can mean that conditions of social injustice, militarism, global income disparities, or even attitudes of modern consumerism can be described as aspects of empire. This rather loose usage invites understandable skepticism. On the other hand, it is one thing to reject rhetorical sleight of hand; it is another to reject categorically the possibility of drawing analogies between ancient imperial realities and aspects of contemporary political and cultural reality. One reason to engage in history is precisely to understand our own historicity, and the work of history inevitably involves making analogies between past and present. The task is not to *avoid* analogies but to be precise and clear about the terms of an analogy and its limits.

Other scholars take the opposite position, insisting that the language of "empire" should be used only when explicit references to the structures, offices, or policies of the Roman Empire, or of a specific emperor or other magistrates, are present in Paul's letters. Inevitably, of course, this more skeptical approach results in a much smaller set of data to be interpreted—practically limited to Paul's comments on the "governing authorities" in Rom 13:1–7, and consequently resulting in a much more muted understanding (see Barclay 2011).

It is important in this regard to note that historians of the Roman Empire—with no vested interest in the interpretation of New Testament writings—discuss under the topic of "empire" a rich and multidimensional reality, including the imperial cult, its relationship to patronage in the cultivation of cooperative provincial elites, the "extractive" nature of the Roman economy and the mechanisms and consequences of integration of local economies into it, the ubiquitous use of images and inscriptions to convey (and "naturalize") imperial ideology, the ideological and visual representation of ethnicity and gender, and a texture of distinctive values, emphasizing honor and including religious piety as aspects of "Augustan culture." Insisting that we may speak of the Roman Empire only

when Paul names specific administrative offices or policies is a remark-
ably narrow approach that flies in the face of current scholarship on the
Roman Empire.[2]

(2) *Affirming the relevance of Roman imperial ideology and culture to
the interpretation of Paul's letters does not depend on Paul's having been a
vocal critic of that empire.* Another way to state this point is that framing the discussion in terms of "Paul *and* empire" is preferable to insisting
that Paul's standpoint was thoroughly and in principle "*against* empire"
or "empire-critical." True, some theologically motivated projects seek to
describe the whole of the biblical legacy *as such* as "resistant" to empire,
a totalizing approach that tends to beg the question by ignoring contradictory data. Since the pioneering work on the Hebrew Bible by Norman
Gottwald (1979), however, we have learned that especially where political
values are in question, the various biblical writings (or the voices partially
expressed in various parts of the biblical writings) represent very different
social locations. When those writings (or parts of writings) were combined
in ways that tended to harmonize, mute, or dilute one or another message,
those efforts also represented particular social locations. I conclude that
there is no single "biblical" attitude for, or against, empire. Nor is there a
theoretically coherent way to identify an empire-critical "core" or "center"
to the biblical testimony.

Further, the rise of postcolonial criticism of Paul's letters has alerted
us to the very real possibilities that Paul's complex identity as a Hellenistic Jew, and (on the evidence of Acts) a Roman citizen as well, may
have involved what contemporary theorists (following Bhabha 1994) call
hybridity, which means more than simply "ambivalence." Seeking to dis-
till a pure and unambiguous pro- or anti-imperial posture from his letters appears, in this light, both misguided and quixotic. The object of our
investigation need not be restricted to an index of Paul's thoughts about the
Roman Empire; it is both more realistic and more responsible to explore
the effects of imperial culture on Paul's communities and on his own self-
presentation and rhetoric.

(3) *Insisting that Paul's letters are "theological" rather than "political" is
a mistake.* Opposing theological and political interpretation, as if these are
methods appropriate to mutually exclusive sets of data or kinds of texts,
not only projects onto the ancient data a categorical binary unknown to

---

2. See the excerpted studies gathered in Horsley 1997.

inhabitants of the Roman Empire; it also misapprehends both the theological and the political. It is a transparently artificial (and, arguably, ten-
dentious) move to protect a domain of discourse, "the theological," from
inquiry into its political contexts or consequences. When a scholar "dou-
bles down" on such a move—insisting, for example, that Paul's message
was theological, *not* political, and at the same time that his message has
political implications that only a theologian can rightly understand (e.g.,
Barclay 2011)—we rightly wonder whether the point is the interpretation
of the ancient sources or some disciplinary turf war today.

(4) *At our present state of knowledge, arguments about implicit meanings in a text remain unfalsifiable and thus require a measure of circum-
spection and modesty on the part of those proposing them.* The perception
of an *implicit* "anti-imperial" message is often in the eye of the beholder.
Whether phrased in terms of what Paul "must have meant" or what his
readers "must have heard," such arguments are inevitably conjectural.
Although N. T. Wright's succinct way of describing the anti-imperial
thrust of Paul's gospel has become very popular—"If Jesus is Lord, then
Caesar is not"—we may well ask whether the ostensible logic of that formula was Paul's own or is only a contemporary (and perhaps contentious) projection onto Paul (see McKnight and Modica 2013). In a public
presentation (now published as a chapter in *Pauline Churches and Diaspora Jews*), John M. G. Barclay (2011) argued that Paul's concern was the
theological proclamation of Christ's lordship, next to which the apparent
power of any particular empire was *implicitly* simply insignificant. Curiously, however, Barclay compares Paul's letters with the theological character of Barth's famous Barmen Declaration—curiously, because everyone
recognizes in that document an implicit refusal of the claims of Nazism in
general and the Deutsche Christen movement in particular, even though
neither Hitler nor the National Socialist Party is ever mentioned in the
document. As the comparison shows, in the first century or today, the
force of an argument can sometimes be precisely an *intended* implication
that is not expressly stated.

Indeed, though it is far more difficult to detect implication or innuendo in an ancient text (where we have neither access to nonverbal performative cues nor the opportunity to interrogate the speaker for clarifi-
cation), contemporary interpreters *routinely* proceed to make inferences
from what is presumed to be implicit in a text, and so long as the inference
does not involve what we might consider "political" realities, no one raises
an eyebrow. The question is not whether arguments regarding implicit

meaning are to be ruled categorically out of bounds, but whether correlations with other information from the social and political context of the text can be adduced to offer a greater or lesser degree of probability. This is, after all, how discussions of "intertextuality" in Paul's letters proceed (pioneered by Richard B. Hays [1989]). But nothing requires us to limit intertextuality to echoes from the Bible, as if we should imagine Paul and his audiences completely closed off from all the other forms of communication going on around them. It is now widely accepted, for example, that Paul's reference to outsiders who "say, 'there is peace and security'" (1 Thess 5:3; all quotations NRSV unless otherwise noted) is an oblique reference to the slogan *pax et securitas* on Roman imperial coinage. Lexical studies and rhetorical criticism alike require us to recognize that Paul's vocabulary potentially carried political connotations that are obscured by the more purely religious translations in our Bibles: for example, *kyrios* (lord, used of the caesars), *ekklēsia* (church, but in Paul's day a civic assembly), *dikaiosynē* (translated "righteousness" in our Bibles but "justice" everywhere else), and *euangelion* (gospel) and *parousia* (appearance), which both had definite civic and imperial resonances. Any of these terms *could* have been heard by the recipients of Paul's letters as carrying political connotations, and taking that possibility seriously is simply a part of responsible exegesis. There is often no way to prove or disprove that a particular connotation was *intended*, of course, but ruling the possibility of one or another implicit meaning out of bounds in preference for a supposedly certain "biblical" meaning would constitute an exercise in theological special pleading.

In fact, we know that significant *implicit* communication of political meanings was not only possible, it was also as important and prevalent in Paul's day as in our own. Theater audiences in Paul's day were attuned to pick up on politically charged innuendo in the pointed reading of a superficially innocuous line. We have clear examples from Paul's world of what political anthropologist James C. Scott (1990) has called "voice under domination," the strategic use of veiled or implied meaning in situations where the less powerful are not free to speak their minds but are not rendered completely mute. One oft-cited example is Philo's distinction of the "untimely frankness" of the reckless with the "caution" that the prudent more usually practice in the presence of powerful adversaries (*Dreams* 2.92). Scott's work has inspired a microdiscipline of investigating "hidden transcripts" in Paul's letters. The theory can of course be abused, as when perceived tensions within a passage (such as Rom 13:1–7) are taken as proof that a "*real*," intended meaning has been "hidden" beneath the surface communication that appears to contradict it. The answer is not to reject the theory, however, which clearly applies to Paul's world, but to apply criteria of contextual correlation in order to establish a degree of probability for a particular reading.[3]

What might these considerations mean for our reading of the three longest of Paul's letters?

1 and 2 Corinthians

The effects of Roman imperial rule are certainly relevant to the interpretation of 1 and 2 Corinthians. After all, Roman forces had destroyed Corinth in 146 BCE, slaughtering its citizens and enslaving their wives and children, as a spectacularly violent example that facilitated the pacification of the rest of Achaia. Julius Caesar established the site a century later as a colony, peopled by freed persons from Rome, whose allegiance and gratitude were thereby assured. Roman Achaia was a showcase of Rome's civilizing power. Abundant inscriptions testify to the close integration of the Roman imperial cult with a system of patronage and benefaction in which local elites competed for prestige in civic and cultic offices (*leitourgiai*). Also evident is a clear hierarchy of peoples, with Romans manifestly superior to the peoples they had conquered, and a certain fluidity of ethnic identities. Through either adoption or manumission, however, a Greek freed person could "become Roman," receiving the Roman name of his father or patron. Through the right expenditure of wealth in civic benefactions, an ambitious freed person could display his generosity and piety and thus gain prestige as a member of the people destined by the gods to "rule the earth."

Such considerations offer a frame of reference different from the assumptions that were brought to the Corinthian letters in much earlier scholarship, which tended to focus on a supposed Corinthian propensity to (especially sexual) immorality, or on a presumed conflict between Paul's law-free gospel and the Jewish Christianity of the Jerusalem apostles, or a Jewish form of Gnosticism. The search for a single unified "opposition" has foundered on lack of clear evidence and the apparent arbitrariness with which select phrases must be assumed through a sort of "mirror reading"

---

3. For example, see Cynthia Briggs Kittredge (2004) and James R. Harrison's discussion in *Paul and the Imperial Authorities* (Harrison 2011b, 30–32).

to represent the views of Paul's putative "opponents." Instead, more recent scholarship has tended toward reading the letters inductively, asking about Paul's relationship with different sectors of the congregation itself.

In the late twentieth century, Wayne A. Meeks (1983) and Gerd Theissen (1980) showed the importance of "social stratification" and "status ambivalence" for understanding social realities in the Corinthian assembly. If "not many" of the first members of the Corinthian assembly had been "wise by human standards, ... powerful, ... of noble birth" (1 Cor 1:26), by implication, these scholars argued, *some* were. It followed that aspects of the Corinthian correspondence could be correlated with socioeconomic inequality in the community. The difference between those who could provide their own (extensive) meals and those who could not was a source of shame at the Lord's Supper (1 Cor 11:17–34). The fact that poorer members could not often afford to purchase meat to eat at home and so encountered meat only as it was slaughtered in the context of pagan ritual meant that the differences between "weak" and "strong" surrounding "idol meat" (*eidōlothyta*) had a socioeconomic basis (1 Cor 8, 10). Respect for rhetorical skill and Paul's suffering in comparison with the more erudite Apollos pointed to the latter's greater success, after Paul had left, among the Corinthian elite (fueling Paul's discussion of wisdom in 1 Cor 2 and the self-defensive tone of parts of both letters). Controversy surrounding Paul's refusal of financial support and his insistence on self-support through manual labor—one cause of friction throughout the correspondence—pointed not only to Corinthian expectation that a legitimate apostle would depend on the community (cf. Matt 10:1–16, 40–42; Luke 10:1–12) but also to the offense Paul gave potential patrons by refusing their support (and the obligation such support would have laid on him). With these postulates, Paul's own social location and his perception, for example, of manual labor, in contrast to perceptions among the Corinthian church, also became objects of study.

More recently, other scholars have challenged the declared "consensus" just described, criticizing the implications of a free and open market of wealth and status in which fluctuation of status and upward social mobility were the norm. Vast inequality characterized the Roman world; the majority in a city like Corinth would have lived near subsistence level (so Meggitt 1998). The point of patronage was precisely to extend inequality, and inequality of obligation, as the structuring principle of civic, economic, and social relationships. Generalizations about the "steep pyramid" of wealth and power in Roman society, with a tiny elite on top and the mass of the people living at subsistence level, can be applied in Roman Corinth as well. Augustus's reforms to marriage laws lubricated the circulation of property and wealth among those who already had it, making it easier (for example) for elite families to retain their wealth through marriages, divorces, and deaths; to describe these laws as "liberalizing" is to mistake their function.

More recent scholarship casts a wary eye at any modern generalization about "new opportunities" for "upward mobility" for a significant Roman "middle class." Those are the anachronistic projections into the past of late twentieth-century United States cultural assumptions. We must take seriously what might be called the precipitating forces of economic relationships in Roman society. We should not imagine life in Roman Corinth, or in the *ekklēsia* within it, as a sort of fluid suspension in which a variety of statuses might circulate in a random and indeterminate way. We should instead think metaphorically of fluid run through a centrifuge, so that the majority of particulates are pressed down, leaving only a small proportion "floating" on top.

Similarly, questions of social stratification are too complex to be addressed by generalizations about "the Corinthians." Differences among different groups, especially differences in socioeconomic status, come to the fore in conflicts there. Feminist interpreters have shattered the possibility that we mighty innocently presume that Paul's letters simply describe the objective situation in Corinth. Responsible interpretation requires that we recognize in Paul's own rhetorical efforts to persuade a respect for the opinions of those he addresses. For some feminist interpreters, the object of attention is the role played by spiritual women in the congregation who may have shared much of Paul's theology but perceived its significance differently, in terms of their own social experience of enhanced honor and spiritual endowment. On this point, Antoinette Clark Wire's (1990) discussion of social location and its correlation with theology is exemplary; its only potential weakness is her conviction that the whole of 1 Corinthians was written with the women prophets of Corinth as its "target." If that was not the case, we must ask the same questions regarding a number of social locations occupied by members of the Corinthian assemblies, including that of men who enjoyed some relative measure of power and prestige on the civic landscape.

I will not attempt here a thorough discussion of the history of Paul's relationship with the Corinthians, though that relationship is obviously an important and complex one, requiring careful reconstruction of the sequence of correspondence (including letters that have not survived, from Paul as well as from the Corinthians, and letters that have survived only fragmentarily in 2 Corinthians). I draw attention to several themes in this correspondence that bear comparison with aspects of Roman imperial culture.

The Turn from Idols

We may assume that part of Paul's initial teaching, at the founding of the *ekklēsia*, included the call to "turn to God from idols" (on the model of 1 Thess 1:8–10). But to what extent did eschewing idolatry mean avoiding the ceremonial aspects of the imperial and civic cult? These were not only the lifeblood of public life but also the channels of advancement in Roman provincial society. So Paul's message is not just a matter of holding the right ideas about the gods; it has eminently practical consequences. But what exactly were those to be? He repudiated the promises of an age destined to pass away (1 Cor 7:31); he warned his hearers away from "the table of demons," referring to the food offered at ceremonial banquets (1 Cor 10). That food, carried away to meals in private homes, apparently was a different subject, however. The idol is no real thing; unless the dinner host declares the food dedicated to a (false) god, Christians should eat what is set before them in equanimity (1 Cor 8). That accommodation was advised, much later, in the Mishnah (Avodah Zarah), so it is hardly scandalous from the point of view of Jewish halakah. More to the point, as Theissen (1980) observed, Paul's advice regarding food in private meals would have been more congenial to the interests of higher-status members of the *ekklēsia*, who might have been invited regularly to "private" dinners—though in sacred precincts, like the excavated dining halls in the precincts of Apollo's temple in Corinth—on a regular basis. (Note that Paul actually contemplates the possibility that one member of the *ekklēsia* might observe another exercising "liberty" by "eating in the temple of an idol": 1 Cor 8:4–12.) Lower-status members would normally encounter consecrated meat only at the public ceremonies where the idolatrous connotations were unavoidable. Because social stratification was so closely intertwined with benefaction and the performance of civic cult, Paul's divergence from some in Corinth may have less to do with differences of theological belief than with the strength of theological convictions to shape, or discipline, civic involvement. In other words, some in Corinth may have understood "wisdom" as consonant with a posture of indifference to social boundaries between the civic ceremonial and the *ekklēsia*. To such individuals, Paul's strident insistence that "what pagans sacrifice, they sacrifice to demons" and that "you cannot drink the cup of the Lord and the cup of demons" (1 Cor 10:14–22) might have seemed unnecessarily austere and provocative.

Head Coverings and Worship

If the previous point appears to involve aspects of Roman imperial cult only indirectly, another subject in 1 Corinthians may have a more direct connection. The almost inscrutable discussion of how women are to present their heads when prophesying in the assembly (1 Cor 11:2–16) has been explained in more than a dozen different ways, none of which has won the day, in part because the several arguments Paul advances about women's heads are inconsistent. But perhaps Paul's chief concern is not with *women's* heads or head coverings. In Roman cult, *men* ordinarily pulled their togas over their heads to offer sacrifice, as demonstrated in the statue of Augustus from Corinth (and elsewhere). Note that Paul begins his discussion by declaring that "the head of every man is Christ" (11:3) and draws the consequence, first, that "any man who prays or prophesies with his head covered dishonors his head [*kephalē*]," that is, Christ (11:4 RSV). Though the passage is a notorious exegetical quagmire, its rhetorical movement at least allows that Paul is relying on tropes of what is "natural" and what is "shameful" for women in order to shame as unnatural specific behaviors on the part of *men*—actions at home precisely in Roman worship. It is possible that Corinthian men are not only dining in sacred precincts but also *offering worship* to Roman gods or even to the genius of Caesar. More would seem to be at stake here than Paul's challenge to idolatry; the language of "headship" suggests that we adapt Wright's famous line to read, "if Christ is the 'head,' then Caesar is not." For Paul, acting otherwise is not merely a matter of sharing honor among different gods (as the Corinthian participants might imagine, in good Roman fashion): it is a direct and shameful affront to Christ (see N. Elliott 1994, 209–11, for my fuller discussion).

Marriage, Divorce, and Sexual Relationships

The topic of marriage and divorce in 1 Cor 7, "matters about which [the Corinthians] wrote" (7:1), likely were linked to issues of social status as well. Higher-status women members of the *ekklēsia* might have been in a better position to withdraw from pagan husbands or fiancés than poorer women, who would have been more dependent on partners for their economic welfare and under more pressure, if abandoned by their pagan husbands, to remarry. If higher-status members, men and women alike, had looked down on such women married to pagan husbands (or divorced by them) as lesser believers because they were not able to actualize the same level of freedom, we might understand Paul's concern both to affirm an ideal ("it is well for a man not to touch a woman," 7:1) and to reassure women in different situations. He urges that living with a pagan spouse does not disqualify the man or woman in Christ; the spouse and the children of such a "mixed" household are sanctified (7:12–16); the separating woman may remain unmarried; the single woman bound to marry does not sin by marrying (7:28). The maxim that each should "remain in the calling to which you were called," regardless of circumstance (7:17, 20, 24), is as widely misunderstood as it is generally mistranslated, as if Paul were advocating a fixity of social roles, when the contrary is evidently the case.[4] The ambivalence of Paul's advice—he would prefer that unmarried members not marry, and married members not separate, but expressly allows exceptions to these ideals—convinces some interpreters that Paul is retreating from ideals he in fact shares with some of the "spiritual women" in Corinth, because he realizes the potential for social disruption their freedom would imply. (The subsequent accounts of Paul's companion Thecla in the third- or possibly second-century CE Acts of Paul show just how disruptive such actions could be: as Thecla preaches her "gospel of virginity," whole cities are "shaken" by the tumult of women's voices [Acts Paul 9].) "The immorality Paul exposes," especially in chapter 6, "is male," Wire (1990, 78–97) writes. "The solution he calls for is marriage," a burden to be borne especially by the women in the assembly (78–97).

On this reading, Paul's sympathy with lower-status members of the *ekklēsia* has a clear limit: he is not willing to foster a situation in which marriages (and other social relationships with which they are intertwined?) are disrupted. Indeed, the differences between Paul and socially superior members of the Corinthian assembly should not be overstated. Paul himself seems to consider his own manual labor as a voluntary self-lowering,

---

4. For further discussion, see N. Elliott 1994, 32–40; Bartchy 1973.

not (as the poor of Rome would perceive it) as a simple necessity of life. He identifies with "the strong" (*hoi dynatoi*) and affirms their freedoms ("All things are lawful," 10:23), though he has "become weak" in order to move among the weak (9:22). But this makes all the more meaningful his insistence that in the (original) calling of the Corinthian *ekklēsia*, God "chose what is foolish, … weak, … low and despised in the world, things that are not, to reduce to nothing things that are" (1 Cor 1:26–29), and his efforts, though limited in some ways, to affirm the position of the "weak" over against the "strong." If there is ambivalence in Paul's language, it reflects, I contend, the ideological limitations of his age: as Dale B. Martin (1995, 67) describes the paradox, Paul "uses assumptions about hierarchy and status to overturn the status expectations of Greco-Roman culture. And, ultimately, he claims the highest status for himself in order to convince those of high status in the Corinthian church to imitate him in accepting a position of low status."

The "Rulers of this Age" Put to Shame

This distinctively Pauline version of a "preferential option for the poor" is not only a reflex of Paul's social location; it expresses his understanding of Christ crucified as "the power of God," an offense to the wise and powerful. Paul goes further: the wisdom revealed in the crucified Christ was, and remains, inscrutable to the "rulers of this age" (1 Cor 2:6, 9) who "crucified the Lord of glory." Paul does not otherwise specify who these "rulers" were and certainly is not concerned here or anywhere else to identify Pontius Pilate or any other specific officeholders involved in Jesus's death. The directness of this phrase is nevertheless irreducibly political: *rulers of this age*, an age that is "passing away" (7:31), crucified Christ, and by that action showed their implacable opposition to God. Paul is not interested in the personalities or policies of particular magistrates; individual culpability is irrelevant to his apocalyptic perspective. At "the end," "every ruler and every authority and power" will be destroyed by Christ as "all things" are subjected to Christ by God (15:24–28). Nowhere in his letters does Paul elaborate on this coming subjection, but the very incidental way in which he affirms it without explanation indicates how basic it is to his beliefs. Such categorical dismissal of worldly rulers stands in dramatic contrast to the subsequent efforts of the gospel writers to mitigate the impression that Pilate himself was responsible for Jesus's fate (see N. Elliott 1994, 109–24).

Paul's Apostolic Weakness

Nor is the contrast Paul makes between his own admittedly unimpressive self-presentation as an apostle and the elite in Corinth (1 Cor 4) or the prestige of his rivals (2 Cor 10–13) merely a matter of different social locations. Here, too, Paul grounds his argument christologically. Paul's rhetorical construal of his own "afflictions"—physical difficulties, like hunger or shipwreck, as well as what we might call "political" afflictions: his record of arrests, imprisonments, and civil punishments ("three times … beaten with rods," 2 Cor 11:23–27; cf. 1 Cor 4:9–13)—are the embodied manifestation of Christ (N. Elliott 2004). By this I mean not only that Paul couches his message as the "demonstration of power" (1 Cor 2:4; cf. 2 Cor 12:12) but also that the physical presence of Paul and his fellow apostles is a "carrying about in the body" of "the dying of Jesus" (1 Cor 4:10). This language of "carrying about," like the language of the apostles becoming a "spectacle" or of "displaying" the crucified Jesus (Gal 3:1), is drawn from the sacred space of civic ceremonial and procession. Paul exploits the language of *Roman* ceremonial when he declares that the public humiliation he shares with all genuine apostles—which is so scandalous to some in Corinth—is to be understood as God leading him "in triumphal procession" (2 Cor 2:14–16). Here the metaphors of military triumph (in which the vanquished were paraded ceremonially to their deaths) and of epiphany processions seem to be mingled. It is perhaps less important to disentangle them than to recognize Paul's rhetorical strategy. He seems to accept his characterization by his opponents as a humiliated, wretched figure but uses it for his own purpose. Even if he has been displayed as a figure of shame and ridicule, it is Christ who has thus triumphed and gained glory: the apostle remains the locus of God's power.

The Collection for "the Saints"

A final contrast with aspects of Roman imperial ideology is evident in Paul's appeal to the Corinthians to participate in his "ministry to the saints," the collection for Jerusalem which is the burden of (two different letters? in) 2 Cor 8 and 9. Noteworthy here is the language in which Paul makes his appeal: "for the purpose [of the collection] is not that there [should be] relief for others and affliction for you, but rather [it should be] out of equality. In the now time, your abundance should supply their lack, in order that their abundance may supply your lack, so that there may be equality" (2

Cor 8:13–14, trans. Welborn). Paul's argument here represents a dramatic divergence from the logic of patronage in the Roman world, according to which "equality" would have meant only an approximation of "balance" (as the NRSV translates the Greek word *isotēs*) "within an unequal friendship." Paul implies that the Corinthians are obligated to the Jerusalem saints, because they have received a spiritual gift from them, and because of their own material abundance. Paul promotes something radical: "the equalization of resources between persons of *different* social classes through voluntary redistribution." More, he goes so far as to suggest that the donation for Jerusalem constitutes the submission of the Achaians to Jerusalem (2 Cor 9:13; for translation and argument, see Welborn 2013). The obligation is more expressly stated in Rom 15:26–27, and in Romans, Paul introduces a new term in referring to the collection: it is not only "ministry," it represents "the offering of the nations" that it is Paul's priestly service to present (Rom 15:16). The last phrase is far grander than the language of gift and obligation; it echoes the language in which the tribute of the nations *to Rome* was described in the *Aeneid* (6.113)—but this is a tribute given by the nations *to Jerusalem* (see N. Elliott 2008, 44–47). Especially given the central significance of the collection to Paul's mission, the characterization of the collection by Sze-Kar Wan (2000, 191–215) as "anti-colonial act" seems apt.

At these points, it is possible to see Paul discussing specific matters, in explicit terms, that bear comparison in one or another way with aspects of Roman imperial cult or ideology. Romans presents a different challenge to the interpreter.

Romans

Except for 13:1–7, Romans offers very little in the way of explicit reference to political realities, and even there the reference to "governing authorities" is quite general. Not surprisingly, for most of the history of interpretation, Romans has not been read as touching on political realities except incidentally. It has been read as a summary of Paul's gospel, involving an explanation of the need for salvation in Christ and a critique of Judaism, as well as a meditation on the fate of Israel (in Rom 9–11).

Scholars tend now to recognize those chapters as the climax of the letter. At the end of the twentieth century, the dominant assumptions of the new perspective shaped a consensus that in Romans Paul was concerned to ameliorate "ethnic tensions" between Jews and gentiles in the Roman church. The historical circumstances that occasioned those tensions were directly connected to Roman policy: according to Suetonius (*Claud.* 25.4), Claudius expelled Jews from Rome, apparently including Jews known to Paul (see Acts 18:1–2). The return of some of these Jews to Rome after Claudius's death, to churches where they were now a vulnerable and, to some extent, a humiliated minority among non-Jews, might have occasioned the disdain and contempt against which Paul warns the non-Jews in Rom 11.

In *The Arrogance of Nations* (N. Elliott 2008), I argued that just that warning was at the heart of the letter and governs its rhetoric from the beginning. I will not recapitulate all those arguments here (nor cite the corroborative work of other scholars on which I gratefully depend!), but I will name several issues that bear directly on the question of Paul and empire.

The Cause of Tension and Paul's Concern

The notice in Suetonius is more ambiguous than usually recognized. *Christian* missionizing was *not* the spark of Jewish agitation named by Suetonius (see Slingerland 1997). That expulsion was simply another episode in recurring Roman crackdowns on "the usual suspects" in episodes of civil unrest. The danger of non-Jewish Christians in Rome "boasting" over Israel—the object of Paul's warning in Rom 11—need not be taken as evidence of a manifest failure on the part of Jews to accept the gospel of Jesus. Rather, it represented the infiltration into the Roman *ekklēsia* of the same contempt for Jews as a "vanquished race" that was common among elite circles from the time of Tiberius onward. The unfortunate circumstances of returning "Claudian exiles" can only have accelerated the spread of such contempt (see N. Elliott 2008, 96–100, 107–19).

The Status of Israel

Despite the long history of Christian interpretation in which Rom 9–11 has been read as including a sort of theological postmortem on a "fallen" Israel, Paul's concern throughout these chapters is the warning to non-Jews. The distinction that structures these chapters—in terms of rhetorical analysis, the "dissociation of concepts"—is not a typological argument about those who are "in" and those who are "out" but between *present* appearances, which may be deceptive, and God's ultimate purposes, which will be manifest only in the future. Israel *seems* to have stumbled, but will be restored, and "all Israel shall be saved" (Rom 11:25–26; see N. Elliott

2008, 111–19). This discussion, which swirls around promises in Israel's prophets that one would "rise to rule the nations" (Rom 15:12, quoting Isa 11:10), contravened the mythology, ubiquitous in Paul's day, that the gods had bestowed the destiny of world supremacy to *the Roman people* and that such rule was exercised by the person of Caesar (Virgil's *Aeneid*; the Res gestae). Here it is important to bear in mind our earlier discussion of *implicit* meanings. Paul never interacts explicitly with that mythology, though it is at least suggestive to compare the narrative of Aeneas—whose unwavering piety to his ancestral gods ensured the world-conquering destiny of his descendants—with what Paul says about Abraham, the "forefather" of Jews and non-Jews alike, who was justified, though *impious* (Rom 4:5—literally so, according to Josh 24:2–4, for he repudiated his ancestors' gods). Paul's insistence that Abraham was not only the ancestor of the circumcised or of descendants "through the law" but of *all* who would "inherit the world" (Rom 4:13) would have sounded like a usurpation of Roman prerogatives to any familiar with the common themes of Roman culture (N. Elliott 2008, 121–41).

No Defense from God's Justice

The early chapters of Romans seem to have nothing to do with the political thematic I have just described. To the contrary, they are usually read, on the strength of Martin Luther's interpretation, as governed by the contrast between justification by faith (which Paul proclaims) and justification by works of law (a characterization of Judaism, which Paul rejects). I contend that this single-minded focus on themes that were central for Luther blinds us to other important themes sounded from the beginning of the letter: for example, the contrast between justice (*dikaiosynē*) and injustice (*adikia*), by which Paul means not to contrast alternative modes of "justification" but to drive a wedge between the claims of those who suppress the truth and those who honor God (1:15–32). This passage is profitably compared with the notions of providence abroad in Paul's day, specifically notions of divine justice being actualized in specific instances of visible, unmistakable punishment of the notoriously wicked. Paul names no individuals, but given the similarities of vocabulary with depictions of the emperors and imperial governors in authors like Philo and Suetonius, the "spiral of depravity" described in Rom 1 would plausibly have evoked for hearers the egregious misdeeds of the spectacularly powerful. Just as other authors could point out the public downfall and destruction of the infamous, so

Paul's theme throughout the letter is God's uncompromising justice and the absence of any possible impunity. Understanding the rhetoric of the letter depends, in my view, on recognizing that this emphasis on justice and refusal of any defense or excuse is connected to the climactic warning against boasting over Israel. That is, it is not necessary to imagine that Paul is trying, in a theoretical, even-handed way, to declare all human beings *equally* lost without Christ—though that reading is crucial, of course, to various forms of Christian evangelism (N. Elliott 2008, 72–85).

Justice, the Jew, and the Law

It is to strengthen the latter point that Paul, through the rhetorical device of conversation with an imaginary interlocutor, calls a Jew to bear witness. The point of this interrogation is not to "demolish Jewish privilege" or to expose some imagined presumption on the part of the Jew but to elicit from the Jew—renowned for his integrity—an unswerving commitment to the principle of justice. (I depend here on the invaluable work of Stanley K. Stowers [1994] on the diatribe, though I apply it to Romans differently.) Instead of a generalized indictment of human depravity in need of salvation in Christ—the customary Christian reading of Rom 1–3—the opening chapters constitute an indirect approach to the warning in Rom 9–11. Paul takes pains to establish a fundamental distinction between (God's) justice and human injustice—even the spectacular injustice of the powerful—because he is opposing a power gradient in which different standards apply to the powerful and their beneficiaries, on one hand, and their ungrateful and undeserving inferiors, on the other. That power gradient, naturalized by Roman ideology, made disregard for the city's Jewish population appear commonsensical; Paul is working to expose it as unjust and an offense to God.

Subjection and the "Idle Sword"

The passage encouraging submission to the governing authorities (Rom 13:1–7) remains a conundrum, not least for the interpretation of Romans that I am advancing here. Scholars have long identified tensions within the passage (does the believer owe "fear," *phobos*, to the authority, or not? Where else in the Pauline corpus does God appear to need the "ministry" of the governing authority to achieve justice?—see 12:19–21). To these comparisons, I would add the contrast between Paul's enigmatic declaration that the authority "does not bear the sword in vain" (13:4) with the theme, abundantly exemplified in literature from the imperial court (Seneca, Calpurnius Siculus, the first *Eclogue* of Calpurnius Piso), that Nero had come to power without bloodshed—evincing superiority even to his hallowed ancestor Augustus—and that peace, "knowing not the drawn sword," now reigned. The juxtaposition suggests at least the possibility that Paul seeks to deny the "harmlessness" of the imperial sword: despite his pretensions of innocence, the ruler does *not* bear the sword in vain (see N. Elliott 2008, 152–59; 1997, 184–204)! But whatever the function of this passage in the letter, it must be balanced against the clear declarations at the beginning and end of Romans that Paul's apostolic commission consists in securing "the obedience of the nations"—surely a prerogative that, according to imperial propaganda, belonged to the emperor alone.

This hardly resolves the tensions in the letter, of course, but especially with regard to this passage it is important to keep in mind the warning that the venerable Leander E. Keck (1993, 16) offered to any interpreter who dared to skate too assuredly on "Romans pond": "Danger: Thin Ice!"

Paul and Empire

The preceding paragraphs have only scratched the surface of interpretive possibility regarding three of Paul's most significant letters (or more, depending on our understanding of the composition of 2 Corinthians). In them, I have intended to make two points: First, that the *realia* of the Roman Empire—including the literary and ideological representations of Roman supremacy and destiny, justice and peace—are indeed relevant to our interpretation of Paul and his letters; second, that any such comparisons should not be stated in simple terms of Paul's opposition to the Roman Empire. Paul was a man of his time; his values—though thoroughly conditioned by the legacy of Jewish apocalypticism and the conviction that God's justice would ultimately triumph over and against all earthly powers—also reflected good Roman virtues of order and harmony (*homonoia*). Paul lived within the "ideological constraints" of his time—as we live in ours (N. Elliott 2008, 157–66). The ultimate responsibility for the appropriations we make of Paul lies not with him, but with us.

For Further Reading

Barclay, John M. G. 2011. *Pauline Churches and Diaspora Jews*. Tübingen: Mohr Siebeck.

Castelli, Elizabeth. 1991. "Interpretations of Power in 1 Corinthians." *Semeia* 54:197–222.

Chow, John K. 1992. *Patronage and Power: A Study of Social Networks in Corinth*. JSNTSup 75. Sheffield: JSOT Press.

Elliott, Neil. 2006. *Liberating Paul: The Justice of God and the Politics of the Apostle*. Maryknoll, NY: Orbis, 1994. Repr., Minneapolis: Fortress.

———. 2008. *The Arrogance of Nations: Reading Romans in the Shadow of Empire*. Paul in Critical Contexts. Minneapolis: Fortress.

Horsley, Richard A. ed. 2004. *Paul and the Roman Imperial Order*. Harrisburg, PA: Trinity Press International.

McKnight, Scot, and Joseph B. Modica, eds. 2013. *Jesus Is Lord, Caesar Is Not: Evaluating Empire in New Testament Studies*. Downers Grove, IL: IVP Academic.

Schüssler Fiorenza, Elisabeth. 1987. "Rhetorical Situation and Historical Reconstruction in 1 Corinthians." *NTS* 33:386–403.

Stowers, Stanley K. 1994. *A Rereading of Romans: Gentiles, Jews, Justice*. New Haven: Yale University Press.

Wire, Antoinette Clark. 1990. *The Corinthian Women Prophets: A Reconstruction through Paul's Rhetoric*. Minneapolis: Fortress.

PAUL AND EMPIRE 2:
NEGOTIATING THE SEDUCTION OF IMPERIAL "PEACE AND SECURITY" IN GALATIANS, THESSALONIANS, AND PHILIPPIANS

James R. Harrison

In seeking to understand Galatians, Philippians, and Thessalonians in their imperial context, this article will concentrate on the archaeological, epigraphic, numismatic, and iconographic evidence for each city. It will be argued that an important issue for the apostle Paul and his house churches was the danger of an idolatrous accommodation with the patronal benefits and values of the Julio-Claudian house on the part of his converts, including the pathways of upward mobility that the Roman ruler and his officials offered to the socially and politically ambitious in the provinces. There was also an ideological collision between the Jewish apocalyptic eschatology of Paul's gospel and the providential, prophetic, and benefaction perspectives espoused regarding the Julio-Claudian house by the Roman ruler and his clients. The versatility and pastoral care with which Paul handled these challenges partially explains why his gospel spread so rapidly throughout the eastern Mediterranean basin from the late 40s to the early 60s.

Imperial Rule and Clientage in North and South Galatia

At the outset, we must recognize that it is a matter of dispute whether Paul is writing to believers in North Galatia or South Galatia. In discussing North Galatia, therefore, I will focus on the inscriptional evidence of Ankara and its district but omit the other major cities of the region. In the case of South Galatia, I will concentrate on the inscriptional, archaeological, and iconographic evidence of Pisidian Antioch, a city visited by Paul in his first missionary journey (Acts 13:14–50), but bypass the other South

Galatian cities of his mission (Iconium, Lystra, and Derbe [Acts 13:51–14:24]). Consequently, the *local* imperial context of Galatians and its relation to Paul's apocalyptic gospel of grace should clearly emerge, irrespective of the letter's destination.

North Galatia:
Ankara and the Inscriptional Evidence for the Imperial Cult

The most important inscription in the city of Ankara, the provincial capital of Galatia, was the Latin and Greek copy of Augustus's self-eulogy, the Res gestae divi Augusti. This bilingual copy of the original inscription at Rome—inscribed in bronze at Augustus's mausoleum in 14 CE—was strategically placed in the Temple of Rome and Augustus in Ankara. The Ankara copy, erected around 19–20 CE, is the most complete text of the three copies of the Res gestae extant in Roman Galatia. Another fragmentary Greek copy was found at Apollonia (ca. 14–19 CE),[1] whereas an extensive Latin copy was discovered at Pisidian Antioch.[2] Justin Hardin (2008, 66–68) has speculated that the concentration of Res gestae inscriptions in Roman Galatia is explained by the decision of the Galatian *koinon* (league) to publish Greek and Latin copies of the text in the imperial sanctuaries across the province in 19–20 CE, replicating the original text at Rome, with the addition of a Greek and Latin appendix for provincial readers.

If Hardin is correct, we have to ask what event precipitated this decision in Roman Galatia. A likely answer is the excitement generated by the mission to the East (18–19 CE) of the charismatic general Germanicus (Tacitus, *Ann.* 73; Cassius Dio, *Hist. rom.* 57.18.6), the Roman conqueror of the Germanic tribes (14–16 CE) and possessor of an impeccable Julio-Claudian pedigree.[3] Germanicus visited Galatia in 19 CE as

---

1. On top of the large base, on which the Res gestae was inscribed, were statues of Augustus, Tiberius, Livia, Germanicus, and Drusus (Cooley 2009, 17), identified by their (fragmentary) inscriptions underneath.

2. None of the major commentators on the Res gestae (Gagé 1935; Ridley 2003; Scheid 2007; Cooley 2009) hazard a guess precisely when the Latin text was erected at Pisidian Antioch after 14 CE. The original context of the monument has been compromised (Cooley 2009, 13–14), with the result that we are uncertain regarding its original location and time of erection.

3. Germanicus (15 BCE–9 CE) was, respectively, great-nephew and nephew of Augustus and Tiberius, as well as the adopted son of the latter and the brother of Claudius and the father of Caligula.

part of a wider tour of subduing feuding and unsettled regions in the East (Tacitus, *Ann.* 2.54, 59), receiving a rapturous response from the Galatian governor Sotidius in preparation for his visit (Judge 2008, 348–54, 390) and stirring up intense excitement among the Egyptian populace upon his arrival.[4] An inscription from Apollonia (*MAMA* 4.142), site of the fragmentary Greek copy of the Res gestae, recounts the diplomatic mission of Apollonius, an imperial priest of the goddess Roma, to meet Germanicus. Presumably Apollonius was either reporting to Germanicus the construction of the Greek monument of the Res gestae during 14–19 CE, as Paul McKechnie (2008, 143) argues, or, alternatively, announcing its imminent erection. Thus the elites of the Galatian cities, with a view to securing Julian patronage (19 CE), pressed the *koinon* to publish the Res gestae throughout the province upon Germanicus's triumphal tour. Undoubtedly the Galatian cities vied among themselves for his recognition.

Why is the erection of Augustus's Res gestae so important for the expansion of the imperial cult throughout Roman Galatia? The Res gestae is a self-eulogy in which Augustus sets out his achievements and accolades: his honors (1–7) and special tributes achieved during his principate (9–13); the honors for his sons (14); his *impensae* (expenses) incurred on behalf of the state and the Roman people (15–24); his *res gestae* (military "achievements") by which he subdued the nations to the power of Rome (25–33); and, last, his preeminence as an example of virtue to all (34–35). Augustus presents his rule as the culmination of republican history, excelling previous great men in virtue (Res gest. divi Aug. 34.2) and representing the yardstick of excellence to which future leaders should aspire (8.5; Suetonius, *Aug.* 35.1). The Julio-Claudian rulers, some more sincerely than others, claimed that they would rule according to Augustan precedent upon their accession to power. Augustus had also maintained meticulous attention to the worship of the traditional Roman gods (Res gest. divi Aug. 8.1; 19.1–2; 20.1, 3–4; 24.1–2) and the great priestly colleges (7.3). Therefore the priests of the imperial cult in Roman Galatia worshiped Augustus and his heirs as "divine" in their rites in conjunction with the Roman gods and their own indigenous deities.

---

4. See Sherk 1988, §34A, B, for Egyptian papyri revealing the inflated responses to Germanicus's visit to Egypt.

An inscription in the inner area of the portico of the Temple of Rome and Augustus at Ankara lists the names of the annually appointed "priests of the god Augustus and of the goddess Roma," as well as their benefactions (feasts, distributions of oil and grain, donations of land, spectacles, gladiatorial and athletic contests, animal hunts and fights). Significantly, the vast majority of the high priests have Celtic names, indicating that the imperial priesthoods were pathways for the acquisition of civic status, providing opportunities for the competitive provincial elites to demonstrate their personal wealth and their faithfulness (*fides*) as clients to the Roman ruler. In this regard, the high priest Albiorex shows his loyalty to the Julian house (Sherk 1988, §28, lines 24–25) by setting up "statues of Caesar and Iulia Augusta" (i.e., the wife of Augustus). Last, a Claudian inscription (41–54 CE), found at Sinanlıköy (50 km west of Ankara), honors the first priest of the divine Augustus and Claudius originating from the Galatian tribe of the Tolistobogii (Mitchell and French 2012, 151–52).

In sum, while the honorific culture of the imperial cult had also penetrated the remote rural areas of the district of Ankara (e.g., Mitchell 1982, §§34, 35, 95, 200, 411), it was in the large North Galatian *urban* centers such as Ankara where the serious cultic activity on behalf of the ruler of Rome and her gods took place.

South Galatia:
The Inscriptional, Archaeological, and Iconographic Evidence

Introduction to the Excavation of Pisidian Antioch

When Paul visited the military colony of Pisidian Antioch in South Galatia (Acts 13:14–50),[5] the precise date of which (34–40 or 43–49? CE) still remains a matter of scholarly dispute—he would have seen two magnificent Augustan monuments. First, near to the two main streets of Pisidian Antioch was the Sebasteion (imperial cult temple). The Sebasteion was built high on the city's eastern acropolis, providing its worshipers a panoramic view of the surrounding countryside. No visitor to the city could miss the Sebasteion and its propylon (gate). Second, the imperial sanctuary was approached by the street called the Tiberia Plateau, which

---

5. For inscriptions honoring legionary veterans of the original *coloni*, see Ramsay 1916.

culminated in twelve steps, above which stood the triple arch of Augustus, constructed in 2/1 BCE (Ossi 2010, 21). This served as a propylon to the sanctuary proper. Between the time of the extensive 1924 expedition of the University of Michigan led by Francis W. Kelsey and the next excavation led by Stephen Mitchell and Marc Waelkens in 1982, the stairs and pavement had almost entirely disappeared. Apparently the modern residents of nearby Yalvaç had removed the stones for their own building projects, with the result that by 2004 the foundations of the arch of Augustus were no longer to be found.

The upper section of the Augustan arch is the best preserved since the lower section had disappeared long before the Michigan excavations. It is a matter of debate from the fragments of the Res gestae found at Pisidian Antioch where its rendering was actually located: was the text inscribed on the faces of the pedestal blocks punctuating the stairway to the arch or on a monument nearby? The Latin Res gestae, published after Augustus's death, would have been inscribed fifteen years after the construction of the arch, if we assume that Ossi's dating is correct (Ossi 2010, 37–40). Further, it is possible—given that a Greek version of the text had been erected at the two other sites in Galatia—that a Greek version was once present in Pisidian Antioch too, even though we have no fragments of its remains.

We turn now to a brief discussion of both monuments. What do they reveal about the imperial cult at Pisidian Antioch?

The Augustan Triple-Arched Propylon at Pisidian Antioch

On the frieze on the western outer face of the Augustan arch and in the spandrels over the archways of the monument, there was rich and complex iconography that articulated the Augustan ideology of rule (Harrison 2011a). First, there was inscribed a *sidus Iulium*, the apotheosis sign of Augustus's adoptive father, Julius Caesar (Ossi 2010, 300). The dedicatory inscription to Augustus on the arch bears the same message of Caesar's apotheosis and Octavian's adoption into the Julian family with the title "son of god."[6]

---

6. The inscription, datable to 2/1 BCE, is as follows (Ossi 2010, 21): "For the imperator Caesar Augustus, son of a god, pontifex maximus, consul for the 13th time, with tribunician power for the 22nd time, imperator for the 14th time, father of the country."

Second, the frieze contained a Capricorn, the astrological sign prophetically associated with Augustus's birth (Suetonius, *Aug.* 94.12; Cassius Dio, *Hist. rom.* 56.25.5; Rubin 2011, 43 fig. 3.9; Ossi 2010, 300 fig. 128). Given that his birth sign on September 23–24 was in reality Libra, Augustus must have chosen Capricorn for other reasons. Rather than its being a case, as some scholars have argued, of Augustus preferring his conception date to his birth date, we should ask why Augustus's clients in Pisidian Antioch, who erected the monument, decided to emphasize the Capricorn motif. It is worth remembering that the iconography of the arch of Augustus interacts ideologically with the text of the Res gestae at the same site. Capricorn was associated with western Europe—especially Spain, Gaul, and Germany—the area that the (then) Octavian had controlled before Actium (31 BCE) (Manilius, *Astronomica* 4.791–796; see also Horace, *Odes* 2.17.19–20). A new age had dawned with the end of the winter solstice traditionally associated with Capricorn. Capricorn now ruled the entire world through Augustus as its savior, since he and his family members—as his Greco-Phrygian and Roman clients at Pisidian Antioch gratefully acknowledged—had conquered the barbarian peoples on the edge of the empire. Thus the appearance of the Capricorn in the iconography of the arch synchronized with the motif of the "conquest of the nations" in the Res gestae (3.1–2; 4.3; 25–33; see the Latin preface).

Third, over the archway of the western facade are placed two kneeling, bound captives in the spandrels. One is nude, while one is partially draped, and scholars have debated their precise identification.[7] Brian Rose (2005) has proposed that Hadrian's arch, built as the ornamental city gate of Pisidian Antioch, had copied motifs already present on the arch of Augustus.[8] It is possible that the two Hadrianic standard-bearing barbarians, one from Gaul and the other from Parthia, had been previously placed on the eastern facade of the Augustan arch (Ossi 2010, 302 figs. 133–34). Thus, if Rose is correct, the "conquest of the nations" motif is visually present on both the eastern and western facades of the arch.

Fourth, naval iconography (ship prows, the ram of a warship, tritons, the god Poseidon) pointed symbolically to Augustus's famous naval victory at Actium (Ossi 2011, 97 fig. 5.15a). Winged figures of victory, of a quasi-supernatural character, feature with garlands on the spandrels of

---

7. Mitchell and Waelkens 1998, 162 fig. 113 (partially draped captive); Rubin 2011, 43 fig. 3.12 (nude captive), 99 fig. 5.19a (partially draped captive).

8. On Hadrian's arch at Pisidian Antioch, see Ossi 2011, 108–85.

the western face (nude males) and on the eastern face (draped females) (Rubin 2011, 43 fig. 3.10). Combining Hellenistic and sacral elements in the iconography, the divinely sanctioned nature of Augustus's rule is powerfully emphasized. This is reinforced by the presence of other prominent deities on the arch, variously identified by scholars (Ossi 2010, 84–86).[9] In the sanctuary proper, the inscriptional dedication of the Sebasteion underscores the superintendence of Augustus's rule by Jupiter.[10] Last, several large statues, each two meters high, crowned the top of the arch, representing Augustus and his family. A headless statue most likely represents Augustus as Zeus (Rubin 2011, 58 fig. 3.23), while another statue perhaps depicts the Roman ruler pinioning a barbarian captive (58 fig. 3.14).

What portrait of victory emerges from the Augustan triumphal arch at Pisidian Antioch? There is little doubt, as Ossi (2010, 71–72) argues, that the Augustan arch at Pisidian Antioch is a "visual *Res Gestae*." It does not just commemorate a single victory like the other Augustan arches in Italy and the Latin West. Its ideological sweep embraces Augustus's ancestry, birth, triumviral years, divinely sanctioned rule from Actium onward, and maintenance of the borders of Rome against the unruly barbarian peoples. What is significant is that his clients in the city have erected the arch, and as its inscription demonstrates, they are conveying an honorific accolade to their imperial benefactor for bringing the city so much prosperity and prestige in Asia Minor. This is not a case of "Romanization" imposed on conquered Galatian provincials, but rather an integration of indigenous Hellenistic and Roman elements in honor of the benefactor of the world.[11]

---

9. For the local god, Men Askaenos, see Rubin 2011, 43 fig. 3.13.

10. Rubin (2008, 63) renders the incomplete inscription thus: "To Jupiter Optimus Maximus Augustus and the Genius of the Colony [ ] the son of Eueius." Rubin (2008, 55–71) argues that the Latin dedication was a collaborative effort on the part of Italian colonists with the local Greco-Phrygian elite, one of whom is mentioned on the inscription ("Eueius"). He observes that Augustus functions as an intermediary—having the same "godlike" status as the Olympian deities—between Jupiter and the genius of the colony, Pisidian Antioch.

11. Ossi (2010, 56) comments that the arch "stands as an attempt to integrate the multicultural population, not by turning Greeks and Phrygians into Romans, but by melding aspects of each cultural tradition into a new provincial culture."

The Augustan Sebasteion at Pisidian Antioch and the Worship of the
Roman Ruler

In the case of the Sebasteion, one proceeded through the propylon to a
large colonnaded plaza called the Augusta Plataea, with a large rectan-
gular courtyard at the front reserved for the rituals and sacrifices of the
imperial cult. In the wall of the western portico were workshops, storage
rooms, and offices for the elite personnel of the cult. The sanctuary, a sev-
enteen- to eighteen-meter structure, stood in front of a two-story semicir-
cular portico cut out from the natural rock of the hillside (Rubin 2011, 48
fig. 3.17). The portico afforded protection from sun and rain, providing
thereby a handy marshaling area for processions and sacrifices in honor
of the Roman ruler, as well as temporary open-air accommodation for pil-
grims from the neighboring countryside. The local elites of the city would
have also used the portico as a convenient place to demonstrate their *fides*
(faithfulness) to the Roman ruler by erecting statues there in honor of the
Roman ruler and the members of his house.

Inscriptions from Pisidian Antioch reveal the identity of some of the
first-century local elites supporting the imperial cult. Three examples will
suffice.[12] First, in a 50 CE Latin inscription, Lucius Calpurnius Longus,
the imperial priest of the city, is honored for funding the construction of
a wooden amphitheater, festivals, fights of wild beasts and gladiators, and
(possibly) hosting a public feast (Ramsay 1924, 178–79 §5). Second, C.
Pepius dedicated a small altar to the Augustan peace in a street of Antioch,
again proving that Augustus's military colony "emulated in a small way the
Ara Pacis at Rome" (Ramsay 1924, 177 §2). Third, C. Caristanius Fronto
Caisianus Iullus—duumvir, pontifex (priest), and military officer—made
a vow to the deities of the city for Claudius's victory and safety during his
invasion of Britain (Mowery 2006, 223–42). He fulfilled his word by means
of four strategic benefactions: a statue (presumably of Claudius), games,
sacrifices, and wild-beast hunts and fights.

Not surprisingly, what we have witnessed in North Galatia has been
mirrored in South Galatia. The colonists replicated the imperial culture
of Rome in their inscriptional, iconographic, and monumental statements at Pisidian Antioch. The attraction of the imperial cult cut across
the social and economic divide. A fusion of indigenous and Roman gods

---

12. For further examples, see Levick 1958; 1967, 101–2 §1, 107 §12, 109 §15.

occurred, whose blessings were mediated by the grace of the Roman ruler as Pontifex Maximus (high priest), in conjunction with his local imperial priests. Last, the imperial *cursus honorum* (course of honors)—with the seduction of its army posts, priesthoods, and magistracies—became an opportunity for upward social mobility and for the enhancement of ancestral fame.

Paul and the Imperial Cult in Galatians

How does Paul's Letter to the Galatians intersect with the imperial culture of North and South Galatia? The issue for Galatians interpreters who posit an imperial critique occurring in Galatians is to reconcile the Julio-Claudian background with the Jewish nature of the "agitation" at Galatia (see Harrison 2004). Bruce Winter (2002; see also Kahl 2010, 218–27) has argued that the agitators' desire to avoid persecution for Christ (Gal 6:12–13) is best understood against the imperial cult, proposing that the agitators in the Galatian churches hoped to gain exemption from observing the imperial cult by sheltering under the Jewish umbrella of being a *religio licita* (permitted religion). By contrast, Hardin (2008, 85–115) argues that the Jews had no such privileges and that the agitators, indigenous to Galatia, were probably navigating a more secure place for the house churches in a hostile Roman society. Either way, by appearing more Jewish through the imposition of circumcision on their gentile members (Gal 2:12; 5:2, 3, 11; 6:13), the agitators hoped to avoid local Jewish and gentile persecution (3:4; 4:29; 5:11; 6:12) and thereby appease the suspicious civil magistrates.

In response, Paul warns the gentile Galatians against spiritual compromise with idolatry by returning to their preconversion observances of special days, months, seasons, and years (Gal 4:8–10), probably referring to the calendrical observance of imperial and indigenous cults, as opposed to the rituals of Jewish calendar (Hardin 2008, 116–47). The inscription in the inner area of the portico of the Temple of Rome and Augustus at Ankara, for example, testifies to the rituals and benefactions that the imperial Celtic priests oversaw, ensuring imperial beneficence toward the city, while the Res gestae highlights Augustus's devotion to the traditional Roman cults. Ideologically, Paul's characterization of the present age as "evil" (Gal 1:4) not only reflects his Jewish apocalyptic worldview but also undermines the boasting of the Roman and indigenous clients at Galatia in the advent of the Augustan "new age," articulated both in the Res gestae and the propylon iconography at Pisidian Antioch.[13] While Paul's language of "grace" (*charis*) would have intersected with the bitter denial of divine "grace" language in some local Galatian gravestones (Harrison 2003, 249; see Gal 2:20), Paul also pivots the unconditioned *charis* of the crucified Christ and Lord over against those compromising with the age of Augustan grace by seeking to evade persecution through Jewish ethnocentrism (Harrison 2003, 226–34; see *charis* in Gal 1:6; 5:4; see also 3:1–5).

In the case of the nations, we have seen that that the local Galatian clients of the Roman ruler and his officials at Pisidian Antioch marginalized the barbarians by depicting them as humiliated victims in their iconography. More intriguingly, in the Res gestae, the rulers of the nations from the ends of the earth send diplomatic missions to Augustus (Res gest. divi Aug. 31.1, 2; 32.2, 3; 33), well aware that Augustus's reputation for "justice" (*iustitia* [*dikaiosynē*]) triggered the "faith" (*fides* [*pistis*]) of his clients in him and in the Roman people (Res gest. divi Aug. 32.3 ["the good faith of the Roman people under my leadership"; *Rōmaiōn pisteōs ep' emou hēgemonos*]; 34:2 [*d*]*ikaiosynēn*; see also Horace, *Saec.* 57–60). *Fides* was the foundation of *iustitia* in Roman thought (Cicero, *Off.* 1.23). In particular, the "justice" of Roman generals, in protecting the conquered nations, established the good "faith" of the Roman people (Cicero, *Off.* 1.35; Livy, *History of Rome* 5.27.11). What is fascinating here for Pauline scholars is the link between "justice" (*dikaiosynē*; Gal 2:21; 3:6, 21; 5:5), "justification" (*dikaioō*; 2:16, 17; 3:8, 11, 24; 5:4), and "faith" language in Galatians (*pistis*: twenty-two occurrences; *pistiseuō*: four).

Over against the Roman metanarrative of the humiliation of the unruly barbarians and the admission of compliant nations to imperial favor, Paul unveils a different narrative of "justice" and "faith" for the nations. Because of the "faithfulness of Christ" to God in his death (*dia pisteōs Iēsou Christou*, Gal 2:16a; 2:16b; *ek pisteōs Christou*, see 2:20; 3:22, 26; Hays 2002, 157–76; Campbell 2005, 90–93; see also Bird and Sprinkle 2009, passim), God has declared his dependents "just" before himself apart from the works of the law (Gal 2:16c, 21), with a view to their acquittal at the eschatological judgment (2:16c). The cruciform faithfulness of Christ (Gal 3:13), founded on his love for his dependents (Gal 2:20c; *tou agapēsantos*

---

13. On Augustus's consciousness that a "new age" for Rome had begun with him (Res gestae 13; 16.1), see Harrison 2013, 28 n. 141.

me; see aslo 5:22), not only fulfilled the covenantal promise to Abraham (3:15–18) but also actualized the promised community in unexpected ways. The gentile offspring of Abraham, declared "just" in the same way as their ancestor (3:6–9; see Isaac in 4:28), would possess the promise of the Spirit through faith (3:14b). Moreover, the extension of "just" status to all of Christ's dependents without qualification contrasted with the ethnic elitism of the Roman model. There Augustus (Res gest. divi Aug. 34.2) and his generals are the *only* "just" individuals who could broker patron-client relations with the conquered nations. Thus the nations, inferior to Rome, were excluded from "just" status, including the much-admired Greeks. Furthermore, through the Spirit, believers could call their heavenly patron "Father" (Gal 4:7; Rom 8:16 [*abba*]), having the same familial access to God as Christ (Mark 14:36 [*abba*]). The gentile believers had experienced a dramatic elevation in status in becoming God's sons and heirs (Gal 4:7). This newly acquired honor rendered insignificant the "paternal" honorific accolade—the culmination of the Res gestae's boasts—accorded to Augustus by a grateful public (Res gest. divi Aug. 35; *patēra patridos* [father of the fatherland]).

In sum, a radical social reordering, invisible to the world, had occurred in the body of Christ. The "fleshly" self-promotion ("selfishness," 5:20b; "conceited," 5:26a; "envying one another," 5:26c; "if anyone thinks they are something," 6:3a) and the competition of imperial culture ("competing against one another," 5:26c; "not boast in the other man," 6:4b), with its hierarchies of esteem and obligation, was replaced by self-effacement ("being nothing," Gal 6:3b) and mutual commitment (6:2a) as the "law of Christ" was expressed among believers (Gal 6:2b). The striking phrase "law of Christ" seized the ideological ground from the opponents who wanted to diminish Christian distinctiveness in the imperial world by retreating behind the law of Moses (Gal 6:12). The new dynamic of Spirit-animated (Gal 6:8b; see also 5:16a, 18a, 22, 25) and eschaton-oriented social relations (6:9) also differentiated the early believers' understanding of benefaction ("we should work the good," 6:10) from imperial patronage. The unqualified extension of benefits "to all" undermined the ancient expectation of reciprocity and stymied the patron's prior evaluation of the "worthiness" of recipients, a precaution central to Greco-Roman gift-giving rituals ("toward all," Gal 6:10; Harrison 2003). Significantly, this occurred without omitting the priority of beneficence toward the household of faith (*malista* [especially], 6:10). Finally, the "new creation" in Christ (Gal 5:6; 6:15; Jewett 2003; Elliott 2013), inaugurated through the cross (6:14; see also 1:4), set aside the religious, ethnic, and cultural divisions expressed in the antinomies of "circumcision" and "uncircumcision" (6:15; De Boer 2011, 401–3). Paul's vision of humanity challenged the Roman hegemony, which, with its clients, demeaned the uncircumcised barbarians and marginalized other contumacious nations.

Paul and the Imperial World in the Epistle to the Philippians

The Archaeological, Epigraphic, and Numismatic Evidence regarding the Imperial Cult at Philippi

Most of the extant archaeological remains of Roman Philippi belong to the second century CE onward. We know extremely little about Philippi of the Claudian era, the time of Paul's arrival at the city (Acts 16:11–40). As Charalambos Bakirtzis (1998, 38) observes, "There remains intact from Paul's time, however, the general site and the surrounding ridges formed by Mounts Pangaion, Symbolon, and Orbelos, as well as the general landscape, though the fertile plain was largely marshland in the early Christian period." Nevertheless, two important fragments of statuary have been found, belonging to what originally was a wide array of statues of Augustus and his family, along with other monuments to the Julio-Claudian rulers. At the forum of Philippi, the marble head of the young boy Augustus was discovered in the basin of a fountain, datable to the first five years of the first century CE (Collart 1937, 353–54). Also, in the Archaeological Museum of Philippi there is a fine marble portrait of Lucius Caesar (Inv. no. Λ31; Bakirtzis and Koester 1998, plate 6.2), who was the adopted son of Augustus, from the Roman period. This attachment to the adopted sons of Augustus, Tiberius and Gaius, is confirmed by the decree erected in their honor, found in Basilika B (36/37 CE; Pilhofer 2009, §282/L270).

The "statue bases" coin issues from Roman Philippi also allow us to imagine what further samples of Julio-Claudian statuary might have existed in the forum of Philippi. A fine example is found on an Augustan coin with the radiate head of Augustus on the obverse. On the reverse, there is a statue group of Augustus standing on the left, right hand raised and clad in military attire, being crowned by a toga-clad Divus Caesar on the right (RPC 1.1650). Each figure is positioned on a central base flanked by smaller bases to the left and right. A Claudian issue, with the bare head of Claudius on the obverse, shows the same scene on the reverse, other than the variation of the central base being inscribed [D] IVVS [AVG] (*RPC* 1.1653; *BMC* 24; Bakirtzis and Koester 1998, plate 10.2a, 2b).

Although the Antonine and Justinian building programs obliterated the edifices of the Julio-Claudian period, Chaido Koukouli-Chrysantiki (1998, 15–16) argues that the general plan of the second-century CE forum most likely replicates the Julio-Claudian version, though the latter had a smaller square. The central square of Paul's day had two temple-shaped buildings on the north side, having the same purpose as the Antonine version, and a temple at the east end dedicated to the imperial cult. This was undoubtedly devoted to the worship of Livia (Augusta), the wife of Augustus whom the Senate had apotheosized in 44 CE (Suetonius, *Claud.* 11). Inscriptions have confirmed the worship of Augusta at Philippi. At the northeast angle of the forum, the remains of an inscriptional honorific monument, erected to the priestess of Augusta, Iulia Auruncina, have been found (Pilhofer 2009, §226/L334[a]).

Last, at the port city of Philippi, Neapolis (Acts 16:11; i.e., modern Kavala), there are inscribed sarcophagi of Julio-Claudian priests (Claudius; Pilhofer 2009, §001/L027) and priestesses (Augusta; §002/L028; cf. §226/ L308), as well as a flamen of Vespasian (§004/L030; cf. §719/L712). There is reference in an inscription to a "flamen of divine Augustus" and "patron of [the] colony," named Caius Oppius Montanus, also based at Kavala (§031/L121; cf. §241/L466; 700/L738). These status-conscious priests, who lived and died at the beautiful port city of Neapolis, are the eminent and wealthy citizens of the colony of Philippi who maintained the rituals of the imperial cult, ensuring the patronage of Rome and the blessing of its gods and ruler.

The elitism, hierarchicalism, and boastfulness of the Philippian priests is seen in the sarcophagus inscription of the Claudian priest, mentioned above, with its *cursus honorum* (course of honors; Hellerman 2005, 51–62, 88–109): "Publius Cornelius Asper Atiarius Montanus, honored with an *equus publicus*, also with the *ornamenta decurionalia*, Duumvir, Priest [*pontifex*], Priest [*flamen*] of divine Claudius in Philippi, twenty-three years old, lies here buried." The *cursus honorum* ascends in status from Publius's military honors (*equus publicus*, public horse) to his civic honors (*ornamenta decurionalia*) and magistracies (*duumvir*), climaxing in his prestigious priesthood of the apotheosized Claudius. It approximates in the civic and religious sphere the similarly stylized boasting in military offices, honors, and achievements that is found in the *cursus honorum* of the veterans of Philippi (e.g., Pilhofer 2009, §221/ L334; Hellerman 2005, 69–79; Nasrallah 2012, 61). The same elevated boasting can also be seen in Augustus's rapid assertion of his absolute precedence, to the exclusion of all others, regarding the Roman victory at Philippi (42 BCE) and, consequently, the establishment of the veteran colony of *Colonia Augusta Iulia Philippensis* (Colony of Philippi [in honor of] Julia Augusta). The coinage of Augustus from 27 BCE onward depicts the ruler as sole founder decreeing the establishment of the colony, supplanting the earlier coinage which had indicated that Antony, not Augustus, was Philippi's primary founder. How does Paul counter this boastful culture at Roman Philippi?

Paul and the Reevaluation of Roman Boasting Culture at Philippi

In two passages of Philippians (2:5–11; 3:4–11), Paul engages the relentless boasting of imperial culture, pinpricking the stylized Roman conventions of self-advertisement characteristic of the Philippian priestly elites and veterans. In each case, the cross of Christ and God's vindication of his obedient and dishonored Son redefines the nature of honor and glory, freeing the Philippian believers from the seduction of power and status associated with imperial clientage. First, Paul engages Jewish boasting culture, and implicitly its Roman equivalent, by setting out his *cursus honorum* of Jewish "confidence in the flesh" (Phil 3:4b). The apostle moves his grounds of boasting from what he had ethnically inherited as a Jew (Phil 3:5) to what he had achieved in a performance-oriented piety (3:5b–6; cf. Acts 26:5; Gal 2:14).

This crescendo of inherited status and personal achievement would have been rhetorically engaging for Philippian readers (see Pilhofer 1995, 122–26). Paul's auditors were probably familiar with the elitist boasting of the Roman nobility in earlier times (Harrison 2011b, 219–25) and, in the context of Philippi, its inflated redefinition through the paths of upward mobility (e.g., military careers, imperial priesthoods) sponsored by the Julio-Claudian ruler for his clients. In Phil 3:7–11, Paul inverts both the Jewish and Roman criteria of inherited status and personal performance by using the accounting language of "profit" (*moi kerdē*, Phil 3:7) and "loss" (*zēmian*, 3:7–8), shocking his readers with his explosive dismissal of flesh-centered achievement as "excrement" (*skybala*, 3:7; Witherington 2011, 202). The apostle pivots negatively his own righteousness ("my righteousness" [*emēn dikaiosunēn*], Phil 3:9a) over against the faithful-

ness of Christ ("through the faithfulness of Christ" [*dia pisteōs Christou*],
3:9a; Witherington 2011, 204–5; contra Reumann 2008, 495–500). His
cruciform obedience (Phil 2:8) secures God's gift of righteousness ("the
righteousness from God" [*tēn ek theou dikaiosunēn*], 3:9b), appropriated
through faith ("[based] on faith" [*epi tēi pistei*], 3:9b) and daily experienced in the believer's dying and rising with Christ (3:10; Tannehill 1967),
with a view to the eschatological resurrection (3:11). Thus Paul punctures
the boasting of the Philippians by stripping away reliance on ancestry and
performance, replacing it with the gift of God's grace and Christ's soteriological accomplishment.

In a trenchant critique of Roman hierarchicalism and self-advertisement, Paul sets forth for the Philippian believers the paradigm of
Christ's self-emptying and self-humbling (Phil 2:7–8)—made all the
more remarkable by his incomparably high status (2:5)—which culminated in the desolation and shame of the cross. Joseph Hellerman (2005)
has argued that Christ's *cursus pudorum* (course of shame) is directed
against the heated competition at Philippi for social precedence through
the imperial *cursus honorum* (course of honors). The cross bore no attraction for the upwardly mobile. However, God intervened to reverse the
shame of the cross: he vindicated Christ's obedience by giving him the
"name above all names" (Phil 2:9b), at which all living beings would bow
(2:10a; cf. Isa 45:23), including, undoubtedly, the imperial authorities "on
earth" (2:10b). The phrase "name above all names" would have reminded
Philippian auditors of the plethora of honorific titles, powers, and offices
attributed to the Roman ruler in many inscriptions (e.g., Braund 1985,
§§6, 28, 66, 87, 105, 117, 118, 144, 214, 216). The confessional name for
the exalted Christ ("Lord" [*kyrios*], Phil 2:11a) also has imperial reference,
given the increasing attribution of *kyrios* language to Nero in inscriptions
and papyri from the sixties onward (Fantin 2011, 196–202). It is likely
that this language was already informally abroad in the early 50s. However, in spite of the universal acclamation of Christ as the plenipotentiary
of all, his total self-effacement is the result: all the glory, from a Jewish
monotheistic perspective, goes to God the Father ("to the glory of God
the Father" [*eis doxan theou patros*], Phil 2:11b). The relentless quest for
glory by the Roman nobility had been totally constricted to the Julio-
Claudian house by the early first century CE (Harrison 2011b, 225–32).
The apostle, however, rejects this myopic concentration of honor in the
person of the Roman ruler in the Philippian Christ hymn by redirecting
all glory to God.

Paul and the Imperial World in the Thessalonian Epistles

The Archaeological, Epigraphic, Numismatic, and Literary Evidence
regarding the Imperial Cult at Thessalonica

To what extent did the imperial cult penetrate Thessalonica? The archaeological and inscriptional remains, while sparse for the Julio-Claudian
period, underscore the centrality of Rome's rule for Thessalonica as the
capital of the Roman province Macedonia Prima (Tellbe 2001, 80–86)
from 146 BCE onward.[14] Holland Lee Hendrix (1984, 1986, 1992) points
out that honors to the traditional gods, Roma and Roman benefactors,
had become increasingly interconnected in the practice of the city (*IG*
12.1.4, 33, 134). This dependence on Roman patronage, expressed in
the cult of "Roma and Roman benefactors," ensured the city's prosperity. Significantly, Paul excludes any such dependence on patronage for the
Thessalonian believers (2 Thess 3:6–10). There is epigraphic record of the
building of a Thessalonian temple to Caesar in the reign of Augustus (*IG*
10.2.1 no. 31). Although no remains of the original temple have survived,
the inscription testifies to the importance of the imperial cult in civic life.
Significantly, the inscription refers to the appointment of a "priest and
ago[nethete of Im]perator Caesar Augustus son [of God]" (*IG* 10.2.1 no.
31 ll. 5–7). It is possible that the imperial cult was located in the western part of the city, because a headless and armless statue of an emperor
was found in that region in 1957 (Vickers 1972). Nearby, to the north/
northeast of the Sarapeion, several fragments of a statue of Augustus were
discovered in 1939 (Hendrix 1991, 116–17). Whether locally produced or
imported, the statue's head was modeled on the famous representation of
Augustus found at Prima Porta. Hendrix (1991) cautions against assuming
that the statue belonged to the original temple of Caesar or that the site of
its discovery was the area devoted to imperial worship. The statue could
well have been executed during the Claudian period and was perhaps an
honorific or administrative monument from the nearby Agora.

The numismatic evidence reinforces the impression that the imperial cult flourished in Thessalonica (Dahmen 2010). Two examples will

---

14. A recently found inscription in the west cemetery of Thessalonica of a Vespa-
sian-era *procurator Augusti*, erected with statues of the Roman official and his daughters, "corroborates the view that Thessalonike was the residence of the imperial procurator of the province" (Nigdelis 2012, 207).

suffice. The obverse of a series of Thessalonian coins shows the laureate head of Caesar and carries the legend THEOS (god). The reverse displays the bare head of Octavian with the legend THESSALONIKEŌN (of the Thessalonians). While the title "son of god" (*theou huios*) does not appear on the reverse, the juxtaposition of Divine Julius with his son probably implies Thessalonian awareness of the honorific title (Hendrix 1984, 170–73). An innovation on a conventional coin issue might point to the divinization of Augustus. On the obverse, the head of Augustus with the legend KAISAR SEBASTOS (Caesar Augustus)—the reverse being a prow with the city legend THESSALONIKEŌN—displaces the head of Zeus on earlier Zeus/prow issues (Hendrix 1984, 179). However, in this instance, the Thessalonians might have only been making the more modest claim that Augustus's exercise of his imperium (power) was "Zeus-like."

Last, Paul's apocalyptic gospel competed with the Augustan conception of rule and its propagandist manipulation by his imperial successors. The Thessalonian politarchs accused Paul, Silas, and their converts of "acting against the decrees of Caesar, saying there is another king, Jesus" (Acts 17:7; cf. 16:21). E. A. Judge (2008, 456–62; *pace* Oakes 2005) contends that the Thessalonian charge is to be understood against the backdrop of the provincial loyalty oaths to the Caesars (e.g., Aritium [Herrmann 1968, 125–26 §6]; Samos [Mitford 1960]; Res gest. divi Aug. 25). Karl Donfried (1985, 349–50) links the persecution of the Thessalonian believers (1 Thess 1:6; 2:14; 3:3b–4) and the deaths mentioned in 1 Thess 4:13–18 to the requirement of the Paphlagonian loyalty oath to Augustus and his descendants (*OGIS* 532; 6 March 3 BCE) that all cases of disloyalty had to be reported and the offenders hunted down. But our text is silent as to whether the combined Jewish and Roman action against the Thessalonian believers did in fact result in martyrdom. There may or may not have been martyrs at Thessalonica. But there can be little doubt that the disciplinary measures undertaken against them would have been severe. Thus the Thessalonian Jews fulfilled the spirit of the imperial loyalty oaths in searching for Paul and Silas at Jason's house (Acts 17:5), reporting the Thessalonian believers to the politarchs (Acts 17:6–9), and then pursuing Paul to Berea with the same intent (17:13; see de Vos 1999, 157–58; Still 1999, 74–78, 150–90). In the view of the Thessalonian Jews, the apostles were preaching a pretender king, Jesus, and had urged the Thessalonian and Berean citizens to violate their oaths of allegiance to the emperor.

The Imperial Context of 1 Thess 4:6–5:11 and 2 Thess 2:1–11

In the much-discussed passage of 1 Thess 4:6–5:11, we need only sum-
marize what has been, until very recently, the broad consensus regarding
the imperial terminological resonances of the pericope (Harrison 2011b,
47–69). In a clever overlap of Jewish apocalyptic (Harrison 2011b, 51 n.
18) and imperial terminology, Paul sets forth the surety of the Christian
hope in the face of the unexpected death of believers. The hope is fulfilled
in the risen Christ of the house of David rather than in the counterfeit
gospel of the Julio-Claudian house, with (at the time of Paul's writing) its
apotheosis of Julius Caesar and Augustus, celebrated on the Thessalonian
coinage, as well as the promise of "peace and security" for its clients. The
terminology—bypassing *kyrios* (Lord), discussed above—is as follows:

- *Parousia* (coming, 1 Thess 4:15): the word was used of the visits
  of imperial dignitaries (e.g., Germanicus, Nero, Hadrian) to cities
  and provinces. Paul's use of *parousia* established the total superiority of Christ's "return" as the risen Lord of all in comparison to
  the much-feted visits of imperial luminaries.
- *Apantēsis* (meeting, 4:17): the word was employed for the civic
  welcome or triumphal entry of a visiting dignitary or new ruler
  to the capital of a city (e.g., Julius Caesar, Titus Caesar). By contrast, nobody in the cosmos would miss the eschatological return
  of Christ to earth.
- *Eirēnē kai asphaleia* (peace and security, 5:3): this (so-called) technical term of imperial propaganda (contra White 2013) sums up
  the benefits offered to the clients of the imperial authorities and
  encapsulates the seductive idolatry of imperial patronage to be
  resisted by believers (see also 2 Thess 3:6–10).
- *Sōtēria* (salvation, 5:8b, 9b): the soteriological language of the
  Hellenistic ruler cult was transferred to the house of the caesars
  in the Greek East by its clients, thereby colliding with Jewish and
  early Christian soteriology.
- *Elpis* (hope, 5:8b): the personified virtue *Spes* (hope) belonged to
  the Claudian numismatic propaganda as early as 41 CE and stood
  in contrast to the eschatological hope in Christ held out by the
  apostle (Míguez 2012).

Last, in 2 Thess 2:8, Paul speaks about the revelation of the "lawless one" thus: "And then the lawless one [*ho anomos*] will be revealed, whom the Lord Jesus will destroy with the breath of his mouth, annihilating him by the manifestation of his coming [*epiphaneia tēs parousias autou*]."

Does Paul's language of Christ's "epiphany" and the destruction of the "lawless one" in 2 Thess 2:8 (see also 2:3; see Harrison 2011b, 71–95) carry imperial overtones for his first-century auditors? The language of "lawlessness" would have reminded auditors of Caligula and, previously, Pompey (Pss. Sol. 17.11–15). The "lawlessness" of the Roman ruler, seen recently in his attempted profanation of the temple in 40 CE (2 Thess 2:3–4; Philo, *Embassy* 203–346; Josephus, *Ant.* 18.2–8 §§261–301; see Mark 13:14, 21–22), pointed to the "mystery of lawlessness" currently engulfing the empire of Rome (2 Thess 2:7). Since Philo had made a similar point about the "lawlessness" of Caligula (*Embassy* 119; see also Pss. Sol. 17.11–15) barely a decade before, it should hardly surprise us to find Paul adapting contemporary Jewish political polemic against the Roman ruler for his own eschatological ends in 2 Thess 2:7.

Finally, the language of epiphany, while having Maccabean precedents (Harrison 2011b, 87–89), was also applied to Caligula, as well as to other Roman rulers (Harrison 2012, 73–75). Before his assassination, the Roman ruler had attempted to erect his gold statue in the Jerusalem temple as "Gaius the new Zeus made manifest" (Philo, *Embassy* 346; *Dios Epiphanous Neou chrēmatizē Gaiou*). *Epiphaneia*, too, was used for the accession of Caligula in an inscription from Cos (LSJ, *epiphaneia* 2.4; *Inscr. Cos* 391: "[the] epiphany of Germanicus Augustus" [*Germnaikou Sebastou epiphaneia*]). In sum, Paul's description of the "epiphany" of the "lawless one" would have recalled several famous figures of hubris (Harrison 2011b, 75–77), including Caligula, alerting his auditors of the present and future dangers of unrestrained human arrogance.

Conclusion

As Paul's missionary outreach moved from Asia Minor into northern Greece, the challenge posed by the ideology of the imperial cult and its offer of peace, security, and prosperity for its clients remained as potent as ever. Paul's eschatological gospel provided him with the ideological and pastoral resources not only to challenge its idolatrous and seductive claims but also to establish within the body of Christ a radical alternative in social relations to the self-seeking, hierarchical, and status-conscious society of the Caesars.

For Further Reading

Bakirtzis, Charalambos, and Helmut Koester, eds. 1998. *Philippi at the Time of Paul and after His Death*. Harrisburg, PA: Trinity Press International.

Fantin, Joseph D. 2011. *The Lord of the Entire World: Lord Jesus, a Challenge to Lord Caesar?* NTMS 31. Sheffield: Sheffield Phoenix.

Hardin, Justin K. 2008. *Galatians and the Imperial Cult: A Critical Analysis of the First-Century Social Context of Paul's Letter*. WUNT 2/237. Tübingen: Mohr Siebeck.

Harrison, James R. 2011. *Paul and the Imperial Authorities at Thessalonica and Rome: A Study in the Conflict of Ideology*. WUNT 273. Tübingen: Mohr Siebeck.

Hellerman, Joseph H. 2005. *Reconstructing Honor in Roman Philippi: Carmen Christi as Cursus Pudorum*. SNTSMS 132. Cambridge: Cambridge University Press.

Judge, E. A. 2008. *The First Christians in the Roman World: Augustan and New Testament Essays*. Edited by James R. Harrison. WUNT 229. Tübingen: Mohr Siebeck.

Kahl, Brigitte. 2010. *Galatians Re-imagined: Reading with the Eyes of the Vanquished*. Minneapolis: Fortress.

Lopez, Davina C. 2008. *Apostle to the Conquered: Reimagining Paul's Mission*. Minneapolis: Fortress.

Mitchell, Stephen, and Marc Waelkens. 1998. *Pisidian Antioch: The Site and Its Monuments*. London: Duckworth.

Still, Todd D. 1999. *Conflict at Thessalonica: A Pauline Church and Its Neighbours*. JSNTSup 183. Sheffield: Sheffield Academic.

COLOSSIANS, EPHESIANS, AND EMPIRE

Harry O. Maier

The quest for Paul in empire has largely passed over Colossians and Ephesians (Lull 2010, 252–62). There are at least two reasons for this. First, the focus on the relationship of Paul to politics in general and the Roman Empire in particular has been directed almost exclusively to the seven letters scholars believe Paul most probably wrote. The Paul and Politics section of the Society of Biblical Literature, which has given attention to the topic for over twenty years, attends to these earlier, not later letters. Many scholars, including this one, argue that Paul did not write Colossians and Ephesians and that the presence of peculiar syntax, ideas, and perspectives not present in the earlier corpus furnish sufficient warrant to question whether the apostle wrote them.[1] The second reason is probably more subtle: these letters espouse a series of ideas that many see as a capitulation to imperial ideas and imperial thinking. Scholars have been more interested in determining how Paul opposed the Roman Empire than the ways he may have embraced it (e.g., Crossan and Reed 2004). This in turn speaks to a number of political commitments many exegetes have that go beyond the traditional limits of biblical exegesis. Some discover a capitulation to empire and betrayal of the "authentic" Paul in the hierarchical household codes of Colossians and Ephesians (Col 3:18–4:1; Eph 5:21–6:9; for example, N. Elliott 2006, 25–54). Whereas an earlier Paul represented all hierarchical institutions as about to be swept away in the imminent second coming of Jesus (1 Cor 7:29–31), these letters appear to adopt the top-down organization of the Hellenistic-Roman household as a chief organizing principle of Pauline

---

1. The reasons for questioning Paul's authorship of Colossians and Ephesians are outlined elsewhere and will not be rehearsed here; for further discussion with bibliography, see MacDonald 2008, 6–29.

churches under a process of institutionalization. I will return to discuss the household codes in due course, but here it is sufficient to observe that for those seeking to discover in the New Testament freedom from hierarchy and traditional institutional ways of thinking, these tables of duties have not been promising.

Although a reading of Colossians and Ephesians in the context of the Roman Empire remains largely unexplored, there is much in these letters that commends them for attention. As the following discussion will show, the letters' vocabulary, metaphor, ideals, theological affirmations, and ethical teachings are heavily indebted to what we may describe broadly as a Roman imperial point of view. The point in what follows is not to argue that the Roman Empire "caused" the disputed letters of Colossians and Ephesians. Talk of "the Roman Empire," which is already a very abstract concept, is fraught with the perils of oversimplification and anachronism. Whatever else the Roman Empire was, it was a social and political order as complicated and contradictory as our own. Further, historical causation is difficult—some might even argue impossible—to determine, especially from a far-removed perspective with such little data as we have when we come to exegete and interpret these letters. The argument in what follows is rather that, when we read Colossians and Ephesians in the context of imperial language, imagery, and conceptualization, we discover how much they are entangled in the political worldview around them, an order that was inscribed in the material culture of everyday life in the peoples and cultures that constituted what today we name the Roman Empire.

A General Imperial Orientation to Colossians and Ephesians

At their most general level, the letters show their imperial provenance. First, they are addressed to urban inhabitants living in cities of western Asia Minor. The writer of Colossians expects his letter will be read to Christ followers in Colossae and neighboring churches in Laodicea and Hierapolis, three cities close to one another at the Lycus Valley in the Roman province of Phrygia. Shared location along a north-south and east-west road network joined these cities. Ephesians, although perhaps not written to the Roman Asian city of Ephesus (see below), reveals itself closely related to Colossians. Shared vocabulary, ecclesiology, eschatology, ethical ideals, and even word-for-word agreement convince many that the writer of Ephesians copied directly from Colossians (MacDonald 2008, 4–6). Others argue these writers belonged to a kind of "Pauline school" and drew on a shared storehouse of teachings in composing their letters (Trebilco 2004, 92–94). At a more general level, however, evidence of shared vocabulary and so on expresses something one fails to see without attention to imperial context. For the Phrygian and Asian cities of western Asia Minor were bound together by treaties, trade, a network of Roman roads, and even rivalries for imperial honors, such as the privilege of hosting the imperial cult or games in the emperor's honor. These letters show evidence of the interconnected world of the Roman Empire; their recurring life situation is city life. It is one of the reasons why we can see so much imperial language and civic vocabulary in these documents. While they invoke battle imagery—another imperial aspect of them, as we will see—their eschatology is otherwise peaceable. There is not the sharp apocalyptic focus of the type we see in 1 Thess 4:13–5:11. There, Jesus's coming is likened to an imperial *adventus* with civic dignitaries going out to meet him (4:17). In Colossians and Ephesians, there is a sense that the eschaton has already arrived and that Christ followers are enjoying its benefits. This would not have been a foreign concept to the Greek, Roman, and indigenous populations of Roman Asia and Phrygia. When these letters were written, these people had not seen war for over a century; the imperial imagery and language that bathed their daily lives expressed that a world of peace and good order had arrived with a Roman rule sanctioned by the gods. Roman rule and colonization were often brutal, of course, but it is notable that no aspect of this appears in the letters. Rather their content might suggest the audiences have absorbed the more irenic aspects of Roman rule. If so, they were not alone. The message of Roman peace and triumph was so ubiquitous and frequent that scholars have argued that it penetrated the very subconscious of the Roman world's inhabitants (see, e.g., Zanker 1988, 265–95). We should not think that Christ followers were exempt from this, even as today we take certain things for granted as just the way things are. Colossians and Ephesians nowhere expressly endorse the imperial order and organization of the world, but the benefits of Christ's present, this-worldly reign were no doubt rendered more comprehensible because of them, even if unconsciously.

Like the rest of the letters that constitute the Pauline corpus, these are occasional writings. They are written for an audience to persuade them of certain things. Colossians conforms to the pattern of a typical Hellenistic-Roman symboleutic/deliberative letter, specifically that of paraenesis or exhortation (Stowers 1989, 91–106). That is, it focuses its attention on advising a body of first-century Christ followers to conform

to a certain set of teachings and behaviors. Its chief interest is polemical: it seeks to persuade listeners (for the letter would have been read
aloud to a congregation of believers, probably meeting in a house church
[4:15]) to avoid teachings the letter describes as "philosophy and empty
deceit" (Col 2:8).

The classification of Ephesians is a far more complex matter, since it is
not clear that it is indeed a letter (for suggestions, see Hendrix 1988, 3–15).
It lacks the typical features of the Greco-Roman letter, not to mention the
characteristic elements one finds in the undisputed Pauline Letters; for
example, it has no greeting section at its closing (Eph 6:23). An important manuscript difference makes it uncertain that the letter was originally
addressed to Christ followers in Ephesus. It falls outside the discussion
here to determine the precise genre of Ephesians. Suffice to state that it
has been championed variously as a letter, an encyclical, a sermon, and
a speech, to name only a few. Nor is it entirely certain what the treatise
is trying to achieve: some argue that is seeks to create a more inclusive
climate for Christ-following Jews and others that is trying to do the same
for Christ-following gentiles (MacDonald 2008, 253–59; Yee 2005, 32–33).
With good reason, it has been called a treatise in search of a setting (R.
Martin 1968, 296–302), and this essay does not attempt to determine that
situation, although my own preference is to read it as a kind of encomium
that celebrates an inclusive community of Jews and gentiles as the preeminent hallmark of Pauline identity.

What is of critical importance for the subject treated here is the recognition that these writings can and should be read against the backdrop
of Roman imperial language, metaphor, and political values. Without
recourse to such a reading, the letters are not as well interpreted as they
might be. This is not to argue that one should only attend to imperial elements in these documents. Other considerations such as the relationship
of the "letters" to the Hebrew Bible are equally necessary and important
for accurate exegesis and interpretation. Attention to Roman imperial
notions serves to enhance and reinforce the richness of readings centered
on comparison with other Jewish documents.

In what follows, I begin by situating each letter in what I describe
as an "imperial situation." I then elucidate the way imperial vocabulary,
especially political language, metaphor, narrative, and imagery, helps to
advance their respective persuasive strategies. I then step back to consider
the documents against a general imperial backdrop to assess their respective place in the urban world of the Roman Empire.

Imperial Situation

In order fully to gauge the presence and role of imperial ideas in Colossians and Ephesians, as well as the letters' relation to larger realities of imperial rule, it is necessary to understand the ways in which they seek to persuade their audiences of particular realities and ideals. I use the phrase "imperial situation" as a means of achieving that goal. At the most general, it acknowledges from the outset that Colossians and Ephesians, whatever their particular goals, represent realities inhabiting and being shaped by an overarching imperial world. The imperial world was inescapable for ancient audiences as the capitalist world is for our own. Moreover, the audiences of these letters lived in cities of the Roman Empire that, like all cities of the time, were particularly attuned to imperial political realities. As city dwellers, they shared with other residents a series of urban experiences, political expectations, civic ideals, and religious ideas that had for many generations been shaped by relations with Rome and the economic and social concerns that went along with them. Not all of these would have been conscious, but some of them were, and we can see evidence of that in the both letters discussed here. Indeed, all of Paul's letters reflect an urban imprint and show how steeped its audiences were in civic realities of their day.

More precisely, "imperial situation" refers to the uses of rhetoric to place the audiences of Colossians and Ephesians in a particular formulation of the world around them. The phrase builds on a concept developed by a modern scholar of rhetorical speech, Lloyd Bitzer (1968, 1–18). He coined the term "rhetorical situation" to describe how rhetoric—the art of persuasion—places speaker and listener in a shared situation that a particular instance of hortatory speech is designed to address and to persuade an audience as true. "Rhetorical situation" describes "a complex of persons, events, objects, and relations presenting an actual or potential exigence which can be completely or partially removed if discourse, introduced into the situation, can so constrain human decision or action as to bring about the significant modification of the exigence" (3). In other words, rhetoric creates a problem or situation that the rhetoric is designed to address and inform or resolve. Central to Bitzer's concept is "exigence," which describes the real or potential challenge to which rhetoric addresses itself. "Rhetorical situation" describes a real setting that requires address: "What is a rhetorical situation? I want to know the nature of those contexts in which speakers or writers create rhetorical discourse: How should they be described? What are their characteristics? Why and how do they result in the creation of rhetoric?" (1). A rhetorical situation mirrors an empirical reality that merits a response: "The presence of rhetorical discourse obviously indicates the presence of a rhetorical situation" (2). Among other examples of rhetorical situation, he cites the occasion of Lincoln's Gettysburg Address and John F. Kennedy's inaugural address and observes that "each is a clear instance of rhetoric and each indicates the presence of a situation" (2).

Building on Bitzer's notion, I use the phrase "imperial situation" to describe the ways in which Paul uses political language, metaphor, and narratives and ideals in his tactics of persuasion. "Situation" here refers to two realities. The first refers to the life situations of the audiences of Colossians and Ephesians as urban life settings. This is the general backdrop of the letters as indicated above. The second sense of situation refers to the ways in which the letters use language, create arguments, and represent the listeners of each of the letters. Here the letters create a world even as they reflect one; they seek to persuade listeners that they inhabit a series of overarching cosmic and ethical realities. To do so they draw on shared experiences, vocabulary, beliefs, and expectations in order to make the arguments and descriptions of each letter persuasive. Central to this sense of imperial situations is a host of terms, concepts, images, and ideals that were well known to and shared by the Roman imperial city dwellers as part of their daily urban experiences and understandings. Imperial cities were awash with images celebrating imperial rule and reminders of Rome's right to rule the world (Whittaker 1997, 145). No one who lived in these cities could have escaped those representations. They accompanied urban dwellers wherever they went: in the market, at the public bath, on coins, through temples and public monuments, and—for those who could read— on the ubiquitous inscriptions that were central to an urban culture of civic honors and benefactions. Paul and his successors could count on—to the degree they were consciously and not simply unconsciously deploying such language and slogans—their audiences to recognize and immediately envision representations of ideas cast in imperial language and metaphor. Paul's letters in general reflect such an urban imperial situation wherever the apostle uses terms at home in the larger civic world of his audiences. The terms are not limited to imperial urban usage and meanings; they also have meanings in other contexts such as Jewish, philosophical, and Greco-Roman religious contexts. Nevertheless, it is important to recognize their political valences so as to place such terms within their widest social and semantic horizons. The uses of political language such as savior (*sōtēr*), salvation (*sōtēria*), Gospel (*euangelion*), peace (*eirēnē*), Son of God (*huios tou theou*), Lord (*kyrios*), parousia (*parousia*), reconciliation and cognates (*katallagē*), ambassador and cognates (*presbeia*), as well as terms such as church (*ekklēsia*), body (of Christ) (*sōma* [*tou christou*]), and citizenship (*politeuma*), are a few more prevalent instances that reflect borrowing and application to his proclamation, instruction, and exhortation. Further, metaphors such as slave of Christ (*doulos tou christou*), going out to meet the Lord (*apantēsin tou kyriou*), citizenship in heaven (*to politeuma en ouranois*), and to lead in triumph (*thrambeuein*) reflect Paul's urban and Roman political context. These are but a few of the instances of political images and vocabulary that pepper Paul's letters. The use of such terms helped to create audiences and to cast them as characters inhabiting overarching political narratives.

It is not surprising the generation of Christ followers who succeeded Paul and who sought to further his aims and promote his understanding of the gospel developed the legacy of imperial vocabulary and conceptualizations the apostle drew on to persuade his audiences. The authors of Colossians and Ephesians placed their audiences in imperial situations, albeit of a very different sort, but with the similar goal of helping them affirm their identity and to live out religious ideals consistent with larger cosmic truths as well as social and theological affirmations.

Vivid Language, Imperial Situation, and Persuasive Strategy

Consideration of the imperial situation Colossians and Ephesians place their audiences within entails recognition of the vivid language the letters use as tools of persuasion. An ancient ideal of rhetoric was to turn listeners into viewers through the use of vivid speech (Robbins 2008, 81–106; Webb 2009, 87–130). The hearers of these letters inhabited an oral/aural culture. Elementary handbooks in rhetorical instruction taught students to learn how to use evocative or graphic speech to help listeners not just hear but also to see subjects treated in declamation (Kennedy 2003, ix–xiv). *Ekphrasis* is a technical term used in this literature to describe the function of vivid speech in making ideas persuasive. First-century handbooks and treatises—that is, literature contemporary with Colossians and Ephesians—define *ekphrasis* as a form of speech through which the speaker brings to sight what is discussed. The mid- to late first-century rhetor Aelius Theon defines *ekphrasis* as "descriptive language, bringing what is portrayed vividly before the sight" (*Progymnasmata* 7; Kennedy 2003, 45). This definition is presumed by other instructors in rhetoric such as the first-century orator Quintilian, who argues that in using vivid speech it is important that the rhetor not depart very far from the experience of listeners even as she or he relies on listeners to fill in details drawn from their own experiences of the topic the speech treats (*Inst.* 8.3.71).

Attention to vivid speech and the role of visualization in Colossians and Ephesians is important, because the letters deploy recognizable political language in passages of vivid description. From a rhetorical standpoint, the authors of these letters invite their audiences to imagine the topics raised. They encourage visualization of a variety of topics, some of them cosmic in scope (Col 1:15–20; Eph 1:3–10), and as they do so they do not range very far from lived civic experiences of political realities, specifically Roman imperial notions of victory, peace, universal rule, and so on. Thus the imperial situations in which the letters place their listeners draw on lived political realities at home in their civic world and experiences. Attention to such realities enables us to recognize the degree to which the letters and their listeners are entangled with imperial realities. A consequence of this is to contest any straightforward formulation of Paul and his successors being "for" or "against" the Roman Empire; rather, all are implicated even at their most oppositional in imperial realities through their use of political language for purposes of teaching, description, exhortation, and instruction. One of the chief challenges of an imperial interpretation of Colossians and Ephesians, as well as of Paul's letters generally, is to understand how such language was borrowed and developed, so as to uncover strategic means by which the apostle and his successors used it to persuade listeners of their teachings.

Imperial Situation in Colossians as Polemical Rhetorical Strategy

Colossians is a polemical letter that places its audiences in an imperial situation in order to demonstrate that their religious identity as converts from Hellenistic-Roman polytheism obliges them to worship and devote themselves to Christ alone. The author represents Christ followers as the beneficiaries of a triumphal rule of God in Christ. It falls outside the limits of this discussion to speculate concerning the precise identity and origins of the teaching that the author calls "philosophy and empty deceit" (Col 2:8; for discussion see Arnold 1996; Sumney 2008, 10–12, with bibliography). He includes in the list false ideas that belong to his opponents' dietary regulations, monthly rituals, worship of angels, and asceticism (2:16, 18, 21–23). These the author relates to "the elements of the universe [*ta stoicheia tou kosmou*]" (2:20) as well as to "principalities and powers [*hai archai kai hai exousiai*]" (2:15). The author's polemical strategy is to assign "the elements of the universe" that direct such beliefs and practices to a middle spatial position below the divine realm, where God rules, and above the earthly realm, where they have exercised power. They have come into being through and for the Son, who is their Creator (1:16), and by the cross they have been defeated and have been led in triumphal procession as the sign of their conquest (2:15). Thus those who are baptized have no reason to submit themselves to any kind of ascetical or devotional practices. Since they have been united in baptism with Christ and they have thus been enthroned with the raised Christ, who is seated at the right hand of God (3:1, 3), they enjoy a spatially superior position with respect to cosmic powers. They must therefore not submit themselves to powers that are below them. The result of the letter is a pronounced verticality. A futurist eschatology one encounters in the earlier Pauline corpus (e.g., 1 Cor 15:21–28) becomes spatialized into a tripartite stratification with God and Christ ruling over the cosmos and all the creation below them.

We can take up Colossian deployment of vivid imperial language and metaphor under three broad headings: cosmic, geopolitical, and moral. Such language runs as a red thread throughout the letter and reflects the imprint of Roman religion in general, where one discovers a similar binding together of universal, political, and ethical claims.

At a cosmic level, the very representation of cosmic creation as designated by the creation of the cosmos, "whether thrones or dominions or principalities or authorities [*eite thronoi eite kyriotētes eite archai eite exousiai*]" (1:16), invokes a series of political terms. In the so-called Christ hymn (Col 1:15–20), where these terms appear, their inherent political valence becomes explicit at two points. First, at 1:19 the author celebrates the death of Christ "making peace by the blood of the cross [*eirēnopoiēsas dia tou haimatos tou staurou autou*]." Second, the author describes this peace as "reconciliation [*apokatallaxai*]," both in 1:19 and 1:22. Such reconciliation is cosmic in 1:19 and social in 1:22: the Colossian listeners were "once estranged and hostile in mind [*pote ontas apēllotriōmenous kai echthrous tē dianoia*]." This represents a complex of ideas a first-century audience would immediately have recognized as shot through with imperial meaning and imagery. Emperors and their supporters regularly championed their divinely appointed right to pacify the nations through diplomacy where possible and violence where necessary (Mazel 1984, 1–20). On this view, the rightly governed world expresses a terrestrial freedom from conflict and political harmony, which mirrors a heavenly concord that expresses the *pax deorum*, or "peace of the gods" (Zanker 1988, 167–238). Pacification describes the subordination of vice by virtue and of rebellion by that power which can impose peace and harmony. Thus when the author describes the audience as "once estranged and hostile in mind" (again with political terms of civic strife and faction), he is carrying the theme forward: those who are rebels and resistant to imperial rule are those removed from peace both internally among themselves and externally with respect to Roman rule. When the author describes reconciliation as both a cosmic (1:19) and social achievement (1:22), he uses the technical vocabulary of diplomacy as the achievement of the end of war through an embassy sent by the vanquished to sue for terms of peace (Breytenbach 2010, 171–86; Bash 1997, 98–99). However, in Colossians the normal ritual of peace is overturned through the invocation of the cross: it is through the blood of the cross that reconciliation unfolds. In the normal application, it would be the cosmic powers that would sue for peace by sending an embassy. In Colossians, in a way that is nowhere precisely explained, it is rather the vanquished on the cross that accomplishes pacification and reconciliation. This is an inversion that no listener of the letter could have failed to notice.

The same paradoxical affirmation appears in Col 2:15, where the author presents a picture of cosmic peace. Here, again, we encounter an image of pacification through the image of a Roman triumph (Maier 2013, 67–71). The NRSV translation reads: "He disarmed the principalities and powers and made a public example of them, triumphing over them in it." The linking of crucifixion with peace in imperial ideology usually represents the pacification of enemies through execution. Triumph, an imperial religious ritual of parading of conquered enemies through the streets of Rome, was a way of celebrating a divinely appointed victory. Here the triumph occurs not through the vanquishing of enemies but through the crucifixion of Jesus, after which there is a triumphal parade. Colossians is clear that the exaltation of Jesus as enthronement at the right hand of God (3:1) confirms all of this. The author nowhere explains the mechanism by which this can be true, and this has given rise to centuries of theological speculation and exploration.

The author invokes a geopolitical achievement at Col 3:11, where he acclaims, "Here there can be neither Greek and Jew, circumcised and uncircumcised, barbarian, Scythian, slave, freedperson, but Christ is all, and in all." This is a significant revision of the baptismal formula of Gal 3:27–29; the Colossian formula notably omits "no longer male and female" from the inherited passage. Colossians' author here transforms the Galatian affirmation of the removal of all social distinctions toward one that expresses a territorial and political reach of Christ's rule. This we can see with the reference to "barbarian, Scythian, slave, freedperson." Again this is vivid language. First-century listeners were well prepared by monumental culture as well as daily experience in the public arena, where brutal spectacles pitted conquered peoples against one another or animals, instantly to imagine barbarians and Scythians as vanquished peoples pacified by imperial rule (see Maier 2013, 77–80, for images). Scythians in imperial imagination were a people at the furthest reach of civilization who inhabited a fantasy space of absolute moral turpitude and indecency (Braund 1986, 31–49). In Col 3:11, the author mirrors a celebration of Roman imperial rule as the geopolitical extension of a divinely arranged order of peace and prosperity. Here, however, it is not the Romans who extend this rule, but Christ, so that there is no portion of the globe where his reign does not reach. The same geopolitical claim appears in 1:6, where "Paul" describes "the gospel" that has come to the audiences "as indeed in the whole world it is bearing fruit and growing." The metaphor is at home in a celebration of imperial rule as "good news" associated with agricultural abundance and human fertility. Taken together with the geopolitical language that appears later in 3:11, it is clear how Colossians places its listeners into an immediately recognizable imperial situation; they are the beneficiaries of an imperial rule of Christ even as they are the audiences he has pacified to incorporate them into his empire-wide reign.

This rule expresses itself in a new moral order. The author uses vivid terms associated with civil strife and faction to describe the listeners' former lives (3:5–8) and exhorts them to pursue virtues that leads to concord (3:12–14). He deploys the striking image of putting off old garments and putting on new clothing and being well dressed. The link between virtue and proper dress was a repeated theme in imperial iconography, where imperial civilization was associated with properly arranged clothing and barbarian identity with improper comportment (Canavan 2012, 67–133). In 3:15, he represents these virtues imperially by exhorting the audience to "let the peace of Christ rule in your hearts [*kai he eirēnē tou christou brabeuetō en tais kardiais hymōn*]." The peace the author promotes is the ethical expression of virtue that reflects the civilizing rule of Christ.

The author outlines the precise behaviors Christ followers are to pursue in the household code (3:18–4:1). The code belongs to a rhetorical topos that recurs in both Jewish and Greek literature to describe the duties owing each rank of the household to its superior, organized typically from the top down (wives to husbands, children to fathers, slaves to masters; Crouch 1972). Colossians' author follows this organization but changes it significantly by introducing reciprocal obligations of husbands to wives, parents to children, and masters to slaves. In the imperial situation the letter places the audience in, the household code functions to identify the ethics that contribute to and express the overarching reign of Christ and the social goods that arise from it. In the larger social theorization of the state, the harmonious household is the chief building block for the rightly functioning state. Here the author draws on the topos to describe the properly governed church. To first-century listeners of the letter living in a Roman province absorbed into the empire, where monuments, coins, and other visual media celebrated the harmonious state with images of the imperial family in harmony with one another (D'Ambra 1993, 78–103), Colossians' vivid topos would have brought a variety of pictures to mind. Combined with the cosmic and geopolitical images of imperial rule, the household code would have urged listeners to imagine their ecclesial communities as inhabiting an ethical order expressive of a divine dominion. The author joined together graphic imperial terms and metaphors to persuade Christ followers inhabiting Roman Phrygia that they were beneficiaries of the cosmic and global rule of God, embodied by them in dedication to harmony-promoting social ideals and patterns of behavior.

An Imperial Situation of Concord in the Letter to the Ephesians

Unlike Colossians, the Letter to the Ephesians is not a polemical letter. While there have been several attempts to identity a rhetorical exigence the letter seeks to resolve, any solution remains hypothetical at best (for different theories, see Maier 2013, 104–6). This treatment does not endorse any of the reigning hypotheses or promote a new one, but rather observes how the letter uses imperial language, image, and concepts to describe its listeners. As literary dependence on Colossians is arguable or even probable, it is no surprise that the repertoire of imperial ideas found in the earlier letter should appear at least in part in Ephesians. But Ephesians does more than quote Colossians. It appropriates Colossians' imperial language and concepts identified above and deploys them to express a unique imperial situation that casts its audiences on a new horizon of identity and meaning. The overarching imperial situation Ephesians casts its audiences within is one in which Christ followers enjoy the benefits of civic concord that has been won through the death and exaltation of Jesus, so that followers inhabit an order that transforms traditional ethnic boundaries and rivalries and fuses all people into an overarching unity. The author draws on imperial, civic, and political vocabulary, imagery, and ideas to celebrate the unity achieved through the Jesus event. We see this in the representation of the church as the site of civic unity, the imagery of cosmic unity in the body of Christ, as well as in the celebration of unity more generally.

I use the term "audiences" in the last paragraph advisedly: it is unclear that the letter's address to an audience in Ephesus is original. Textual variants may indicate that the reference to Ephesus in 1:1 is a later addition to the text. Without taking up theories that the letter originated as an encyclical (for discussion, MacDonald 2008, 191–96), it is possible that the document was heard in various communities. The textual evidence is too ambiguous to determine the validity of such a theory one way or the other, but it points to an imperial situation of universal concord that frames the letter as a whole. Roman imperial propagandists celebrated both the imperial family as well as the unity of peoples brought under its imperium as evidencing and sharing an empire-wide civic harmony and the end of faction. The cities of western Asia Minor, where Ephesus is located, issued coins to mark an end to rivalries that sometimes divided them. These are called *homonoia* issues, and they communicate an ideal of freedom from faction and rivalry (Lotz 1999, 173–88). Alongside these coins was a series of speeches by orators contemporary with the letter to the Ephesians designed to promote cooperation between cities and the cessation of hostilities that contributed to faction and rivalry (for discussion with literature, see Maier 2013, 107–18). In these speeches, as on the coins marking treaties, the theme that dominates is that humans are to imitate nature by living civic relationships marked by social harmony, an identity that imitates various forms of natural, cosmic, and indeed divine unity, and a concord that arises out of a shared humankind.

Ephesians shows the imprint of a political theology of concord where it celebrates the Christ event as the end of ethnic rivalry between Jews and gentiles. In 2:11–21, the author deploys a series of vivid images to invite listeners to envision civic concord: the breaking down of a dividing wall of hostility (2:14), the creation of one body through the cross (2:16), the creation of a new building or temple that celebrates an organic unity of believers (2:19–21). The passage reinforces concord imagery by drawing on Jewish representation of the division of humankind: Paul represents listeners as "gentiles in the flesh" alienated from "the commonwealth of Israel and strangers to the covenants of promise [*apēllotriōmenoi tēs politeias tou Israēl kai xenoi tōn diathēkōn tēs epangelias*]" (2:11–12). Scholars rightly identify this passage as the very center of Ephesians but have not adequately assessed the presence of imperial ideas in these critical verses (exceptions include Faust 1993; Gupta and Long 2010; Muddiman 2001, 114–37). The author supplements Jewish designations to portray non-Jewish listeners with a host of political terms to describe the former divisions and the new identity of unity Jews and gentiles enjoy. Thus on the one side non-Jews are aliens and strangers (2:11–12, 19) and "sojourners [*paroikoi*]"; Jews and non-Jews were hostile to one another (2:16). The death of Jesus has made former rivals "co-citizens [*sympolitai*]" (2:19). What makes this a particularly imperial presentation is the author's reference to the Jesus event as making and proclaiming peace (*poiōn eirēnēn*; *euēngelisato eirēnēn*, 2:15, 17).

As in Colossians, the author invokes a Roman imperial ideology of pacification as well as the "gospel" of peace to show how rivals have become co-citizens. Also like Colossians, the author transforms a Roman ideology of imposed peace as the sign of cessation of hostility to a peace won through the death of Jesus (2:13, 15, 16). "He is our peace" (2:14). This is an inversion no less dramatic than the one we encounter in Col 2:15. That inversion Ephesians makes even more startling where it casts Paul in the role of "ambassador in chains" (6:20). As I indicated above, ambassadors were typically sent out by the defeated party to the victorious one to sue for peace; Ephesians here mirrors typical expectations. But it is clear from the overall logic of the letter that it is the defeated one who brings about peace as a mode of pacification. This again is paradoxical when considered in the light of normal imperial experience. Ephesians is the one, after all, that promotes the preaching of peace to those far and those near of Eph 2:17. Taken as a whole, Ephesians appropriates ideals of civic and imperial concord realized in the church, which it celebrates as the site of the realization of one new humanity. Like Colossians, Ephesians spatializes a temporal formulation and also makes a transformation of creation in the earlier Pauline letters (Rom 8:18–23; 1 Cor 15:28; 2 Cor 5:17) into an achievement found specifically in the church (Eph 2:19–21).

Pacification themes also appear in a remarkable appropriation of divine-victory motifs. In Eph 4:8–14, the author cites Ps 68:18, which is itself an invocation of victory theology: here a royal psalm celebrates the king as leading a triumphal procession of conquered captives to Zion and receiving gifts, namely, seized booty, from them. Ephesians reverses this by portraying the death and ascension of Jesus as a triumphal procession where gifts are distributed; the spoils of victory here are spiritual gifts and offices for the building of the church. A first-century audience primed by triumphal imagery in a variety of media in urban settings would have been impressed by this application of victory theology. Closer to the victory motif is the ritual enactment of triumph where the conqueror dispenses spoils of victory and payment to his army, a motif that recurs in imperial art across the empire (for images and discussion, see Maier 2013, 135–36).

On the other side of military imagery, namely, that of ongoing battle, one sees further borrowing from a theology of victory. Ephesians offers an ekphrastic depiction of the armor of God (6:10–17), where the author enjoins believers to fight against "the world rulers of this present darkness, chains the spiritual hosts of wickedness in the heavenly places." Ubiquitous images of trophies and despoiled weapons primed a first-century audience both to envision what the author exhorts here and to experience emotions associated with military battle and victory.

Like Colossians, Ephesians offers what we might call a "cosmic Christology," and here again we may detect the influence of political and imperial ideas. Like the earlier letters by Paul (Rom 12:4–8; 1 Cor 12:12–27), Colossians and Ephesians represent the church as the body of Christ. Unlike them, however, these letters expressly make Christ the head of that body (Col 1:18; 3:15; Eph 1:22–23; 4:1–16; 5:23, 30). The body as a motif for the properly functioning state was an ancient topos, but the idea of Christ as head of the church finds a direct parallel in political representation of the emperor as head of his body, the empire. Seneca, in a moral treatise dedicated to convincing the emperor Nero to pursue the virtue of mercy, informs the young emperor that he is obliged to care for his moral health, for if the head of the empire is healthy, his body will be as well (*Clem.* 1.3.5). In Colossians, the presentation takes a directly polemical meaning to affirm the superior position of the baptized, who form the body united to the exalted head, Christ, above the principalities and powers. In Ephesians, there is also a cosmic application, but the role is not polemical; it rather belongs to the larger celebration of the unity of believers, which now mirrors a divine fullness that brings harmony and unity to everything (Eph 1:16–23).

Finally, it is unity that marks the overarching theme of Ephesians' ethical teachings. Here again a civic imagery dominates. In Eph 4:4–6, the paratactic use of the term "one" expresses the results of "the bond of peace" of 4:3. In the imperial ideal of concord, unity in virtue and civic identity arises from recognition of unity of origins and political goals. Ephesians furnishes the same basis for unity in affirming that there is one God and Father of us all as well as a shared humankind in the one baptism that makes all together into one body. The author again transforms a universal imperial civic image into an ecclesial one. Later in the household code (5:21–6:9), the author reinforces the theme of unity (Dawes 1998, 195–216). Like Colossians, Ephesians draws on the topos and changes its traditional contours by reminding husbands, parents, and masters of their responsibilities to wives, children, and slaves. Ephesians, however, adds significantly to the Colossian duties by representing the love of husband for wives as modeled after the love of Christ for the church (5:25–32). The language here moves far beyond the strict parameters of political ideals of the unity of the household promoting that of the state. Nevertheless, there is here an application of the household topos as an image of civic concord (Gombis 2005, 317–30; Julien Smith 2011, 235–38). The idealization of the concord of Christ with the church—what we may conceive broadly as an overarching, universal social order—one sees lived out in the obedience of wives to husbands and the love of husbands for wives. In the visual urban world of the Ephesian listeners, iconographers regularly depicted the marital harmony of emperors and their wives and the concord of the imperial household in general. This was a vision for the harmony of the empire as a whole: the concord of Caesar's household is the basis of the harmony of the state writ large as the emperor's dominion. This is a universalizing application of an ancient set of beliefs about the intimate connection of the health of the household as indispensable to the state's health. In Ephesians, the same set of analogies works together, but here it is the harmony of husband and wife who make up the harmony of the church and the concord of Christ with his church rendered as a husband-wife unity that models that of the husband-wife.

Concluding Observations

I conclude with three observations that arise from the preceding discussion. The first is to notice how important the creation of an imperial situation is to the strategies of persuasion of the authors of these letters. We

COLOSSIANS, EPHESIANS, AND EMPIRE   201

should not reduce these letters to a monocular imperial reading, but to ignore their deployment of recognizably imperial vocabulary, imagery, and conceptualization is to miss a key rhetorical strategy, and to ignore a critical component of first-century audiences' reception of the letters. Karl Galinsky (2011, 222) describes the New Testament uses of imperial imagery as the creation of a "supraimperial" vision of the reign of Christ. The Christology encountered in Colossians and Ephesians is supraimperial, and it is so because of how steeped it is in recognizably political language. Second, we can see that the letters celebrate their audiences as having broken off from a Greco-Roman past (Eph 2:1–10; Col 3:5–11) and how religious belief enfolds them in a new rule of God in Christ, described with the help of imperial language, images, and ideals. This had a paradoxical effect of removing listeners from a former past while at the same time integrating them into their urban world through the invocation of recognizably imperial ideas to describe their new identity. An important consequence of this leads to a third concluding observation. It is important to note the ways these letters draw on an inherited Pauline set of universal declarations about all of creation and consistently turn them into statements about achievements that occur in the church. This relieves them of the eschatological pressure of the earlier Pauline letters even as it renders them more parochial. Such a development was critical for the survival of Pauline theology as we find it in the New Testament canon and the Christian theology based on it that developed in later centuries. The effect of that vision was to help promote a statist version of Pauline theology that would in due course be a useful means of forging the allegiance of church and state in a new imperial and civil order. The outcome of that development is a set of social and political ideals that frame—usually unconsciously—modern Western identity, even in their most secular manifestations (Badiou 2003; Breton 2011; Žižek 2003).

For Further Reading

Canavan, Rosemary. 2012. *Clothing the Body of Christ at Colossae: A Visual Construction of Identity*. WUNT 2/334. Tübingen: Mohr Siebeck.

Faust, Eberhard. 1993. *Pax Christi et Pax Caesaris: Religionsgeschichtliche, traditionsgeschichtliche und sozialgeschichtliche Studien zum Epheserbrief*. NTOA 24. Göttingen: Vandenhoeck & Ruprecht.

Gupta, Nijay K., and Frederick J. Long. 2010. "The Politics of Ephesians and Empire: Accommodation or Resistance?" *JGRChJ* 7:112–36.

Lotz, John Paul. 1999. "The HOMONOIA Coins of Asia Minor and Ephesians 1.21." *TynBul* 50:173–88.

MacDonald, Margaret Y. 2004. "The Politics of Identity in Ephesians." *JSNT* 26:419–44.

Maier, Harry O. 2013. *Picturing Paul in Empire: Imperial Image, Text and Persuasion in Colossians, Ephesians and the Pastoral Epistles.* New York: T&T Clark.

Walsh, Brian J., and Sylvia C. Keesmaat. 2004. *Colossians Remixed: Subverting the Empire.* Downers Grove, IL: IVP Academic.

Construing and Containing an Imperial Paul: Rhetoric and the Politics of Representation in the Pastoral Epistles

Deborah Krause

A subject as expansive as empire would seem to occlude attention to three brief apparently personal pieces of correspondence between an aging leader of religious communities and his trusted emissaries. The Pastoral Epistles 1 and 2 Timothy and Titus and their canonical location at the conclusion of the Pauline Letters hardly seem worthy of an empire-critical examination. What could these scant and ostensibly temporal artifacts of the Jesus movement have to offer such a review? Indeed, empire criticism seems more appropriate for texts such as Luke's Acts of the Apostles with its coverage of the Jesus movement in its journey from Jerusalem across the imperial territory of the Mediterranean or for John of Patmos's Apocalypse in its thinly veiled attack against "Babylon" and its imagination for the ultimate destruction of Rome's violent and unjust imperial rule. Nonetheless, a critical reading of the Pastoral Epistles in light of the development of the Pauline tradition and their place within the New Testament canon reveals their disproportionate significance. In fact, a reading of the Pastoral Epistles through the lens of empire reveals that their stealth composition and canonical placement play an important role in shaping the legacy of Paul in terms of the church and its ministry.

For most of their history of interpretation, the Pastoral Epistles have been viewed as legitimate letters sent from Paul at the conclusion of his ministry to his emissaries Timothy and Titus in Ephesus and Crete. In the last two hundred years, biblical scholars in light of advances in historical-critical methods have questioned their authorship and begun to appreciate these writings as more than personal missives on matters of ecclesial leadership. Identifying the writings as examples of ancient pseudepigraphy, scholars have surmised that they were composed by a leader of the church within the Pauline tradition as a single corpus sometime in the late first or early second century. This hypothesis of their composition offers insight to help account for their manuscript history, as well as the discrepancies in vocabulary, syntax, ecclesial structure, and emphasis in comparison with the likely historical letters of Paul. While some have argued that this critical perspective has diminished the authority of the writings as a collection of forgeries and fakes (e.g., Ehrman 2011, 93–105), others have understood that as pseudepigraphical texts the Pastoral Epistles provide a window into the early Christian interpretation of Paul and his representation from struggling Jesus-movement missionary into an authoritative leader of the church universal (e.g., Pervo 2010, 63–118). It is this latter sense of appreciating how the Pastoral Epistles represent Paul and thereby construe his legacy within the context of the Jesus movement in the Roman Empire with which this reading is engaged.

Representation as a practice of rhetoric and a mode of power is an area of concern of postcolonial theorists. Edward Said in his groundbreaking work *Orientalism* (1978) identified the use of representational language as an act of power in portraying "the Oriental other" in his analysis of Western European and American literature. Said unveiled the dynamics of power at work in the ostensibly neutral act of "describing" colonized subjects as a strategy of colonialist discourse and vision. Gayatri Spivak in her essay "Can the Subaltern Speak?" (1988) developed Said's insight toward attending to different forms of representation in colonial discourse, namely, the representation of others as a political act (as "proxy," speaking for those who cannot speak for themselves) and the representation of the other as "portrait." In both cases, attending to representation in texts and images offers the opportunity to discern such artifacts as performances with particular interests and purposes.

Engaging the Pastoral Epistles as pseudepigraphical texts of the late first- and early second-century Roman imperial context offers the opportunity to see them as complex performances of Paul. Spivak's taxonomy of "proxy" and "portrait" sheds light on their complexity. The Pastoral Epistles writer "stands in" for Paul, speaking for him in his absence, representing him when he is not able (due to death) to represent himself. Yet, in the act of standing in for Paul, the Pastoral Epistles writer also constructs a portrait of Paul, offering a representation of Paul as a leader discussing concerns about the administration of the church with two of his most trusted coworkers.

Importantly, the Pastoral Epistles writer's act of standing in for Paul is not transparent about how the writer is Paul's proxy. Rather, the writer subsumes Paul's identity. In this sense, the dynamic of power at work in the Pastoral Epistles' rhetoric of representation is highly charged with a sense of entitlement and privilege. Not only does the writer of the Pastoral Epistles presume to speak "for" Paul, but he also presumes to speak "as" Paul. In this sense, the mechanics of pseudepigraphy offer the Pastoral Epistles writer a way to stand in and perform Paul that enables the capacity to erase and rewrite Paul as he had been formerly known in the tradition. Charged with the authorial "I" of Paul, the Pastoral Epistles writer stands in a position to manage the reception of all of Paul's thought and work in the church ("all his letters," 2 Pet 3:16) and to promote the Pastoral Epistles writer's agenda for the belief and practice of the church and its leadership in the name of Paul. Seen in this light, the relatively scant pages of the Pastoral Epistles in relationship to the overall Pauline corpus play a powerful role in defining and packaging the Pauline tradition. Three little letters that are not even really letters have never had so much to say.

In addition to insight about representation, postcolonial analysis offers the study of the Pastoral Epistles in their Roman imperial context a way out of the binary that has plagued so much of their historical analysis—between seeing Paul's likely historical writings as the "real Paul" and the Pastoral Epistles (and other pseudepigraphical texts, such as 2 Thessalonians) as "fake Paul." Leery of the power dynamics at work in constructing a sense of pristine origin and asserting "the real Paul," a postcolonial analysis of the Pauline tradition within the Roman imperial context would understand all of the Pauline writings to be engaged in rhetorics of representation. As such, the Epistle to the Romans is every bit as much a "performance" of Paul as 2 Timothy. Second Corinthians, with its multiple letter fragments edited into a single "letter," is every bit as much a construction of Paul as a letter-writing leader as Titus and 1 Timothy.

Additionally, no division can be neatly placed between the likely historical letters of Paul and the Pastoral Epistles around the issue of their connection to matters of empire. Both the mid-first-century writings of Paul and the late first- or early second-century writings of the Pastoral Epistles are products of the Roman imperial context. While the historical letters of Paul have been noted for containing anti-imperial rhetoric (using terms often connected with the cult of the Roman ruler, such as "Savior," "gospel," and "Lord,"), so too do the Pastoral Epistles. Beyond this, both the historical letters of Paul and the Pastoral Epistles are very much products of the technologies and infrastructure of the Roman Empire (i.e., writing on papyrus, and the distribution of letters via roads and trade routes). Finally, both Paul and the Pastoral Epistles issue calls to be "subject" to civil authority (Rom 13:1; Titus 3:1). In this sense, the study of the Pastoral Epistles as imperial writings, and as a construal of Paul within an imperial context, does not distinguish them from the historical letters of Paul.

Where the Pastoral Epistles and Paul's Letters do divide is in how their representations of Paul and his teaching are directed. Paul in the likely seven historical letters speaks to communities (or in the case of Philemon, a person) in particular contexts in which they face particular issues and challenges. The Pastoral Epistles writer, however, presents Paul directing his teaching toward his trusted emissaries (Timothy and Titus), ostensibly located in Ephesus and Crete, about general rules for leadership and administration in the church. It is in this sense that the Pastoral Epistles first got their name as "Pastoral" Epistles—in that Thomas Aquinas noted that they are "virtually a pastoral rule" (*In omnes S. Pauli Apostoli epistolas commentaria*, at 1 Tim 1:4). As such, their form as "epistles" is determined by the mimicry of Paul's leadership as a "letter writer," and their content as a set of guidelines for church leaders is their primary purpose and function.

The letters of Paul seek to "stand in" for Paul's leadership in communities such as Corinth, Thessalonica, Philippi, and Galatia while he is absent and convey Paul's attempts to offer insight and guidance on how to be the church in those contexts. By contrast, the Pastoral Epistles convey a church leader's attempt (writing in the name of Paul) to establish a set of comprehensive guidelines for ministry and church order. In this sense, the consolidation of power at work in the Pastoral Epistles is remarkable. They perform Paul (who was a leader) writing to leaders about subjects related to the formation and compensation of leadership. Additionally, standing at the conclusion of the corpus of the Pauline tradition (both historically and canonically), they serve to focus and construe all of its contextual particularity toward the function of what Aquinas discerned as a pastoral rule. As such, the Pastoral Epistles writer creates not only a portrait of Paul as a dying leader imparting his final words of wisdom to his most trusted emissaries, but also, through it, a construal and rewriting of the entire Pauline tradition. In their powerful performance of representational rhetoric, the Pastoral Epistles accomplish an appropriation of the Pauline tradition toward the production and administration of an orderly church within the Roman imperial context.

The following analysis explores a comparative reading of Paul's likely historical writings with the Pastoral Epistles around four areas that have significant connection with Roman imperial infrastructure and culture: the collection project, governing authorities, metaphors for the life of the church, and compensation for church leadership. Each of these areas offers a setting in which to appreciate how Paul is presented as a church leader in both his own letters and the Pastoral Epistles. In comparing the representation of Paul in each of these areas, the distinctive ways in which the Pastoral Epistles writer construes the Pauline tradition toward a general vision of church leadership come into view. Paul is ever more removed from his own leadership in particular contexts of ministry and represented as a mediator of practices of church leadership and ministry. In the process, Paul is rendered portable, becoming a general authority for managing the church in its development throughout the Roman Empire.

The Collection for the Church in Jerusalem

Paul's seven likely historical letters are artifacts of his contextually engaged responses to communities of the Jesus movement. While they were ultimately collected and circulated as a corpus, they stand independent of one another as witnesses to Paul's attempts to speak directly with communities about matters pertaining to their worship, fellowship, and life "in the Spirit of Christ." While interpreters of Paul (such as the writers of Ephesians and Colossians) would adapt his central metaphor of "the body of Christ" into a universal cosmic idea, for Paul each local community was just such a body. Rarely does he reflect on ways in which these different communities in Greece, Asia Minor, Jerusalem, Syria, and Italy are interconnected with one another as a geo-ecclesial and cross-imperial entity. Certainly he understands that God's sovereignty and the Spirit's vitality connect these communities, but he does not offer much insight into how they are related to one another in an overall universal mission.

One area in which Paul begins to transcend his fierce local attention to each community and to develop connections between them as interrelated to one another is his project of collecting funds to support the "saints" or the "poor" in Jerusalem. The collection project is widely referenced among Paul's letters (Rom 15; 1 Cor 16; 2 Cor 8–9; Gal 2:10), and its delivery to Jerusalem marked a pivotal point in his transition from his ministry in the Aegean toward his westward mission to Rome, and beyond that to Spain. Through the project, Paul solicited the generosity of his Greek congregations (in Macedonia and Achaia) in the service of extending financial relief to the "saints" in Jerusalem who were likely in the 50s and early 60s experiencing the economic deprivation of Roman imperial action against the Jewish rebel resistance in Jerusalem in the buildup to the Jewish War of 66–70 CE.

While the majority of biblical scholars focus on the intramural role that Paul's collection played in mediating his relationship with the Jerusalem church, its significance within the context of the Roman Empire should not be ignored (Friesen 2010). With this project, Paul garnered funds from communities of the Jesus movement in northern and southern Greece (playing those regions off one another in his bid to raise more funds) and prepared to deliver the gift as evidence of the fruit of God's work in and through Paul's ministry among the gentiles. As such, Paul imagined the resources of Greek gentiles in relief of the suffering Jerusalem Jewish Jesus movement as evidence of God's work of reconciliation in and through the Spirit of Jesus Christ. The collection was a deeply theological and eschatological artifact for Paul (something he referred to as "a fruit," Rom 15:28) that united gentiles with Jews in material support that mirrored their spiritual connection (Rom 15:29). As such, in Paul's theological imagination it bore witness to the sovereign reconciliatory work of God in God's world.

Warren Carter (2006b) has noted that the collection project both in its geographical scope (Macedonia and Achaia to Jerusalem) and its economic significance (a trans-imperial redistribution of wealth) functioned as a kind of reverse flow of the taxes and tributes from the colonies to Rome. The work of redistributing resources from one region of the empire to another and the act of offering relief to those in a city and among a people whom Rome found to be rebellious might well have been understood as a form of sedition. While Luke does not associate the collection with Paul's arrest in Jerusalem, Paul himself expresses concern in Rom 15:31–32 about his reception in the city among "the disobedient" as well as "the saints." From the perspective of the Roman civil authorities in Jerusalem, all parties among these two groups would be considered "Jews," and Paul's delivery of the funds could well be perceived as aiding and abetting the enemy.

As important as the collection project was to Paul's ministry, the Pastoral Epistles' representation of Paul in 1 and 2 Timothy and Titus does not mention it. This is particularly striking given that 2 Cor 8–9 discuss that Titus is Paul's primary proxy in Achaia for the collection of the offering. Moreover, the Pastoral Epistles are constructed to portray Paul via 2 Timothy as within the context of the city of Rome and under arrest. As such, the Pastoral Epistles writer prepares a portrait of Paul that focuses on his biography at the conclusion of his Aegean ministry and in the midst of his imprisonment in Rome, but that does not mention the most significant event in his ministry to that point. While arguments from silence are always tenuous, the silence of the Pastoral Epistles on the collection project is remarkable. It is as if the Pastoral Epistles writer has erased this aspect of Paul's mission and ministry from his portrait of Paul.

In comparing the portrait of Paul in his historical correspondence with the Pastoral Epistles in relation to the collection project, it is not accurate to say that Paul's portrait is anti-imperial while the Pastoral Epistles writer's portrait is pro-imperial. Both are no doubt infused with responses to and engagements with the presence of empire. To send and receive his letters, dispatch his emissaries, solicit funds, and deliver the collection, Paul depended on culturally engaged social relationships, as well as Roman roads and trade routes (which were elements of the military and economic infrastructure of the Roman Empire). If indeed the project functioned as a "reverse flow" of taxes collected by Rome, sent to support the members of the Jerusalem church, then it may have occupied Paul's imagination as a counterimperial witness to the sovereign and creative presence of God over the world. As such, Paul's engagement with the collection shows his embedded and ambiguous relationship to empire.

The Pastoral Epistles draw on prior traditions about Paul (from his letters and Acts) to refer to Paul's travels, his relationships with various churches, and even his hardships and persecutions. In 2 Timothy, the Pastoral Epistles writer dramatizes Paul's hardship as he represents Paul in the midst of his imprisonment in Rome, and yet the journey to Jerusalem, the hardship Paul faced there, and his delivery of the collection are not mentioned in the in 2 Timothy or the rest of the Pastoral Epistles. Luke's portrait of Paul in the Acts of the Apostles does dramatize the journey to Jerusalem and the subsequent arrest, but it downplays the act of delivering the collection to Jerusalem. In that narrative (which repeatedly references the journey to Jerusalem), the only reference to Paul's tribute is made in his trial before Felix (Acts 24:17), where Paul is portrayed describing that he came to Jerusalem bearing alms and offerings for "his nation." Attending to the portrait of Paul in Acts and the Pastoral Epistles, it seems as though some of Paul's interpreters sought to represent Paul in a way that distanced him from the collection project. Luke's portrait underscores the journey as pilgrimage and the offering as pious religious practice for a good Jew visiting Jerusalem—a matter of religious observance more than imperial engagement. In the Pastoral Epistles, the journey to Jerusalem and the collection do not appear at all. Paul is imprisoned in Rome, but the context and ground for that imprisonment is not detailed. The portrait is denuded of its political and even religious connections. Paul's imprisonment stands on its own, as a poignant signifier of the trials, opposition, and difficulty he has faced in his ministry all along.

Relationship of the Church to Governing Authorities

Imperial explorations of Paul's worldview assert repeatedly that as an apocalyptic Jewish theologian, Paul held the perspective that God alone is the sovereign judge of all creation, and that this current age is "evil" (Gal 1:4). As such, Paul's letters regularly make claims that would likely stand in contradiction to imperial propaganda and the claims of the cult of the Roman ruler (Georgi 1997). If God is sovereign over creation and will judge all of creation, and Jesus Christ, his "Son," is the firstfruits of the resurrection—the new age of God's sovereign rule—then it must be understood at some level that the power of the Roman Empire is in every sense subject to God. Yet, for Paul, that very claim to God's sovereignty, alongside the reality of Roman imperial rule, required the negotiation of authority that God's creative sovereignty and the ruling presence of Rome were in some sense compatible. Romans 13:1–7, especially as read within the broader theological discourse of Rom 11–15, articulates a tense negotiation of Paul's understanding of divine sovereignty within the reality of Roman rule.

The conclusion of Paul's Aegean ministry coincided with Emperor Nero's repeal of Claudius's edict that had evicted Jews from the city of Rome. With this repeal, Roman Jews who had lived in exile around the Mediterranean (e.g., Prisca and Aquila) began to return to Rome. Paul's letter to the Roman church coincided with these events. As such, the context of his address to the Roman church meets a mixed population of Jewish and gentile Jesus-movement members and not only that but a predominantly gentile community receiving back (after a number of years) its Jewish members. It is in this context that Paul's classification of the "strong" and the "weak" makes sense. While gentile members may have been considered "newer" in many contexts, in the Roman church they were the established group. The returning Jews were both culturally marginal to the community and ethnically and politically vulnerable within the setting of the imperial capital. In this context, Paul's rhetoric about the coinciding of divine sovereignty and civil authority offers those established members a call to remember the vulnerability of their returning members and to comport themselves in ways that offered protection to one and all. In this sense, while Paul's words reflect a conciliatory tone toward imperial rule, his rhetoric in context bespeaks an ethic of belonging that communicates deeply to the Roman church about what it means to be a member of the body of Christ (Rom 12) and what it means to live in love and equal regard toward one another (Rom 14).

Paul's teaching in Rom 13:1–7 offers insight into his assessment of the civil governing authorities in relation to the Roman church. While he asserts that God is sovereign and that the authorities that exist are "appointed by God," Paul describes the exercise of that authority in a way that underscores its violence and terror. He concedes, "Do good and you will receive commendation" (Rom 13:3), but to that one affirmation he asserts four times (Rom 13:2, 4a, 4b, 5) that such authorities will bring wrath and retribution and will condemn those who resist their authority. Furthermore, he details just how that wrath will be delivered with reference to the "sword" (Rom 13:4). As such, on the surface, Paul's rhetoric is a call to obey civil authorities, but that call bears a code that describes in detail the violence with which Roman civil authority governs. The very bodies of the Roman church are at risk, and Paul at once performs a conciliatory posture toward civil authority even as he describes its brutality.

Just what Paul may be performing in Rom 13:1–7 with regard to his posture toward Rome has consumed much scholarly effort (N. Elliott 1997, 184–86). Whether overtly "pro-Roman" or deftly providing a screen of safety for Jews who were at risk in the city, Paul's performance is tense—charged with multiple layers of meaning and deeply engaged in addressing the particular context of the Roman church as it navigates its own transition under the vagaries of Roman imperial rule.

The performance of Paul in the Pastoral Epistles regarding obedience to civil authority is broader and less deep than Paul's performance in Rom 13:1–7. In 1 Tim 2:1–2, the Pastoral Epistles writer portrays Paul urging Timothy to see to it that "prayers and intercessions" be offered on behalf of "all people" and further "for kings and all who are in authority" (1 Tim 2:2). This liturgical call for alliance with civil authority is further bolstered in the Pastoral Epistles performance of Paul in Titus 3:1, where the Pastoral Epistles writer presents Paul offering a more general challenge to Titus to "remind them" (ostensibly the ministers under "Titus's" authority) to "be subject to rulers and authorities." This reminder evokes Paul's teaching in Rom 13:1–7—whereby the Pastoral Epistles writer represents Paul by drawing on the content of Paul's known letters. As such, the Pastoral Epistles writer constructs a portrait of Paul that mimics the teaching about obedience to civil authority in Romans and offers a kind of "last word" on that subject. The Pastoral Epistles amplify the subject of obedience to civil authority as a general instruction on proper behavior in the church.

In addition to generalizing the call of obedience to civil authority as a "Pauline instruction," the Pastoral Epistles writer performs a less dense representation of civil rule than Paul in Rom 13:1–7. Where Paul details the violence of civil authority no fewer than four times and names the relative benevolence of such authority only once, in 1 Tim 2:1–2 and Titus 3:1, the instruction mentions only the good that can come of such alliance and obedience for the community. In Rom 13:1–7, Paul bases his call to obedience for civil authority in a larger understanding of divine sovereignty, but in the Pastoral Epistles the writer envisions prayer for those in civil authority as a part of God's saving work, the church's practice of evangelism (1 Tim 2:3–4) and as a means toward a "quiet and peaceful" life for those in the church (1 Tim 2:2).

Metaphors for the Life the Church

Paul attended to the local lives of his communities. His letters are artifacts of that attention. They are, in fact, performances of his leadership directed toward the challenges and concerns of each of the Jesus movement communities in the cities and regions for which the letters are now named—Corinth, Galatia, Philippi, Thessalonica, and Rome. Only Philemon stands out as a "personal letter," but this writing is addressed to Philemon (and Apphia and Archippus) along with "the church that meets in your house." As such, even Philemon's ostensible personal business regarding his relationship with Onesimus is addressed within a local-communal context.

Paul's most highly developed and represented (both by Paul and his interpreters) metaphor for the life of his communities was related to the organism of the human body. Complex, multifaceted, interrelated, and necessarily (for proper functioning) united—the body offered a basis for challenging first the Corinthian and later the Roman church to see themselves as diverse members and yet one community united in the Spirit of Christ. True to his attention to the life of local communities, Paul envisioned the body metaphor as a basis for representing the relationships and life of particular churches. While his interpreters in Ephesians and Colossians would render the body metaphor as a cosmic entity (in which the church is the body whose head is Christ), Paul's engagement of the body to describe the life of local communities insisted on the nonhierarchical, interdependent functioning of all the diverse parts of the body (inclusive of the head) in order to underscore the call to Corinth and Rome to live in peace and unity amid their diverse gifts and membership.

In 1 Cor 12:12, Paul introduces the concept of the unity and diversity of the body to speak to the unity and diversity of the church within the Spirit. Earlier he notes that there are different gifts, but that they arise from the same Spirit (1 Cor 12:4). The metaphor works to challenge members of the community who are elevating their gift of speaking in tongues over other expressions of giftedness in the church. By drawing on the metaphor of the body, Paul engages a well-known trope for unity in cosmopolitan relationships seen especially in Stoic philosophical thought (M. Lee 2006). In 1 Cor 12, Paul teaches through the body metaphor that each part of the body has an important role for the proper functioning of the whole. In other words, every part of the body has a place—all are equally important to the proper functioning of the whole. With this imagery, Paul is able to challenge the Corinthians in their practice of lording their gifts over one another, and to call them as a body unified by God through the Spirit to have "mutual concern for each other" (1 Cor 12:24–25). He at once challenges them in their boasting among themselves, and instructs the church on its alternative formation to the broader culture within the Spirit of Christ.

In Rom 12 Paul represents his metaphor of the body of Christ into a different local context of the church. Where the Corinthians had divided around competitively ranking their gifts, the Roman church faced the challenge of being a multiethnic community of gentiles and Jews in a context that had been particularly inhospitable to Jews. Paul takes the metaphor and reapplies it to the Roman context, calling on the members to understand that the body of Christ is one and that they are individually members of it (Rom 12:5).

In both Corinth and Rome, Paul draws on the body metaphor to speak to the unity and diversity of the life of the local congregation. The deutero-Pauline interpreters of Ephesians and Colossians pick up on the metaphor and expand its application from local churches to the universal church (Eph 4:12; 5:23; Col 1:18). In these applications, the body of

Christ is the church, and the head of the body is Christ. Undoubtedly the metaphor is radically altered by this reapplication, but it underscores the importance of the metaphor of the body for describing the life of the church in the Pauline tradition. This is what makes the absence of the body metaphor from the Pastoral Epistles striking. Indeed, the subject matter of the Pastoral Epistles is almost entirely ecclesiological, and yet the central Pauline metaphor for the life of the church, the body of Christ, does not appear in them.

In the place of the body metaphor, the Pastoral Epistles writer presents Paul reflecting on the life of the church in light of a different organizing metaphor—the household (2 Tim 2:20–26). As Paul used the body to describe the interdependent relationship of members to the whole community, the Pastoral Epistles writer draws on the structure of the Greco-Roman household to characterize how the members of the church can be honorable or dishonorable vessels. The writer calls for members to be honorable, set apart for the master of the household. Paul's direct instruction from the body metaphor, in which he has argued that the "dishonorable" members of the body are honored by additional clothing (1 Cor 12:23), is reversed in this passage. Only the honorable vessels are worthy of the Lord's use. Members are challenged to be honorable and not dishonorable.

The comparison of the body metaphor in Paul and the household metaphor in the Pastoral Epistles is instructive for understanding the ecclesiologies at work in these different writings. Paul employs the metaphor of the body to emphasize the idea of honor through belonging and to correct a tendency in the local communities to hierarchical social organization. The Pastoral Epistles writer engages the metaphor of the household to focus on the "honorability" and "usefulness" of each member of the community. The Lord of the house has expectations for the vessels within the household. The summons in 2 Tim 2:20–26 is to be a valuable vessel and to serve the household well in one's capacity (be it gold, silver, clay, or wood). While a classist division between members can be transgressed by right behavior (a clay jar can be as honorable as a silver pot), the members of the body have been rendered as discrete objects of the household—all subject to the Lord's use—and retain their given social and economic condition (gold, silver, clay, wood) even as they all serve honorably. Within such a structure, members each have their place. Slaves can be called on to serve nobly (1 Tim 6:1), and women can be promised salvation through submission to their designated role of wife and mother (1 Tim 2:8–15).

Church Leadership and Compensation

Perhaps nowhere else does the Pastoral Epistles writer reanimate Paul's own presentation of himself more powerfully than in 1 Tim 5:17–18. In that text, the Pastoral Epistles writer draws on Paul's performance of his own example of forsaking his right to apostolic compensation in order to serve the common good. In the midst of a long discussion of the subject of the consumption of idol meat within Corinth (1 Cor 8–10), Paul chooses to confront the claim that "all things are lawful" in the gospel with an example from his own practice of ministry. In doing so, he manages to establish the authority for the apostolic right to compensation and his entitlement to that right, even while he presents himself as an example of one who has forsaken this right for the benefit of the greater community. It is a complex rhetorical performance, at once a declaration of his apostolic authority and a description of his ministerial practice in the service of teaching in the church. The Pastoral Epistles writer's reanimation of this Pauline performance compresses some of the content of Paul's teaching into an assertion of the authority for apostolic compensation. In this sense, the Pastoral Epistles writer represents Paul using many of Paul's words, but divorces the rhetoric from the particularities of Paul's context and his practice.

In 1 Cor 9:8–14 Paul draws on two traditions in order to assert the apostolic right to compensation. The first he sources from "the law of Moses" in 1 Cor 9:9, a quote from Deut 25:4: "You shall not muzzle the ox while it is treading the grain." After his interpretation and application of this text to the practice of ministry in general and his in particular (1 Cor 9:10–12), Paul offers an additional tradition to bolster the authority of his claim in 1 Cor 9:14. Here he sources that tradition as "the Lord commanded"; in other words, he offers a rare example of his citation of Jesus's teaching as authority for his practice of ministry. The command of the Lord that Paul references is a logion found also in Luke 10:7: "The laborer deserves his own wages." For Paul, the "law of Moses" and the "command of the Lord" offer two distinct traditions on which he establishes the authority of the practice of apostolic compensation. Of course, he goes through this grand demonstration of authorizing apostolic compensation in 1 Cor 9:8–14 only to assert that, in spite of this, he "makes the gospel free of charge, not making full use of my right in the gospel" (1 Cor 9:18). In this sense, he puts his personal example in service to his summons to the community in 1 Cor 10:23–24: "'All things are lawful,' but not all things are helpful.

'All things are lawful,' but not all things build up. Let no one seek his own good, but the good of his neighbor."

In 1 Tim 5:17–18, the Pastoral Epistles writer represents this complex performance of Paul's apostolic authority and ministerial practice as a means toward establishing a general teaching about the compensation of elders who "rule well" within the church. Compressing the two traditions that Paul sources distinctly from the "law of Moses" and a "commandment from the Lord," the Pastoral Epistles writer quotes both of them with the preface: "Scripture says." In this way, the Pastoral Epistles writer has rendered Paul as one who would understand both Deut 25:4 and Jesus's saying (now located in Luke 10:7) as "Scripture" (*graphē*). Beyond this remarkable hermeneutical makeover, the Pastoral Epistles writer has also managed to use Paul's own rhetoric to establish a rule that runs contrary to his ministerial practice, and that undermines his rhetorical purpose in 1 Cor 8–10. Where Paul asserted his own right in order to illustrate the value of not exercising it for the good of the community, the Pastoral Epistles writer in the name of Paul appropriates Paul's language to assert simply that elders who rule well are worthy of double compensation. Moreover, the writer performs this representation of Paul in the midst of a larger discussion of church offices and compensation in which he has argued forcefully for curtailing the church's financial support of widows (1 Tim 5:3–16). As such, he asserts the importance of compensation for male leaders while arguing for the curtailing of widow's support. With this portrayal, the Pastoral Epistles writer has managed to streamline the Pauline tradition of its ambivalence regarding financial compensation for church leadership (the historical particularity of Paul's ministry practice in context) and establish in the words of Paul the unequivocal "scriptural" authority for the financial compensation of church elders.

Conclusion: Paul in the Box—Representing Paul in the Imperial Context

This survey of the Pastoral Epistles writer's performance of Paul in comparison with Paul's performance of his own leadership in his letters offers insight into how the representation of Paul's deeply contextual and ambivalent relationship with empire is clarified by one Pauline interpreter. In each area surveyed (the collection project, the church's relation to civil authorities, the description of church membership, and the understanding of compensation for ministerial leaders), the Pastoral Epistles writer construes Paul away from the particularities of his engagement with the mechanisms of empire—such as the socioeconomic particularities of the collection or the realities of social membership—and toward an idealized expression of imperial values. Jennifer Glancy in her analysis of the performance of masculinity in the Pastoral Epistles has identified a similar trend in the Pastoral Epistles' writer's engagement with issues of gender. In a comparative study of the Pastoral Epistles writer's moral argument and that of other Greco-Roman writers, Glancy (2003, 237) notes that the "Pastoral Epistles codify a protocol for proper Christian masculinity consistent with coeval pagan articulations of masculinity." That protocol is primarily concerned with control, both of one's household, and of one's own self, particularly around one's passions. In this sense, the Pastoral Epistles writer's preoccupation with religious leadership (i.e., bishops and deacons) who rule their houses well and who avoid anger, arguments, and controversies, is illustrative of the ideal of Greco-Roman masculinity.

The representation of Paul in the Pastoral Epistles coincides with Glancy's analysis of the performance of ideal elite Greco-Roman masculinity. As Paul is denuded of the particularities of his contextual and ambivalent engagement with Roman imperial structures and culture, he is portrayed as in ever more control of his church (characterized now as a "household" and not a body) and of his own self. At the close of his life, he is portrayed as imprisoned but without particular imperial charges or concerns. His suffering is decontextualized and idealized. His relationship to Rome has been emptied of its tense ambivalence (as expressed in Rom 13:1–7) and replaced with calls for obedience and affirmations of civil benevolence. His imagination for the church's membership has transformed from the biological metaphor of the body and its many integral parts to the architectural understanding of the household and its various objects of service. Finally, his understanding of church leadership has been emptied of his vocational struggle for authority and the particularity of his practice in Corinth to generalized calls for Greco-Roman idealized masculinity— ruling well over one's household and one's passions.

The representation of Paul in the Pastoral Epistles renders an authoritative religious leader who is spared the potential complications of his contextual engagement. He is noble in his suffering, secure in his leadership, clinical in his understanding of the church, and certain in his direction of matters of church leadership. Devoid of the intramural challenges to his own authority, the Pastoral Epistles writer's Paul bears many of the components of an idealized Greco-Roman masculinity to which he calls church leaders—he is in control, both of his own household (in his case the church) and his own passions. The Pastoral Epistles writer has managed to package Paul not only within his own writings but also through them by discrete references to them (e.g., Titus 3:1, referring to Rom 13:1–7; and 1 Tim 5:17–18, referring to 1 Cor 9:8–18), the writings of the broader Pauline tradition. The Pastoral Epistles offer a portrait of Paul, and it is a portrait that manages to draw in and re-present the entire Pauline tradition.

Seen in this light, the Pastoral Epistles' representation of Paul marks a significant innovation in the presentation of the apostle as an authoritative leader for the church ecumenical. Spivak's double-edged notion of representation—proxy and portrait—offers insight into ingenuity of the Pastoral Epistles writer's performance. The writings serve to "stand in" for the apostle in his absence in a late first- or early second-century context, and in their canonical location they offer a "makeover" (portrait) of the apostle in the entire Pauline corpus. This innovation in representing Paul provides a means of containing the Pauline tradition and managing it in the direction of, as Aquinas noted, "a general pastoral rule." This powerful act of containment evokes an analogical connection for me between the imperial context of the ancient Mediterranean world and our own. As I consider how the Pastoral Epistles, in spite of their diminutive size and theological scope, manage to enfold the Pauline tradition and serve to transport it to new ecclesial contexts, I am reminded of another seemingly humble twentieth-century innovation in global trade, the shipping container.

In his analysis of the role of this innovation in global trade, *The Box: How the Shipping Container Made the World Smaller and the World's Economy Bigger*, Marc Levinson (2006) notes that the shipping container—while apparently modest in its design and humble in its appearance—has since its development and implementation completely transformed the process of global trade. The container has offered a means whereby goods can be transported to and from ports seamlessly, making the routes between manufacturing and distributing much more efficient. Whereas prior to containerized shipping, goods had to be loaded and offloaded onto ships one at a time, with containerization goods preloaded after manufacturing into containers that are then transported either by truck or train to port, by crane to ship, and then offloaded and distributed in reverse. Shipping containers do more than merely hold the goods they carry; they manage the flow of goods and streamline the entire process of the contemporary global economy.

Analogously, the Pastoral Epistles in their historical and canonical location serve as a kind of containerizing mechanism for Paul. When the corpus of the Pauline tradition is gathered up into the Pastoral Epistles, Paul is represented in a way that his teachings are streamlined into an authority for the broader church that transcends context and authorizes a "general" rule for ministry. As such, the Pastoral Epistles exercise their significant influence on the Pauline tradition not so much through their content as through the mechanics of their representation and packaging of the apostle. They contain the Pauline tradition in a way that offers Paul's authority and teaching portability, efficiency, and broad-based applicability. They streamline Paul from the vagaries of his contexts of ministry and the details of his personal challenges toward an authoritative rule for leadership and management of the church.

Reading the Pastoral Epistles through their rhetoric of representation illumines their strategic role in the interpretation of Paul toward the process of canonization. Evoking Paul's leadership as letter writer and containing his particularity as leader, the writings both draw in and cap the Pauline tradition into a portable collection for the management of the church. While Luke's Acts of the Apostles may have narrated Paul's global journeys across the map of the Roman Empire, the Pastoral Epistles writer constructed a mechanism for the transport of the Pauline corpus for the church in its development in the Roman imperial world.

For Further Reading

Elliott, Neil. 2008. *The Arrogance of the Nations: Reading Romans in the Shadow of Empire*. Minneapolis: Fortress.

Friesen, Steven J. 2010. "Paul and Economics: The Jerusalem Collection as an Alternative to Patronage." Pages 27–54 in *Paul Unbound: Other Perspectives on the Apostle*. Edited by Mark D. Given. Peabody, MA: Hendrickson.

Georgi, Dieter. 1997. "God Turned Upside Down." Pages 148–57 in *Paul and Empire: Religion and Power in Imperial Society*. Edited by Richard A Horsley. Harrisburg, PA: Trinity Press International.

Glancy, Jennifer. 2003. "Protocols of Masculinity in the Pastoral Epistles." Pages 235–64 in *New Testament Masculinities*. Edited by Stephen D. Moore and Janice Capel Anderson. Leiden: Brill.

Lee, Michelle. 2006. *Paul, the Stoics, and the Body of Christ*. Cambridge: Cambridge University Press.

Pervo, Richard L. 2010. *The Making of Paul: Constructions of the Apostle in Early Christianity*. Minneapolis: Fortress.

Spivak, Gayatri Chakravorty. 1988. "Can the Subaltern Speak?" Pages 271–
313 in *Marxism and the Interpretation of Culture*. Edited by Cary Nelson
and Lawrence Grossberg. Urbana, IL: University of Illinois Press.

RESISTING EMPIRE IN HEBREWS

Jason A. Whitlark

The Letter to the Hebrews was written under the hegemonic rule of imperial Rome. Among studies of the Roman imperial context in the New Testament, the Letter to the Hebrews has attracted relatively little attention. In
the twentieth century, Ernst Käsemann's (1982, 17) classic study found in
Hebrews a valuable resource with which the confessing church could resist
the political power and propaganda of Nazi Germany. This essay contends
that Hebrews was a similar resource for its original audience, providing
a sober message that resisted the propaganda and pressures of imperial
Rome in order to preserve faithfulness to Jesus Christ and his community
of followers.

Considering the Imperial Context of Hebrews

Three broad observations suggest that an examination of the Roman
imperial milieu is an apt area of inquiry for the study of Hebrews. The
audience (1) is suffering from official action, (2) is tempted to return to
their pagan identities, and (3) is living in Rome in the latter half of the
first century CE. First, Hebrews offers some clues that the audience is
struggling with pressures arising from official action against members of
the community. For example, some among the audience had experienced
imprisonment and confiscation of their property (see Heb 10:34). Imprisonment with torture continued in the present for others (see Heb 13:3,
23). These experiences point to both the involvement of authorities and
the precarious status of the community.[1] The author also seems to believe

---

1. For the use of torture by authorities, especially of slaves, see Suetonius, *Tib.* 58;
Tacitus, *Ann.* 6.47. For Christians suffering torture by authorities after being revealed
by informants, see Tacitus, *Ann.* 15.44; Pliny, *Ep.* 10.96.8; Mart. Pol. 2.

that these official responses could potentially escalate, leading to martyrdom or exile. Though no one in the audience has currently "resisted to
the point of shedding blood," the threat of death that the audience feels
is a recurrent motif in Hebrews. For example, in Heb 2:14–15, the author
speaks of the "fear of death" that enslaves humans to the devil. In Heb 11,
the author continually points to the experience of death or the threat of
death that puts in jeopardy the promises of God or tests the faithfulness
of his followers. It is worth noting that the author concludes his list of
exempla with those who were not only mocked, imprisoned, destitute,
oppressed, and tortured but also martyred, sawn in two, and killed by the
sword in order to remain faithful to God (see 11:35–38). His final exemplum is Jesus Christ, who was killed by Roman crucifixion.

Second, these negative pressures appear to have made defection to or
identification with the pagan imperil culture an attractive alternative to
the audience, especially if we are willing to allow that many in the audience of Hebrews are former pagans who have had their "consciences
cleansed from dead works [idolatry] so that they [now] serve the living
God" (9:14).[2] Defection would have been a way of restoring honor and
finding safety outside a community that suffered from shame and was sus-
ceptible to loss of possessions or even life for its identification with a crucified savior. The author's consistent appeal to texts and images from the
Old Testament that warn against idolatry—especially in the latter half of
the discourse—indicates that the author is concerned about defection for
the purpose of identifying with the pagan imperial milieu. For example,
in Heb 12:15, the author exhorts the community not to let a "root of bitterness" grow up and thus defile many. The imagery echoes Deut 28:17
(LXX), where the people are warned not to turn away from God and serve
the gods of the nations. Such apostasy will lead to "a root which grows
in gall and bitterness" among the Israelite community. This potent imagery from the Old Testament is fitting for members of the audience who
might be considering returning to their former pagan lives (Whitlark
2014, 49–76). If this is indeed the case, Hebrews suitably depicts Moses as
one who chose mistreatment and reproach with God's people rather than
enjoy the momentary pleasures of sin that identification with the pagan,
even imperial, Egypt offered him (see Heb 11:24–26).

---

2. Unless otherwise indicated, all translations are my own.

Third, there are some good (even if not conclusive) reasons to locate the original audience of Hebrews in Rome in the latter half of the first century CE. First, the epistolary conclusion, "those from Italy send greetings," likely refers to those who are sending greetings back to Christians who are in Rome (Brown and Meier 1983, 146). Second, the earliest witness we have to Hebrews is a late first-century or early second-century document of Roman provenance, 1 Clement (1 Clem. 36.1–5 // Heb 1:3–14).[3] Third, if we consider other documents of Roman provenance such as the Gospel of Mark, the Shepherd of Hermas, and 1 Peter, these documents not only address the issue of suffering for allegiance to Christ and his community but also wrestle in varying degrees with the consequences of defection to avoid suffering.[4] Such issues are central in Hebrews, which is especially severe with regard to the consequences of apostasy (e.g., Heb 6:4–6). Fourth, many of the previous considerations fit the context of Rome, especially post-Neronian Rome. Confiscation of property for treason against the Roman state was part of life in the imperial capital (e.g., Tacitus, *Ann.* 3.28; 4.19–20; 4.30; Suetonius, *Dom.* 9.3; 12.1–2).[5] Furthermore, the charge of atheism (rejecting the Roman gods) could lead to prosecution for treason. For example, Cassius Dio records that Flavius Clemens, Domitilla, and many others were charged with atheism and thus treason during the reign of Domitian. They had their property confiscated; Clemens was executed; and Domitilla was exiled (*Hist. rom.* 67.14.2; cf. 68.1.1–2).[6] Even though there is no evidence that Christians in Rome regularly suffered pogroms like the one implemented by Nero, it is not difficult to imagine the lingering anxiety that could accompany a confession of Jesus Christ not long after that time in Rome. Such lingering anxieties

---

3. Both 1 Clement and Hebrews also refer to Jesus as "high priest." Other potential connections between Hebrews and 1 Clement are 1 Clem. 17.1 = Heb 11:37, 39; 1 Clem. 17.5 = Heb 3:5; 1 Clem. 21.9 = Heb 4:12; 1 Clem. 27.2 = Heb 6:8; and 1 Clem. 31.3 = Heb 11:20. Eusebius noted as well Clement's dependence on Hebrews (see *Hist. eccl.* 3.38.1–3).

4. E.g., Mark Allan Powell (1998, 58), following Ernest Best, states that the negative portrayal of the disciples in Mark addresses the pastoral concern of a community that has suffered persecution, with the result that some had lapsed. See 1 Pet 4:1–6; 5:8–9; Shepherd of Hermas, Sim. 9.20–21.3; Vis. 5.7; Mand. 4.3.

5. Similar experiences also occurred in the Roman provinces (see Josephus, *J.W.* 7.11.1–4 §§437–453).

6. See also Cassius Dio, *Hist. rom.* 63.11.1–12.1, for similar penalties of execution, exile, and confiscation under Nero.

makes good sense of the "fear of death" that the author addresses in the opening of his sermon. In sum, if the recipients of Hebrews are suffering, in part, from official action in Rome and if they are tempted to deny their confession of Jesus Christ in order to (re)identify with their former pagan lives, then Rome and its propaganda should warrant careful consideration for the study of Hebrews.

Understanding the Rhetoric of Resistance in Hebrews

Even in light of the considerations above, we still might wonder if Rome and its propaganda are a concern to the author or his audience since Hebrews never explicitly mentions Rome but frames its discourse around a comparison between the old and the new covenants (Martin and Whitlark 2011, 415–39). We should note, however, that all of the comparative topics in Hebrews are employed for a deliberative end in order to address the overriding concern of the author that his audience continue firm in its hope in Jesus Christ until the end (Martin and Whitlark 2012, 379–400). This deliberative focus coheres well with a community that is tempted to compromise its Christian confession to identify more closely with Rome. Even so, is it possible that, within this exhortation to ongoing faithfulness, the audience would have recognized resistance to Rome and its claims? One answer to this question has been the insights drawn from James C. Scott's discussion of hidden transcripts and his observation that resistance to imperial power occurs along a spectrum, from compliance to open rebellion. According to Scott, the hidden transcript that expresses the opposition of the subordinate is often veiled and smuggled into public interactions. Coding the hidden transcript is done in the interest of safety, because the subordinate group cannot afford direct confrontation with the dominant.[7] Scott's observations have encouraged New Testament scholars to discern within the New Testament more subtle and sophisticated resistance by early Christians to their imperial culture.

This essay, however, offers another approach, namely, to ask what the rhetorical expectations of first-century audiences were with regard to the critique of authority. If we examine these rhetorical expectations, we will find that the authorial audience of Hebrews would have anticipated

---

7. One of Scott's most influential works, though not his earliest, has been *Domination and the Arts of Resistance: Hidden Transcripts* (1990).

critiques of authority to be oblique, implicit, or covert, that is, "figured." Figured speech was a much-discussed topic in ancient rhetorical hand-books.[8] Quintilian acknowledges that this type of figured communication was common in his day (Flavian Rome), and he thought that his read-ers were especially eager for him to address it (see *Inst.* 9.1.14; 9.2.65). At its heart, figured speech was a way of saying something without having to say it directly or plainly or even at all. Furthermore, it was the rec-ommended "art of safe criticism" (Ahl 1984, 174–208).[9] In the Roman Empire, speaking against the emperor or Rome could be regarded as a treasonable offense, thus any strategic critique would require the sophis-tication of figured speaking (Rudich 2006, 7–28; e.g., Suetonius, *Aug.* 55; *Dom.* 12.2). The surveillance or informant culture of imperial Rome also made figured forms of communication popular.[10] We would, then, antici-pate that the rhetorically sophisticated author of Hebrews would not take on Rome directly in his critiques of its propaganda. Moreover, the audi-ence of Hebrews would expect critiques of Rome's hegemonic authority to be figured. They may even have been eager to hear these messages of covert resistance. Recognizing figured critiques, then, requires us both to pay attention to places where the author of Hebrews is oblique and to con-sider whether we are able to hear resistance to Rome and its propaganda after an examination of the imperial culture of the audience.

Resisting Rome's Rhetoric in Hebrews

In this section I will offer three areas of resistance in Hebrews where the author, in a figured manner, has challenged Rome and its propaganda with the gospel of Jesus Christ. These locations of resistance center on (1) the Christians' superior hope, (2) the nullification of Roman power to coerce

---

8. See those handbooks attributed to Demetrius (*Eloc.* 287–94), Quintilian (*Inst.* 9.1.14; 9.2.65–99), Dionysius ([*Rhet.*] 8–9), and Hermogenes (*On Invention* 4.13). Figured critiques could take three basic forms: implication, deflection, or irony (see Hermogenes, *On Invention* 4.13). Heath (2003, 88) thinks that these three were stan-dard classifications since these forms are paralleled in both treatises by Dionysius on figured speech.

9. See Quintilian, *Inst.* 9.2.66, and Demetrius, *Eloc.* 287, who identify the need for safety and propriety as situations that called for figured speech.

10. Suetonius records unsuccessful attempts to curb the prevalence of informants in Rome under Nero (*Nero* 10.1) and at the beginning of Domitian's rule (*Dom.* 9.3). Cassius Dio also relates similar efforts attempted under Nerva (*Hist. rom.* 68.1.2).

loyalty through fear, and (3) the theodicean challenge presented by Rome's
destruction of the Jerusalem temple.

Proclaiming a Superior Hope

The first site of resistance to consider in Hebrews involves a hope the
author claims for his audience. The author of Hebrews in his final exhortations calls for his audience to bear the reproach of Jesus, because "here
we have a city that does not remain but are looking for one to come" (Heb
13:14). This elliptical statement illustrates a form of figured speech where
the explicit referent (in this case two cities) is implied (Whitlark 2014,
23–25; see Demetrius, *Eloc.* 287; Quintilian, *Inst.* 9.2.64 [cf. 8.6.21]). The
city to come which is the hope of the audience is readily identifiable from
the context of the sermon. In the preceding final *synkrisis*, the author
described the inviolable heavenly Jerusalem that awaits the faithful, where
they will gather forever in joyful assembly (Heb 12:22–24). The author
contrasts the heavenly Jerusalem with the present city of the audience.
That earthly city is not eternal, therefore it will not remain.

If we listen to such a statement in the wider context of first-century
Rome, then we can discern that this rather oblique and seemingly innocuous statement resists important imperial claims. By the first century, Rome
was being touted as the eternal city. Tibullus, in his *Elegies* 2.5.23, refers
to Rome as the eternal city. Under Vespasian, ROMA PERPTVA (eternal
Rome) and AETERNITAS (eternity) appeared on coin legends. The eternity of Rome was an important message in Flavian propaganda, especially
in view of the political upheavals that had resulted after Nero's death. The
far-reaching influence of this claim is illustrated in a decree from Acmo-
nia in Phrygia during the Flavian period. The decree is validated with
the statement "by the eternity of Rome."[11] During this period as well, it
was not uncommon to find the image of Vesta holding the palladium on
coins.[12] The palladium was allegedly kept in the Temple of Vesta in Rome
in order to affirm, as the coins depicted, the tradition that the city which
possessed the palladium would never cease to exist. By the early second
century, when Hadrian built his Temple to Roma Aeternitas and Venus

---

11. *IGR* 4.661.14–15; see also *CIG* 2.2715.
12. *BMC* 2:46 nos. 260–62, 47 no. 263, 237 no. 83, 238 no. 87, 247 no. 144, 253 no.
150, 261 no. 189, 264 no. 200, 265 nos. 201–2, 267 no. 216, 272 no. 234, 276 no. 248,
277 no. 251, 279 nos. 256–58, 295 no. 313, 353 no. 258.

Felix, *aeterna* becomes increasingly fixed as a modifier of Roma and *urbs* (Pratt 1965, 28).

Proclaiming Rome as the eternal city was one way to assert the unending and indomitable rule of Rome. Virgil has Jupiter famously promise the eternity of Roman dominion at the beginning of the *Aeneid*: "For these I have set neither bounds nor periods of Empire. *Imperium* without end I have bestowed" (1.278–279 [Fairclough, LCL]). Aristides, in his *Roman Oration*, praises the unending rule of Rome as the hope for the world: "For the eternal duration of the Empire the whole civilized world prays" (29).[13] Aristides goes on to pity all those born before the rise of Roman rule that has returned Justice to the earth in a new golden age (106).

It was typically not safe to prophesy the end of Rome. Some Roman emperors had even forbidden such prophecies like those that arose among the Gauls predicting the end of Roman rule and the rise of a new Gallic hegemony (Janssen 1979, 148–49; see Tacitus, *Hist.* 4.54). The author of Hebrews, however, announces in a figured manner the end of Rome and its rule while holding out the hope of an eternal city and kingdom established by God for his people. The one who holds on to this hope will share in the joyful celebration in the heavenly Jerusalem at the end of the age. For the author of Hebrews, Rome stands under the imminent judgment of God, who will once more shake the heavens and the earth, leaving only the unshakeable kingdom, which the faithful will inherit (Heb 12:25–29). The boast of eternal Rome is thus vacuous.[14]

Nullifying the Threat of Death

The second area of resistance involves the limitation of Roman power to coerce loyalty. In Heb 2:14–15, the author declares that Jesus has destroyed or nullified "the one who holds the power of death." Like Heb 13:14, this elliptical statement implies its referent. The author, however, immediately identifies his referent as the devil, who by this power enslaves those who fear death. The description of the devil as "the one who holds the power of

---

13. The translation of the Greek text of Aristides's encomium is by Oliver 1953, 895–907.

14. Other supra-imperial claims in Hebrews may also be found in the use of *oikoumenē* in 1:6 and 2:15 and in the use of *patris* in 11:13–16. Both refer the place of the believers' hope but also were common terms used to refer to the world that was ruled by Rome (Whitlark 2014, 77–93).

death" is a curious description, seeing that the author recognizes God as the ultimate giver of life and death. Examining the imperial context of the audience will uncover that the author has engaged in a figured critique of Rome's own claim to exercise the power of death over those under its rule.

Roman imperium was understood to lie in the ability to take life. There were several ways in which this idea was communicated. First, only the holder of imperium in the provinces could conduct capital trials (SEG 9.8; Pliny, *Ep.* 10.30). When Josephus describes the authority Augustus granted Coponius over Judea, Josephus writes that Coponius was given "power to kill" (*J. W.* 2.8.1 §117). Second, the conceptual framework for Roman imperium was that of the power and rights of the paterfamilias (Lacey 1986, 121–44). This framework is reinforced by the emperor, who regularly took the title *pater patriae* (father of the fatherland)—a title printed ubiquitously on coin legends as P.P. Consequently, Seneca relates the authority of the emperor to that of a father (*Clem.* 1.14.2). The all-encompassing nature of the paterfamilias's authority to care for his household and to protect its honor was expressed in the paterfamilias's absolute power over life and death (see Dionysius of Halicarnassus, *Ant. rom.* 2.26). Thus the emperor as the father of the Roman state and the holder of imperium was also, as Seneca writes, "the arbiter of life and death for the nations. It rests in [his] power what each person's lot and state shall be" (*Clem.* 1.1.2 [Basore, LCL]). Third, the insignia of Roman imperium were the fasces. The fasces were a bound group of rods in which an ax was inserted. Lictors carried the fasces as part of the entourage of one who held imperium. The message was clear—the one accused and convicted was liable to immediate punishment, either to be beaten or to be beheaded. Thus one of the most cherished rights of Roman citizenship was the right to appeal a verdict (Marshall 1984, 130). The fasces were symbols of terror that elicited fear when they were paraded in public. Words such as *timeo* (to dread), *terror* (terror), *terribilis* (dreadful), *terreo* (to terrify), *metus* (dread), and *vereor* (to fear/to revere) were commonly used to describe the fasces as the death-dealing emblems of Roman power (137). Supposedly Antony, after mingling with the Alexandrians for a time, appeared suddenly in public in his traditional Roman dress and with his lictors, which inspired terror and awe among the citizenry (Appian, *Bell. civ.* 5.76). Dionysius of Halicarnassus records that Romulus invented the fasces in order to inspire fear so as to restrain the city's inhabitants (*Ant. rom.* 2.29.1). Horace writes that the "Mede dreads our mighty hands and the axes of Alba that are powerful over land and sea" (*Saec.* 54 [Rudd, LCL]). Silius

Italicus writes that the fasces were "a badge of power that all men feared" (*Punica* 10.563–64 [Duff, LCL]). Holding the ax of the fasces to the throat was used as an expression of complete subjugation to Roman power (see Plutarch, *Praec. ger. rei publ.* 17 (813F); Livy, *Ab urbe condita* 26.13.15; 28.24.14, 16). The audience of Hebrews, upon hearing the elliptical phrase "the one who holds the power of death," likely heard a figured reference to Rome's claim to authority and its demand for loyalty.

The oblique description is transformed into a figured critique, in part, when the author identifies the referent of his elliptical statement as the devil. It was not uncommon for early Christians to associate persecuting authorities with the devil's activities. Paul attributes the persecution of the Thessalonian Christians to the devil, who was trying to destroy the faith and loyalty of the fledgling community. Revelation 13 depicts the devil as standing behind the persecution of the Christian community, in part, by Roman authorities. The dragon (i.e., the devil) gives authority over all nations to the first beast (Rome) so that it has the power to kill the saints (esp. 13:5–7, 15). Texts recounting Christian martyrdoms commonly linked the devil with the Roman authorities who persecuted them. For example, in the Mart. Pol. 2.4–3.1, the tortures afflicted by the imperial authorities are attributed to the schemes of the devil. In the Martyrs of Lyons 1.5, the persecution of Christians by the city's inhabitants and its imperial authorities is because of the "evil one." By allying Roman imperium with the demonic, the author of Hebrews locates his audience's struggle in an apocalyptic framework. Their contest is not with the flesh-and-blood representatives of Roman authority. Their contest is with the devil, who attempts to dislodge the community from its confession of Jesus Christ through the threat of death at the hands of Roman authorities. The contest, then, is one that calls for persevering confidence in God's promised future in the face of privation, torture, and even death.

Rome's power of death was used to coerce obedience or submission to its rule. The fear of death made Rome's threats effective. Unless the audience of Hebrews is free from this fear, Rome could always coerce their ultimate loyalties. The author of Hebrews completes his figured critique by announcing abolition from Rome's coercive power through Jesus's own death and subsequent exaltation to immortal life in the world to come.[15]

---

15. Jesus's victory over the devil in Heb 2:14–15 is also reminiscent of the labors of Hercules, especially his labors to bring certain individuals back from the realm of the dead. Moreover, at the conclusion of Hercules's labors, he is taken up at his death

The author's entire focus of Heb 2:5–18 is to amplify the implications of Jesus's exaltation for his audience. Like Jesus, they too will be crowned with glory and honor. Because of Jesus's own exaltation by overcoming death—even death by Roman execution—through resurrection, he is able to lead God's children into the abundance of the coming world that God has promised. Thus Rome's power to coerce loyalty by threatening death can no longer determine the allegiance of the audience. Instead, the author goes on to exhort his audience to heed the word of God, which is like a sword held to an exposed throat (Heb 4:12–13). Thus the audience is not to fear the Roman axes on their necks. In the conclusion of his sermon, the author exhorts his audience to steadfast faith even in the face of loss. He quotes Ps 117:6 (LXX): "The Lord is my help and I will not fear. What can humans do to me?" In the psalm, the psalmist recounts the help and victory of God that counters the threats of his enemies. Thus, with the psalmist, the audience of Hebrews is to remember the help and victory of God. They are to recall the triumphant exaltation of Jesus and not fear what any earthly power can do to them (Whitlark 2014, 122–41).

Undermining Flavian Triumph

The final site of resistance considered in this essay requires us to be willing to locate the audience of Hebrews in Flavian Rome and thus after the destruction of the Jerusalem temple (Whitlark 2014, 8–12). Flavian Rome presented significant theodicean challenges to both Jews and Christians, because the Flavians made central their victory in the Jewish War in efforts to support their claim to rule. For example, the Flavians celebrated a triumph in 71 CE in order to commemorate their victory. During the triumph, items from the Jerusalem temple were displayed in the parade, signifying a conquered deity. In 75 CE, the Temple of Peace, which was built

---

to live among the gods, where he continues to give aid to those who call on him. Likewise, the author of Hebrews in chapters 1 and 2 has depicted Jesus's own apotheosis, which occurred at the conclusion of his labors. Jesus has ascended into the immortal realm, where he is now seated at the right hand of God as helper of Abraham's seed. It might be that the author takes aim at the Roman emperors who modeled their rule and apotheosis after Hercules. Jesus's victory over the devil on behalf of God's faithful legitimated his heavenly ascent. He is the true ruler of the cosmos, not the emperor in Rome, nor the devil who wields death-dealing Roman imperium. For other ways that the Christology of Heb 1–2 possibly resists imperial propaganda surrounding the emperor, see Muir 2008, 170–86.

from the spoils of the Jewish War, was dedicated. The Temple of Peace displayed the golden vessels taken from the Jerusalem temple. In 80 CE, the Colosseum was dedicated. It contained an inscription stating that the amphitheater had been built from the spoils of war, most likely the Jewish War. In 81 CE, two triumphal arches were dedicated to Titus—one in the Circus Maximus and one on the Via Sacra. Both arches celebrated Rome's victory in the Jewish War. Additionally, the Flavians redirected the temple tax paid by every Jewish male for the rebuilding and maintaining of the Temple of Jupiter Optimus Maximus in Rome (Josephus, *J. W.* 7.6.6 §218; Cassius Dio, *Hist. rom.* epitome 65[66].7.2). The *fiscus Judaicus* was aggressively collected at times under the Flavians. Also the *capta* coin type, which had disappeared after Augustus, returned under the Flavians. On these coins, the subjugation of the Judean rebels was depicted often showing Jewish captives bound next to a palm tree (the Flavain symbol for Judea).[16]

The Flavians emphasized their victory in the Jewish War, because they had no family connection to Augustus, which had been the basis of succession to power under the Julio-Claudians. Victory was a revelation of divine approval, thus legitimating new and untraditional claimants to power (Fears 1981, 736–826). Victory in the Jewish War had been achieved under the auspices of Vespasian, indicating that Vespasian and his son were favored by Jupiter, the protector of the Roman state.[17] Moreover, the triumphal procession celebrated in 71 CE was more than a celebration of the *triumphator*. It was a celebration of the gods and especially Jupiter Optimus Maximus, who gave victory over Rome's enemies (see Livy, *Ab urbe condita* 45.30.10; Josephus, *J. W.* 7.5.5 §136). Supposedly the *triumphator* wore the insignia of Jupiter Optimus Maximus and concluded the triumphal procession at his temple in recognition of the favor Jupiter had bestowed on his earthly representative.[18] It is no sur-

---

16. From 69 CE to 85 CE, series of coins were issued that proclaimed Roman victory over Judea. From 69 to 73 CE: *RIC* 2:16 nos. 15–16, 18 no. 34, 19 no. 41a, 20 nos. 45 and 53, 44 nos. 254 and 266, 48 no. 287, 49 nos. 288–89, 63 no. 393, 68 nos. 424–26, 73 nos. 489–91, 86 no. 608, 87 no. 620, 101 no. 733. 77–78 CE: *RIC* 2:84 nos. 596–96; 104 no. 762; 107 no. 784. From 80 to 81 CE: *RIC* 2:127 nos. 91–93, 133 no. 141, 131 no. 128. From 85 CE: *RIC* 2:180 no. 280.

17. This claim can be found on the triumphal arch in the Circus Maximus; see *CIL* 6.944 = *ILS* 264.

18. For the *triumphator* wearing the garb of Jupiter Optimus Maximus, see Livy,

prise, then, that divine grant of victory appears as a major theme on the imperial coinage of the Flavians.[19] Coins issued under Vespasian show Victoria handing the palladium to Vespasian.[20] On other coins, Victoria is in the extended right hand of Roma, signifying the bestowal of victory on the emperor.[21] Furthermore, Flavian victory brought peace and abundance. Consequently, imperial coinage from this time regularly depicts Pax holding the cornucopia.[22]

The claim that the gods of Rome prevailed over the God of the Jews (and Christians)—profoundly symbolized in the destruction of his temple in Jerusalem—posed a significant challenge for Christians and Jews. From the pagan perspective, Rome's victory and destruction of the Jerusalem temple brought great shame on the God not only of Jews but also of Christians. Even a century later, for Christians who continued to identify the God of the Jews with the God of Jesus Christ, Irenaeus still had to defend God's power and sovereignty against his gnostic opponents who point to Rome's destruction of the temple as impugning both (*Haer.* 4.4.1–2).

How, then, does the author of Hebrews respond to this theodicean challenge faced by Christians in Flavian Rome? First, the author refocuses the loci of God's honor in the enthroned Son, whom he appointed heir of all things (Heb 1:2–3), and in the persevering community, who holds on to its confidence in God's promise (12:28; 13:15–16). These loci affirm God's power to override any verdict of Rome as well as God's continued sovereignty to fulfill his plans for his creation. Second, the author interprets the suffering that his audience is experiencing as God's instrument for their training or education in holiness (Heb 12:4–11). Here, Rome's power is made subservient to God's purposes. Third, the author engages in a sophisticated figured critique of Rome's boast. In this case, we need to consider what the structural framework or comparative project of Hebrews might have meant to a Christian audience in Flavian Rome. Two points

---

Ab urbe condita 10.7.10, and Suetonius, *Aug.* 94. Josephus only mentions the triumphal garments (*J.W.* 7.5.4 §131).

19. A glance at the index in *BMC* 2:451–52 demonstrates the ubiquity of victory on Flavian coinage.

20. *BMC* 2:126 no. 586, 191 no. 786, 194 no. 793, 198 no. 805.

21. *BMC* 2:111 no. 526, 295 no. 316.

22. *RIC* 2:64 no. 403, 65 no. 410, 69 nos. 435–37 and 440, 76 nos. 515 and 517, 78 no. 534, 80 no. 552, 81 no. 564, 82 no. 573, 84 no. 589, 86 no. 609, 93 no. 673, 96 no. 693, 99 no. 718, 102 no. 748, 106 no. 779, 125 no. 77, 127 no. 94, 135 no. 155, 140 no. 181, 210 nos. 444 and 448.

about figured speech are important for our consideration: (1) rhetorical theorists recognized that whole speeches could be figured (Dionysius, [*Rhet.*] 8 [295.2–14]),[23] and (2) speeches could have multiple purposes, both overt and covert or figured (Dionysius, [*Rhet.*] 8 [296.14–20]; Heath 2003, 83). With regard to Hebrews, the sermon has an overt deliberative aim that calls its audience to covenant faithfulness even in the midst of suffering and shame. That deliberative aim is accomplished through structuring the exhortations around a comparison of covenants where the new covenant is shown to be superior to the old covenant. One function of that comparison is to amplify the reasons that the community has for faithfulness. If certain consequences resulted from fidelity or infidelity under the old covenant how much more these are true for those under the new. A complementary covert objective also emerges if we consider an aspect of this comparative project in the context of Flavian Rome. The author argues that the old covenant was designed by God to anticipate the realities of the new covenant inaugurated by Jesus's enthronement. Moses had been a witness to those realities (Heb 3:5). The earthly cultic ministry of the tabernacle, which served as the pattern for the temple, was brought to an end through Jesus's heavenly priestly ministry (Heb 8:5, 13; 9:6–14). In fact, Jesus was God's plan "from the foundation of the world" to perfect his people (implied in Heb 9:26). By arguing in this manner, the author of Hebrews holds forth God's sovereignty over the world. His plans are being fulfilled. Additionally, the author makes void Rome's claim to have ended the worship and honor of the God of Jews (and Christians) by destroying his temple. Long before Rome ever got to Jerusalem, God had brought to an end the ministry of the temple when he enthroned Jesus as the Son at his right hand. In fact, its end had been prefigured in the tabernacle and its ministry even before the first temple had been built. Interestingly, Irenaeus takes the same line of argument against the theodicean challenge of his opponents. He states that they misunderstand the function of the temple. The temple and old-covenant institutions were always meant to come to an end in their fulfillment (Whitlark 2014, 160–88).[24]

---

23. The text consulted and referenced here is from Radermacher and Usener 1967.

24. Aitken (2005, 131–48) pioneered this area of inquiry in the study of Hebrews. She argued that Hebrews was a response to the Flavian triumph and the celebration of the apotheosis of Titus in its own celebration of Jesus's enthronement and victory procession of freedpersons to the true heavenly temple. The author ironically bestows

Conclusion

Empires are maintained both by superior power and stories that justify that power. Certainly this is true of imperial Rome during the emergence of Christian communities in the first century. The Letter to the Hebrews engages the pressures its audience is experiencing within the Roman imperial culture. The author in a rhetorically appropriate and anticipated manner combats some of the powerful myths of Rome with the gospel of Jesus Christ in an effort to address the spiritual fatigue and drift some in the community were experiencing through the ongoing experience of fear and shame. The use of figured critiques accomplishes two purposes. First, they provided a measure of safety for the community and author by not taking on Roman propaganda directly. The author knows that the persevering faith to which he calls members of his audience will signal ongoing resistance to authorities, in part, by continuing to identify with the community that confesses the enthroned Son who was crucified. That identification includes caring for those imprisoned, tortured, and possibly threatened with exile or death. The author, however, is not promoting a lust for martyrdom through inflammatory rhetoric against Roman authority. Hebrews is not a call for open rebellion but patient suffering. Second, the use of figured speech is rhetorically effective in diminishing the self-importance of Rome. Rome is not central to the author's exhortation. Instead, Jesus Christ and the hope God offers through him is the focus. The audience above all is to consider, not Rome, but Jesus—their apostle and high priest and the author and perfect of faith (3:1; 12:2). In sum, the author of Hebrews summons his audience to follow Jesus patiently "through endless wastes," resisting the tyranny of Rome on their way to God's promised future (Käsemann 1982, 17).

For Further Reading

Aitken, Ellen Bradshaw. 2005. "Portraying the Temple in Stone and Text: The Arch of Titus and the Epistle to the Hebrews." Pages 131–48 in *Hebrews: Contemporary Methods—New Insights*. Edited by Gabriella Gelardini. Leiden: Brill.

---

honor on Jesus and his community by co-opting and employing echoes of the Roman triumph that had been used to shame the Jews and their God.

Maier, Harry O. Forthcoming. "'For Here We Have No Lasting City...':
Flavian Iconography, Roman Imperial Sacrificial Iconography, and the
Epistle to the Hebrews." In *Hebrews in Context*. Edited by Gabriella
Gelardini and Harold W. Attridge. AJEC 91. Leiden: Brill.

Muir, Steven. 2008. "The Anti-imperial Rhetoric of Hebrews 1:3: Χαρακτήρ
as a 'Double-edged Sword.'" Pages 170–86 in *A Cloud of Witnesses: The
Theology of Hebrews in Its Ancient Context*. Edited by Richard Bauckham, Daniel Driver, Trevor Hart, and Nathan MacDonald. LNTS 387.
London: T&T Clark.

Punt, Jeremy. 2007. "The Letter to the Hebrews." Pages 338–68 in *Postcolonial Commentary on the New Testament Writings*. Edited by Fernando
F. Segovia and Rasiah S. Sugirtharajah. New York: Continuum.

Westfall, Cynthia Long. 2011. "Running the Gamut: The Varied Responses
to Empire in Jewish Christianity." Pages 230–58 in *Empire in the New
Testament*. Edited by Stanley E. Porter and Cynthia Long Westfall.
MNTSS 10. Eugene, OR: Pickwick.

Whitlark, Jason A. 2014. *Resisting Empire: Rethinking the Purpose of the
Letter to "the Hebrews."* LNTS 484. London: T&T Clark.

———. Forthcoming. "The God of Peace and His Victorious King:
Hebrews 13:20–21 in Its Roman Imperial Context." In *Hebrews in
Context*. Edited by Gabriella Gelardini and Harold W. Attridge. AJEC
91. Leiden: Brill.

Empire in James: The Crown of Life

Matthew Ryan Hauge

The book of James stands at the forefront of the so-called Catholic Epistles, which also includes the two letters of Peter, the three letters of John, and Jude. These writings were thought to have been written for the catholic, or "whole," church, in contrast to the occasional letters of Paul, which were intended for specific communities and persons. Unfortunately, this collection of mass mail within the New Testament is often overshadowed by the Gospels and the Pauline corpus, but for those who have eyes to see and ears to hear they are an invaluable source of early reflection on Christian faith and practice.[1]

The "father of church history," Eusebius of Caesarea (263–339 CE), identified the author of the book of James as the brother of Jesus (see Gal 1:19) and leader of the early church in Jerusalem (see Acts 15:13; 21:18). Modern translations render the Greek name *Iakōbos* as "James" in the salutation, but the book itself suggests that a more appropriate translation would be "Jacob," the father of the twelve tribes to whom the letter is written. These are the words from a father to his children who have been scattered and dispersed.

The Crown of Life (1:2–21)

Jacob begins by identifying the nature of his concern, namely, trials his children are suffering, but this suffering is not in vain. These trials are

---

1. Pheme Perkins notes that these epistles have always occupied the outer edges of the canon; in the *Revised Common Lectionary*, for example, there are eight selections of 1 Peter, five from James, two from 2 Peter, and none from Jude (Perkins 1995, 1–2). In other words, for over a millennium, lay Christians were seldom exposed to these disregarded members of the New Testament.

instrumental for the maturation of their faith. In the light of these trials, he advises them to seek wisdom from God, who gives generously to those who seek it. At the same time, he warns them of the danger of hypocrisy, drawing on the image of the wave of the sea being tossed back and forth by the wind. They must trust the wisdom that is given, but that is not as easy as it may sound, especially if that wisdom calls for inaction.

Immediately after the call for wisdom, the content of these trials is identified as socioeconomic injustice. The "lowly" children, who will be raised up, are contrasted with the "rich," who will be brought low and perish like a fragile flower in the field under the scorching heat of the sun (Jas 1:9–10).[2] The beauty of the flower is seductive and alluring, but its beauty is fleeting and will disappear. The lowly do not need to take matters into their own hands; they are to seek the wisdom necessary to endure, and their needs will be addressed and their situation made right.

Given the fate that awaits the rich, which Jacob will describe in greater detail toward the conclusion of the book, the lowly are blessed if they endure this socioeconomic injustice. Jacob warns his children that they will be tested by the desires within them, but these desires do not come from God despite their allure and seductive qualities. Rather, they are conceived within Jacob's children, and that desire gives birth to imbalance and error in judgment, which leads to death. If they act on this desire, they act on a deception and will die, but if they resist the temptation to raise themselves up and wait patiently to be raised up, they will be rewarded. The elucidation of this deception is the key task of the remainder of the book, but for now it would be wise for the lowly to consider their prize—the "crown of life" (1:12).

The "crown of life" is an unusual phrase in the New Testament. Outside of James, it occurs one other time, in Rev 2:10: "Do not fear what you are about to suffer. Beware, the devil is about to throw some of you into prison so that you may be tested, and for ten days you will have affliction. Be faithful until death, and I will give you the crown of life." Both authors are deeply concerned with the suffering of the faithful, but if the faithful defeat these trials through perseverance they are promised the gift of the crown of life. But what exactly is the crown of life?

"Crown" is a translation of the Greek word *stephanos* (Lat. *corona*), which occurs only once in James, meaning "to surround or encompass." In

---

2. Unless otherwise noted, all Scripture quotations are from the NRSV.

the context of Jas 1:9–18, it is clear this term refers to an award or prize for the lowly who endure the trial and pass the test. During the classical Greek and Hellenistic era, crowns were worn by priests, actors, orators, symposiasts, and most importantly victors at the games. These crowns were constructed from branches and plants, and the type of material used was often associated with a certain deity or deities. The most prized crown was made of an olive branch, reserved for those victorious at the Olympian games.

The games at Olympia were held in honor of Zeus, the sky god, once every four years in August or September. Pindar (ca. 522–443 BCE), the revered lyric poet from Thebes, records two possible origins for the games. In his first *Olympian Ode*, Pindar recalls the victory of Pelops in his chariot race against King Oenomaus and his ensuing fame: "My duty is to crown [*stephanōnsai*] that man with an equestrian tune in Aeolic song" (*Ol.* 100–102 [Race, LCL]). Pelops would later be venerated at the sanctuary of Olympia. Blood was poured into the sacrificial pit in the evening for Pelops ("dark-face"), and the next day sacrifice was made to the god of light, Zeus (Burkert 1983, 97).

The Olympian Games were also thought to have been founded by Heracles, the son of Zeus and Alcmene. In the tenth *Olympian Ode*, Pindar commemorates the military victory of the hero and how he established the first Olympiad. "Who then won the new crown [*stephanon*] with hands or feet or with chariot, after fixing in his thoughts a triumph in the context and achieving it in deed?" (*Ol.* 60–64 [Race, LCL]). Pindar continues, naming the victors and describing the cheers from their fellow soldiers.

The Olympian Games, regardless of their origin, were a celebration of the greatest warriors of the age. Each of the contests, including the sprint, chariot, and single-horse races, the long jump, discus, javelin, wrestling, boxing, and the *pankration* (a combination of boxing and wrestling), were intended to measure the key qualities of the ideal warrior. They were games of combat, and the most violent was awarded the crown.

During the Roman era, crowns were awarded in recognition of valor in battle, most notably, the *corona obsidionalis* or *graminea*—the "blockade crown" or the "grass crown" (Maxfield 1981, 67). There were many crowns awarded for various acts of military courage but only the grass crown was awarded by the soldiers to a single individual for rescuing an entire army from certain disaster. Often, the grass itself was given by the vanquished people to their conqueror as a symbol of their surrender—their soil (land) now belonged to the victor.

Pliny the Elder (23/24–79 CE), the Roman naturalist, comments on the significance of this crown in his compendium of ancient knowledge, the *Natural History*.

> No crown indeed has been a higher honour than the crown of grass among the rewards for glorious deeds given by the sovereign people, lords of the earth. Jeweled crowns, golden crowns, crowns for scaling enemy ramparts or walls, or for boarding men-of-war, the civic crown for saving the life of a citizen, the triumph crown—these were instituted later than this grass crown, and all differ from it greatly, in distinction as in character. (*Nat.* 22.4 [Jones, LCL])

Pliny records only eight recipients of this most distinguished award, the final of whom was Augustus (63 BCE–14 CE), the first emperor at Rome who is "now in Heaven" (*Nat.* 22.6 [Jones, LCL]).

Pliny does not indicate why the emperor was given this honor, but the Priene Calendar Inscription (*OGIS* 458; ca. 9 BCE) at the Temple of Athena provides some illustrative context. In this dedicatory inscription, Augustus is celebrated by the Greeks of Asia as the culmination of the divine order, the patron of virtue, and the savior (*sōtēr*) of humanity—the day of his birth was the beginning of the good news (*euangelion*) for the cosmos—high praise indeed!

Upon Augustus's death, the Roman biographer Suetonius (ca. 69–after 122 CE) records the various honors that were considered to recognize his achievements as emperor, including transferring the month of August to September, because he died in the latter. After his body was carried by the senators to the funeral pyre, a man of praetorian rank testified that "he had seen the form of the Emperor, after he had been reduced to ashes, on its way to heaven" (*Aug.* 100.4 [Rolfe, LCL]). The flames that consumed his broken body could not ultimately defeat this final recipient of the crown of grass—his spirit rose up and ascended into heaven as a god.

The Greeks and Romans awarded crowns of olive, vine and ivy, roses, oak leaves, laurel, myrtle, and gold for heroic feats in the games and on the battlefield, but none were composed of "life." What is this material, and what merit does it indicate? Unfortunately, the author of James only uses this Greek term for "life" (*zōē*) twice. Interestingly, the second occurrence is within the context of a critique of the merchant class who year after year pursue wealth in 4:13–17. Jacob pauses to remind them of their misplaced values: "What is your life [*zōē*]? For you are a mist that appears for a little while and then vanishes" (4:14b). This caveat, reminiscent of the wisdom of the teacher in the book of Ecclesiastes (see 1:2–11), recalls the condemnation of the rich in Jas 1:10–11 who will disappear suddenly amid their busyness.

Outside of the book of James, this term often refers to one's living or property, but given his critique of the rich and the merchant class, this cannot be what Jacob has in mind. In some other occurrences of this term in Greek literature, it is used as the opposite of death, as in existence. Is the crown of life a reward of life without death, and if so, who has the power and authority to grant such a gift?

The location and title of the gift-giver are identified immediately after Jacob warns his children not to be deceived by the desire within them that gives birth to death. If they endure the trial and test before them, the lowly will be rewarded the crown of life by the "Father of lights [*patros tōn phōtōn*]," who is "from above" (1:17). This title is unusual, so it is difficult to know with any degree of certainty what the author intends by this phrase.

The location of the gift-giver suggests that he may be the creator of the visible lights "above"—the sun, the moon, the five wandering lights (i.e., planets), and the fixed lights (i.e., stars). Indeed, Jacob contrasts the fixed (consistent) position of the Father with these moving (inconsistent) lights, which turn and cast shadows.[3] Many may turn to the heavenly bodies as a medium of divination, but Jacob calls his children to place their faith in the purposes of the creator of these lights. He is the progenitor of the "word of truth [*logō alētheias*]"—a new kind of world and wisdom—giving birth not to a deception crowned by victory, violence, and death, but to a truth crowned by faith, endurance, and life (1:18).

If the lowly are to receive this crown of life, they must listen to the wisdom from above and persevere under trial. In contrast to the Romans, who crowned the greatest warriors of the age for their deliberate violence, the Father of lights will crown the greatest listeners of the age for their deliberate submission. The injustice of the socioeconomic situation of the lowly can easily lead to a diseased mind, and a diseased mind is filthy, defective, and cannot be trusted. If they welcome the "word of truth,"

---

3. "Light" is also used as a metaphor for deliverance, happiness, victory, or glory (see Homer, *Il.* 6.6; 16.95; 15.741; 17.615; 21.538; Pindar, *Ol.* 4.11; Aeschylus, *Pers.* 300; Sophocles, *Ant.* 600; *Aj.* 709), which given the promise of the crown is possible, but the plural form and the critique of the movement of the "lights" suggests that the metaphoric use is unlikely in this context.

placing their trust in the divine impartation of the Father of lights, they will live as new creations and be delivered from certain death.

The Mirror (1:22–2:26)

In 1:22, Jacob transitions from listening to doing, but what exactly are the lowly expected to do? If they are not called to rise up and defeat the rich, but rather to endure the trial that is set before them as a test of their trust in the wisdom of God—the word of truth—then how are they expected to live?

There are some who hear the word of truth, but they are not "doers" (*poiētēs*, "composer of a poem") of the word (1:22). They are frauds and charlatans who look in the mirror and immediately forget what they look like. But why are they looking in a mirror in the first place? "Mirror" is a translation of the Greek word *eisoptron*, which refers to a looking glass that reflects something. This is not a common term in Greek literature, but it does occur in the seventh *Nemean Ode*, in which Pindar describes poetry and song as the looking glass through which the great deeds of those who have died can be remembered, although he also recognizes the qualitative difference between the reflection and the object (*Nem.* 7.14).

Eisoptron is only used one other time in the New Testament. Paul, like Pindar, comments on the limitations of the "mirror" in 1 Corinthians: "For now we see in a mirror, dimly [*ainigmati*, "dark saying"], but then we will see face to face. Now I know only in part; then I will know fully, even as I have been fully known" (1 Cor 13:12). In 13:10, Paul warns of the limitations of what can be known until the arrival of the "complete [*teleios*]"; after all, we see in the looking glass a dark saying (i.e., an enigma). In the light of this unknowing, the apostle admonishes the community to love one another. Love is the definitive demarcation of the one who serves God.

Jacob agrees. The mirror is deceptive, but he contrasts the mirror with the "perfect [*teleion*]" law—ways or customs of God—that can be seen (Jas 1:25). If they become composers of the word of truth, they will be free of the mirror that deceives and disguises. There are some who are held in the grip of that deception. Their tongues never stop moving. Their hearts never stop cheating. They are vain, empty, and idle. They are "religious" (*thrēskos*, "superstitious"), but their religion is vain, empty, and idle (1:26). The "religion" (*thrēkeia*, "service of God") that is unstained by the cosmic pollution that deceives and destroys looks on and considers the needs of the powerless—the orphan and widow. This is the worship God desires (1:27).

Sadly, the superstitious continue to act on the reflection in the mirror, the deception of this world, which (ironically; see 1:9–11) privileges the rich and humiliates the poor. Even the "assembly" (*synagōgē*, "synagogue") has been polluted (2:2). In antiquity, there were two primary social markers of wealth—clothing and diet. Jacob employs the former to demonstrate the hypocrisy of the synagogue. He condemns the superstitious for their lack of trust and their lack of imagination. Why do they prefer the one with the gold ring and clean clothing over the one whose clothing is filthy, greasy, and uncultured?

These socioeconomic indicators are dividing the synagogue, but this should not be. They are based in thoughtless reasoning that reflects the kingdom in the mirror, not the kingdom of the perfect. The rich may possess fine jewelry and garments, but it is the lowly whom God has chosen to be rich in the one commodity of any value in the kingdom that is coming—faith. It is the rich who blaspheme; that is to say, it is the rich who speak ill of God, utter rash prayers, and make common the creator of the heavenly lights.

As a result, the superstitious trample on the most important custom of God—"You shall love your neighbor as yourself" (2:8). These members of the synagogue suffer from a failure of judgment; they fail to understand that one who violates a single way of God violates all the ways of God. The God who said, "You shall not commit adultery," also said, "You shall not murder" (2:11). The superstitious would never commit adultery, but they would kill the rich who oppress them. The mirror has deceived them, and they act on that deception. They fail to understand the ways of God. Judgment has been defeated. Mercy wears the crown of victory.

God has chosen the poor to be rich in faith, but what exactly is faith? The Greek term for faith, *pistis*, is common and tends to infer trust or confidence, but what is the object of that trust and how does that trust manifest itself? Jacob begins by warning his children that faith cannot deliver them from death. If they do not care for the widow and orphan—the one who lacks clothing and food—their faith is already dead. If faith is merely a verbal claim—"Go in peace; keep warm and eat your fill"—it has no life, no vitality, no anima (2:15).

The faith of the superstitious is bankrupt and useless. Actually, it is worse than that. As proof, Jacob alludes to the opening line of the Shema, the Jewish confessionary prayer recited daily: "You believe [*pisteueis*] that God is one" (2:19). They have placed their trust in the oneness of God, but in this regard they are no different from the demons (*daimonion*). These lower divinities also believe in the oneness of God, but cognitive recognition and verbal assent cannot save you from death. If the superstitious do not bring their faith to life through deeds of mercy, they are functionally demonic.

Faith that is fertile and life-giving is exemplified in two figures from the past, Abraham and Rahab. Abram had begun to lose hope in the promises of Yahweh. In Gen 12:1–3, Yahweh promised that Abram would be given offspring and land, but three chapters later he remained childless and complained that a slave would be his heir. The word of Yahweh came to the troubled man in a vision, and the "Father of lights" renewed his promise: "'Look toward heaven and count the stars, if you are able to count them.' Then he said to him, 'So shall your descendants be.' And he believed the LORD; and the LORD reckoned it to him as righteousness" (Gen 15:5b–6; see Jas 2:23).

According to Jacob, the "righteousness," or justness, of Abram was not truly fulfilled until several chapters later, when the Lord tested the faith of Abraham by commanding him to sacrifice his son on the altar. Abraham did not hesitate (see Jub. 19:9; 1 Macc 2:52; Sir 44:20–21; Philo, *Abr.* 32.170; LAB 18.5). As fate (or the Lord) would have it, a ram was in the wrong place at the wrong time. Abram believed the divine promise in Gen 15, but Abraham acted on that faith in Gen 22: "Because you have done this, and have not withheld your son, your only son, I will indeed bless you, and I will make your offspring as numerous as the stars of heaven and as the sand that is on the seashore" (22:16b–17). Abraham believed and obeyed God; he was a friend of God (see 2 Chr 20:7; Isa 41:8). Without obedience (works), faith is dead.

This obedience is also exemplified by the lesser-known Rahab, a curiously significant character in the New Testament despite the minor role she plays in the book of Joshua (see Josh 2:1–24; 6:22–25; Matt 1:5; Heb 11:31). Like the "lowly," Rahab is defined by her socioeconomic situation—a harlot (*pornē*)—but she is not bound to it. She was vindicated by her hospitality, welcoming and entertaining those in need of shelter and food (see Jas 2:16). Without the animating force of the spirit, the body lies still and lifeless. Likewise, as Abraham and Rahab demonstrate, without the animating force of acts of mercy, faith lies still and lifeless.

The Wisdom from Below (3:1–4:12)

Acts of violence begin with violent speech. In 3:1, Jacob directs his rhetorical gaze on the leadership in the community, namely, those who teach and shape the trajectory of communal life. These teachers will be held to a stricter standard of judgment than those who are led astray by their teaching. Influence and power do not come without consequence. In fact, those in positions of influence and power should be worried—deeply worried—for everyone makes mistakes, especially mistakes of the fiery tongue from below.

Teachers, consider the horse. Or, more properly, consider the chariot. The plural form of *hippos* ("horses") in 3:3 is often associated in Greek literature with a team of chariot horses. Prior to the eighth century CE, chariots were often used to transport infantry units, but soon they became a symbol of violence and wealth. Aristocratic Romans rode them in battle, in the games, and for hunting (see Horace, *Ep.* 1.15.10–13; Plutarch, *Quaest. rom.* 83; Apuleius, *Metam.* 1.2). A chariot race was the featured ritual, for example, during the annual festival in celebration of Mars, the Roman god of war and agrarian fertility (see Jas 5:1–11). The right-hand horse of the winning chariot was sacrificed to the deity on the Campus Martius (Field of Mars) in October; hence, this sacrifice became known as the "October Horse" (Pascal 1981, 261).

Teachers, consider the ship. Or, more properly, consider large ships. Large ships were used in antiquity for the transportation of goods and for the purposes of war. Strictly speaking, the "rudder" was not used in the ancient world (3:4). Sailing vessels were guided by one or two steering oars in the stern, controlled by the most important member of the crew—the pilot. The teacher, like the pilot, directs and governs the course of the people, whether to life or death. Ancient shipwrecks were common, especially from the period between the first century BCE and the first century CE (see Acts 27:39–44). Over a thousand shipwreck sites are scattered throughout the Mediterranean; these watery graveyards bear witness to the dangers of being driven by a crooked course (Parker 1992, 5).

Teachers, consider the tongue. Or more properly, consider the fiery tongue from below. The tongue is a unique member of the body. There are approximately 642 skeletal muscles in the average human body, but only one is capable of forming sounds—sounds that convey socially constructed meaning. Only one member of the body possesses this kind of untamable power. Only one member of the body can boast (*auxeō*), but boasting is a dangerous game to play and is often met with retribution and disaster.

In this particular case, the disaster comes in the form of a forest (*hylē*) raging with a consuming fire (*pyr*; see Jas 5:3). In book 11 of the *Iliad*,

Homer describes the violent retribution of Agamemnon on the Trojans in a similar vein.

> And lord Agamemnon, ever slaying, followed after, calling to the Argives. And as when consuming fire [*pyr*] falls on a thick wood [*hylē*], and the whirling wind carries it everywhere, and the thickets fall uprooted as they are assailed by the onrush of the fire [*pyros*]; so beneath Agamemnon, son of Atreus, fell the heads of the Trojans as they fled, and many horses [*hippoi*] with high-arched necks rattled empty chariots along the lines of battle, longing for their incomparable charioteers; but they lay on the ground dearer far to vultures than to their wives. (*Il.* 11.153–162 [Murray, LCL])

In this scene, the bard describes the violent king as a great fire that consumes the forest, but this once glorious and victorious warrior would ultimately be brought down and undone by hubris and arrogance (see Aeschylus, *Agamemnon*).

The theme of hubris is prevalent in ancient Greek literature, especially in the works of Herodotus (484–428 BCE), Aeschylus (525–456 BCE), Sophocles (496–406 BCE), and Euripides (484–406 BCE). The "father of history" and the Athenian tragedians routinely explore the corruptive nature of positions of power and influence. Without exception, power leads to satiety, and satiety to insolence, and insolence to hubris, and hubris to error (i.e., sin), and hubris must be punished (Dodds 1951, 31). Teachers, you have been warned. The desires within you once fully conceived give birth to sin, and sin (i.e., error) leads to death (see Jas 1:14–15).

In the Greco-Roman period, the Homeric epics (i.e., the *Iliad* and the *Odyssey*) functioned as the unofficial literary "canon" in ancient education and literary composition. During the imperial identity crisis of the Augustan age, for example, the Homeric epics provided the literary template for the composition of the foundational epic of the Roman Empire—the *Aeneid*. Virgil created his epic by appropriating and transforming Homer (Bonz 2000, 19). Like the magnificently tragic Agamemnon, the teachers have set the community ablaze, but what is the source of this fire that has been unleashed by the hubris of this small member?

The cosmic injustice of the tongue defiles and stains (see Jas 1:27) the body that empowers it and enflames the potter's wheel from which all things were formed—this fire is from below, the fires of the valley. "Gehenna [*geenna*]" is the Greek form of the Hebrew name for the "Valley of Hinnom [*hinnōm gê*]" (see Josh 15:8; 18:16; Neh 11:30).[4] This is the name of the valley south of Jerusalem where sacrifices were offered to Molech during the reign of Ahaz and Manasseh (see 2 Kgs 16:3; 21:6; Jer 7:31; 19:1–5; 32:35).

Outside of the book of James, the Greek term *geenna* appears exclusively in the Synoptic Gospels (see Matt 5:22, 29, 30; 10:28, 18:9; 23:15, 33; Mark 9:43, 45, 47; Luke 12:5) within the New Testament. In the opening chapters of the Gospel of Matthew, a male child is born and miraculously escapes a fierce tyrant, passing through waters to be tested in the wilderness for a time of forty days. This new Moses ascends the mountain and delivers a new law, a reimagining of the law for a different time and place, including the prohibiting of anger and desire as the embryonic forms of murder and adultery (see Jas 2:11).

It is within this context that the new Moses warns of the fire from below, a warning shared by the new Jacob. Murder and adultery corrupt and disrupt the social bonds that are necessary for communal life, but anger and lust violently threaten the life of the *ethnos*—an insidious disease that infects the people. Jesus recommends selective amputation rather than suffer the annihilating force of the fires of Gehenna. Jacob is less optimistic.

In the book of James, this disease has spread through the community like a forest ravaged by fire, but the tongue reveals the true nature of these teachers. They eulogize the master and father of humanity, but they call down curses on those who resemble the creator. "God damn the lords of land and wealth!" The mouth opens and this small member of the body reveals the poison within. Sweet and bitter (*pikros*) waters cannot flow from the mouth of the same fountain.

Consider the fig tree. The *Ficus Ruminalis* (Rumina was the goddess of suckling animals) was the sacred fig tree located near the small cave known as the Lupercal on the Palatine Hill, the centermost of the seven hills of Rome (Hadzsits 1936, 319). This wild fig signified the spot where Romulus and Remus washed ashore and were nursed by the she-wolf (Pliny, *Nat.* 15.77; Plutarch, *Rom.* 4). Romulus and Remus were twin brothers and the primary characters of the foundational myth of the Roman Empire. Like the synagogue, the brothers were divided and anger gave birth to

---

4. *Hinnōm gê* is not the typical formulation in the Hebrew Bible for the "Valley of Hinnom," but it is what the LXX seems to be reading.

murder and death. The city of Rome itself takes its name from the surviving brother, but the sacred fig tree drooped and withered—a bad omen of things to come for the "lords of land and wealth" (Tacitus, *Ann.* 13.58). Cursed is the Roman "tree of life" and the teachers who conjure the fires of hell (Hadzsits 1936, 319; see Matt 21:18–22; Mark 11:12–14, 20–25).

The fig tree and the bitter waters are from below. Wisdom from above is unstained by blood (*hagnos*; see Sophocles, *Ant.* 889; Euripides, *Orest.* 1604), nonviolent, equitable, satisfied, compassionate; it produces gentle, courageous, and good fruit. Wisdom from below creeps on the ground like an animal or demon (*daimoniōdēs*; see Jas 2:19). Bitter (*pikros*; see Jas 3:11) waters flow from the desire and purpose of this wisdom—it is jealous, factious, and boastful (*katakauchaomai*; see Jas 2:13) of false truth (*alētheia*; see Jas 5:19). The fruit of this divisive and jealous wisdom is instability (see Jas. 1:6) and acts of pettiness. Who is wise among you? The one who plants and reaps the fruit of justice in peace.

What is the source of these bitter waters that flow from below and pour out of the mouth of the cursed fountain? War. The forest is engaged in mortal combat, waging war with the fiery weapons of Gehenna. Jealousy has blinded the forest. It desires and yearns for that which it cannot possess, and this desire has conceived and given birth to murder (see Jas 1:14–15). The forest asks for wealth and opulence, but what the forest truly lacks is wisdom (see Jas 1:5), which flows freely from above from the generous giver of gifts. Orphans and widows wander unseen through the woods while violent pollution spreads through this forest of death.

"God damn the adulteresses!" In Jas 2:8–13, Jacob reminds the synagogue that the ways of God are defined by love of neighbor—adultery and murder are diseases that can plague and devour the community. One cannot freely choose to obey one and disobey the other. Adulteresses are murderers. Murderers are adulteresses. The forest wages war against the "lords of the land," rather than waiting patiently for the flower in the field to wither from the heat of the sun (see Jas 1:10–11). These adulteresses have been seduced by the ways of the adversary and have cultivated a friendship (*philia*) with the cosmos. As a result, they have become enemies (*echthros*) of God.

The infamous enemy of God in antiquity was Prometheus—the offender of the divine order. The Greek tragedy *Prometheus Bound*, traditionally attributed to the playwright Aeschylus, was the most influential treatment of the Prometheus legend during the Greco-Roman age. In this play, under orders from Zeus, Hephaestus binds Prometheus with chains to a rock for stealing fire and giving it to humanity. Prometheus laments, "Behold me, an ill-fated god, chained, the foe [*echthron*] of Zeus [*dios*, "God"], hated of all who enter the court of Zeus, because of my very great love [*philotēta*, "friendship"] for mankind" (118–122 [Smyth, LCL]). A friend of this world is an enemy of God. Prometheus chose unwisely.

As support for this claim, Jacob draws from the text that says, "God yearns jealously [*phthonon*] for the spirit that he has made to dwell in us" (Jas 4:5). The source of these words has not been identified, but the jealousy (*phthonos*) of the gods has been well-documented.[5] This motif is found most prominently in the Athenian tragedians and Herodotus, but it is already present in the Homeric age: "For on this wise have the gods spun the thread for wretched mortals, that they should live in pain; and themselves are sorrowless. For two urns are set upon the floor of Zeus of gifts that he giveth, the one of ills, the other of blessings" (Homer, *Il.* 24.526–528 [Murray, LCL]). Achilles laments, for the gods give to some mixed good and evil and others unmixed evil, but none enjoy unmixed good except the immortals. Although the punishment of the gods appears random at times, it is those who boast of their great wealth and prosperity who are the chosen recipients of the wrath of the gods.

In this vein, Jacob turns to the proverb, "God opposes the proud [*hyperēphanois*], but gives grace to the humble" (Jas 4:6; see Prov 3:34). The Greek term *hyperēphanos* can denote "arrogance" or "pride," but often that arrogance and pride is associated with an extravagant lifestyle. For example, in the Platonic dialogue *Laws*, the Athenian Stranger, the Spartan Megillus, and the Cretan politician Clinias are on a journey from Cnosus to the cave of Zeus to consult the divine lawgiver. On the way, Clinias issues this critique of monarchy and empire: "Probably this is, in the main, a disease of kings, in whom luxury breeds pride [*hyperēphanōs*] of life" (*Leg.* 691a [Bury, LCL]).

The teachers and the forest have chosen unwisely, and as a result their pride and desire have stained their hands and polluted their hearts. But there is still time. If the double-minded (see Jas 1:5–8) choose the wisdom from above and resist the wisdom from below, the one who defames (*diabolos*, "devil"; see Jas 2:7) will take flight (*pheugō*) and become their slave. Listen to the wisdom of the Athenian:

---

5. For an extensive treatment of the jealousy of the gods in antiquity, see Ranulf 1933–1934.

> You alone of Greeks and barbarians, so far as I can discover, possess
> a lawgiver who charged you to abstain from the greatest of pleasures
> and amusements and taste them not; but concerning pains and fears,
> as we said before, he held the view that anyone who shuns them con-
> tinuously from childhood onward, when confronted with unavoidable
> hardships and fears and pains, will be put to flight [*pheuxeisthai*] by the
> men who are trained in such things, and will become their slave. (Plato,
> *Leg.* 635b–c [Bury, LCL])

Lament, mourn, and weep. The lowly—the ones trained in hardship and
pain—will be raised up by the divine lawgiver (see Jas 1:9).

Do they not know there is only one lawgiver (*nomothetēs*)? Tragically, these murderers and adulteresses have chosen to imitate the wisdom
from below—the wisdom of Rome—the *decemviri*. The *decemviri* (Gk.
nomothetēs; see Diodorus Siculus, *Bib. hist.* 12.24.1; Dionysius of Halicarnassus, *Ant. rom.* 10.57.1) was a board of ten charged with consular
power to form Roman law. According to tradition, the Decemvirate com-
piled the legendary Twelve Tables that provided the foundation of Roman
legislation. The Twelve Tables were particularly concerned with relations
between individuals and the relations between individuals and the community, especially as it regards the socioeconomic tension between the
plebeians and the patricians.

The Roman historian Livy (59 BCE–17 CE) recounts that the patricians were the first one hundred senators chosen by Romulus to help
govern Rome (*Ab urbe condita* 1.8). The "fathers" and their families held
exclusive rights to the priestly offices and dominated the Senate. In contrast, the plebeians were a heterogeneous collection of people, ranging
from the day laborer to the wealthy non-noble citizen. For centuries, the
tension between these two groups was an ongoing concern of the republic
and the empire. The Twelve Tables and their legacy attempted to mitigate
this tension, but the threat of revolution was always present.

Within the synagogue, the same tension exists (see Jas 2:1–7). The rich
and the poor occupy the same social space, but their socioeconomic status
functions as a dividing line that has set the community ablaze. In this
case, however, there is only one lawgiver and judge and only one law. The
Decemvirate and the Twelve Tables are unnecessary. "You shall love your
neighbor as yourself" (Jas 2:8). The patricians and the plebeians babble
loudly against each other and the royal custom of the divine lawgiver.
Deliverance and destruction is coming. Choose wisely.

YHWH of Armies (4:13–5:20)

The economy of the Roman Empire was inextricably linked to local agriculture. This was common among all ancient Mediterranean economies, but the sophistication and scale of the Roman system was unparalleled in antiquity. During the periods of Roman expansion, enemy territories were conquered and the land designated as *ager publicus* (public land). These public lands remained, in theory, the property of the state, but the plebeians and the patricians disputed whether these properties ought to be made available via lease to the wealthy (*possessores*) or divided up among the poorer classes. In Italy, little public land remained by the time of the imperium, but in the provinces enormous swaths of the land were under the permanent control and management of *possessores*.

The private ownership of these public lands paved the way for the emergence of the *latifundium* (large estate) during the Julio-Claudian dynasty (27 BCE–68 CE), which specialized in the exportation of agrarian products like grain, olive oil, and wine. Needless to say, smaller farms could not compete with these *latifundia*, and economic consolidation was well underway. Peasant farmers were forced from the land, and small villas gave way to expansive farms tended by slaves and tenants with reaping machines and long-handled scythes. By the second century CE, the *latifundium* had replaced the small farm as the agricultural foundation of the Roman economy.

The vast wealth generated by these large estates and the consolidation of land within the hands of the few fueled social instability and unrest, especially in the provinces. In the *Natural History*, Pliny the Elder laments to his friend Emperor Titus (79–81 CE) that the *latifundia* will be the ruin of Rome.

> In old times it was thought that to observe moderation in the size of a farm was of primary importance, inasmuch as the view was held that it was more satisfactory to sow less land and plough it better; and I observe that Virgil was of this opinion. And if the truth be confessed, large estates [*latifundia*] have been the ruin of Italy, and are now proving the ruin of the provinces too—half of Africa was owned by six landlords, when the Emperor Nero put them to death; though Gnaeus Pompeius must not be cheated out of this mark of his greatness also: he never bought land belonging to a neighboring estate. (*Nat.* 18.7.35 [Rackham, LCL])

This form of industrialized agriculture filled the pockets of the Roman senatorial class but displaced the landless, dispossessed peasantry and conceived a landscape that was ripe for revolution.

With the emergence of these larges estates, exportation of their respective goods throughout the Mediterranean became increasingly common. The *Pax Romana* (Roman peace), during the Augustan age and beyond, guaranteed the safety and security of travel and trade throughout the empire on an unprecedented scale. Trade was carried out by agents of the *latifundia*, who occupied one of the few social positions available to those not born into the elite class of landowners for economic advancement, but they were required to travel often and widely.

In Jas 4:13, Jacob turns his rhetorical gaze on these agents—the pursuers of wealth. They have been hypnotized by the wisdom from below and become servants of the wrong master. They travel from city to city, year in and year out, in the pursuit of that which is temporal, fleeting, and worthless—"mist [*atmis*]." In the Platonic dialogue on the properties of nature, Timaeus comments on the effect of this smoky vapor on the soul.

> For whenever the humors which arise from acid and saline phlegms, and all humors that are bitter and bilious wander through the body and find no external vent but are confined within, and mingle their vapor [*atmida*] with the movement of the soul and are blended therewith, they implant diseases of the soul of all kinds, varying in intensity and in extent; and as these humors penetrate to the three regions of the Soul, according to the region which they severally attack, they give rise to all varieties of bad temper and bad spirits, and they give rise to all manner of rashness and cowardice, and of forgetfulness also, as well as of stupidity. (*Tim.* 86e–87a [Bury, LCL])

These agents of the *latifundia* brag loudly of their enterprise, but they are deceived by their misty life (*zōē*) that poisons their soul and is good for nothing.

The "lords of land and wealth"—the landed gentry—are doomed. Their only option is to cry and lament the inevitability of their fate. The crops of their fields (*ploutos*, riches) harvested from these large estates decay, rot, and molder like a diseased body or a garment in the warm embrace of a ravenous moth (see Plato, *Tim.* 84d; Job 13:28; Arrian, *Epict. diss.* 4.6). These lords amass precious metals from their ever-expanding empires, but "gold and silver" do not in fact "rust" (Jas 5:3). Rather, these lords bear the stigmata of corrosion and rust that is the by-product of their greed and excess (see Lucian, *Cat.* 28). These landlords steal and rob from the day laborers who work their massive fields, but the stains of their hedonism are witness to the crime and the sound of the mowers is rising. The lawgiver is coming. The judge is coming. The "Lord of hosts [*sabaōth*]" is coming (Jas 5:4).

Sabaōth is a rare Greek term and only occurs twice in the New Testament (see Rom 9:29), but it is generally considered to be a rendering of the Hebrew—*yhwh ṣəbāʾôt* ("YHWH of armies"). This divine name appears frequently in Jewish texts that are concerned with Zion, the sacred mountain fortress of Yahweh. This mountain abode is not the domain of mortal kings, which is the subject of the satirical lamentation of the king of Babylon in Isaiah.

> How you are fallen from heaven,
> O Day Star, son of Dawn!
> How you are cut down to the ground,
> you who laid the nations low!
> You said in your heart,
> "I will ascend to heaven;
> I will raise my throne
> above the stars of God;
> I will sit on the mount of assembly
> on the heights of Zaphon;
> I will ascend to the tops of the clouds,
> I will make myself like the Most High."
> But you are brought down to Sheol,
> to the depths of the Pit. (Isa 14:12–15)

The hubris of this Babylonian tyrant is his ultimate undoing, for the "Father of lights" will bring down all those who desire to rise above the "stars of God."

In the New Testament, "Babylon" functions as a cryptogram for "Rome," indicting the empire as the source of oppression of the people of God (see 1 Pet 5:13). The revelator identifies Babylon (i.e., Rome) as the ruler of the kings of the earth sitting on seven mountains from which her agents have become rich and powerful (see Rev 17:9, 18; 18:2–3). Despite appearances, there is an unseen reality beneath the soil, poised to erupt and break into this age of oppression. Rome, the city on seven hills, is going to be brought low, and the *latifundia* will wither like a scorched flower.

Do not take oaths and band together to defeat this great dragon of chaos, for that path leads to certain defeat and certain death. Consider the innocent suffering of Job. Like the seeds beneath the soil, Job was unaware of the cosmic dispute taking place concerning his faithfulness. In the end,

HAUGE

Job remained faithful, his enemies were judged, and his suffering was vindicated. Job cried out to God amid his sufferings, and his cries were heard. The sounds of the faithful are rising. The cries of the mowers. The cries of the hopeful. The cries of the weak.

Job was not extraordinary, and neither was Elijah. Like the eschatological charioteer, the crown of life awaits all those who are not deceived by the mirror and seek wisdom from above. There is only one lawgiver. There is only one law. There is only one judge. There is only one Lord of hosts. YHWH of armies is coming. Soon.

For Further Reading

Champion, Craige B. 2003. *Roman Imperialism: Readings and Sources*. Chichester, UK: Wiley-Blackwell.

Finley, Moses I. 1999. *The Ancient Economy*. Berkeley: University of California Press.

Gutiérrez, Gustavo. 1987. *On Job: God-Talk and the Suffering of the Innocent*. Maryknoll, NY: Orbis.

Longman, Tremper, III, and Daniel G. Reid. 1995. *God Is a Warrior*. Studies in Old Testament Theology. Grand Rapids: Zondervan.

Miller, Stephen G. 2004. *Ancient Greek Athletics*. New Haven: Yale University Press.

Confronting Roman Imperial Claims: Following the Footsteps (and the Narrative) of 1 Peter's Eschatological Davidic Shepherd

Kelly D. Liebengood

The injunction to "honor the emperor" (1 Pet 2:17) would seem to be a clear indication that 1 Peter is a text that promotes an accommodating strategy in negotiating the claims of Jesus Christ and the demands of Rome. It is perhaps unsurprising, then, that in an important study that compares the place of diverse associations, synagogues, and assemblies under Roman rule in Asia Minor, Philip Harland (2003, 229–35) points to 1 Peter as one example of literary evidence that Christian assemblies in Asia Minor could participate positively in certain imperial practices, such as erecting inscriptions ("doing good"; 1 Pet 2:12) to honor the emperor.[1] Harland further argues that 1 Peter reflects a clearly positive view regarding the position of the emperor and other imperial officials within God's ordained order of existence (234).

There is, however, reason to suspect that 1 Peter is more nuanced than Harland has suggested. For example, even in 1 Pet 2:17 ("Honor everyone. Love the family of believers. Fear God. Honor the emperor."), the passage that many scholars appeal to as evidence for an assimilating posture toward the Roman Empire, the injunction to honor the emperor is framed by other directives that generate at least two subversive effects.[2] First, the honor that is due to the emperor is equalized such that it is in no way more unique than what is owed to everyone else (including slaves; 1

---

1. For a thorough analysis of the social context of Christian suffering in 1 Peter, see T. Williams 2012, especially his critique of the claim that "good works" in 1 Peter is a reference to the accommodating strategy of setting up imperial honorary inscriptions.

2. All English Bible citations are from the NRSV.

Pet 2:18). Second, the meaning of "honor" has been subtly nuanced, with
the result that it cannot refer to "worship" (as it often did in the East).
Instead, worship (*timaō*, fear) is to be exclusively offered to God alone
(Horrell 2007, 135).

Harland is not the first to suggest that 1 Peter encourages an accommodating approach to culture. In the early 1980s, David Balch (1981) offered
a study of the household code (1 Pet 2:11–3:12) in which he argued that
the pastoral strategy of 1 Peter is to urge Christians to assimilate to social
norms as much as possible in order to minimize conflict and hostility. His
study sparked a sustained conversation within 1 Peter studies, in which a
second, contrary appraisal emerged, epitomized by the work of John Elliot.
Drawing on sociological studies of religious sects, Elliott (1981) contends
that the pastoral strategy of 1 Peter is to develop a strong sense of internal
cohesion within the Christian community and to encourage the community to resist conforming to social norms.[3] Subsequent attempts at advancing the contrasting proposals of Balch and Elliott have tended to further
entrench the discussion such that only an either/or solution is envisioned:
either the pastoral strategy is assimilation, or it is resistance.

Horrell (2007, 114–17) has helpfully moved the conversation beyond
the present impasse by suggesting the need for a different methodology for
making sense of what likely is a more nuanced approach between church
and culture than has been previously recognized. Perhaps most importantly, he points out that the assimilation/resistance debate has either over-
looked or underemphasized "the central fact about the particular world
in which the addressees lived and which most fundamentally determines
their difficult relationship with it: the fact of empire" (117).[4]

With that in view, Horrell suggests that the insights from postcolonial criticism can illuminate the complex and subtle ways in which dominated peoples seek to negotiate their identity and existence. In particular, he highlights three significant observations from postcolonial studies

---

3. For a concise survey of what has been deemed "the Balch-Elliott debate," see
Horrell 2007, 111–17.

4. In his seminal work on imperial cult, Simon R. F. Price concludes that "the
imperial cult stabilized the religions of the world. The system of ritual was carefully
structured; the symbolism evoked a picture of the relationship between the emperor
and the gods. The ritual was also structuring; it imposed a definition of the world. The
imperial cult, along with politics and diplomacy, constructed the reality of the Roman
empire" (1984, 248).

that help orient what we might expect from subordinates as they seek to express resistance in a context of cultural dominance. First, dominated people rarely resort to outright physical and/or verbal resistance as a way of confronting dominance, since that strategy is certainly to be short-lived and thus ineffective in the long haul.

Second, subordinates make use of a variety of hidden and subversive forms of resistance that are generally concealed from the dominator's gaze. Here, Horrell draws particular attention to the work of James Scott (1990), a political scientist who has dedicated much of his research to studying ways in which subordinated people resist their dominators in "everyday" life. A number of biblical scholars have found Scott's insights to be relevant for understanding the way in which the gospel material and the Pauline Letters express resistance to various aspects of Roman imperial ideology.[5] According to Scott, since subordinate groups "confront elaborate ideologies [which he refers to as the 'public transcript'] that justify inequality, bondage, monarchy, caste, and so on … resistance to ideological domination requires a counter-ideology—a negation—that will effectively provide a general normative form to the host of resistant practices invented in self-defense by any subordinate group" (118). Scott refers to this counterideology as "hidden transcripts," the critique of power that goes on backstage, beyond the observation of power holders.[6] Often hidden transcripts take the form of "symbolic inversion," where the social ordering maintained in the public transcript is turned upside down and in which an alternative social structure can be imagined (166–82).

Third, Horrell has drawn on the work of Homi Bhabha (1994, 102–22) to point out that ambivalence and complexity often characterize the manner in which the subordinated resist their dominators. Bhabha describes this complex process as "hybridity," and perhaps the most helpful insight from Bhabha's analysis for the purposes of this essay is that subordinates must affiliate or assimilate to some degree *in order to faithfully resist.*

Horrell thus suggests that these three insights invite us to read 1 Peter with our ears attuned to the ways in which identity formation and "expressions of resistance may be subtle and ambivalent, woven in complex ways

---

5. See especially Horsley 2004 and the bibliography therein.
6. See Barclay 2011, 379–83, for a critique of the application of Scott's "hidden transcripts" to New Testament epistles.

into a discourse which may also be complicit and conformist, constructed in the encounter between colonizer and colonized" (Horrell 2007, 123).

In what follows, I seek to demonstrate the nuanced way in which 1 Peter confronts and subverts the claims and demands of Rome. In particular, I will underscore that expressions of resistance are not discerned *primarily* in terminology that can be interpreted as having an antithetical relationship to Rome (such as *lord, savior, gospel,* or *kingdom*) but rather that a more profound confrontation can be ascertained at the level of the implied narrative of 1 Peter. That is to say, I will show the manner in which an implicit narrative in 1 Peter turns the public transcript of Roman imperial ideology upside down ("symbolic inversion"). I will develop this, first, by drawing attention to the realized eschatology (or hope) characteristic of Roman imperial ideology and then by underscoring the way in which 1 Peter defers hope to the eschaton by anchoring it within the unfolding narrative of the eschatological Davidic shepherd.

The "Public Transcript": Rome's Realized Eschatology

In the past four decades, classical historians have produced a wellspring of research that has detailed, to use Scott's terminology, the public transcripts of Roman hegemony in the first century CE and the ways in which Rome's message was communicated across the empire. Given the scope and aims of this essay, I am only able to highlight three key conclusions that have emerged from these studies, which will help illuminate the way in which the implicit narrative of 1 Peter confronts and subverts Roman imperial claims by symbolically inverting the public transcripts.

I begin first by calling attention to one of the more remarkable facts about the Roman Empire in the first century CE, namely, that it did not maintain imperial order in Asia Minor through military conquest or even military presence.[7] Instead, as Simon Price (1984), Clifford Ando (2000), Paul Zanker (1988), Karl Galinsky (1996; 2005), and Beth Severy (2003) have thoroughly demonstrated in their own ways, in Asia Minor, Roman imperial order was maintained "through the symbolic arrangement of public space, the presence of images, and the performance of rituals" (Horsley 2004, 6). Said in another way, beginning with Augustus, rather

---

7. Price (1984, 54) notes: "No Roman legion was stationed in the province of Asia during the first three centuries."

than conquering through military might, Rome mounted an intentional and unprecedented propaganda campaign, especially in Asia Minor, as the means by which it would extend and secure its dominion. In his research on the innovative use of imperial imagery in the age of Augustus, Zanker (1988, 4) concludes that "through visual imagery a new mythology of Rome and, for the emperor, a new ritual of power were created. Built on relatively simple foundations, the myth perpetuated itself and transcended the realities of everyday life to project onto future generations the impression that they lived in the best of all possible worlds in the best of all times."

Ando has compellingly highlighted the way Rome exerted this "soft power" in order to maintain imperial order, in particular by explaining the bidirectional nature of Roman hegemony; that is to say, that imperial loyalty was not imposed from some hierarchy in Rome, but rather was initiated by local communities, especially in the East, who wished to get in on the prosperity and social recognition that went along with honoring the emperor and the Roman way of life. The responsibility of the empire was to provide peace, security, economic prosperity, social status, and communal honor. In exchange, communities offered loyal allegiance to the emperor, expressed in a variety of forms, not least through the imperial cult, but also in attending imperial festivals, erecting honorary inscriptions, and more generally by upholding the Roman way of life in the provinces. As Ando argues,

> It was Rome that supplied the initial articulation of the values to which residents of the empire oriented themselves as members of its community, and it was the belief that others shared those values that legitimized Rome's representation of social order. Acquiescence and, ultimately, loyalty to Rome thus required recognition that the Roman construction of society, in relations between provinces, cities, individuals, emperors, and empire, adequately mapped the collective value commitments of its residents. (2000, 5)

Similarly, Galinsky has shown that each community in the empire had something invested in its relationship with Rome. One result of this arrangement, which is significant for understanding the nature of suffering in 1 Peter, is the fact that anyone who was seen as deviating from this new construct of Roman life, anyone who did not express loyalty to the emperor in the proper way, was seen as a threat to the stability of the community, a stability secured by Rome. "Leadership," Galinsky (2005, 6) notes, "is thus inseparable from followers' needs and goals." All this to say that Roman imperial order was sustained, in grand measure, because the adherents—local communities—were convinced that Rome helped them meet their needs and realize their hopes and dreams.

A second significant (and related) conclusion that has emerged from four decades of research on the Roman Empire in the first century CE is a more acute awareness that the symbolization of dominance was undergirded by a narrative that professed realized hope for those who loyally aligned themselves with Rome and all that it represented (or at least promised). Through this complex ideological program, which included imperial temples, festivals, statues, shrines and monuments, coins, theater, and literature, first-century inhabitants of Asia Minor were, in a variety of manners, unrelentingly told that they were fortunate to live in a unique moment in history, a time of restoration, peace, and prosperity. Although imperial worship was expressed in a number of ways, as the archaeological, epigraphic, and literary evidence bears witness, Rome's narrative remained constant: thanks to one man, a man sent by god, a new age had dawned. No longer were Romans being punished for their impiety and their disregard for the ways of their forefathers. For, through this one man, the enemy had been defeated; *pax deorum* (peace with the gods) had been restored; and prosperity awaited all who proved themselves loyal to the new lord and savior of the universe. Two important inscriptions illustrate the consistency of this narrative of realized hope: the Res gestae, and the Priene Calendar Inscription.

Zanker (1988) and Edwin Ramage (1987) independently have argued that the Res gestae divi Augusti is perhaps the most important artifact to help us understand the ideology of the Roman Empire in the first century CE. The inscription, which tells the story of how Augustus restored peace and prosperity to the world, was distributed throughout the empire. It is certainly significant for our discussion of 1 Peter that our only extant remains of the Res gestae are from Asia Minor (Ancyra, Apollonia, and Pisidian Antioch).

The Priene Calendar Inscription narrates a more condensed version of this narrative: providence has given the world Augustus, sending him as a savior, who has established a dynasty that brings peace and order to the world. According to Price (1984), all of Asia Minor instituted a calendar that began the New Year on Augustus's birthday with similar inscriptions that declared that a new epoch, a golden age, was initiated with Augustus.

Finally, classics historians have demonstrated that the aggressive propaganda program along with its consistent narrative of realized eschatology, which was initiated by Augustus, was foundational for the rest of the Julio-Claudian and Flavian lines, and was appropriated in order to establish a narrative of imperial dynasty (see especially Severy 2003; Crossan and Reed 2004, 142–52; and Millar 1993). That is to say, all of the emperors that followed Augustus in the first century, in one way or another, appealed to the dawning of the golden age initiated by Augustus as a way of legitimizing their own rule and in an effort to compel loyalty that would in turn generate peace, security, and prosperity for all.[8]

The Davidic Imperial Narrative of 1 Peter

This narrative of Rome's golden age is the setting in which Peter seeks to help Anatolian (residents of Asia Minor) Christians negotiate their professed loyalty to Jesus Christ.[9] As we will see, in a variety of manners, the strategy of 1 Peter is to encourage readers to understand themselves as displaced people who are dislocated from the values, practices, and false (realized) hopes of the Roman Empire and instead are encouraged to inhabit a different way of life that is grounded in a different telos.

Horrell (2007, 124–29) has demonstrated the way in which the letter frame sets the tone for the manner in which the readers ought to understand their circumstances and identity. In the opening of the letter, Peter strategically refers to the recipients as "elect sojourners [i.e., chosen refugees] of the Diaspora" (1 Pet 1:1). Here Peter draws on the Jewish experience of being exiled and exported to foreign lands (the diaspora or dispersion), in order to depict the addressees, who seem to be native to Asia Minor, as those who must now think of themselves as outsiders, foreigners in their own land.[10] Horrell encourages us to read this opening depiction of the addressees along with the closing verses of the letter, in which Peter

---

8. Galinsky (2005) argues that under Augustus a foundation was laid for a system of belief that lasted for more than two hundred years, which would also include the Flavian dynasty. According to scholarly consensus, 1 Peter was written sometime between 64 and 92 CE.

9. In this essay, I have not concerned myself with the historical figure of Peter who exists outside of the letter. Instead, I have chosen to focus on Peter who manifests himself within the letter, that is, the author who is revealed as we interpret 1 Peter. For convenience, I will refer to the author as Peter, as he has identified himself at the beginning of the letter.

10. See Horrell 2007, 127, for a condensed argument regarding the alienation of the addressees, which is a result of their conversion.

sends greetings to the Anatolian Christians from "Babylon" (1 Pet 5:13). There is a strong consensus that 1 Peter was written in Rome and that the Babylon reference is meant to characterize Rome in a particularly negative light. Since the book of Daniel, Babylon was a symbolic name for the world power that oppressed and displaced God's people. It is likely that Peter refers to Rome as Babylon in order to align himself and his readers to a different narrative about Rome, one that claims that this seemingly invincible, universal power, whose influence on the world seems to negate the very claims that Peter is making in his letter (i.e., that restoration has begun in Jesus Christ), will in fact be judged and destroyed, because it has oppressed the people of God and opposed God's ways. In other words, what lies behind the Babylon reference is a call to interpret Rome's rule as fleeting, its judgment and destruction as pending. Thus, while to some the reference to Babylon might work to conceal the identity of Rome, for those who have ears to hear, the term "Babylon" does not actually conceal but rather reveals the real nature of Rome's alluring and tenuous reign.[11] Lutz Doering (2009, 233) advances a similar point: "If Rome were indeed meant here [1 Pet 5:13], it would be more likely a *qualification* of Rome as ultimately responsible for persecution and dispersion, than an oblique reference by code name." As Horrell (2007, 126–27) has noted, this "view of the empire as godless power, scattering and displacing the people of God, stands in stark contrast to the narrative promoted by the architects of empire, for whom their divinely appointed vocation is to bring peace to warring tribes and civilization to uncultured barbarians."

For the purposes of this essay, what perhaps is most significant about the manner in which the letter seeks to orient the readers, especially in light of Rome's public script of realized eschatology, is the fact that real, enduring hope is deferred to the eschaton. We can see this most immediately in the opening section of the letter (1:3–9), where the readers are reminded that God is to be praised for a variety of reasons, all of which center on a hope that is to be actualized at the return of Jesus Christ. Those who align themselves with the resurrected Jesus Christ, Peter writes, are born anew to a living hope, to an inheritance that will not perish, to a prepared salvation that will be revealed in the last time (1:3–5). Furthermore, Peter explains, those who love and believe in Jesus Christ rejoice

---

11. It should be noted that the book of Revelation also appropriates apocalyptic imagery and refers to Rome as Babylon with a similar aim in view.

with inexpressible joy, because the outcome of their faithfulness will result in none other than the salvation of their souls (1:8–9).

After providing his readers with an orientation that is foundationally eschatological in nature, Peter then offers his first exhortation in what most consider to be the opening line of the body of the letter: "Set all your hope on the grace that Jesus Christ will bring you when he is revealed (i.e., "when he returns"; 1:13). The importance of having a legitimate, enduring hope seems to be a primary concern of Peter elsewhere in the letter as well. In 1 Pet 1:21, he reminds his readers that the resurrection of Jesus from the dead means that their faith and hope are in God; in 1 Pet 2:11, his exhortation to abstain from the passions of the flesh is based, in part, on the fact that God will vindicate their good behavior on the day of his visitation. In 1 Pet 3:15, readers who are undergoing hardship because of their loyalty to Jesus Christ are exhorted to be prepared to make a defense for the *hope* that they share among one another. Finally, the letter body ends with one final word of hope: readers are encouraged to endure suffering "for a little while," because the God of all grace will restore and establish them in due course.

This optimism, however, is tempered with the reminder that this living hope, this incorruptible inheritance, this already-prepared salvation, is yet to dawn; instead, it must be realized through fiery trials that will test one's true loyalty (1 Pet 1:6–7; 4:12–17). In other words, Peter portrays his readers as living in a period of transition. This in-between period is characterized as a time in which faithful followers of the Christ must (*dei*, "it is necessary") pass through various trials (1 Pet 1:6), though not without God's protection (1 Pet 1:5). In 1 Pet 1:7, this transition period of various trials is further characterized as a time in which their "proven faithfulness" (*to dokimion hymōn tēs pisteōs*) will result in their being honored at the revelation (return) of Jesus Christ.[12]

---

12. The genitive *tēs pisteōs* in the phrase *to dokimion hymōn tēs pisteōs* is best understood as an attributed genitive. As such, the head noun, *to dokimion* (understood as "genuineness as result of a test," functions as the adjective, and the genitive, *tēs pisteōs*, syntactically speaking functions as the head noun; the phrase, then, should be translated "proven faithfulness." Read in this way, 1 Pet 1:7 highlights with confidence the proven fidelity of the readers with respect to their allegiance to Jesus in the midst of trials. Thus, the basis for rejoicing is not because of the inherent value of trials (e.g., Jas 1:2–4) but rather because of the certainty of salvation for those who maintain faithfulness.

In light of this brief survey, it is not difficult to discern a rudimentary narrative that undergirds the discourse of 1 Peter, nor is it too much to see that the schema of deferred hope in 1 Peter competes with, even subverts, the public transcript of the Roman Empire. In recent years, a number of scholars have underscored (some more explicitly than others) that a narrative undergirds the theological orientation that Peter offers. Steven Bechtler (1998), for example, demonstrates that a foundational element of Peter's strategy for helping the addressees deal with their alienation and suffering is essentially narrative in character.[13] In particular, Bechtler reveals the manner in which Peter constructs, as he calls it, a "symbolic universe" of temporal liminality:[14] "1 Peter presupposes a temporal context for Christian life that is liminal in the literal sense; the addressees are living in that ambiguous time between Christ's death and resurrection on the one hand and the imminent manifestation of the fullness of his glory on the other" (126). In his work on the paraenetic strategies of 1 Peter, Jeff Dryden is much more explicit about the narrative aspects within the letter.

> The author's aim in 1 Peter is to encourage young Anatolian churches to live out their beliefs in the midst of social hostility.... Before giving them moral instructions, he gives them a moral vision that places them within a moral universe. He does this by depicting not simply a theological worldview, but a *narrative* theological worldview. He is not giving simply ontological statements about how the world is, but weaving together a *story* of how the world is; and this becomes the context for their own stories as individuals and as a community. This is the sense in which the narrative world of 1 Peter contextualizes the lives of the readers and their moral choices. It places their lives within a story of the world conceived on the largest possible canvas—a story of creation, fall, redemption, and consummation. What God is doing in their midst is part of the grand narrative of his plan to redeem his creation and a people for himself. Thus, the world is not spinning aimlessly, but headed toward a goal. In this context, daily choices, as the means by which they appropriate their salvation in the present, take on truly cosmic significance. (Dryden 2006, 64)

---

13. He does not, however, use the terminology "narrative."

14. "1 Peter's depiction of the temporal liminality of Christian existence provides part of the letter's answer" to their social liminality (Bechtler 1998, 126). To be clear, Bechtler does not grant Petrine authorship and would thus not attribute this strategy to the historical Peter.

He further underscores that the author only refers to key elements of the story of salvation to evoke an entire narrative worldview that is familiar to both author and readers. This sort of shorthand description of key elements is, as we have noted before, typical of paraenesis, where only a few key points need to be reviewed and emphasized. Thus what we have access to in the epistle is that portion of the entire presupposed narrative theological worldview that the author found it useful to highlight (Dryden 2006, 66).

This recognition of the narrative character of 1 Peter is significant for the aims of this essay, in part because confrontation or subversion is often best discerned at the level of competing narratives. Although my own reading of 1 Peter resonates with many of the observations made by Bechtler and Dryden, I regard each account in its own way to be too generic: that is, each describes in a one-dimensional fashion a narrative that has more texture and depth than has been indicated. Defining the narrative within 1 Peter with generic terms like creation, fall, redemption, and consummation (as Dryden has) is akin to identifying the kingdom and perhaps the phylum of a living creature but electing to say nothing about its class, order, family, genus, or species when such an identification can be made. In particular, narrative approaches to 1 Peter have regularly neglected to connect the narrative to its roots in Israel's Scriptures, and more specifically to the prominent expectations of Jewish restoration eschatology—this in spite of the predominance of Old Testament citations in the letter.[15]

Following the Footsteps of 1 Peter's Eschatological Davidic Shepherd-King

In what remains, I will sketch the manner in which the competing narrative of 1 Peter is implicitly Davidic at its core. That is to say, the accomplishments of Jesus Christ (whether past or future), the identity of the Anatolian Christians, and the rationale for Christian suffering (that is, suffering because of one's allegiance to Jesus Christ) are all explained in relation to Davidic themes, especially as they are mediated through Zech 9–14.

There is a strong sense that an eschatological Davidic program is nowhere explicitly mentioned and yet everywhere present in 1 Peter. For

15. To be fair to both Bechtler and Dryden, this falls outside of the scope of their projects. My point is not to minimize their work but rather to show where their work, helpful as it is, can be taken further.

example, in the central section of the letter (1 Pet 2:4–10), which many
scholars have noted is where the fundamental indicatives of the letter are
found, Jesus is presented as the chosen and precious stone of stumbling,
which the builders have rejected. These references, sometimes referred to
as the "stone catena" (Isa 28:16; Ps 118:22; and Isa 8:14), have an interpretive history in certain forms of Judaism and in early Christianity that are
associated with God's promise to restore his people through an eschatological Davidic king (see, e.g., Kim 1987). Additionally, the "house" language of 1 Pet 2:5 (and 4:14–17), while often regarded to be temple imagery, can also be understood as a reference to the reestablishment of the
Davidic house (or dynasty) in keeping with the promises found in such
places as 2 Sam 7, Ps 132, and Zech 12:9–10 (see Hillyer 1969; Liebengood
2014, 164–70). It is also significant that, in 1 Pet 2:25, Jesus is identified as
the "shepherd" who gives his life in order to return straying sheep. Prior
to Jesus, no Israelite leader ever bore the title "shepherd," which, as we will
soon see, was exclusively reserved for the eschatological Davidic king.

In order to discern the manner in which these Davidic themes in
1 Peter are brought together in a coherent pattern, we must first briefly
consider the development of the eschatological Davidic tradition in the
prophets and the way it was received, especially in the passion narratives,
in the book of Revelation, and, as I have argued elsewhere, in 1 Peter.

The Eschatological Davidic Tradition and Its Reception

In the Old Testament Historical Books and the Psalms, the title "shepherd"
is reserved for YHWH alone, and although Israelite leadership (most notably that of Moses and David) was periodically described with shepherding
terminology, the title of shepherd seems to have been intentionally avoided.[16] In the prophetic material, the term "shepherd" has three distinct
reference points, which are all integrally connected to Israel's restoration
from exile, often depicted in terms of a second exodus and accomplished
in conjunction with the rule of a Davidic shepherd-king.[17] The Prophets

---

16. For references of YHWH as the shepherd of Israel, see Gen 48:15; 49:24; Pss
23; 28:9; 74:1; 77:20; 78:52–55; 79:13; 80:1; 95:7. For shepherding terminology used to
describe Moses's leadership, see Ps 77:20; Hos 12:13. For shepherding terminology to
describe David's leadership, see, e.g., 2 Sam 7:8; Ps 78:70–71.

17. For a full development of this, see Laniak 2006, 115–70. For a full develop-

announce that (1) YHWH is the good shepherd[18] who will judge the (2) bad shepherds (unnamed and unfaithful Israelite leadership), regather the straying sheep of Israel, renew his covenant, and appoint for his people (3) a new shepherd (king) from the house of David, who will bring about healing and restoration, and usher in the new age of universal peace. It can be shown that the shepherd tradition of the prophets, with its eschatological framework, is first developed in Jer 23, elaborated in Ezek 34,[19] and then is significantly expanded in Zech 9–14, where YHWH not only affirms the unworthiness of the "bad shepherds," but also reveals that the people themselves share responsibility for the deterioration of the community (Zech 11:7–9). In what appears to be a reversal of the shepherd tradition of Jer 23/Ezek 34, the coming of YHWH's appointed good shepherd does not bring immediate restoration and renewal; instead, the shepherd will be rejected by not only the leaders but also by the people (11:4–14) and struck by a sword (13:7). His affliction will bring about a time of trouble, described as "fiery trials"—even for those who are faithful. The remnant "one-third" that makes it through the time of trouble will be reestablished with YHWH through covenant renewal (13:8–9; cf. 1 Pet 2:9–10) and will worship him in purity as a renewed "house" (14:3–20; cf. 1 Pet 2:4–5; 4:14–17).

While the reception of the eschatological Davidic program of Zech 9–14 in the Jewish Second Temple period was sparse, there is enough evidence to suggest that it was known and available for theological reflection, though without any uniform approach for interpreting and appropriating the eschatological program. In contrast, in early Christianity, Zech 9–14 was a prominent and integral source for explaining how Jesus's rejection, suffering, and death as Messiah were in keeping with the Scriptures (as is witnessed in the passion narratives) and for indicating signs that pointed to the imminent and consummated restoration of YHWH's people (e.g., Revelation; see Liebengood 2014, 61–78; Jauhiainen 2005).

---

ment of the Davidic shepherd-king tradition, see Willitts 2007, 58–67; Chae 2006, 32–94.

18. For YHWH as shepherd in the prophetic material, see Isa 40:10–11; 49:9–13; Jer 23:2; 31:10; 50:19; Ezek 34:31; Mic 2:12–13; 4:6–8; 7:14–15; implied in Zech 9:16; 10:8–10.

19. Echoes of the Jer 23/Ezek 34 tradition can be found in Isa 40:1–11 and Mic 4:14–5:5.

The Eschatological Davidic Shepherd in 1 Peter

Elsewhere, I have argued that there are a number of unique parallels between 1 Peter and Zech 9–14 that strongly suggest the latter functions as the substructure for 1 Peter's eschatological program (Liebengood 2014). What is significant for our purposes is that the eschatological program of Zech 9–14 is foundationally a Davidic program that 1 Peter draws on to explain why Jesus was rejected and why his loyal followers should expect the same if they are to follow in his footsteps.[20] Given the limited scope of this essay, I will simply highlight a few of these parallels, which give texture and dimension to the narrative of deferred hope that I have already highlighted:

1. The community that aligns itself with God's royal figure is described as the house of God (Zech 12:8; 1 Pet 2:4; 4:17).
2. The royal/messianic agent is described variously as a slain shepherd (Zech 13:7; 1 Pet 2:23–35), a stone (Zech 10:3; 1 Pet 2:6–8), and the shoot of David (implied in Zech 9–14 from Zech 3:8; 6:12; and in 1 Pet 4:14 from Isa 11:2).
3. The house of God will undergo a period of fiery trials that are likened to a wilderness/new exodus journey and that is designed to test fidelity to God (Zech 10:4–12; 1 Pet 1:3–2:10).
4. The Spirit will be poured out/now rests on the house of God (Zech 12:10; 1 Pet 4:14; "spiritual" house in 2:5).
5. Restoration is described in terms of scattered/straying sheep being gathered from exile and returned to the shepherd-king (Zech 9:16; 10:8–12; 1 Pet 1:1; 2:24–25).
6. Metallurgy imagery is used to describe trials in terms of an assaying/sifting process rather than as mere purgation (Zech 13:7–9; 1 Pet 1:5–7; 4:12–19).
7. God declares, "You are my people" to his ingathered/remnant sheep, who are called to endure the fiery trials (Zech 13:7–9; 1 Pet 2:10; both Zechariah and 1 Peter drawn on Hos 2:23 to make this point).

---

20. For a comprehensive development of the Davidic contours of the eschatological program of Zech 9–14, see Liebengood 2014, 23–52. Here I will simply note that the coming king (Zech 9:9–10), the pierced one (Zech 12:10), and the slain shepherd (Zech 13:7) are all depicted in terms of an eschatological Davidic king.

8. There is an optimism concerning those who have aligned themselves with God's appointed agent/shepherd; they will journey
   faithfully through the fiery trials/second exodus on to their sal-
   vation/inheritance/glory through God's enabling (Zech 10:6–12;
   13:7–9; 1 Pet 1:5–7; 4:12–19; 5:10).

9. God, through his agent, will restore a rightly functioning royal
   house/temple where acceptable offerings are presented to God
   (Zech 14; 1 Pet 2:4–10; 2:23–24).

What is most significant, perhaps even determinative, when the implicit
narrative of 1 Peter is read in light of Zech 9–14 is that only 1 Peter and
Zech 9–14 offer an eschatological program that develops the notion of
a transition (or liminal) period subsequent to the coming of YHWH's
redemptive agent and prior to consummation that is described both as
a period of fiery trials as well as a second-exodus journey.[21] In other
words, Zech 9–14 offers the unique solution to the precise issue with
which Peter and his addressees are concerned: if Jesus is in fact the
Christ, the agent appointed to bring about restoration, then why are we
suffering *after* his coming?

Often, Peter's appropriation of Old Testament texts and early Christian traditions is characterized as being eclectic in nature. However, when
we analyze Peter's appropriation in light of the eschatological program
of Zech 9–14, a coherent pattern emerges. Peter has drawn on particular Old Testament passages and themes such as fiery trials, stone, house,
new exodus, and shepherd in order to support and affirm the substructure provided by Zech 9–14. Said in another way, Peter uses a variety of
Old Testament passages and even sayings from the Jesus tradition (1 Pet
2:11–12) and early Christian traditions (e.g., stone catena in 1 Pet 2:4–8)
in order to fortify, explain, illustrate, and corroborate the very substructure that undergirds and generates his eschatological program of deferred
hope. In this regard, we could say that Zech 9–14 functions as the frame on
which the bricks of Old Testament citations and Christian traditions have

---

21. Isaiah 40–55, for example, cannot account for shepherd imagery in 1 Peter or
the transition period of suffering that comes after the suffering servant has suffered
and died and prior to consummation. While Ezekiel shares the shepherd imagery that
is found in both 1 Peter and Zech 9–14, as I have sketched above, Zech 9–14 develops
the Ezekiel program in a unique fashion, underscoring a transition period of fiery
trials prior to consummation.

been laid. Additionally, Peter's fragmentary allusions and echoes derive coherence from their relation to the eschatological program of Zech 9–14: they are allusive recollections of the foundational eschatological narrative. The eschatological program of Zech 9–14 is thus a springboard for his understanding and presentation of the outworking of God's restoration, in which he feels the freedom to draw on texts from the Old Testament that accord with his reading of Zech 9–14.

What this means for the purpose of this essay is that the narrative of deferred hope found in 1 Peter, which stands in contrast to the narrative of Rome's realized hope, is more specifically a narrative about a different king and a different empire and the way in which this king's people ought to faithfully orient themselves while living under foreign (and alluring) rule. Said in another way, the primary aim of 1 Peter is to help Anatolian Christians learn how to negotiate their allegiance to King Jesus in a social context that, for a number of reasons, is antagonistic to such a commitment. It is a letter written to encourage Christ followers to interpret their suffering and social alienation in light of the fact that they live in an in-between, inaugurated-but-not-yet-fully-realized time, to help them understand that *Christian* suffering, that is, suffering because of one's allegiance to Jesus, is in fact in keeping with God's will—for now.

It is important to make one final point about the way 1 Peter frames Christian suffering and faithful discipleship: the primary enemy with whom Christians struggle is not Rome or its loyal citizens! Instead, Peter paints the narrative of deferred hope and faithful allegiance on a much wider canvas, the cosmic struggle between God and the devil. The addressees are called to be on the lookout for an enemy more powerful than Rome, namely, the devil, who roams all over the world seeking for someone to devour (1 Pet 5:8–9). Identifying the devil as the true source behind the addressees' social alienation and suffering actually functions to deflate Rome's overexalted and totalizing self-understanding as the divinely appointed agent through whom the world is blessed with peace, prosperity, and justice. It minimizes Rome by depicting it as just another fleeting manifestation of the devil's schemes against God and his people. What is more, in 1 Peter, loyal allegiance to the true king in this in-between time of deferred hope is most fully and faithfully expressed by following Jesus's pattern of enemy-love, who when he suffered did not threaten in return, and who when he was reviled did not return revile in return, but instead entrusted himself to the one who judges justly (2:23). Likewise, Christians are exhorted to not repay evil for evil but instead to bless those who revile them (3:9) and to entrust themselves to the faithful creator while continuing to do good (4:19). This way of life that is rooted in enemy-love establishes an alternative social structure that runs counter to the fundamental way in which *Pax Romana* was administered.

Conclusion

In the end it is difficult, if not impossible, to adjudicate whether 1 Peter is a text that deliberately sets out to target Roman imperial claims of realized eschatology.[22] This, in fact, has not been the primary aim of this essay. We can say with certainty, however, that the implicit narrative of 1 Peter, with its deferred hope that is mediated through the eschatological Davidic shepherd, Jesus Christ, does in fact contradict, confront, and subvert the notion that the golden age has dawned and is sustained through loyalty to Rome. That is to say, 1 Peter clearly does not promote an accommodating strategy in negotiating the claims of Jesus Christ and the demands of Rome. I have sought to demonstrate this by highlighting the way the embedded narrative of 1 Peter symbolically inverts the public transcript of Rome by placing hope in the eschaton, by lifting up another king as the means by which that true, enduring hope will be secured and realized, and by underscoring that in 1 Peter, Christian suffering, that is, suffering because of one's allegiance to Jesus Christ, is regarded as a sign of future blessing in the age to come.

There are other strategies in 1 Peter that could be highlighted, which (intentionally or not) seem to put the claims of Rome in tension with the demands of following Jesus Christ. But in underscoring the implicit narrative of deferred hope in 1 Peter, we see the way in which our author deals with the most pressing pastoral need of the moment: for in pointing his readers, in a variety of ways, to the eschatological Davidic program of Zech 9–14 as it is realized through Jesus Christ, he helps his readers understand that their suffering, far from being a sign of God's rejection, is a necessary feature of faithful allegiance to King Jesus, the promised Davidic shepherd-king, in whose footsteps they follow, and for whose return they await.

---

22. If Rome is in fact not the primary target of 1 Peter, this opens up space for the text to confront and subvert any number of ideologies that profess an alternative hope and/or make totalizing claims in contradistinction to those made in 1 Peter.

For Further Reading

Carter, Warren. 2004. "Going All the Way? Honoring the Emperor and
    Sacrificing Wives and Slaves in 1 Peter 2.13–3.6." Pages 14–33 in *A
    Feminist Companion to the Catholic Epistles*. Edited by Amy-Jill Levine
    and Maria Mayo Robbins. London: T&T Clark.
Green, Joel B. 2007. *1 Peter*. Two Horizons New Testament Commentary.
    Grand Rapids: Eerdmans.
Horrell, David. 2007. "Between Conformity and Resistance: Beyond the
    Balch-Elliott Debate towards a Postcolonial Reading of 1 Peter." Pages
    111–43 in *Reading 1 Peter with New Eyes: Methodological Reassess-
    ments of the Letter of First Peter*. Edited by Robert L. Webb and Betsy
    J. Bauman-Martin. London: T&T Clark.
———. 2008. *1 Peter*. New Testament Guides. London: T&T Clark. Espe-
    cially 77–96.
Liebengood, Kelly D. 2014. *The Eschatology of First Peter: Considering the
    Influence of Zechariah 9–14*. SNTSMS 157. Cambridge: Cambridge
    University Press.
Williams, Travis. 2012. *Persecution in 1 Peter: Differentiating and Contex-
    tualizing Early Christian Suffering*. SNTSMS 145. Leiden: Brill.

Victory and Visibility: Revelation's Imperial Textures and Monumental Logics*

Davina C. Lopez

The spectacle is not a collection of images, but a social relation among people, mediated by images.
—Guy Debord (1977)

The horrible, terrible, and magisterial imagery permeating the only apocalypse of the canonical New Testament has occasioned innumerable imaginative responses within and beyond biblical scholarship. Alongside a vibrant and persistent afterlife as a potent predictor of "the end times" in ecclesial and popular cultures, the world of powerful pictures in Revelation has been the focus of much interpretive attention about the relationship between the New Testament, early Christianity, and the Roman Empire. In some respects, Revelation is a contemporary "ground zero" for exploring and exploiting the intersection of the New Testament texts and their Roman imperial contexts, as well as questions that arise out of modern life in imperial regimes. Herein a focus has been on the response to suffering and persecution of a small group of insiders ("Christians") at the hands of a much greater earthly power ("Rome"). In John's imagination, that earthly power is decisively and violently punished for enacting punishments, and that retribution comes "from above," that is, from a divine

* I am grateful to Adam Winn for enduring his tribulations as editor of this important volume. Conversations about "the end" and "the beginning" with Juan Hernández Jr., Milton Moreland, and Suzanne Watts Henderson have been most helpful and pleasurable. Todd Penner deserves special credit for his deftness in helping me to sharpen some of the methodological issues I explore herein, as well as for his critical acumen and imagination about empires then and now.

throne room in the sky. To this end, some interpreters, especially those using postcolonial and "empire-critical" analytics, have configured Revelation as "the most explicitly counter-imperial book in the New Testament" (Carey 2008, 157), one that constitutes a hidden transcript of "deviant knowledge" from dominant cultural norms (Thompson 1997, 181). In this schema, it has been easy to pit the Roman Empire against the New Testament/early Christians, with the latter representing an oppressed minority group engaged in fantasies of "striking back," "subverting," or "resisting" oppression and celebrating the establishment of a new, more just world where they might flourish.

Such observations about Revelation's imperial resonances, however, are not new. The German history of religions scholar Wilhelm Bousset (1865–1920) detected a tension between the Roman Empire and the "people of God," describing Revelation as a nascent Christian nationalist polemic against all enemies of the church (Bousset 1896, 189–90). Sir William Ramsay (1852–1916), the British classical archaeologist and New Testament scholar, claimed that focusing solely on Jewish backgrounds of Revelation and ignoring the Roman imperial elements of its compositional context resulted in John's letter being "the most misunderstood book in the New Testament," a book that in Ramsay's view spoke clearly to the "clash of east and west" in ancient and modern settings (Ramsay 1904, vi). Friedrich Engels (1820–1895), an admirer of historical criticism, called Revelation an "authentic" picture of early Christianity that was "worth more than the rest of the New Testament put together" on account of what he saw as a mirror portrait of an ancient revolutionary sect akin to the socialist movements of his time (Engels and Marx 1957, 112). Regardless of one's orientation to Revelation, it has long been difficult to ignore "empire," ancient and modern, in relation to this most charged of New Testament texts.

Empire, then, is a long-standing prism through which to view Revelation, given the role that imperial ideology plays in multiple times and places. It is tempting to read this material as symptomatic of an intractable conflict between early Christianity and the Roman Empire, with Christians imagining a world in which the "evil empire" is destroyed for good and a "counter-empire" inaugurated. Such a reading can occasion the question of whether the New Testament as a whole can be seen as anti-imperial. The perspective that the early Christians were a persecuted religious minority group under Roman political rule who sought to oppose their imperial oppressors also gives weight to appropriations of Revelation that appear to be politically progressive, even radical, in our own situation. Reading Revelation with empire is a potent way to emphasize the "political," as opposed to "theological" or "dogmatic," dimensions of early Christian discourses. Indeed, over the last several decades the topic of "New Testament and Roman Empire" has become a signifier for discussions about the relation between religion and politics in ancient and contemporary contexts. Herein a primary question hinges on whether and how the authors and audiences of texts such as Revelation negotiated Roman imperial power structures, marking these texts out as potentially having political as well as theological dimensions.

Within empire-critical studies, debates about the possible political dimensions of the New Testament texts tends to focus on their characterization as pro- or anti-imperial, along with the implications of such questions for contemporary ethics and theologies that deploy the New Testament as a scriptural resource.[1] However, such interpretive trajectories have relied on neat distinctions between theology, history, religion, and politics that were quite likely nonexistent in the ancient world. Oppositional discourses wherein theology is opposed to history and religion (Judaism and/ or Christianity) and politics (empire) downplay important aspects of the Roman world, namely, the interdependence of mythological, historical, and theological narratives that the Romans themselves constructed and maintained. It may very well be the case that John and his ancient colleagues deployed similar narrativizing strategies as a means to negotiate their world.

Contemporary empire-focused biblical scholarship offers an investigative site where texts, contexts, histories of interpretation, and identities and ideologies of readers coalesce. Herein I will leave aside the question of whether and how Revelation resists or accommodates the Roman imperial world in which it was clearly written and to which it responds. Rather, through accenting the imperial textures of Revelation's various fantastic (and sometimes fantastically frayed) threads, I will explore several interrelated issues at the intersection of the New Testament and the Roman Empire. In my estimation, the multivalence of mytho-historical rhetoric and the politics of visuality and visibility in the Roman imperial world provide a "way in" to thinking with Revelation and empire.

---

1. For an appraisal of this trajectory, see Penner and Lopez 2015, esp. 97–110 and 145–60.

Roman Representation: Imagining Empire between Myth and History

As with the rest of the canonical New Testament and much early Christian literature, Revelation was written in the Roman Empire, which is the world in which the text is situated. Understanding the Roman imperial world with which Revelation interacts and to which it might suggest alternatives involves understanding something of the matrices of power and signification at work therein.[2] Read in this light, it is quite likely no accident that the discourse of Revelation privileges the power of seeing and the monumental imagination. In being told what John sees, readers are constantly asked to look, gaze, and otherwise interact with monumental figures and spaces: thrones, winged messengers, cities, fantastic creatures, mountains, stars falling, and so on. This pattern resonates with the rhetorical and historical context. The ancient Roman world in which Revelation was composed was primarily a world of visual imagery. Far from neutral or irrelevant, visual representation—art, archaeological remains, material culture—serves as a powerful means of constructing, and not simply reflecting, narratives about history, relations of power, and national and ideological boundaries. In this respect, visual representation functions no less *rhetorically* than literary representation—the task is to persuade audiences of arguments, ideas, sets of values, and/or courses of action. Rhetoric creates a sense of reality through representation and, if persuasive, is at least in part due to an elision of the two.

No Roman imperial city was without a visual architectural program that affirmed the legitimacy of the world as it is. In this world, the Romans (especially the emperor and his family) were configured as people who worked wonders, saved nations, fought righteous wars, and ensured cosmic friend-

---

2. In this essay I leave aside traditional questions about Revelation's date of composition and focus on imperial resonances and the rhetorical configurations thereof. Some scholars have tried to give Revelation a precise temporal location by attending to the language of persecution and attempting to decipher the beast symbolism in the text. The most popular dating decisions lie with the imperium of Nero (54–68 CE) and Domitian (81–96 CE), the last of the Julio-Claudian and Flavian dynasties, respectively. Each of these "bad emperor" reigns is characterized by tyranny, injustice, and persecution of peoples at both the center and periphery of Roman territory. While it is tempting to fix the date of Revelation to a period in which maximum imperial persecution of its ancient minority audience might be prevalent—thus providing credence to the observation that John is writing about actual historical events and circumstances from the perspective of the oppressed—it is notoriously difficult to do so.

ship and peace—and were destined to do so from time immemorial. In a sense, these visual rhetorical programs rewrote history to include Roman rule "without limits on space or time" (Virgil, *Aen.* 1.279 [Goold, LCL]) as its inevitable culmination. From the coins changing hands every day, to domestic decor and practices, to large-scale public buildings, to games and entertainments that visually reenacted mythological and historical events, inhabitants of the spaces of empire were constantly reminded of their social position, the values and virtues ideally held by the populace, and powerful suggestions as to the events that led to that place and arrangement of social relations. The pervasiveness of the Roman power of images serves the ideological function of rendering empire as natural, universal, and divinely ordained, as having no boundaries and constituting the world itself. While exactly how persuasive such monuments and images were to ordinary people in antiquity is an open question, as is the extent to which such visual representations coalesce with "what really happened," it is not outlandish to suggest that viewers constantly contended with the visual landscape. For our purposes, I will focus on themes that come to the forefront most readily in Roman visual rhetoric: imperial cult, victory, barbarians and personifications of nations, and fertility motifs. As we shall see, these overlapping areas are of notable importance to locating Revelation's imperial textures.

Imperial Cult

Of particular interest to readers of Revelation, and perhaps the whole New Testament, is a preponderance of visual representations of emperors as divine figures or "sons of god" in the imperial landscape, especially in Asia Minor. Such images are thought to be a major part of what contemporary scholars have termed "imperial cult." Broadly speaking, "imperial cult" denotes a "religious" phenomenon in which the emperor (and his family) is identified with the divinely mandated authority of the Roman state. The populace may have given honors or worship to these entities, in multiple forms and settings, alongside traditional patron deities. This means that in many cases images of people were the focus of devotion. Some scholars note a difference between the presence and practices of imperial cult at Rome, where an emperor could be called "divine" after his death, and the muddier waters of eastern provinces that had a longer history of interaction with Hellenistic ruler cults and would venerate emperors while alive.[3]

---

3. While the rise of the identification of the emperor with a divine figure might

Further complicating the picture is the alignment of imperial cult with long-standing cults of local deities such as Artemis of Ephesus and Aphrodite of Aphrodisias, suggesting that emperor worship was folded into local practices. At the very least, evidence suggests that images of emperors were displayed alongside more familiar civic deities in already-established temple complexes. As such, imperial cult represents a rich amalgam of traditions, performed in various settings and initiated both by the center of empire and by peripheral provincial local elites.

Imperial cult is often anachronistically called a form of "political religion." Modern distinctions between "politics" and "religion" have led to downplaying this phenomenon as merely "political honors," obscuring the ways in which imperial cult intersects with so-called nonpolitical early Christians. A further caution must be exercised in using imperial cult as a heuristic through which to see Roman domination and potential conflicts with ancient Jewish and Christian practices. It would be an oversimplification to suggest that imperial cult was simply designed by the emperor and imposed from the capital city (above) onto subject territories (below). There was probably some measure of collaboration and compromise among rulers and subjects throughout the empire, mostly through local elite families but also among ordinary people as well. Regardless of the interpretive problems presented by the sheer diversity of practices and ritual settings denoted as belonging to imperial cult, the pervasiveness of the material record containing visual imagery from all over the empire brings these phenomena into focus. That is, the spatial vastness of the Roman Empire—along with the number of foreign cultures incorporated into its territory, hierarchy, and ideological narrative of victory and grandeur—shared the ubiquitous, likely inescapable image of the emperor, and by extension Roman power. Such ubiquity suggests from an ideological standpoint that a sense of belonging to Roman world order—as slave, family member, collaborator, and quite possibly all three—tied these peoples and places together in what Keith Hopkins (1981, 197–242) calls "symbolic unity." Whether nude and striding land and sea, as Augustus does at the Aphrodisias Sebasteion, or towering over the city, as a colossal

---

appear to be a departure from traditional Roman republican values, it could also be said that imperial cult accented the concept of *genius*, or innate divine spirit in each person, alongside features common to Roman ancestor-worship practices as well as reverence for absent external rulers in the eastern territories, a tradition at least as old as the time of Alexander the Great (died ca. 323 BCE).

Domitian did in Ephesus, or shaking hands with provinces, as Hadrian does on his *adventus* coin series, there was no shortage of emperor images with which ancient people could interact.

Victory as Messenger

It is important to remember that imperial cult is a part of a larger system of Roman signification rendered through visual representation. Herein images of the emperor align with a rhetorical framework justifying Roman world order. This larger framework can be characterized by the broad theme of eternal war and guaranteed, even predestined, victory. The Romans were good at narrating the events of war visually, transforming a series of spatially and temporally bounded events into cosmic stories. Communicative practices about specific battles were not just news but ways of reinforcing the idea of "empire without end." Images large and small, public and domestic, commemorated the conquest and humiliation of national enemies. Beyond coinage, these were depicted in narrative reliefs on arches, columns, altars, temples, tombs, and sarcophagi that constituted a long pattern of communicating success in specific battles as a means of communicating eternal victory. If one posits that the author of Revelation drew on existing discourses of war and violence, one need look no further than coins in hand or the local visual landscape for potent and pervasive inspiration. War and its spoils were everywhere; the Roman Empire was built out of images of triumph and glory.

A primary example of the Roman visual rhetoric of victory is representations of the moment in a battle when it is finished and the winners (usually the Romans) and losers (everyone else, regardless of the "actual" outcome) are evident. Such trophy monuments are traces of specific events. Erecting trophies out of weapons and armor of the defeated to mark victory has a long history in the Mediterranean. The Romans made this practice part of their visual rhetoric more broadly, rendering a specific event into part of a grammar of universal victory across time and space. One visual form of the trophy is a representation of enemy armor hung on a tree stump, reminiscent of battle sites. Along with captives, the Romans would return from war with the armor, weapons, and other accouterments of the defeated, showing them in triumphal processions and even displaying them in homes. Sculpted piles of enemy weapons and armor are also common, such as the haphazardly ordered bounty of Dacian spoils adorning the bottom of Trajan's Column in Rome.

Sometimes, a personification or goddess of victory accompanies a trophy monument. These "Nike/Victoria" figures were typically winged and are portrayed flying above, around, or standing in a scene. As a character in Roman visual narratives, Victory is imaged in poses that signify her role in announcing battle-related matters. Representations of Victory were common in imperial cult complexes, marking a connection between reverence for the emperor and his role in winning wars. In a relief from the Aphrodisias Sebasteion, for example, Victory places a trophy near a captured barbarian at its base. On the Arch of Titus in Rome, a similar figure accompanies the emperor on his four-horse chariot ride through the triumphal procession with the Jews/Judeans, who carry representative objects from their plundered Jerusalem temple. Victory figures also fly in the spandrels, flanking the archway (fig. 1). On the left, Victory carries a trophy, and on the right, she carries a small object. Trajan's Column features a larger-than-life Victory (fig. 2) standing between two trophies, writing on a shield—perhaps announcing the end of one Dacian war and the beginning of the second. Victory appears on the so-called Boscoreale cups, handing a miniature statue of herself to an enthroned Augustus. The British Museum collections include several terracotta reliefs of nude Victory figures wrestling and sacrificing animals. As part of the Roman imperial visual landscape framing Revelation, it is difficult to overlook these winged messengers as resonating with the "angels" who constantly relate noises, images, instructions, and actions to John, including those that lead to the destruction of "Babylon the Great" and the "beast(s)" along with the introduction of "New Jerusalem."

Captive Barbarians and Personifications of Nations

The Roman visual landscape contains numerous representations of conquered peoples—barbarians, nations, and barbarian nations. These constitute a core element of Roman visual rhetoric that emphasizes endless and divinely ordained victory as a natural part of the world order. Such figures are marked as "other" through symbolic posture, clothing, hairstyle, and attributes, and yet, through conquest and enslavement, they visually become part of the international Roman "family" and "household." Barbarians are featured on every kind of media: coins, domestic items, gemstones, cuirassed statues, public monuments, and imperial cult complexes throughout the empire. They are rarely shown in postures that visually suggest freedom. At times, their likenesses fight against the Romans,

Figure 1. Arch of Titus, Via Sacra, Rome. This first-century triumphal arch commemorates Titus's victories in battle—most notably against the Jews/Judeans in Jerusalem. The interior features a triumphal procession through another arch and includes Titus being led in a four-horse-drawn chariot by the armor-clad female personification Roma. Victory figures flank the spandrels on the outside of the arch. Photo by Davina C. Lopez.

Figure 2. Trajan's Column, Forum of Trajan, Rome. On this second-century column narrating the Roman-Dacian wars, a winged Victory stands between two trophy monuments, writing on a shield. Noticeably larger than other figures (except a personified Danube River at the bottom), she appears as a marker between the two campaigns. Photo by Davina C. Lopez.

or, in the case of Trajan's Column, fight for Rome against the Dacians. Conquered barbarians are commonly depicted at the moment of defeat or soon afterward: crouching alone, in couples, or with children; handing children to an emperor; parading together in triumph; stepped on by emperors; run over by horses; dying and dead; buried up to their waists; sitting underneath Nike/Victoria figures. These images may, and may not, represent actual captives. That said, the sheer number of barbarians in Roman art renders this visual trope difficult to ignore as a justification of power relationships. That the world appears to be divided into "Romans" and "others" would be a suggestive thread to follow in Revelation.

While images of barbarians are omnipresent in the world that produced Revelation, also quite prominent are personifications of cities and nations as female figures. Herein the Romans combined the visual grammatical elements associated with (1) visualizing female barbarian others and (2) imagining cities and countries as women. In the Hellenistic period, we see both "ideal" conquered figures (e.g., Gauls, Amazons, giants) and representations of the "spirit" of the *dēmos* or *polis*, often called "Tyche" (or "Fortuna," luck/fortune), who is thought to signify the destiny and fertility of a given people. Cities adopted and venerated their own versions of Tyche, who could be shown standing or enthroned, wearing a mural crown (made of city walls), and holding agricultural bounty, a ship's rudder, or the wheel of fortune. According to Libanius, Tyche of Alexandria dwelled in one of the world's most beautiful temples, wherein she was depicted crowning Earth (*Gē*), who was shown crowning her "conqueror" (*ta nikēsanta*; likely Alexander; see Libanius, *Prog.* 1114). Tyche of Antioch is usually portrayed as enthroned or sitting on a male personification of a body of water, wearing a mural crown, and holding a handful of grain. As the "fortune" of the city, Tyche was a popular visual rhetorical element in the Greek world.

As conquered figures and cities were represented as separate entities in the Hellenistic period, the Romans often represented cities and nations *as* conquered figures. Such entities were displayed alone, as on coins and triumphal monuments and in series of multiple nations, each with distinctive clothing, hairstyle, and national attributes. In the Sebasteion at Aphrodisias, a row of more than fifty different nations, including "Judea," constituted a long portico on the approach to an imperial temple. Displaying personified nations in series resonates with lists of conquered and/or "saved" peoples in inscriptions and ethnographic writings. Not all of these figures were imaged in conquered or humiliated postures—some stand "freely," as in this relief from the second-century Hadrianeum thought to portray Egypt (fig. 3). This woman stands alone without the usual decor denoting captivity, is draped in a manner vaguely suggestive of her geographical location and ethnic orientation, and holds symbols of the local harvest. Each of the Hadrianeum's surviving "faithful provinces" stands similarly. However, other panels thought to be part of this complex display trophy monuments and enemy armor, signifying a dimension of conquest that resulted in fidelity. Again, displaying nations in this manner need not betray a one-to-one correspondence between historical events and public narratives. By the time the Hadrianeum was erected, the display of barbarians and nations was oft-repeated throughout the imperial visual landscape. Such display buttresses the core message of "empire without end" and the cosmopolitanism afforded through conquest by, and international cooperation with, Rome.

Figure 3. Personification of Egypt from the Hadrianeum, Palazzo Massimo alle Terme, Rome. One of nineteen surviving reliefs from the second-century Temple of Hadrian. This standing and fully draped female figure holds a cluster of branches with fruits (perhaps olives) in her left hand and a pomegranate with exposed arils in her outstretched right hand. A series of standing nations such as this one were displayed alongside stylized reliefs of enemy armor and weapons. Photo by Davina C. Lopez.

"Just" Fertility

Roman personification of nations was not limited to others who were conquered, assimilated, and/or "faithful." Roma, the personification of Rome, often appears dressed as an Amazonian military figure shown in various poses, including standing near or sitting on piles of captured weapons, offering a tiny Victory figure with an outstretched arm, approving an emperor's apotheosis, or leading a quadriga in triumph. A suggestive idea that personifications offer is that conquest results in peace and fertility. This visual dimension includes agriculture (plants and animals), as well human fertility (infants and small children). A famous such image appears on the Ara Pacis Augustae in Rome, dedicated in 9 BCE to commemorate Augustus's return to Rome after a successful campaign against the Gauls and Spaniards.[4] Upon approaching the doorway leading to the festooned interior of this altar, one would ascend a bank of stairs and notice that reliefs of scrolling plants give way to two female-centered allegorical mythological scenes on either side of the entry opening. The panel on the left (fig. 4) features a veiled woman sitting on a stone pedestal, holding two babies and fruits on her lap. Farm animals graze at her feet, and plants shoot up around her. Two female figures, clothed from the waist down, flank the central woman and ride on the backs of a waterbird (left) and dragon-like creature (right). Plants on the left and water on the right associate the bird-riding figure with land and the sea-creature-riding figure with sea. This is supported by

Figure 4. Ara Pacis Augustae, Rome. Relief featuring a veiled woman sitting on a stone throne. Infants sit in her lap, as does a collection of various fruits. She is flanked by two personifications, perhaps of land and sea. This figure has been identified as the earth mother Tellus, the nation of Italia, and a variety of other goddesses/personified virtues. Photo by Davina C. Lopez.

---

4. For further exploration of the Ara Pacis Augustae, its mytho-historical imagery, and its resonances with New Testament (especially Pauline) rhetoric, see Lopez forthcoming.

images of Augustus striding "land and sea" in the Aphrodisias Sebasteion, for example, as well as his publicly displayed statement of successful deeds: "I many times waged civil and foreign wars by land and sea
over the whole world, and as victor I spared all citizens who asked for
pardon" (Res gest. divi Aug. 3.1 [Shipley, LCL]). The critical focus is the
association of the emperor and empire with a blossoming, fertile, near-
paradisiacal habitus as befits a new "golden age."

The relationship between war and imperial abundance is a theme
developed further in visual rhetoric. Plants and vines springing up everywhere, including at the tops of columns and in historical reliefs, bolster
the notion that the "golden age" brings marvelous bounties from the earth,
who gives of herself freely. To this end, the scroll reliefs around the bottom
register of the Ara Pacis are more than decorative. The relief comprises
a hybrid vine and can be seen as emphasizing miraculous fertility (see
Pollini 2012, 271–308), born from many plants (of the nations) tied to
a common acanthus (Roman) root, brought by the *pax Augusta*. In fact,
the rehabilitated Augustan golden age is a mythological construct partially
defined by a miraculous agricultural abundance wherein humans would
not need to work the land for food. Herein one notes some overlap between
allegorical personification of nations and so-called earth mother fertility
figures that complicates interpretations of rhetorics of power under imperial conditions. At times the nations, such as Egypt pictured above, are
shown handing their fruits to viewers. Just as the display of weapons and
armor or women in mourning poses is not ornamental, so too with plants.
Egypt was annexed through conquest, to be sure, and yet she is shown as
a willing collaborator in imperial abundance. In the Hadrianeum, several
other nations are shown similarly extending their hands with representative agricultural products, reminiscent both of Tyche, who holds agricultural fortune in her hand, as well as the earth figures holding cornucopias
and other harvested bounties.

Revelation harnesses a fertility trope in John's visions as well: elements
of the natural (imperial) world such as trees and grasses are destroyed,
stars are swept to the ground, and rivers, springs, and the sea are ruined
with fire, blood, and falling mountains. The earth, for her part, provides a
sheltering wilderness for the single woman who gives birth in Revelation
and swallows the dragon pursuing her and her "seed" (Rev 12). The "tree
of life" sprouting whole in the new Jerusalem has twelve fruits and abundant leaves (and perhaps has Jesus as the "root" [*rhidza*]; see Rev 22:16);
the "river of life" flows clear as crystal, and the light shines always.

Summary

Interrelationships between visual representations associated with imperial cult; victory, war, and conquest; barbarians and personified nations; and international fertility and peace are powerfully suggestive about Roman imperial discourses. These tropes are part of a foundational narrative that lies, in my view, somewhere between myth and history and yet are presented as more "true" than either history or myth. As terrible as war might be, the idea that violence leads to abundance can be alluring, and the rhetorical result of fertility and international cooperation justifies constant and unrelenting conquest. Narratives of the miraculous, predestined founding and flourishing of the Roman state, the rehabilitation of the "golden age" under Augustus, and invitations to give honors to the imperial family and related deities as providers of "empire without end" defy easy categorization as political stories. The discursive power of such narratives can be highlighted as a major potential *comparandum* with the rhetoric of Revelation.

I have briefly explored some of the architectural structures of imperial rhetoric, especially in Roman monuments. Many of these themes appear in Roman imperial literature, which in some sense provides a corollary to visual representation. What is helpful about using Roman imperial visual rhetoric to think with is that, unlike literature written by elites, it is clear that a cross section of people saw and interacted with imperial monuments. These images communicate something grandiose and multivalent about empire—they provide an imperial texture that was easily accessed. Such visual rhetoric helps to imagine, nurture, and sustain desired social relationships—ones that were quite necessary to ensure that empire was, in fact, without end. Through the lens of imperial textures we can think about and with Revelation. Below I will delineate several of the probably many imperial resonances between the visual rhetoric of the Roman Empire and John's Apocalypse.

Imperial Resonances and the Logics of Empire

The beast(s) and dragon. The bride and whore. The lamb and locust-king. The throne and trumpet. Like many disaster scenes, it is difficult to "look away" from Revelation. Readers of this letter are invited to peer into a busy, noisy world of spectacular imagery and symbolism, catching glimpses of persecution, war, and retribution on a grand, fantastic scale that affects not just the addressees but also the whole world, as well as under and above it.

The visual onslaught culminates in the "faithful" being invited to a wedding feast between the new Jerusalem, who descends from a mountain fully decked out in bridal attire and serves as a replacement city for the fallen Babylon, and the many-horned and-eyed Lamb residing in the sky. Throughout John's narrative, imperatives to look and to *see* in the face of uncertainty and danger persist. Revelation at once gazes on the boundless and draws strict boundaries: between now and soon, between selves and others, and between pure and profane. Particular social relations, mediated by images, are reimagined as universal cosmic views.

As Christopher Frilingos (2004, 5) suggests, Revelation can be read as "a cultural product of the Roman Empire, a book that shares with contemporaneous texts and institutions specific techniques for defining world and self." In this light, Revelation can also be seen as "a work of visionary rhetoric," in Elisabeth Schüssler Fiorenza's (1985, 187) words, wherein the author constructs an "alternative symbolic universe" from a social position of dissatisfaction with the world. However horrifying Revelation's pervasive imagery might seem, such imagery should not be surprising given what I have been exploring about Roman imperial visual representation. Visual rhetoric is part of a system of Roman signification about the way the world is and ought to be. This world constitutes the rhetorical situation of Revelation—"seeing" Rome, or what Rome was thought to represent, all around was part of daily experience and ideological imagination. A note of caution is necessary, though, for examining the rhetorical dimensions of the Roman world requires recognizing distance between representation and reality. That is, in Roman visual representation, we can "see" history rewritten to include empire as its natural and inevitable apex, as well as the adoption of genealogical and mythological tropes in order to communicate universal and eternal victory and international cooperation. Such representation may or may not signify a one-to-one historical correspondence with Revelation. However, Roman use of mythological tropes to support claims about reality does not render their stories about themselves and their world untrue. That is, I am not saying that war and conquest never happened, nor would I suppose that fertility was impossible in the Roman Empire. Rather, deploying myths of origins denotes rhetorical textures with a deep level of recognizability and persuasiveness. As Bruce Lincoln (2014, 115–17) notes, foundation stories, particularly when articulated by the state—whether from the capital or from provincial elites—serve to stabilize a past and present that are fundamentally unstable. Such rhetoric is multivalent, and the success (or demise) of historical and mythological narratives, regardless of media form, depends in part on the type of relationship the narrators and audience have with the story and with one another.

Just as Roman monuments convey powerful arguments, Revelation's discourse has monumental dimensions that resonate with imperial rhetoric. One might take many directions with this line of thinking in relation to the text. I offer here two points of resonance between Revelation and the Roman Empire that rely on monumental visibility as a methodological thread. While war and conquest, victory symbols, and imperial cult imagery would be obvious avenues to pursue, I focus on the related issues of personifications ("Babylon"/"New Jerusalem") and the larger function of ubiquitous visibility and its implications for thinking about Revelation.

"Babylon"/"New Jerusalem" as Personifications

Roman identification of nations, peoples, and cities with female figures allows for a wide range of imaginings such as the allegorical depictions of "Babylon/whore" and "New Jerusalem/bride" in Revelation. Connecting these characters with the Roman visual rhetoric of personifying cities and nations raises some interesting questions about imperial resonances and logics. "Babylon" is described as a woman dressed opulently whose attribute is a cup of abomination and fornication (Rev 17:4). She has a mark on her forehead that delineates who she is: "Babylon the Great, the mother of prostitutes and of the abominations of the earth" (17:5). She is "the city that rules over the kings of the earth" (18:18) and a "whore" to whom kings, merchants, and sea workers (18:9, 11, 17) showed "allegiance" through "committing fornication." However, the mark on her head could identify her as someone's property, and specifically as an imperial brothel slave, thus building on the gendered, sexualized, racialized, and economic dimensions of her representation (Moore and Glancy 2011, 551–69; S. Smith 2014). Additionally, she is a city sitting on waters that represent "the peoples and crowds and nations and tongues" (Rev 18:15). Revelation clearly asserts that Babylon has not been good for humanity or the earth, and John sees divine demands that she be "terminated." Personified Babylon is not a warrior (like Roma) but is dressed as an elite woman. She loses that clothing to become a conquered city, reminiscent of the Roman personifications that feature half-clothed or naked nations such as the reliefs of Claudius over Britannia and Nero over Armenia at Aphrodisias. The destruction of Babylon is completed not by her "ene-

mies" or those who do not "fornicate" with her, but is prophesied to John
as being accomplished by the "ten horns" and the "beast" she is shown
riding (17:3), who will strip her naked, eat her flesh, and burn her (17:16)
after making a deal with God that the beast will receive a kingdom in
return for this violence (17:17). Babylon, it seems, is devoured by the very
entity who serves her and whom she services, even as beast(s) and city
roll into John's line of vision together and belong to the same semantic
universe as enemies.

The stripping, eating, and burning of Babylon makes room for New
Jerusalem, whom John sees in the last two chapters of Revelation. As part
of a "new heaven and new earth," this "bride" comes down from a mountain dressed no less opulently than the "whore" whose remains were left
smoldering in the distance. New Jerusalem is the bringer of abundance in
the "river of life" flowing through the streets (Rev 22:1). Near the river is
the "tree of life" (22:2) producing twelve fruits, one each month, with leaves
for "the healing of the nations" (22:2). Aside from obvious resonances with
the restoration tradition of the Hebrew Bible prophets, this fertility trope
is reminiscent of the abundance brought by Roman conquest. The defeat
of Babylon is part of what enables this fruitfulness to blossom.

New Jerusalem could be read in empire-conscious terms as an antidote to imperialism, a city free of domination. But that does not mean
this city lacks domination of any sort. Indeed, while this bride-to-be city
would be free from corruption, she apparently is not free from hierarchical
power relationships. Perhaps most striking, her citizens—"slaves" to her
husband-to-be—will be visibly marked on their foreheads with the name
of their master (Rev 22:4), which recalls that Roman slaves and prisoners
of war were often marked with tattoos on their foreheads and/or hands as
both a visible declaration of their status as property and as a deterrent from
flight. Such an imperial texture suggests a logic of belonging: as imperial
households would be filled with slaves, and the Roman Empire is imaged
metaphorically as relating to the nations with the latter forming a "worldwide, age-old slave-gang" (Tacitus, *Agr.* 31.2 [Hutton and Peterson, LCL]),
so, too, is a household of belonging writ large in New Jerusalem. The logic,
though, has limits, especially if one imagines New Jerusalem to be a haven
after empire "falls." What do we make of the final transformation of these
bodies into visible monuments of servitude? Should we understand this
image of the body politic as constituting "captives" or a "slave-gang," as
the Roman Empire does? That the inhabitants of New Jerusalem will be
marked as slaves for all to see is reminiscent of imperial patterns to be

sure. Such rhetoric is, after all, part of the world of tropes available to the author of Revelation. To this end, New Jerusalem appears like a reincarnation of the imperial landscape, and it should not be surprising that Revelation alludes to imagery associated with slavery therein.

The Romans' pervasive use of allegorical personifications to denote peoples, virtues, and power relationships further complicates the picture concerning what we ought to do with these images in relation to Revelation. Given the ubiquity of these representations as constructions of reality, it is not surprising that such depictions are deployed therein, nor is it surprising that Revelation's image catalog functions similarly to Roman visual rhetoric. Both the visual rhetoric and mythological flavor of Revelation resist a single interpretation or either/or juxtaposition; such is the point of allegory. As in Roman imaging, adding gendered and enslaved personifications to the mix in Revelation could function as a means of communicating power relationships rather than signifying much in terms of historical women's and men's issues, thus bolstering an elastic view of the rhetorical situation. Methodologically, it is easy to pit the terrible "whore" and awesome "bride" against one another, or in hierarchical relationship to one another. However, city or hierarchy as such is not necessarily the problem in Revelation. After all, it appears that more pastoral nature scenes and are targets for annihilation, and it is telling that New Jerusalem is a walled city and not, say, a desert or village. It is who has relationships with the city, and on what terms, that configures that power. No merchants, sea workers, or kings can traffic in their wares, including human bodies, in New Jerusalem, as they did in Babylon; they practice abominations outside her splendid walls (Rev 21:27). She appears as a city without the usual commercial endeavors common to empire, but again, that does not mean without hierarchy as such. What of the nations? They are pictured as objects, as the waters underneath Babylon and in need of "healing" and "light" that New Jerusalem provides. This might resonate with portrayals of the nations as both conquered entities whose display bolsters imperial prowess and willing collaborators whose fidelity supports imperial plentitude. One might ask whether the two main personifications, Babylon and New Jerusalem, represent two sides of the same imperial coin, so to speak.

Visibility and Surveillance

Images of war, personifications of cities, and fertility discussed above are critical components for seeing Revelation's imperial resonances. Also important for detecting imperial logic in Revelation is the notion that these spectacular events happen publicly, where they can be seen. Just as Roman monuments such as the Ara Pacis and Arch of Titus feature processions with crowds of witnesses that viewers can join just by walking past and seeing the images, and just as the Romans were invited to become audiences to spectacles such as gladiator battles and reenactments of war, so too with Revelation's visions. While John is the one seeing, readers are invited to become viewers of the sights he vividly narrates "before their eyes," and for its mysteriousness Revelation at times suggests particular ways in which its pictures are to be seen. The "angels"/messengers of victory show John many things and manage his line of vision and construction as a viewer and narrator.[5] Similarly, crowds and multitudes and peoples gather to see and participate in what happens throughout the narration of John's visions. While visions "belong" to John, they also have built-in audiences that readers can join. Managing the ways in which viewers negotiate imagery coheres with imperial logics.

While Revelation appears to construct what Frilingos (2004, 120) terms an "empire of viewers," it also constructs what I would designate as a panoptic empire of the viewed. Eyes "above" abound. Hybrid creatures in the heavenly throne room are filled with eyes in "front and back" (Rev 4:6–8). The "Lamb" has seven eyes (5:6). More striking than eyes seeing all from above, however, is how surveillance is written into the letters to the seven assemblies of Asia. Together, these letters serve as a prelude to the cacophony of sounds and panoply of sights/sites in what follows. Each is dictated to John by the "Son of Man" (1:13) to be written formulaically. First, the messenger of the assembly to whom the letter is addressed is told

---

5. Interestingly, at the same time that John is constructed as a viewer, his actions are under surveillance by the messenger(s). John is told what to write for his viewers, and, suspiciously, what not to write (Rev 10:4). He falls down afraid, and is told not to have fear and to write (1:19). He weeps as a response to the vision in which no one is found worthy to open the scroll in the right hand of the one on the throne (5:4), and is told not to weep. He "marvels" at Babylon, is asked why he does so (17:7), and is told that her mystery will be revealed. When John reveals himself to be the narrator and viewer and falls down at the feet of the messenger who showed him his visions, the messenger tells him not to do that and that the messenger is a "fellow slave" (*syndoulos*) with John's "brothers" the prophets and "those who keep the words of this book" (22:8–9). The construction of John as a character could serve as a model of how to view Revelation's visions: do what you are told, do not weep, do not marvel, do not worship the wrong entity.

to describe an image of the "Son of Man," for example, "the one who has eyes of flames" (2:12), and each assembly receives a different descriptor. Second, the sender directs each messenger to tell their assembly that "I know/see" (*oida*) what they are doing; in each case the activity is either condoned or condemned, and the assembly is told what to do differently. Third, each assembly is told what "the one who conquers" (*ta nikōn*) will get as a reward for such "good behavior."

Taken together, these letters to Asia suggest a politics of being monitored and shaped from afar. Declarations of surveillance—"I see what you are doing down there, cities of Asia"—have an effect of helping to manage subjectivity in a manner similar to what Michel Foucault (1995) called a "technology of the self." For Foucault, such are disciplinary practices that subjects perform to manage their own self-presentation at least partially as a result of being constantly visible and viewed.[6] In such situations, one need not be watched by personally present ruling powers. Relentless visibility renders it possible to exercise power in the physical absence of rulers. Between the management of John's visions and the suggestion that viewers are being viewed, it is difficult not to submit that Revelation offers a technology of the self to its readers. Further, the panoptic power construct in Revelation echoes that of the Roman Empire. The emperor was physically absent from most of imperial territory most of the time, and yet his presence was everywhere visually, "watching." The eyes of Victory, barbarians, and nations also "see" their viewers. Imperial subjects collaborated to inscribe disciplinary power relations that perpetuated their subjection under such circumstances. It is not surprising that the logic of Revelation includes among its spectacles the spectacle of being visible and being watched. Such monitoring, and the call to monitor one's self, is even emphasized at the end of Revelation, where readers/viewers are implored not to add anything to or subtract anything from the book under threat of being written out of it and thus out of a place in New Jerusalem and her "tree of life" (Rev 22:18–19). Even in the end, imagination and vision are managed in view of consequences. The book itself becomes a monument—to victory, fertility, visibility, to imperial logics generally.

---

6. Foucault (1995, 203) suggests that, when one is placed in a constant field of visibility, one "assumes responsibility for the constraints of power; he makes them play spontaneously upon himself; he inscribes in himself the power relation in which he simultaneously plays both roles; he becomes the principle of his own subjection."

When thinking through imperial resonances in Revelation, I suggest that it is less important to identify specific points of historical cohesion and collision than it is to explore broad rhetorical contours. Rhetoric does not necessarily work through one-to-one correspondence (e.g., Babylon = Rome in the 60s CE), but through persuasive strategies. Perhaps this point is no more evident than in scholarly preoccupation with the crisis theme in Revelation that has dominated and controlled analyses of the letter, assessments of its historical situation, and redeployments in its reception over time. This theme has in some sense sustained readings of Revelation as "anti-imperial" from the inception of modern historical-critical inquiry into the text. However, the theme of oppression is critical to heightening the urgent, "coming-soon" quality of the rhetoric—whether or not the communities addressed in the letter were actually persecuted by external entities. Thus, whether reflecting historical realities, imagined by John and his audience, or even manufactured by the author, continual appeals to the imminent threat of violence against "Christians" heightens the surveillance motif and the need to be on one's guard and "watchful." One is being "watched" by the various nefarious entities that arise from land and sea throughout Revelation, but also, more importantly, the angelic armies of God and inhabitants of the heavenly throne room see all. Unless one "conquers," one will not be rewarded. This is not unlike the implications of Roman visual rhetoric: by virtue of the emperor bringing and sustaining peace, an ever-present threat underlies the manufactured appearance. At any moment, the peace may well come to an end, and for that reason the Romans stand guard and remain ever-watchful over imperial subjects. In this rhetorical environment, then, it is not surprising that people would develop notions of crisis and persecution as essential components of identity, and that so-called counterdiscourses would exhibit similar qualities to their own rhetoric from the standpoint of marginalization.

Even in some core elements of Revelation, considered by many scholars to be the bedrock of historical *realia* in the text, it is critical to see the Roman Empire as a historical force at work with and through imperial textures and logics. Insofar as Revelation imagines something "new," it does so at least in part by interacting with available discourses that were thought to be persuasive or at least those with which an audience would be familiar. Roman imperial visual rhetoric offers an abundance of tropes and themes with which to imagine "new" cities, images, and practices of belonging and nonbelonging. That this imagination is violent and features total destruction of this world should not be surprising. For many of the Roman Empire's inhabitants—especially those formerly "foreign"—their world "ended" with conquest and war and began again when they became subjects, even "slaves," to a "new" city. The thrust of Revelation resonates, and powerfully so, especially with those who are used to worlds ending and beginning again.

Conclusion: Empires of Imagination

It might be common for empire-conscious New Testament scholars to interpret the Roman Empire as a monolithic and relentless war machine that successfully used force on every single one of its inhabitants, not to mention the earth itself, and Revelation as a text that proposes a thorough-going anti-imperial view and resistance from all sides and at all costs. But the story is probably more complex and unstable than what a simple Revelation/Roman Empire opposition affords. To be sure, the Roman Empire offers an "official" narrative of history and power relationships, whereas Revelation may offer an "alternative" or "revisionist" version of that narrative. However, and this is critical for interrogating the relationship between Revelation and the Roman Empire, "official" and "alternative" histories are similar in that both narratives deploy tropes in strategic ways to shape the present and future. Likewise, it is worth noting that "alternative" mytho-historical narratives can all too easily become "official" narratives—as is the case with both the Roman Empire, which had its own revisions to make following the collapse of the republic and consolidation of power into the hands of an emperor, and the New Testament, which underwent its own power consolidation of sorts when it became part of state-sponsored theological and religious projects. Thus I suggest that while Revelation may entertain resistance as an option in relation to empire, its rhetoric also appears to be thoroughly textured with imperial resonances in both "official" and "alternative" threads.

Ultimately, it may be the case that imperial logics and theology are present on both sides, that of the Roman Empire and that of the New Testament. In other words, if we want to examine the relationship between Revelation and the Roman Empire in terms of pro-/anti-imperial questions, then we need to entertain the possibility that Revelation might be pro-imperial, or at least pro-Roman. After all, Rome was not the only imperial game in town as far as the ancients were concerned. The Parthians to the south, where Babylon was located geographically, were an

ever-present threat to "the world" as such, and Asia was contentious territory located between two empires. For the Romans, however important
it was to keep the nations in check, it was even more critical to neutralize
Parthian threats. In this sense, perhaps the choice readers of Revelation are
asked to see is not between empire and counterempire but between two
imperial paradigms.

It could also very well be that what Revelation resists is not empire
itself, but the stability, cohesion, comfort, and desire that empire appears
to provide. In revealing what the world looks like, and what viewers should
see, Revelation reveals the world as a spectacularly ugly image—even
when it appears opulent and fertile and even when the multitudes serve it.
In revealing the book to be "closed," Revelation reveals itself, and perhaps
empire, to be uncontainable—without limits on space or time. As Debord
notes, the society of the spectacle is less about the image than about relations between people that are mediated through images. It is the spectacle
of imagining constructions of selves, others, and social relations that is at
the heart of Revelation, and perhaps of the human experience as a whole.
If we take imperial resonances seriously, no matter the historical context,
then we must question whether such imagination, in the end, has failed us,
or we have failed it, and whether we are surprised by such failures.

For Further Reading

Friesen, Steven J. 2001. *Imperial Cults and the Apocalypse of John: Reading
    Revelation in the Ruins*. New York: Oxford University Press.
Howard-Brook, Wes, and Anthony Gwyther. 1999. *Unveiling Empire: Read-
    ing Revelation Then and Now*. Bible and Liberation Series. Maryknoll,
    NY: Orbis.
Levine, Amy-Jill, and Maria Mayo Robbins, eds. 2009. *A Feminist Com-
    panion to the Apocalypse of John*. Feminist Companions to the Bible.
    New York: T&T Clark.
Moore, Stephen D. 2015. *Untold Tales from the Book of Revelation: Sex and
    Gender, Empire and Ecology*. RBS 79. Atlanta: SBL Press.
Sánchez, David A. 2008. *From Patmos to the Barrio: Subverting Imperial
    Myths*. Minneapolis: Fortress.
Schüssler Fiorenza, Elisabeth. 1985. *The Book of Revelation: Justice and
    Judgment*. Philadelphia: Fortress.
Thompson, Leonard L. 1997. *The Book of Revelation: Apocalypse and
    Empire*. New York: Oxford University Press.

Bibliography

Aeschylus. 1922–1926. Translated by H. W. Smyth. 2 vols. LCL. Cambridge: Harvard University Press.

Ahl, Frederick. 1984. "The Art of Safe Criticism in Greece and Rome." *AJP* 105:174–208.

Aitken, Ellen Bradshaw. 2005. "Portraying the Temple in Stone and Text: The Arch of Titus and the Epistle to the Hebrews." Pages 131–48 in *Hebrews: Contemporary Methods—New Insights.* Edited by Gabriella Gelardini. Leiden: Brill.

Alcock, Susan E. 1997. "The Problem of Romanization, the Power of Athens." Pages 1–7 in *The Romanization of Athens.* Edited by Michael C. Hoff and Susan I. Rotroff. Oxford: Oxbow.

Allison, Dale. 1998. *Jesus of Nazareth: Millenarian Prophet.* Minneapolis: Fortress.

Ando, Clifford. 2000. *Imperial Ideology and Provincial Loyalty in the Roman Empire.* Berkeley: University of California Press.

Arnold, Clinton E. 1996. *The Colossian Syncretism: The Interface between Christianity and Folk Belief at Colossae.* WUNT 2/77. Tübingen: Mohr Siebeck.

Badiou, Alain. 2003. *Saint Paul: The Foundation of Universalism.* Translated by Ray Brassier. Stanford: Stanford University Press.

Bakirtzis, Charalambos. 1998. "Paul and Philippi: The Archaeological Evidence." Pages 37–48 in *Philippi at the Time of Paul and after His Death.* Edited by Charalambos Bakirtzis and Helmut Koester. Harrisburg, PA: Trinity Press International.

Bakirtzis, Charalambos, and Helmut Koester, eds. 1998. *Philippi at the Time of Paul and after His Death.* Harrisburg, PA: Trinity Press International.

Balch, David. L. 1981. *Let Wives Be Submissive: The Domestic Code in 1 Peter.* SBLDS 26. Chico, CA: Scholars Press.

Barclay, John M. G. 2011. *Pauline Churches and Diaspora Jews*. WUNT 275. Tübingen: Mohr Siebeck.

Bartchy, S. Scott. 1973. *Mallon Chresai: First Century Slavery and 1 Corinthians 7:21*. SBLDS 11. Missoula, MT: Scholars Press.

Barreto, Eric D. 2010. *Ethnic Negotiations: The Function of Race and Ethnicity in Acts 16*. WUNT 2/294. Tübingen: Mohr Siebeck.

———. 2013. "Negotiating Difference: Theology and Ethnicity in the Acts of the Apostles." Pages 97–106 in *Soundings in Cultural Criticism: Perspectives and Methods in Culture, Power, and Identity in the New Testament*. Edited by Greg Carey and Francisco Lozada. Minneapolis: Fortress.

Bash, Anthony. 1997. *Ambassadors for Christ: An Exploration of Ambassadorial Language in the New Testament*. WUNT 2/92. Tübingen: Mohr Siebeck.

Bassler, Jouette M., David M. Hay, and E. Elizabeth Johnson, eds. 1991–1997. *Pauline Theology*. 4 vols. SymS 4. Minneapolis: Fortress.

Bechtler, Steven Richard. 1998. *Following in His Steps: Suffering, Community, and Christology in 1 Peter*. SBLDS 162. Atlanta: Scholars Press.

Beebe, H. Keith. 1983. "Caesarea Maritima: Its Strategic and Political Significance to Rome." *JNES* 42:195-207.

Bhabha, Homi K. 1984. "Of Mimicry and Man: The Ambivalence of Colonial Discourse." *October* 28:125–33.

———. 1985. "Signs Taken for Wonders: Questions of Ambivalence and Authority under a Tree Outside Delhi, May 1817." *Critical Inquiry* 12:144–65.

———. 1994. *The Location of Culture*. New York: Routledge.

Bilde, Per. 1988. *Flavius Josephus between Jerusalem and Rome: His Life, His Works, and Their Importance*. JSPSup 2. Sheffield: Sheffield Academic.

Bird, Michael F., and Preston M. Sprinkle, eds. 2009. *The Pistis Christou Debate: The Faith of Christ. Exegetical, Biblical and Theological Studies*. Peabody, MA: Hendrickson.

Bitzer, Lloyd. 1968. "The Rhetorical Situation." *Ph&Rh* 1:1–18.

Bolt, Peter. 2003. *Jesus' Defeat of Death: Persuading Mark's Early Readers*. Cambridge: Cambridge University Press.

Bonz, Marianne Palmer. 2000. *The Past as Legacy: Luke-Acts and Ancient Epic*. Minneapolis: Fortress.

Bousset, Wilhelm. 1896. *Die Offenbarung Johannis*. Göttingen: Vandenhoeck & Ruprecht.

Braund, David C. 1985. *Augustus to Nero: A Sourcebook on Roman History 31 BC–AD 68*. London: Croom Helm.

———. 1986. "The Caucasian Frontier: Myth, Exploration and the Dynamics of Imperialism." Pages 31–49 in volume 1 of *The Defence of the Roman Byzantine East*. BAR International Series 297. Edited by Philip Freeman and David Kennedy. Oxford: British Archaeological Report.

Brennan, T. Corey. 2012. "Perceptions of Women's Power in the Late Republic: Terentia, Fluvia, and the Generation of 63 BCE." Pages 354-55 in *A Companion to Women in the Ancient World*. Edited by Sharon L. James and Sheila Dillon. Chichester, UK: Wiley-Blackwell.

Breton, Stanislas. 2011. *A Radical Philosophy of Saint Paul*. Translated by Joseph N. Ballan. New York: Columbia University Press.

Breytenbach, Cilliers. 2010. *Grace, Reconciliation, Concord: The Death of Christ in Graeco-Roman Metaphors*. NovTSup 135. Leiden: Brill.

Broshi, Magen. 1987. "The Role of the Temple in the Herodian Economy." *JJS* 38:31–37.

Brown, Raymond E., and John P. Meier. 1983. *Antioch and Rome: New Testament Cradles of Catholic Christianity*. New York: Paulist.

Burkert, Walter. 1983. *Homo Necans: The Anthropology of Ancient Greek and Sacrificial Ritual and Myth*. Berkeley: University of California Press.

Burridge, Richard A. 2004. *What Are the Gospels? A Comparison with Graeco-Roman Biography*. 2nd ed. Grand Rapids: Eerdmans.

Campbell, Douglas A. 2005. *The Quest for Paul's Gospel: A Suggested Strategy*. London: T&T Clark.

Canavan, Rosemary. 2012. *Clothing the Body of Christ at Colossae: A Visual Construction of Identity*. WUNT 2/334. Tübingen: Mohr Siebeck.

Carey, Greg. 2008. "The Book of Revelation as Counter-Imperial Script." Pages 157–76 in *In the Shadow of Empire: Reading the Bible as a History of Faithful Resistance*. Edited by Richard A. Horsley. Louisville: Westminster John Knox.

Carter, Warren. 2000. *Matthew and the Margins: A Sociopolitical and Religious Reading*. Maryknoll, NY: Orbis.

———. 2001. *Matthew and Empire: Initial Explorations*. Harrisburg, PA: Trinity Press International.

———. 2003. "Are There Imperial Texts in the Class? Intertextual Eagles and Matthean Eschatology as 'Lights Out' Time for Imperial Rome (Matt 24:27–31)." *JBL* 122:467–87.

———. 2005a. "Construction of Violence and Identities in Matthew's Gospel." Pages 81–108 in *Violence in the New Testament*. Edited by Shelly Matthews and Leigh Gibson. New York: T&T Clark.

———. 2005b. "Matthew's People." Pages 138–61 in *A People's History of Christianity: Christian Origins*. Edited by Richard Horsley. Minneapolis: Fortress.

———. 2006a. *John: Storyteller, Interpreter, Evangelist*. Peabody, MA: Hendrickson.

———. 2006b. *The Roman Empire and the New Testament: An Essential Guide*. Nashville: Abingdon.

———. 2008. *John and Empire: Initial Explorations*. New York: T&T Clark.

———. 2013. "Postcolonial Criticism." Pages 97–116 in *New Meanings for Ancient Texts*. Edited by Steven MacKenzie and John Kaltner. Louisville: Westminster John Knox.

Cassidy, Richard J. 1992. *John's Gospel in New Perspective*. Maryknoll, NY: Orbis.

Cassius Dio. 1914–1927. *Roman History*. Translated by Earnest Cary and Herbert Foster. 9 vols. LCL. Cambridge: Harvard University Press.

Castelli, Elizabeth. 1991. "Interpretations of Power in 1 Corinthians." *Semeia* 54:197–222.

Chae, Young S. 2006. *Jesus as the Eschatological Davidic Shepherd*. WUNT 2/216. Tübingen: Mohr Siebeck.

Chancey, Mark A. 2005. *Greco-Roman Culture and the Galilee of Jesus*. Cambridge: Cambridge University Press.

Collart, Paul. 1937. *Philippes ville de Macédoine de ses origines jusqu'à la fin de l'époque romaine*. Paris: de Boccard.

Collins, Adela Yarbro. 2000. "Mark and His Readers: The Son of God among Greeks and Romans." *HTR* 93:85–100.

Collins, Raymond. 1999. *1 Corinthians*. SP. Collegeville, MN: Liturgical Press.

Coloe, Mary L. 2013. "The Mother of Jesus: A Woman Possessed." Pages 202–13 in *Character Studies in the Fourth Gospel*. Edited by Stephen A. Hunt, D. Francois Tolmie, and Ruben Zimmermann. WUNT 314. Tübingen: Mohr Siebeck.

Cooley, Alison E. 2009. *Res Gestae Divi Augusti: Text, Translation, and Commentary*. Cambridge: Cambridge University Press.

Cooley, Alison E., and M. G. L. Cooley. 2013. *Pompeii: A Sourcebook*. 2nd ed. London: Routledge.

Cotter, Wendy. 1999. *Miracles in Greco-Roman Antiquity: A Sourcebook for the Study of the New Testament Miracle Stories*. London: Rutledge.

Crossan, John Dominic. 1991. *The Historical Jesus: The Life of a Mediterranean Jewish Peasant*. San Francisco: HarperSanFrancisco.

Crossan, John Dominic, and Jonathan L. Reed. 2004. *In Search of Paul: How Jesus's Apostle Opposed Rome's Empire with God's Kingdom*. San Francisco: HarperSanFrancisco.

Crouch, James E. 1972. *The Origin and Intention of the Colossian Haustafel*. Göttingen: Vandenhoeck & Ruprecht.

Cullmann, Oscar. 1970. *Jesus and the Revolutionaries*. New York: Harper & Row.

D'Ambra, Eve. 1993. *Private Lives, Imperial Virtues: The Frieze of the Forum Transitorium in Rome*. Princeton: Princeton University Press.

Dahmen, Karsten. 2010. "The Numismatic Evidence." Pages 41–62 in *A Companion to Ancient Macedonia*. Edited by Joseph Roisman and Ian Worthington. Chichester, UK: Wiley-Blackwell.

Dawes, Gregory W. 1998. *The Body in Question: Metaphor and Meaning in the Interpretation of Ephesians 5:21–33*. BibInt 30. Leiden: Brill, 1998.

De Boer, Martinus C. 2011. *Galatians: A Commentary*. NTL. Louisville: Westminster John Knox.

De Jong, Lidewijde. 2007. *Becoming a Roman Province: An Analysis of Funerary Practices in Roman Syria in the Context of Empire*. PhD diss., Stanford University.

De Vos, Craig S. 1999. *Church and Community Conflicts: The Relationships of the Thessalonian, Corinthians, and Philippian Churches in Their Wider Civic Communities*. SBLDS 168. Atlanta: Scholars Press.

Debord, Guy. 1977. *The Society of the Spectacle*. Translated by Fredy Perlman et al. Detroit: Red & Black.

Deissmann, Adolf. 1908. *Licht vom Osten: Das Neue Testament und die neuentdeckten Texte der hellenistisch-römischen Welt*. Tübingen: Mohr Siebeck.

Dionysius of Halicarnassus. 1937–1985. *Roman Antiquities*. Translated by Earnest Cary. 7 vols. LCL. Cambridge: Harvard University Press.

Dodds, Eric R. 1951. *The Greeks and the Irrational*. Berkeley: University of California Press.

Doering, Lutz. 2009. "First Peter as Early Christian Diaspora Letter." Pages 215–36 in *The Catholic Epistles and Apostolic Tradition: A New Perspective on James to Jude*. Edited by Karl-Wilhelm Niebuhr and Robert W. Wall. Waco, TX: Baylor University Press.

Donfried, Karl P. 1985. "The Cults of Thessalonica and the Thessalonian Correspondence." *NTS* 31:336–56.

Dryden, Jeffrey de Waal. 2006. *Theology and Ethics in 1 Peter: Paraenetic Strategies for Christian Character Formation.* WUNT 209. Tübingen: Mohr Siebeck.

Duling, Dennis. 2005. "Empire: Theories, Methods, Models." Pages 49–74 in *The Gospel of Matthew in Its Roman Imperial Context.* Edited by John Riches and David Sim. London: T&T Clark.

Egger, Brigitte. 1988. "Zu den Fruenrollen in griechischen Roman: Die Frau as Heldin und Leserin." Pages 33–66 in vol. 1 of *Groningen Colloquia on the Novel.* Edited by Heinz Hofmann. Groningen: Forsten.

Elliott, John H. 1981. *A Home for the Homeless: A Sociological Exegesis of 1 Peter; Its Situation and Strategy.* Philadelphia: Fortress.

Elliott, Neil. 1994. *The Justice of God and the Politics of the Apostle.* Maryknoll, NY: Orbis.

———. 1997. "Romans 13:1–7 in the Context of Roman Imperial Propaganda." Pages 184–204 in *Paul and Empire: Religion and Power in Imperial Society.* Edited by Richard A. Horsley. Harrisburg, PA: Trinity Press International.

———. 2004. "Strategies of Resistance and Hidden Transcripts in the Pauline Communities." Pages 97–122 in *Hidden Transcripts and the Arts of Resistance.* Edited by Richard Horsley. SemeiaSt 48. Atlanta: Society of Biblical Literature.

———. 2006. *Liberating Paul: The Justice of God and the Politics of the Apostle.* Minneapolis: Fortress.

———. 2008. *The Arrogance of the Nations: Reading Romans in the Shadow of Empire.* Minneapolis: Fortress.

———. 2013. "Creation, Cosmos, and Conflict in Romans 8–9." Pages 131–56 in *Apocalyptic Paul: Creation and Anthropos in Romans 5–8.* Edited by Beverly Roberts Gaventa. Waco, TX: Baylor University Press.

Engels, Friedrich, and Karl Marx. 1957. *On Religion.* Moscow: Foreign Languages Publishing House.

Epictetus. 1925–1928. Translated by W. A. Oldfather. 2 vols. LCL. Cambridge: Harvard University Press.

Ehrman, Bart D. 2011. *Forged: Writing in the Name of God; Why the Bible's Authors Are Not Who We Think They Are.* New York: HarperCollins.

Evans, Craig A. 2000. "Mark's Incipit and the Priene Calendar Inscription: From Jewish Gospel to Greco-Roman Gospel." *JGRChJ* 1:67–81.

———. 2001. *Mark 8:27–16:20*. WBC 34b. Nashville: Nelson.

Fanon, Frantz. 1968. *The Wretched of the Earth*. Translated by Richard Philcox. New York: Grove.

Fantin, Joseph D. 2011. *The Lord of the Entire World: Lord Jesus, a Challenge to Lord Caesar?* NTMS 31. Sheffield: Sheffield Phoenix.

Faust, Eberhard. 1993. *Pax Christi et Pax Caesaris: Religionsgeschichtliche, traditionsgeschichtliche und sozialgeschichtliche Studien zum Epheserbrief*. NTOA 24. Göttingen: Vandenhoeck & Ruprecht.

Fears, J. Rufus. 1981. "Theology of Victory at Rome: Approaches and Problems." *ANRW* 17.2:736–826.

Foucault, Michel. 1995. *Technologies of the Self: A Seminar with Michel Foucault*. Edited by Luther Martin et al. Amherst: University of Massachusetts Press.

France, R. T. 2002. *The Gospel of Mark*. NIGTC. Grand Rapids: Eerdmans.

Freyne, Sean. 1999. "Behind the Names Galileans, Samaritans, Ioudaioi." Pages 39–56 in *Galilee through the Centuries: Confluence of Cultures*. Edited by Eric Meyers. Winona Lake, IN: Eisenbrauns.

Friesen, Steven J. 2004. "Poverty in Pauline Studies: Beyond the So-Called New Consensus." *JSNT* 26:323–61.

———. 2010. "Paul and Economics: The Jerusalem Collection as an Alternative to Patronage." Pages 27–54 in *Paul Unbound: Other Perspectives on the Apostle*. Edited by Mark D. Given. Peabody, MA: Hendrickson.

Frilingos, Christopher A. 2004. *Spectacles of Empire: Monsters, Martyrs, and the Book of Revelation*. Divinations. Philadelphia: University of Pennsylvania Press.

Fuchs, Harald. 1965. *Augustin und der antike Friedensgedanke*. Berlin: Weidmann.

Gagé, Jean. 1935. *Res Gestae Divi Augustae ex Monumentis Ancyrano et Antiocheno Latinis Ancyrano et Apolloniensi Graecis*. Paris: Les Belles Lettres.

Galinsky, Karl. 1996. *Augustan Culture*. Princeton: Princeton University Press.

———, ed. 2005. *The Cambridge Companion to the Age of Augustus*. Cambridge: Cambridge University Press.

———. 2011. "The Cult of the Roman Emperor: Uniter or Divider?" Pages 1–22 in *Rome and Religion: A Cross-Disciplinary Dialogue on the Imperial Cult*. Edited by Jeffrey Brodd and Jonathan L. Reed. WGRWSup 5. Atlanta: Society of Biblical Literature.

García Martínez, Florentino, and Eibert J. C. Tigchelaar, eds. and trans. 1997–1998. *The Dead Sea Scrolls: Study Edition*. 2 vols. Leiden: Brill; Grand Rapids: Eerdmans.

Garnsey, Peter. 1999. *Food and Society in Classical Antiquity*. Cambridge: Cambridge University Press.

Georgi, Dieter. 1991. *Theocracy in Paul's Praxis and Theology*. Minneapolis: Fortress.

———. 1997. "God Turned Upside Down." Pages 148–57 in *Paul and Empire: Religion and Power in Imperial Society*. Edited by Richard A Horsley. Harrisburg, PA: Trinity Press International.

Gilbert, Gary. 2004. "Roman Propaganda and Christian Identity in the Worldview of Luke-Acts." Pages 233–56 in *Contextualizing Acts: Lukan Narrative and Greco-Roman Discourse*. Edited by Todd C. Penner and Caroline Vander Stichele. Leiden: Brill.

Glancy, Jennifer A. 2003. "Protocols of Masculinity in the Pastoral Epistles." Pages 235–64 in *New Testament Masculinities*. Edited by Stephen D. Moore and Janice Capel Anderson. Atlanta: Society of Biblical Literature.

Gombis, Timothy G. 2005. "A Radically New Humanity: The Function of the Haustafel in Ephesians." *JETS* 48:317–30.

Goodman, Martin. 1982. "The First Jewish Revolt: Social Conflict and the Problem of Debt." *JJS* 33:422–34.

———. 1987. *The Ruling Class of Judea: The Origins of the Jewish Revolt against Rome; A.D. 66–70*. Cambridge: Cambridge University Press.

Gottwald, Norman K. 1979. *The Tribes of Yahweh: A Sociology of Liberated Israel*. Maryknoll, NY: Orbis.

Grant, Michael. 1995. *Greek and Roman Historians: Information and Misinformation*. London: Routledge.

Green, Joel B. 1997. *The Gospel of Luke*. NICNT. Grand Rapids: Eerdmans.

Gupta, Nijay K., and Frederick J. Long. 2010. "The Politics of Ephesians and Empire: Accommodation or Resistance?" *JGRChJ* 7:112–36.

Hadzsits, G. D. 1936. "The Vera Historia of the Palatine Ficus Ruminalis." *CP* 31:305–19.

Hanson, K. C., and Douglas E. Oakman. 1998. *Palestine in the Time of Jesus*. Minneapolis: Fortress.

Hardin, Justin K. 2008. *Galatians and the Imperial Cult: A Critical Analysis of the First-Century Social Context of Paul's Letter*. WUNT 2/237: Tübingen: Mohr Siebeck.

Harland, Philip. 2003. *Associations, Synagogues, and Congregations: Claiming a Place in Ancient Mediterranean Society*. Minneapolis: Fortress.

Harrison, James R. 2003. *Paul's Language of Grace in Its Graeco-Roman Context*. WUNT 2/172. Tübingen: Mohr Siebeck.

———. 2004. "Why Did Josephus and Paul Refuse to Circumcise?" *Pacifica* 17:137–58.

———. 2011a. "'More Than Conquerors' (Rom 8:37): Paul's Gospel and the Augustan Triumphal Arches of the Greek and Latin West." *BurH* 47:3–21.

———. 2011b. *Paul and the Imperial Authorities at Thessalonica and Rome: A Study in the Conflict of Ideology*. WUNT 273. Tübingen: Mohr Siebeck.

———. 2012. "Diplomacy over Tiberius' Accession." Pages 64–75 in vol. 10 of *New Documents Illustrating Early Christianity*. Edited by Stephen Llewelyn and James R. Harrison. Grand Rapids: Eerdmans.

———. 2013. "Augustan Rome and the Body of Christ: A Comparison of the Social Vision of the *Res Gestae* and Paul's Letter to the Romans." *HTR* 106:1–36.

Hays, Richard B. 1989. *Echoes of Scripture in the Letters of Paul*. New Haven: Yale University Press.

———. 2002. *The Faith of Jesus Christ: An Investigation of the Narrative Substructure of Galatians 3:1–4:11*. 2nd ed. Grand Rapids: Eerdmans.

Heath, Malcolm. 2003. "Pseudo-Dionysius *Art of Rhetoric* 8–11: Figured Speech, Declamation and Criticism." *AJP* 124:81–105.

Hellerman, Joseph H. 2005. *Reconstructing Honor in Roman Philippi: Carmen Christi as Cursus Pudorum*. SNTSMS 132. Cambridge: Cambridge University Press.

Hendrix, Holland Lee. 1984. "Thessalonicans Honor Romans." PhD diss., Harvard University.

———. 1986. "Beyond 'Imperial Cult' and 'Cults of Magistrates.'" Pages 301–8 in *Society of Biblical Literature 1986 Seminar Papers*. SBLSP 25. Edited by Kent Harold Richards. Atlanta: Scholars Press.

———. 1988. "On the Form and Ethos of Ephesians." *USQR* 42:3–15.

———. 1991. "Archaeology and Eschatology at Thessalonica." Pages 107–28 in *The Future of Early Christianity: Essays in Honor of Helmut Koester*. Edited by Birger A. Pearson, A. Thomas Kraabel, George W. E. Nickelsburg, and Norman R. Petersen. Minneapolis: Fortress.

———. 1992. "Benefactor/Patron Networks in the Urban Environment" *Semeia* 56:39–58.

Hengel, Martin. 1961. *Die Zeloten.* Leiden: Brill.

———. 1971. *Was Jesus a Revolutionist?* Philadelphia: Fortress.

———. 1973. *Victory over Violence.* Philadelphia: Fortress.

Herrmann, Peter. 1968. *Der römische Kaisereid.* Göttingen: Vandenhoeck & Ruprecht.

Hezser, Catherine. 2001. *Jewish Literacy in Roman Palestine.* Tübingen: Mohr Siebeck.

Hillyer, C. N. 1969. "Spiritual Milk … Spiritual House." *TynBul* 20:126–27.

Hirschfeld, Gustav, ed. 1893. *The Collection of Ancient Greek Inscriptions in the British Museum.* Vol. 4. London: Clarendon.

Homer. 1924–1925. *Iliad.* Translated by A. T. Murray. 2 vols. LCL. Cambridge: Harvard University Press.

Hooker, Morna. 1991. *The Gospel according to St. Mark.* Peabody, MA: Hendrickson.

Hopkins, Keith. 1981. *Conquerors and Slaves.* Sociological Studies in Roman History 1. Cambridge: Cambridge University Press.

Horace. 1926–2004. Translated by H. Rushton Fairclough and Niall Rudd. 2 vols. LCL. Cambridge: Harvard University Press.

Horrell, David. 2007. "Between Conformity and Resistance: Beyond the Balch-Elliott Debate towards a Postcolonial Reading of 1 Peter." Pages 111–43 in *Reading First Peter with New Eyes: Methodological Reassessments of the Letter of First Peter.* Edited by Robert L. Webb and Betsy J. Bauman-Martin. London: T&T Clark.

Horsley, Richard A. 1981. "Ancient Jewish Banditry and the Revolt against Rome." *CBQ* 43:409–32.

———. 1984. "Popular Messianic Movements around the Time of Jesus." *CBQ* 46:471–95.

———. 1985. "'Like One of the Prophets of Old': Two Types of Popular Prophets at the Time of Jesus." *CBQ* 47:435–63.

———. 1986. "High Priests and the Politics of Roman Palestine." *JSJ* 17:23–55.

———. 1987. *Jesus and the Spiral of Violence: Popular Jewish Resistance in Roman Palestine.* San Francisco: Harper & Row.

———. 1989a. *The Liberation of Christmas: The Infancy Narratives in Social Context.* New York: Crossroad.

———. 1989b. *Sociology and the Jesus Movement.* New York: Crossroad.

———. 1995. *Galilee: History, Politics, People.* Valley Forge, PA: Trinity Press International.

———, ed. 1997. *Paul and Empire: Religion and Power in Roman Imperial Society.* Harrisburg, PA: Trinity Press International.

———. 2001. *Hearing the Whole Story: The Politics of Plot in Mark's Gospel.* Louisville: Westminster John Knox.

———. 2002. "Power Vacuum and Power Struggle in 66–67 C.E." Pages 87–109 in *The First Jewish Revolt: Archaeology, History, and Ideology.* Edited by Andrea M. Berlin and J. Andrew Overman. London: Routledge.

———. 2003. *Jesus and Empire: The Kingdom of God and the New World Disorder.* Minneapolis: Fortress.

———, ed. 2004. *Hidden Transcripts and the Arts of Resistance: Applying the Work of James C. Scott to Jesus and Paul.* SemeiaSt 48. Atlanta: Society of Biblical Literature.

———. 2007. *Scribes, Visionaries, and the Politics of Second Temple Judea.* Louisville: Westminster John Knox.

———. 2011a. *Jesus and the Powers: Conflict, Covenant, and the Hope of the Poor.* Minneapolis: Fortress.

———. 2011b. "Oral Communication, Oral Performance, and New Testament Interpretation." Pages 125–55 in *Method and Meaning: Essays on New Testament Interpretation in Honor of Harold W. Attridge.* Edited by Andrew B. McGowan and Kent Harold Richards. RBS 67. Atlanta: Society of Biblical Literature.

———. 2014. *Jesus and the Politics of Roman Palestine.* Columbia: University of South Carolina Press.

Horsley, Richard A., with Jonathan Draper. 1999. *Whoever Hears You Hears Me: Prophecy, Performance, and Tradition in Q.* Harrisburg, PA: Trinity Press International.

Horsley, Richard A., and Tom Thatcher. 2013. *John, Jesus, and the Renewal of Israel.* Grand Rapids: Eerdmans.

Incigneri, Brian J. 2003. *The Gospel to the Romans: The Setting and Rhetoric of Mark's Gospel.* BibInt 65. Leiden: Brill.

Jauhiainen, Marko. 2005. *The Use of Zechariah in Revelation.* WUNT 2/199. Tübingen: Mohr Siebeck.

Jervis, L. Ann. 2004. "Reading Romans 7 in Conversation with Post-colonial Theory: Paul's Struggle towards a Christian Identity of Hybridity." *ThJ* 35:173–93.

Jewett, Robert. 2003. "The Corruption and Redemption of Creation: Reading Rom 8:18–23 within the Imperial Context." Pages 25–46 *Paul and the Roman Imperial Order.* Edited by Richard A. Horsley. Harrisburg, PA: Trinity Press International.

Janssen, Laurens F. 1979. "'Superstitio' and the Persecution of Christians." *VC* 33:131–59.

Johne, Renate. 1996. "Women in the Ancient Novel." Pages 151–207 in *The Novel in the Ancient World.* Edited by Gareth Schmeling. Leiden: Brill.

Johnson, Luke Timothy. 2011. *Sharing Possessions: What Faith Demands.* 2nd ed. Grand Rapids: Eerdmans.

Josephus. 1926–1965. Translated by Henry St. J. Thackeray et al. 13 vols. LCL. Cambridge: Harvard University Press.

Judge, E. A. 2008. *The First Christians in the Roman World: Augustan and New Testament Essays.* Edited by James R. Harrison. WUNT 229. Tübingen: Mohr Siebeck.

Juvenal and Persius. 1928. Translated by G. G. Ramsay. LCL. Cambridge: Harvard University Press.

Kahl, Brigitte. 2008. "Acts of the Apostles: Pro(to)-imperial Script and Hidden Transcript." Pages 137–56 in *In the Shadow of Empire: Reclaiming the Bible as a History of Faithful Resistance.* Edited by Richard A. Horsley. Louisville: Westminster John Knox.

———. 2010. *Galatians Re-imagined: Reading with the Eyes of the Vanquished.* Minneapolis: Fortress.

Kallet-Marx, Robert M. 1995. *Hegemony to Empire: The Development of the Roman Imperium in the East from 148–62 BC.* Berkeley: University of California Press.

Käsemann, Ernst. 1982. *Kirchliche Konflikte.* Vol. 1. Göttingen: Vandenhoeck & Ruprecht.

Kautsky, John. 1984. *The Politics of Aristocratic Empires.* Chapel Hill: University of North Carolina Press.

Keck, Leander E. 1993. "What Makes Romans Tick?" Pages 3–29 in *Romans.* Vol. 3 of *Pauline Theology.* Edited by David M. Hay and E. Elizabeth Johnson. Minneapolis: Fortress.

Keener, Craig S. 2003. *The Gospel of John: A Commentary.* Vol. 1. Peabody, MA: Hendrickson.

Kelber, Werner. 1979. *Mark's Story of Jesus.* Philadelphia: Fortress.

Kennedy, George A. 2003. *Progymnasmata: Greek Textbooks of Prose Composition and Rhetoric.* WGRW 10. Atlanta: Society of Biblical Literature.

Kim, Seyoon. 1987. "Jesus—The Son of God, the Stone, the Son of Man, and the Servant: The Role of Zechariah in the Self-Identification of

Jesus." Pages 134–48 in *Tradition and Interpretation in the New Testament: Essays in Honor of E. Earle Ellis for His Sixtieth Birthday*. Edited by Otto Betz and Gerald F. Hawthorne. Grand Rapids: Eerdmans.

Kittredge, Cynthia Briggs. 2004. "Reconstructing 'Resistance' or Reading to Resist: James C. Scott and the Politics of Interpretation." Pages 145–55 in *Hidden Transcripts and the Arts of Resistance*. Edited by Richard A. Horsley. SemeiaSt 48. Atlanta: Society of Biblical Literature.

Koukouli-Chrysantiki, Chaido C. 1998. "Colonia Iulia Augusta Philippensis." Pages 5–36 in *Philippi at the Time of Paul and after His Death*. Edited by Charalambos Bakirtzis and Helmut Koester. Harrisburg, PA: Trinity Press International.

Lacey, Walter K. 1986. *Patria Potestas*. Pages 121–44 in *The Family in Ancient Rome: New Perspectives*. Edited by Beryl Rawson. Ithaca, NY: Cornell University Press.

Lamberton, Robert. 1997. "Plutarch and the Romanization of Athens." Pages 151-60 in *The Romanization of Athens*. Edited by Michael C. Hoff and Susan I. Rotroff. Oxford: Oxbow.

Laniak, Timothy S. 2006. *Shepherds after My Own Heart*. SBT 20. Downers Grove, IL: InterVarsity Press.

Lee, Dorothy. 2013. "Martha and Mary: Levels of Characterization in Luke and John." Pages 197-220 in *Characters and Characterization in the Gospel of John*. Edited by Christopher W. Skinner. LNTS 461. London: Bloomsbury.

Lee, Michelle. 2006. *Paul, the Stoics, and the Body of Christ*. Cambridge: Cambridge University Press.

Lenski, Gerhard. 1984. *Power and Privilege: A Theory of Social Stratification*. Chapel Hill: University of North Carolina Press.

Levick, Barbara. 1958. "An Honorific Inscription from Pisidian Antioch." *AnSt* 8:219–22.

———. 1967. "Unpublished Inscriptions from Pisidia Antioch." *AnSt* 17:101–21.

———. 1999. *Vespasian*. New York: Routledge.

Levinson, Marc. 2006. *The Box: How the Shipping Container Made the World Smaller and the World Economy Bigger*. Princeton: Princeton University Press.

Liebengood, Kelly D. 2014. *The Eschatology of First Peter: Considering the Influence of Zechariah 9–14*. SNTSMS 157. Cambridge: Cambridge University Press.

Lieber, Laura S. 2012. "Jewish Women: Texts and Contexts." Pages 329-42 in *A Companion to Women in the Ancient World*. Edited by Sharon L. James and Sheila Dillon. Chichester, UK: Wiley-Blackwell.

Lincoln, Bruce. 2014. *Between History and Myth: Stories of Harold Fairhair and the Founding of the State*. Chicago: University of Chicago Press.

Longenecker, Bruce. 2010. *Remember the Poor: Paul, Poverty, and the Greco-Roman World*. Grand Rapids: Eerdmans.

Lopez, Davina C. Forthcoming. "Grafting Rhetoric: Myth and Methodological Multivalence in Romans 11." In *Did God Reject God's People? Studies in Romans 9–11*. Edited by Todd D. Still, Bruce Longenecker, and Beverly Roberts Gaventa. Waco, TX: Baylor University Press.

Lotz, John Paul. 1999. "The HOMONOIA Coins of Asia Minor and Ephesians 1.21." *TynBul* 50:173–88.

Lucian. 1913–1967. Translated by A. M. Harmon, K. Kilburn, and M. D. MacLeod. 8 vols. LCL. Cambridge: Harvard University Press.

Lull, David J. 2010. "Paul and Empire." *RSR* 36:252–62.

MacDonald, Margaret Y. 2008. *Colossians and Ephesians*. SP 17. Collegeville, MN: Liturgical Press.

MacDonald, William L. 1982–1986. *The Architecture of the Roman Empire*. 2 vols. New Haven: Yale University Press.

MacMullen, Ramsay. 2000. *Romanization in the Time of Augustus*. New Haven: Yale University Press.

Macurdy, Grace Harriet. 1937. *Vassal-Queens and Some Contemporary Women in the Roman Empire*. Baltimore: Johns Hopkins University Press.

Maddox, Robert. 1982. *The Purpose of Luke-Acts*. Edinburgh: T&T Clark.

Maier, Harry O. 2013. *Picturing Paul in Empire: Imperial Image, Text and Persuasion in Colossians, Ephesians and the Pastorals Epistles*. London: T&T Clark.

Mann, Michael. 1986. *A History of Power from the Beginning to AD 1760*. Vol. 1 of *The Sources of Social Power*. Cambridge: Cambridge University Press.

Marshall, Anthony J. 1984. "Symbols of Showmanship in Roman Public Life: The Fasces." *Phoenix* 38:120–41.

Marshall, John W. 2008. "Hybridity and Reading Romans 13." *JSNT* 31:157–78.

Martin, Dale B. 1995. *The Corinthian Body*. New Haven: Yale University Press.

Martin, Michael W., and Jason A. Whitlark. 2011. "The Encomiastic Topics of Syncrisis as the Key to the Structure and Argument of Hebrews." *NTS* 57:415–39.

———. 2012. "Choosing What Is Advantageous: The Relationship between Epideictic and Deliberative Syncrisis in Hebrews." *NTS* 58:379–400.

Martin, Ralph P. 1968. "An Epistle in Search of a Life-Setting." *ExpTim* 79:296–302.

Mattern, Susan P. 1999. *Rome and the Enemy: Imperial Strategy in the Principate*. Berkeley: University of California Press.

Maxfield, Valerie A. 1981. *The Military Decorations of the Roman Army*. Berkeley: University of California Press.

Mazel, M. 1984. "Some Aspects of the Concept of Peace in Military Thought." Pages 1–20 in *Frieden und Friedensicherungen in Vergangenheit und Gegenwart*. Edited by Manfred Schenke and Klaus-Jürgen Matz. Munich: Fink.

McKechnie, Paul. 2008. "Apollonia: An Early Testimony for Christianity in Anatolia." *Epigraphica Anatolica* 41:141–46.

McKnight, Scot, and Joseph B. Modica, eds. 2013. *Jesus Is Lord, Caesar Is Not: Evaluating Empire in New Testament Studies*. Downers Grove, IL: IVP Academic.

Meeks, Wayne A. 1983. *The First Urban Christians: The Social World of the Apostle Paul*. New Haven: Yale University Press.

Meggitt, Justin J. 1998. *Paul, Poverty, and Survival*. Edinburgh: T&T Clark.

Metzger, Bruce M. 2002. *A Textual Commentary on the Greek New Testament*. 2nd ed. Stuttgart: United Bible Societies.

Míguez, Néstor O. 2012. *The Practice of Hope: Ideology and Intention in First Thessalonians*. Minneapolis: Fortress.

Millar, Fergus. 1993. "Ovid and the Domus Augusta: Rome Seen from Tomoi." *JRS* 83:1–17.

Milnor, Kristina. 2009. "Women in Roman Historiography." Pages 276–87 in *The Cambridge Companion to the Roman Historians*. Edited by Andrew Feldherr. Cambridge: Cambridge University Press.

Mitchell, Stephen. 1982. *The Ankara District: The Inscriptions of North Galatia*. Vol. 2 of *Regional Epigraphic Catalogues of Asia Minor*. London: BAR International.

Mitchell, Stephen, and David French, eds. 2012. *From Augustus to the End of the Third Century AD*. Vol. 1 of *The Greek and Latin Inscriptions of Ankara (Ancyra)*. Munich: Beck.

Mitchell, Stephen, and Marc Waelkens. 1998. *Pisidian Antioch: The Site and Its Monuments*. London: Duckworth.

Mitford, T. B. 1960. "A Cypriot Oath of Allegiance to Tiberius." *JRS* 50:75–79.

Moore, Stephen D. 1989. *Literary Criticism and the Gospels*. New Haven: Yale University Press.

———. 2006. *Empire and Apocalypse: Postcolonialism and the New Testament*. BMW. Sheffield: Sheffield Phoenix.

Moore, Stephen D., and Jennifer A. Glancy. 2011. "How Typical a Roman Prostitute Is Revelation's 'Great Whore'?" *JBL* 130:551–69.

Mowery, Robert L. 2006. "Paul and Caristanius at Pisidian Antioch." *Bib* 87:223–42.

Muddiman, John. 2001. *A Commentary on the Epistle to the Ephesians*. BNTC. New York: Continuum.

Muir, Steven. 2008. "The Anti-imperial Rhetoric of Hebrews 1:3: Χαρακτήρ as a 'Double-Edged Sword.'" Pages 170–86 in *A Cloud of Witnesses: The Theology of Hebrews in Its Ancient Context*. Edited by Richard Bauckham, Trevor Hart, Nathan MacDonald, and Daniel Driver. LNTS 387. London: T&T Clark.

Myers, Ched. 1992. *Binding the Strong Man: A Political Reading of Mark's Story of Jesus*. Maryknoll, NY: Orbis.

Nasrallah, Laura. 2012. "Spacial Perspectives: Space and Archaeology in Roman Philippi." Pages 54–74 in *Studying Paul's Letters: Contemporary Perspectives and Methods*. Edited by Joseph A. Marchal. Minneapolis: Fortress.

Nigdelis, Pantelis M. 2012. "A New *Procurator Augusti* in the Province of Macedonia." *GRBS* 52:198–207.

Oakes, Peter. 2005. "Re-mapping the Universe: Paul and the Emperor in 1 Thessalonians and Philippians." *JSNT* 27:301–22.

Oliver, James H. 1953. "The Ruling Power: A Study of the Roman Empire in the Second Century after Christ through the Roman Oration of Aelius Aristides." *TAPS* 43:871–1003.

Ossi, Adrian J. 2010. "The Roman Honorific Arches of Pisidian Antioch: Reconstruction and Contextualization." PhD diss., University of Michigan.

———. 2011. "The Arch of Hadrian and Sabina at Pisidian Antioch: Imperial Associations, Ritual Connections, and Civic Euergetism." Pages 85–108 in *Building a New Rome: The Roman Colony of Pisidian Antioch*

(25 BC–300 AD). Edited by Elaine K. Gazda and Diana Y. Ng. Ann Arbor: Kelsey Museum of Archaeology.

Parker, A. J. 1992. *Ancient Shipwrecks of the Mediterranean and the Roman Provinces*. Oxford: Tempus Reparatum.

Parkin, Tim, and Arthur Pomeroy. 2007. *Roman Social History: A Sourcebook*. London: Routledge.

Pascal, C. Bennett. 1981. "October Horse." *HSCP* 85:261–91.

Penner, Todd, and Davina C. Lopez. 2015. *De-introducing the New Testament: Texts, Worlds, Methods, Stories*. Oxford: Wiley-Blackwell.

Perkins, Pheme. 1995. *First and Second Peter, James, and Jude*. IBC. Louisville: Westminster John Knox.

Pervo, Richard L. 2010. *The Making of Paul: Constructions of the Apostle in Early Christianity*. Minneapolis: Fortress.

Philo. 1929–1962. Translated by G. H. Whitaker, F. H. Colson, and Ralph Marcus. 12 vols. LCL. Cambridge: Harvard University Press.

Pilhofer, Peter. 1995. *Die erste christliche Gemeinde Europas*. Vol. 1 of *Philippi*. WUNT 87. Tübingen: Mohr Siebeck.

———. 2009. *Katalog der Inschriften von Philippi*. Vol. 2 of *Philippi*. 2nd ed. WUNT 119. Tübingen: Mohr Siebeck.

Pindar. 1997. *Odes*. Translated by William H. Race. 2 vols. LCL. Cambridge: Harvard University Press.

Plato. 1914–2013. Translated by Harold North Fowler et al. 12 vols. LCL. Cambridge: Harvard University Press.

Pliny the Elder. 1938–1963. *Natural History*. Translated by H. Rackham, W. H. S. Jones, and D. E. Eichholz. 10 vols. LCL. Cambridge: Harvard University Press.

Pliny the Younger. 1969. Translated by Betty Radice. 2 vols. LCL. Cambridge: Harvard University Press.

Plutarch. 1914–2004. Translated by Bernadotte Perrin et al. 28 vols. LCL. Cambridge: Harvard University Press.

Pollini, John. 2012. *From Republic to Empire: Rhetoric, Religion, and Power in the Visual Culture of Ancient Rome*. Oklahoma Series in Classical Culture 48. Norman: University of Oklahoma Press.

Powell, Mark Allan. 1998. *Fortress Introduction to the Gospels*. Minneapolis: Fortress.

Pratt, Kenneth. 1965. "Rome as Eternal." *JHI* 26:25–44.

Price, Simon R. F. 1984. *Rituals and Power: The Roman Imperial Cult in Asia Minor*. Cambridge: Cambridge University Press.

Propertius. 1912. Translated by H. E. Butler. LCL. Cambridge: Harvard University Press.

Radermacher, Ludwig, and Hermann Usener. 1967. *Dionysii Halicarnasei quae exstant.* Vol. 6. BSGRT. Stuttgart: Teubner.

Ramage, Edwin S. 1987. *The Nature and Purpose of Augustus' "Res Gestae."* Stuttgart: Steiner.

Ramsay, William M. 1904. *The Letters to the Seven Churches in Asia Minor and Their Place in the Plan of the Apocalypse.* London: Hodder & Stoughton.

———. 1907. *The Cities of Paul: Their Influence on His Life and Thought.* The Dale Memorial Lectures in Mansfield College, Oxford. New York: Hodder & Stoughton.

———. 1916. "Colonia Caesarea (Pisidian Antioch) in the Augustan Age." *JRS* 6:84–134.

———. 1924. "Studies in the Roman Province Galatia: VI. Some Inscriptions of Colonia Caesarea Antiochea." *JRS* 14:172–205.

Ranulf, Svend. 1933–1934. *The Jealousy of the Gods and Criminal Law at Athens: A Contribution to the Sociology of Moral Indignation.* 2 vols. London: Williams & Norgate.

Reed, Jonathan L. 1992. "The Population of Capernaum." Occasional Papers of the Institute for Antiquity and Christianity 24. Claremont: Institute for Antiquity and Christianity.

Reinhartz, Adele. 2003. "Women in the Johannine Community: An Exercise in Historical Imagination." Pages 14–33 in vol. 2 of *A Feminist Companion to John.* Edited by Amy-Jill Levine and Marianne Blickenstaff. Cleveland: Pilgrim.

Rensberger, David. 1988. *Johannine Faith and Liberating Community.* Philadelphia: Westminster.

Reumann, John H. P. 2008. *Philippians: A New Translation with Introduction and Commentary.* AYB. New Haven: Yale University Press.

Rhoads, David, and Donald Michie. 1982. *Mark as Story: An Introduction to the Narrative of a Gospel.* Philadelphia: Fortress.

Richey, Lance Byron. 2007. *Roman Imperial Ideology and the Gospel of John.* Washington, DC: Catholic Biblical Association.

Ridley, Ronald. 2003. *The Emperor's Retrospect: Augustus' Res Gestae in Epigraphy, Historiography and Commentary.* Leuven: Peeters.

Robbins, Vernon K. 2008. "Rhetography: A New Way of Seeing the Familiar Text." Pages 81–106 in *Words Well Spoken: George Kennedy's Rhet-*

oric of the New Testament. Edited by C. Clifton Black and Duane F. Watson. Waco, TX: Baylor University Press.

Rose, C. Brian. 2005. "The Parthians in Augustan Rome." *AJA* 109:21–75.

Rubin, Benjamin B. 2008. "(Re)presenting Empire: The Roman Imperial Cult in Asia Minor, 31 BC–AD 63." PhD diss., University of Michigan.

———. 2011. "Ruler Cult and Colonial Identity: The Imperial Sanctuary at Pisidian Antioch." Pages 33–60 in *Building a New Rome: The Roman Colony of Pisidian Antioch (25 BC–300 AD)*. Edited by Elaine K. Gazda and Diana Y. Ng. Ann Arbor: Kelsey Museum of Archaeology.

Rudich, Vasily. 2006. "Navigating the Uncertain: Literature and Censorship in the Early Roman Empire." *Arion* 14:7–28.

Said, Edward W. 1978. *Orientalism*. New York: Random House.

———. 1993. *Culture and Imperialism*. New York: Random House.

Saldarini, Anthony J. 1988. *Pharisees, Scribes, and Sadducees in Palestinian Society: A Sociological Approach*. Wilmington, DE: Michael Glazier.

Sallust. Translated by J. C. Rolfe and John T. Ramsey. 2 vols. LCL. Cambridge: Harvard University Press.

Sals, Ulrike. 2008. "The Hybrid Story of Balaam (Numbers 22–24): Theology for the Diaspora in the Torah." *BibInt* 16:315–35.

Sanders, E. P. 1985. *Jesus and Judaism*. Philadelphia: Fortress.

Santoro L'Hoir, Francesca. 1994. "Tacitus and Women's Usurpation of Power." *CW* 88:5–25.

Schmidt, Thomas E. 1995. "Mark 15: 16–32: The Crucifixion Narrative and the Roman Triumphal Procession." *NTS* 41:1–18.

Scheid, John. 2007. *Res gestae divi Avgvsti: Hauts Faits du Divin Auguste*. Paris: Les Belles Lettres.

Schüssler Fiorenza, Elisabeth. 1983. *In Memory of Her*. New York: Crossroad.

———. 1985. *The Book of Revelation: Justice and Judgment*. Philadelphia: Fortress.

———. 1987. "Rhetorical Situation and Historical Reconstruction in 1 Corinthians." *NTS* 33:386–403.

———. 2007. *The Power of the Word: Scripture and the Rhetoric of Empire*. Minneapolis: Fortress.

Scott, James C. 1977. "Protest and Profanation: Agrarian Revolt and the Little Tradition." *Theory and Society* 4:1–38, 211–46.

———. 1985. *Weapons of the Weak: Everyday Forms of Peasant Resistance*. New Haven: Yale University Press.

———. 1990. *Domination and the Arts of Resistance.* New Haven: Yale University Press.

Segovia, Fernando. 2005. "Mapping the Postcolonial Optic in Biblical Criticism: Meaning and Scope." Pages 23–78 in *Postcolonial Biblical Criticism: Interdisciplinary Intersections.* Edited by Stephen Moore and Fernando Segovia. London: T&T Clark.

Seneca. 1913–2004. Translated by W. H. D. Rouse et al. 11 vols. LCL. Cambridge: Harvard University Press.

Severy, Beth. 2003. *Augustus and the Family at the Birth of the Roman Empire.* New York: Routledge.

Sherk, Robert K., ed. 1988. *The Roman Empire: Augustus to Hadrian.* Cambridge: Cambridge University.

Silius Italicus. 1934. *Punica.* Translated by J. D. Duff. 2 vols. LCL. Cambridge: Harvard University Press.

Slingerland, H. Dixon. 1997. *Claudian Policymaking and the Early Imperial Repression of Judaism at Rome.* Atlanta: Scholars Press.

Smith, Dennis E. 1990. "Narrative Beginnings in Ancient Literature and Theory." *Semeia* 52:1–9.

Smith, Julien. 2011. *Christ the Ideal King: Cultural Context, Rhetorical Strategy, and the Power of Divine Monarchy in Ephesians.* WUNT 313. Tübingen: Mohr Siebeck.

Smith, Justin. M. 2007. "Genre, Sub-genre and Questions of Audience: A Proposed Typology for Greco-Roman Biography." *JGRChJ* 4:184–216.

Smith, Shanell T. 2014. *The Woman Babylon and the Marks of Empire: Reading Revelation with a Postcolonial Womanist Hermeneutics of Ambiveilence.* Emerging Scholars. Minneapolis: Fortress.

Spivak, Gayatri Chakravorty. 1988. "Can the Subaltern Speak?" Pages 271–313 in *Marxism and the Interpretation of Culture.* Edited by Cary Nelson and Lawrence Grossberg. Urbana: University of Illinois Press.

Still, Todd. D. 1999. *Conflict at Thessalonica: A Pauline Church and Its Neighbours.* JSNTSup 183. Sheffield: Sheffield Academic.

Stowers, Stanley. 1989. *Letter Writing in Greco-Roman Antiquity.* LEC 6. Philadelphia: Westminster.

———. 1994. *A Rereading of Romans: Gentiles, Jews, Justice.* New Haven: Yale University Press.

Suetonius. 1914. *Lives of the Caesars.* Translated by J. C. Rolfe. 2 vols. LCL. Cambridge: Harvard University Press.

Sugirtharajah, Rasiah S. 2001. "Postcolonial Theory and Biblical Studies." Pages 541–52 in *Fair Play: Diversity and Conflicts in Early Christianity.*

Edited by Ismo Dunderberg, Christopher Tuckett, and Kari Syreeni. Leiden: Brill.

Sumney, Jerry L. 2008. *Colossians: A Commentary*. NTL. Louisville: Westminster John Knox.

Tacitus. 1914. *Agricola; Germania; Dialogue on Oratory*. Translated by M. Hutton and W. Peterson. LCL. Cambridge: Harvard University Press.

———. 1925–1937. *The Histories and the Annals*. Translated by Clifford H. Moore and John Jackson. 4 vols. LCL. Cambridge: Harvard University Press.

———. 1991. *Tacitus' Agricola, Germany, and Dialogue on Orators*. Translated by Herbert W. Benario. Oklahoma Series in Classical Culture 8. Norman: University of Oklahoma Press.

Tannehill, Robert C. 1967. *Dying and Rising in Christ: A Study in Pauline Theology*. Berlin: Töpelmann.

Taubes, Jacob. 2004. *The Political Theology of Paul*. Edited by Aleida Assmann and Jan Assmann, in conjunction with Horst Folkers, Wolf-Daniel Hartwich, and Christopher Schulte. Translated by Dana Hollander. Stanford, CA: Stanford University Press.

Tellbe, Mikael. 2001. *Paul between Synagogue and State: Christians, Jews, and Civic Authorities in 1 Thessalonians, Romans and Philippians*. CBNTS 34. Stockholm: Almqvist & Wiksell.

Thatcher, Tom. 2009. *Greater Than Caesar: Christology and Empire in the Fourth Gospel*. Minneapolis: Fortress.

Theissen, Gerd. 1980. *The Social Setting of Pauline Christianity: Essays on Corinth*. Translated by John Schütz. Philadelphia: Fortress.

Thompson, Leonard L. 1997. *The Book of Revelation: Apocalypse and Empire*. New York: Oxford University Press.

Ulrich, Eugene. 1999. *The Dead Sea Scrolls and the Origins of the Bible*. Grand Rapids: Eerdmans.

Trebilco, Paul. 2004. *The Early Christians in Ephesus from Paul to Ignatius*. WUNT 166. Tübingen: Mohr Siebeck.

Velleus Paterculus. 1924. *Compendium of Roman History: Res Gestae Divi Augusti*. Translated by Frederick W. Shipley. LCL. Cambridge: Harvard University Press.

Vickers, Michael. 1972. "Hellenistic Thessaloniki." *JHS* 92:156–70.

Virgil. 1999–2001. Translated by H. Rushton Fairclough. 2 vols. LCL. Cambridge: Harvard University Press.

Von Wahlde, Urban C. 2010. *The Gospel and Letters of John*. Vol. 1. Grand Rapids: Eerdmans.

Walasky, Paul. 1983. *"And So We Came to Rome": The Political Perspective of St. Luke*. SNTSMS 49. Cambridge: Cambridge University Press.

Wallace-Hadrill, Andrew. 1990. "The Social Spread of Roman Luxury: Sampling Pompeii and Herculaneum." *Papers of the British School at Rome* 58:145–92.

———. 1994. *Houses and Society in Pompeii and Herculaneum*. Princeton: Princeton University Press.

———. 2011. *Herculaneum: Past and Future*. London: Lincoln.

Wan, Sze-Kar. 2000. "Collection as Anti-colonial Act: The Implications of Paul's Ethnic Reconstruction." Pages 191–215 in *Paul and Politics: Ekklesia, Israel, Imperium, Interpretation*. Edited by Richard A. Horsley. Harrisburg, PA: Trinity Press International.

Watts, Rikki E. 2000. *Isaiah's New Exodus in Mark*. WUNT 2/88. Tübingen: Mohr Siebeck, 1997. Repr., Grand Rapids: Baker.

Webb, Ruth. 2009. *Ekphrasis, Imagination, and Persuasion in Ancient Rhetorical Theory and Practice*. Surrey, UK: Ashgate.

Welborn, L. L. 2013. " 'That There May Be Equality': The Contexts and Consequences of a Pauline Ideal." *NTS* 59:73–90.

Wengst, Klaus. 1987. *Pax Romana and the Peace of Jesus Christ*. Translated by John Bowden. London: SCM.

White, Joel R. 2013. " 'Peace and Security' (1 Thessalonians 5:3): Is It Really a Roman Slogan?" *NTS* 59:382–95.

Whitlark, Jason A. 2014. *Resisting Empire: Rethinking the Purpose of the Letter to "the Hebrews."* LNTS 484. London: T&T Clark.

Whittaker, C. R. 1997. "Imperialism and Culture: The Roman Initiative." Pages 143–64 in *Dialogues in Roman Imperialism: Power, Discourse and Discrepant Experience in the Roman Empire*. JRASS 23. Edited by David J. Mattingly and Susan E. Alcock. Portsmouth, RI: Cushing-Malloy.

Williams, David John. 1990. *Acts*. NIBCNT. Peabody, MA: Hendrickson.

Williams, Travis. 2012. *Persecution in 1 Peter: Differentiating and Contextualizing Early Christian Suffering*. SNT 145. Leiden, Brill.

Willitts, Joel. 2007. *Matthew's Messianic Shepherd-King: In Search of "The Lost Sheep of the House of Israel."* BZNW 147. Berlin: de Gruyter.

Winn, Adam. 2008. *The Purpose of Mark's Gospel*. WUNT 2/245. Tübingen: Mohr Siebeck.

Winter, Bruce W. 2002. "The Imperial Cult and the Early Christians in Pisidian Antioch (Acts XIII 13–50 and Gal VI 11–18)." Pages 67–75 in *Actes du 1er Congrès International sur Antioche de Pisidie*. Edited by Thomas Drew-Bear, Mehmet Taşlıalan, and Christine M. Thomas. Lyon: Université Lumière.

Wire, Antoinette Clark. 1990. *The Corinthian Women Prophets: A Reconstruction through Paul's Rhetoric*. Minneapolis: Fortress.

Witherington, Ben, III. 2011. *Paul's Letter to the Philippians: A Socio-rhetorical Commentary*. Grand Rapids: Eerdmans.

Wright, N. T. 2013. *Paul and the Faithfulness of God*. Minneapolis: Fortress.

Yee, Tet-Lim N. 2005. *Jews, Gentiles and Ethnic Reconciliation: Paul's Jewish Identity and Ephesians*. SNTSMS 130. Cambridge: Cambridge University Press.

Zanker, Paul. 1988. *The Power of Images in the Age of Augustus*. Ann Arbor: University of Michigan Press.

Žižek, Slavoj. 2003. *The Puppet and the Dwarf: The Perverse Core of Christianity*. Cambridge: MIT Press.

CONTRIBUTORS

Eric D. Barreto is associate professor of New Testament at Luther Seminary in St. Paul, Minnesota. The author of *Ethnic Negotiations: The Function of Race and Ethnicity in Acts 16* (Mohr Siebeck, 2010), the coauthor of *New Proclamation Year C 2013: Easter through Christ the King* (Augsburg Fortress, 2013), and editor of *Reading Theologically* (Fortress, 2014) and *Thinking Theologically* (Fortress, 2015), he is also a regular contributor to ONScripture.org, the *Huffington Post*, WorkingPreacher.org, and EntertheBible.org.

Warren Carter is professor of New Testament at Brite Divinity School at Texas Christian University in Fort Worth, Texas. He is the author of numerous books and articles that engage the question of the various ways that New Testament texts negotiate Roman imperial power. His books include *Israel and Empires: Postcolonial Approaches* coauthored with Leo G. Perdue (Bloomsbury, 2014); *Seven Events that Shaped the New Testament World* (Baker Academic, 2013); *What Does Revelation Reveal?* (Abingdon, 2011); *John and Empire: Initial Explorations* (T&T Clark, 2008); *The Roman Empire and the New Testament: An Essential Guide* (Abingdon, 2006); *Pontius Pilate: Portraits of a Roman Governor* (Liturgical Press, 2003); *Matthew and Empire: Initial Explorations* (Trinity Press International, 2001); and *Matthew and the Margins: A Religious and Sociopolitical Reading* (Orbis; Sheffield Academic, 2000).

Neil Elliott is biblical studies editor at Fortress Press and the author of *The Rhetoric of Romans* (Fortress, 1990); *Liberating Paul: The Justice of God and the Politics of the Apostle* (Fortress, 1994); *The Arrogance of Nations: Reading Romans in the Shadow of Empire* (Fortress, 2008); with Mark Reasoner, *Documents and Images for the Study of Paul* (Fortress, 2010); and *The Bodies of Christ: A Materialist Approach to the Theology of the New Testament* (forthcoming).

James R. Harrison studied ancient history at Macquarie University and graduated from the doctoral program in 1997. He is the research director at the Sydney College of Divinity, Australia and an honorary associate in the Macquarie University Ancient History Department. His publications include *Paul's Language of Grace in Its Graeco-Roman Context* (Mohr Siebeck, 2003) and *Paul and the Imperial Authorities at Thessalonica and Rome* (Mohr Siebeck, 2011). He also is, with Professor Larry Welborn (Fordham), editor of the new sequence of volumes, *The First Urban Churches*, in the Society of Biblical Literature Writings from the Greco-Roman World Supplement Series.

Matthew Ryan Hauge is associate professor of biblical studies at Azusa Pacific University in Azusa, California. He is the author of *The Biblical Tour of Hell* (T&T Clark, 2013) and the coeditor of *Characters Studies and the Gospel of Mark* (T&T Clark, 2014) and *Ancient Education and Early Christianity* (T&T Clark, 2016). He is also an active member of the Society of Biblical Literature and serves on the steering unit for the Seminar on Markan Literary Sources.

Richard A. Horsley, Distinguished Professor of Liberal Arts at the University of Massachusetts Boston (emeritus), is author and editor of many books, including *Galilee: History, Politics, People*; *Jesus and Empire*; *Jesus and the Powers*; *Jesus and the Politics of Roman Palestine*; and *Scribes, Visionaries, and the Politics of Second Temple Judea*.

Deborah Krause is professor of New Testament and academic dean at Eden Theological Seminary in St. Louis. She is the author of several articles and commentaries on the Pastoral Epistles (e.g., *1 Timothy* [T&T Clark, 2004]; "The Pastoral Epistles," in *Fortress Commentary on the Bible* [Fortress, 2014]). Deborah focuses her scholarship and teaching on the Bible at intersections of identity, power, and struggles for human freedom. In the last year, her activism has been dedicated to the Black Lives Matter movement in response to addressing issues of structural racism and dismantling white supremacy in light of the killing of Michael Brown and the uprising for justice in Ferguson, Missouri.

Kelly D. Liebengood is associate professor of biblical studies at LeTourneau University in Longview, Texas. His publications includes *The Eschatology of 1 Peter: Considering the Influence of Zechariah 9–14* (Cambridge

University Press, 2014). Together with Bruce Longenecker, he edited *Engaging Economics: New Testament Scenarios and Early Christian Reception* (Eerdmans, 2009).

Bruce W. Longenecker is professor of early Christianity and the W. W. Melton Chair of Religion at Baylor University in Waco, Texas, having formerly taught in Britain at St. Andrews, Cambridge, and Durham Universities. Some of his recent publications include *Remember the Poor: Paul, Poverty, and the Greco-Roman World* (Eerdmans, 2010); *The Cross before Constantine: The Early Life of a Christian Symbol* (Fortress, 2015); and *The Crosses of Pompeii: Jesus-Devotion in a Vesuvian Town* (Fortress, 2016).

Davina C. Lopez is an associate professor of religious studies at Eckerd College in St. Petersburg, Florida, where she teaches courses in biblical and ancient studies as well as method and theory in the study of religion. She is the author of *Apostle to the Conquered: Reimagining Paul's Mission* (Fortress, 2008) and the coauthor (with Todd Penner) of *De-introducing the New Testament: Texts, Worlds, Methods, Stories* (Wiley-Blackwell, 2015). She is also a senior editor for the Greek World, Roman World, New Testament, and Early Christianity sections of *The Oxford Encyclopedia of the Bible and Gender Studies* (Oxford University Press, 2014).

Harry O. Maier is professor of New Testament and early Christian studies at Vancouver School of Theology, Vancouver, Canada. He is author of several books, including *Picturing Paul in Empire: Imperial Image, Text, and Persuasion in Colossians, Ephesians and the Pastoral Epistles* (T&T Clark, 2013) and *Apocalypse Recalled: The Book of Revelation after Christendom* (Fortress, 2002), as well as a number of edited volumes.

Beth M. Sheppard is associate professor for the practice of theological bibliography and director of the Duke Divinity School Library. She holds a PhD in biblical studies from the University of Sheffield, and her research interests include not only library administration and practice but also the Fourth Gospel. She is particularly intrigued with the ins and outs of everyday life for early Christians. Her dual research agenda is reflected in the diversity of the journals in which her recent articles have appeared, including *Theological Librarianship* and *Sapientia Logos*. Her book titled *The Craft of History for the Study of the New Testament* was published by the Society of Biblical Literature in 2012.

Jason A. Whitlark is an associate professor of New Testament at Baylor University, where he teaches in the Baylor Interdisciplinary Core Program. His other publications include *Enabling Fidelity to God* (Paternoster, 2008), *Getting "Saved"* (with Charles Talbert; Eerdmans, 2011), *Interpretation and the Claims of the Text* (coedited with Bruce Longenecker, Lidija Novakovic, and Mikeal Parsons; Baylor University Press, 2014), and *Resisting Empire* (Paternoster, 2008).

Adam Winn is assistant professor of New Testament at Azusa Pacific University, in Azusa, California. He serves as an affiliate faculty member for Fuller Theological Seminary. He is the author of numerous academic articles as well as two monographs on Mark's Gospel: *The Purpose of Mark's Gospel: An Early Christian Response to Roman Imperial Propaganda* (Mohr Siebeck, 2008) and *Mark and the Elijah-Elisha Narrative: Considering the Practice of Greco-Roman Imitation in the Search for Markan Source Material* (Pickwick, 2010).

ANCIENT SOURCES INDEX

Modern Authors Index

Subject Index

accommodation, 11–13, 71, 77–78, 86, 89, 107–8, 110, 114, 120, 126, 153, 165, 172, 201

Antiochus IV, 49, 89, 101

apocalyptic(ism), 39, 47, 55, 60, 62–63, 156, 162, 165–66, 173, 181–82, 187, 210, 229, 262,

Aramaic, 103, 127, 135

artisans, 29, 31–32, 74, 81–82

Asia Minor, 171, 183, 186–87, 197, 202, 207, 255, 258–61, 277

Babylon, 5–6, 35, 84–85, 203, 253, 262, 280, 287–91, 293–94

benefaction, benefactor, 17, 25, 73, 76, 92, 102, 105, 150, 153, 165, 168, 171–73, 175, 180, 190

Caesar(s), 6–7, 15, 17–18, 24, 35, 42, 48, 51–52, 55, 58, 68, 92–93, 95–96, 101–2, 105, 111, 121, 125, 144, 148–49, 154, 160, 163, 168, 176, 180–82, 184, 200. *See also* emperor(s)

centurion, 6–7, 95–96, 104–5, 109, 113, 115, 118

Christ, 1, 4, 6–7, 10, 45, 92–93, 99, 127, 139, 148, 154–58, 161, 173–75, 178–79, 182–83, 186–88, 191–93, 195–97, 199–201, 207–8, 210–14, 221–25, 229, 232, 234, 255, 261–65, 269–71. *See also* Messiah

Christian(s), 1–5, 10–11, 13, 47, 53, 59, 63, 91, 97, 99, 106–9, 119, 144, 153, 159, 161, 175–76, 182, 201, 204, 217, 221, 223–25, 229–30, 232–34, 237, 255–56, 261–62, 264–65, 269–71, 273–76, 278, 293

Christology, 199, 201, 230

Clients, 9–10, 24–25, 30, 48, 102, 165, 168, 170–71, 173–76, 178, 182–83

coins, coinage, 4, 7, 26, 30, 37, 73, 149, 176, 178, 181–82, 189–90, 196–97, 226, 228, 231–32, 260, 277, 279, 280, 282, 290

Colossae, 186, 201

colonial(ism), 12–13, 48, 50, 52, 107–8, 110, 158. *See also* postcolonialism

co-opted language, 6–7, 13

Corinth(ian), 10, 73, 125, 146, 150–57, 206, 212–13, 215, 217

denarius, denarii, 17, 127

devil, 83, 86, 89, 113, 222, 227, 229–30, 238, 249, 270

disciples(hip), 47, 65, 81, 84, 130, 134–35, 137–38, 140–41, 223, 270

divorce, 152, 154–55, 215

elite(s), 9, 19, 20, 22–32, 41, 43–44, 58, 72–78, 80–83, 86, 88, 103, 127, 130, 146, 150–52, 157, 159, 167–68, 171–72, 178, 217, 252, 278, 286–88

emperor(s), 6, 9–11, 15, 17–20, 23, 26, 28, 34, 36–38, 42–43, 49, 57–58, 75, 78–79, 81–82, 84, 86–88, 92–105, 109, 112, 124–25, 131, 133–34, 136–38, 146, 160, 162, 180–81, 187, 193, 199–200, 210, 225, 227–28, 230, 232, 240, 251, 255–56, 259, 261, 276–80, 282–83, 285, 292–294

Augustus, 15–24, 27, 37, 42–44, 78–79, 92–93, 101–2, 112, 125, 130–39, 152–54, 162, 166–78, 180–83, 228, 231, 240, 258–61, 278, 280, 284–86

Sadducees, 52, 69

Satan. *See* devil

Savior, savior, 6, 8, 18, 55, 57, 92, 112, 142, 170, 191, 205, 222, 240, 258, 260

Sebastos, Sebastoi, 17, 168, 171–72, 181, 183, 278, 280, 282, 285

Senate, sentator, 16, 19, 32, 49, 75, 98, 124, 129, 134, 137, 177, 240, 250

sex(uality), 23, 32–33, 36, 71, 76, 150, 154, 288

shame, 48, 104, 132, 151, 154, 156–57, 179, 222, 232–34

slave(ry), 9–11, 23, 27–28, 30, 32–33, 36, 41, 56, 65, 73–76, 80–81, 84, 86, 191, 195–96, 200, 214, 221, 244, 249–51, 255, 278, 288–89, 291, 294

Son of God, 6–7, 17–18, 55, 84, 92–93, 95–96, 97, 104–5, 127, 169, 181, 191

Son of Man, 87, 291, 292

subversion, 8, 10, 265

Thessalonica, 180–81, 206, 212

triumph, 17, 38, 102–5, 157, 162, 167, 171, 182, 187, 191, 193–94, 199, 230–34, 239–40, 279–83

urban, 17, 20, 22–24, 26, 28, 31–32, 58, 73–75, 83, 168, 186, 188–91, 199–201

wife, 10–11, 27, 130–34, 136–37, 141, 168, 177, 200, 214

wealth(y), 2, 5, 9–10, 23, 25, 27–29, 41–42, 44, 49, 66–67, 72–76, 79, 81, 84, 86, 110, 114–15, 150,–51, 168, 177, 208, 240, 243, 245, 247–52

woman, women, 4, 25, 27, 37, 65, 73, 123–29, 131–42, 152, 154–55, 214, 282–85, 288, 290

CPSIA information can be obtained
at www.ICGtesting.com
Printed in the USA
LVHW110753250123
737546LV00001B/2